THESE THINGS ARE MINE

PLATS BY GEORGE MIDDLETON

(author or part-author)

That Was Balzac
Polly with a Past
Adam and Eva
Hiss! Boom!! Blah!!!
The Big Pond
Hit-the-Trail-Holliday
The Road Together
The Cavalier
Nowadays
The Cave Girl
The Sinner
Blood Money
Accused (*from the French of Brieux*)

A Wife's Strategy
The Other Rose (*from the French of Bourdet*)
The Light of the World
The Prodigal Judge (*from the novel*)
Barriers Burned Away (*from the novel*)
Rosalind at Red Gate (*from the novel*)
The House of a Thousand Candles (*from the novel*)
The Bride
Madame Capet (*from the French*)

Published One-Act Plays

Embers (*collection*)
Possession (*collection*)
Masks (*collection*)

Tradition (*collection*)
Back of the Ballot
Criminals

The Unknown Lady (Collusion)

Portrait by Gordon Stevenson

GEORGE MIDDLETON

These Things Are Mine

THE AUTOBIOGRAPHY OF A
JOURNEYMAN PLAYWRIGHT

THESE THINGS ARE MINE AS THEY WERE, AND
ALWAYS WILL BE AS LONG AS I REMEMBER.

1947

THE MACMILLAN COMPANY · NEW YORK

Copyright, 1947, by
GEORGE MIDDLETON

First Printing

PRINTED IN THE UNITED STATES OF AMERICA
BY J. J. LITTLE & IVES COMPANY, NEW YORK

TO MY WIFE

FOLA LA FOLLETTE

ASIDE TO THE READER

THE RECORD of a journeyman playwright necessarily treats of professional activities. Merely to unload the cargo of recollections, which a full life has stowed away from many ports of call, might be reason enough for this venture. But activity outside the theatre, and the privileged seat for watching various worlds which it has been my good fortune to occupy, have brought me further excitements. Early, I realized that the livelihood gained as a playwright was only one of the compensations I received. The work trained my selective instinct, for example, sharpened my zest for the drama in the daily show and shifting scene at Washington (intermittently my base for decades) and abroad, which only the freedom of the literary life permitted me to enjoy. Perhaps, too, that selective instinct has helped me to appreciate the comedy enacted in both public and private life—including, I hasten to add, my own life, for no one should attempt an autobiography without being able to smile at himself, whether in the scrimmage or on the side lines.

Autobiography must be selective. Some chosen path is needful, even if one occasionally wanders off into tempting byways. Only with the perspective of the sixties can one draw a magnet over the past to pick up the particles of revealing experience. This tale will focus mainly upon the happenings which influenced the making of a writing man, upon the friends who enriched the days or whose collaboration added pleasure and profit to my calling, and upon my wife, without whom most of this would not have been possible.

Discounting whatever "posthumous vanity" is implicit in using so many personal experiences to disclose seldom considered aspects and technic of my craft, this narrative modestly claims some value not elsewhere found in stage annals or in academic appraisals from the outside looking in. I seek to describe as a practicing playwright the constantly changing market place, here and abroad, in which we had to peddle our dramatic wares: from the days of charming chaos in the theatre I first knew, to its present struggle to survive amid the mechanized intrusions of movie and radio, with their eye- and ear-arresting appeals.

To present such a tale mainly through the provocative personalities with whom I was inevitably associated in New York, London, Paris, Berlin, and Hollywood, is perhaps the most attractive way to give some facets of our world of make-believe. Having also had some part in organizing that exciting and hitherto unwritten adventure which became the powerful Dramatists' Guild of the Authors' League, and having twice represented it officially abroad, I was privileged, more than most, to meet my colleagues of several lands in their work clothes. Though I loved the art of the theatre in all its phases, I happened to care about the terms and conditions upon which authors, actors, and producers carried on their trade. As Shaw once put it to me: "It's art when you're writing a play, but it's business when you're selling it."

I was writing this book when the war came. Each word seemed to shrink in importance as part of a mere individual's story. Many another writer, I am sure, paused often to wonder whether it were worth while to push on to the end of the page. Yet I knew that authors, willy-nilly, would continue to pen their visions of the world before them, just as they had done of other worlds that had passed. To portray realities or to escape them, through their own experiences or dreams, writers would always dip into the dateless stream of life for inspiration. A scribbler could only write of whatever little world he knew and had a part in. So, for what it may be worth, I have finished my personal story.

Much of this story, however, was written as occasion permitted, away from an office job—the first and only one I ever had, except in Hollywood; for, in trying to find how I might be useful, after war broke, my mind recalled what Arthur Schnitzler, the Austrian dramatist, had told me in Vienna, in 1928: When settlements were made after the First World War, he said, he failed to receive royalties from the United States which he believed were due. With so many helpless countries overrun, including the France I loved, it came to me then that all foreign authors and composers might similarly suffer from some unscrupulous exploiters here or, more likely, from the inevitable chaos of the years ahead. With this in mind, I was able to suggest to the Alien Property Custodian some directives for a copyright program, little emphasized in the last war, which might assist in the administrative problems arising out of the highly specialized trade customs and diversified rights which stemmed from the many thousands of copyrighted properties he would have to take over.

With the sympathetic cooperation and guidance of the Custodian and his staff, I have been able for five years now to contribute, out of my knowledge of trade practices here and abroad, to the collection of royalties and the administration of prewar contracts between American firms and designated foreign nationals. Every such contract, in which there are live copyright interests, has come under my eye. But, oddest of all, amid the royalty reports which have accompanied the nearly two millions of dollars collected, I have frequently come across the names of writers who were friends or associates in calmer days, of refugees happily here, or of some tersely prefixed, "Estate of." Thus have these formal reports become alive and also awakened recollection.

Though I have ended my personal tale in the Hollywood afterglow, since parts of my professional activities there seem to be completed, this Aside to the Reader may supplement the epilogue, now unfolding, to a lifetime of interest and experience in matters of concern to us writers.

G. M.

WASHINGTON, OCTOBER 1, 1946

ACKNOWLEDGMENTS

I WISH to express my indebtedness to Frank Archer for permission to use a letter to me from William Archer; to Lady Asquith for a letter from Sir James Barrie; to Henri Claudel for a letter from Paul Claudel; to John Rumsey for a letter from Edward Knoblock; to Eva Le Gallienne for a letter from Richard Le Gallienne; to Constable & Co. for a letter from George Meredith; to Wallis Clark for a letter from Ada Rehan (supplied through courtesy of Harold Moulton); to Eleanor Roosevelt for a letter from Franklin Delano Roosevelt; to Ella Winter for letters from Lincoln Steffens; to Harrison Smith for a letter from Winchell Smith; to Lady Tweedsmuir for a letter from Lord Tweedsmuir (John Buchan); to Mrs. Charles Woodberry for letters from Professor George Edward Woodberry; and to his estate for a letter from Stefan Zweig. Also my gratitude to Julia Marlowe for the use of her own letters to me and those of E. H. Sothern.

My appreciation is further expressed for like permission, personally granted me on various occasions, by the following:

S. N. Behrman, David Belasco, Arnold Bennett, Alice Stone Blackwell, Edouard Bourdet, Major Edward Bowes, Van Wyck Brooks, Witter Bynner, Irvin S. Cobb, George M. Cohan, John Corbin, Noel Coward, Owen Davis, Professor John Dewey, John Drinkwater, Walter Prichard Eaton, John Erskine, St. John Ervine, Martin Flavin, Firmin Gémier, Charlotte Perkins Gilman, Emma Goldman, Harley Granville-Barker, Sydney Greenstreet, Clayton Hamilton, James Huneker, George S. Kaufman, Emmet Lavery, Judge Ben Lindsey, Percy MacKaye, Dr. Thomas Mann, Don Marquis, Gilbert Miller, Ferenc Molnár, Alla Nazimova, Eugene O'Neill, Professor William Lyon Phelps, Sir Arthur Pinero, Arthur Schnitzler, Bernard Shaw, and Robert Sherwood.

Other obligations should be acknowledged to Gordon Stevenson, for permission to use his portrait of me and to Austin Strong and Jeanne de Lanux, for unpublished drawings; also to the late Ralph Curtis Ringwalt and Arthur Richman, as well as to Dr. Horace Kallen, A. E. Thomas, Harold Freedman, and D. Kilham Roberts of the

Society of British Authors, for helpful comments on certain chapters. To this should be added, George H. Milne and his staff at the Congressional Reading Room, in the Library of Congress, for unfailing courtesy and assistance. The chapter on David Belasco was in large part published in *Town and Country*. Other acknowledgments to books, magazines and newspapers are noted where used.

And, of course, to my wife, who quite wisely would not read a line of this manuscript until it was finished and then gave hours to patient suggestion and to correction of errors in the detail of the many experiences we shared and to the recollection of others, now incorporated, which I had overlooked.

CONTENTS

ILLUSTRATIONS

ILLUSTRATIONS

CHAPTER I

OVERTURE

MY MOTHER and father eloped. They were married in Trinity Parish, New York City, by the Rev. Thomas H. Sill, on December 27, 1879. As I began there, I begin here.

I still have Dad's telegram of October 27, 1880, to my mother's mother in Philadelphia, announcing that an "eight pound son" was born. Two days later, addressing her as "My dear Madame," he wrote: "We have a dear little baby. I think it looks very much like his mother. The baby has light hair, dark blue eyes, well proportioned and perfect in every particular." It happened at her mother-in-law's home in Paterson, N. J. No one of her own was with my mother. Her family had not approved of the marriage.

Dad and Mother were said to be far-distant cousins. They both came from solid pioneer stock—nearly all Anglo-Saxon, with enough Irish to make me contentious. I wish a little Latin or Oriental had filtered in; but all the family unions appear to have been legal, and the recorded offspring legitimate. My mother's sister, desiring to join the D.A.R., spaded about till she dug up an eligible ancestor, my great-great-grandfather, Sergeant Gresham Flagg Lane. Fortunately for her, he had shouldered his New England musket at the proper historical moment. Like so many of our ancestors, however, he did not enlist for the duration. Even so, this appears to be the only revolutionary thing any of my male relatives ever did.

Those who were to come within my personal ken, on both sides, included the usual assortment of lawyers, doctors, ministers, stockbrokers, businessmen and loose-living what-nots, of varying degrees of prominence and probity. But there was not a writing man among them. My brother, Scudder Middleton, with his fine poetic gift, and I, a dramatist, were sports on the family tree.

Of all my relatives, I best loved Grandma Blakeslee, my mother's mother. About 1830, when she was a girl, she and her mother—who, oddly enough, had been born a Middleton—were painted together by the well-known Bass Otis. In his Philadelphia studio he had made portraits of Jefferson and Madison, as well as the first lithograph in America. The companion portrait of my great-grandfather, John Joseph Joyce—also highly appreciated by its restorers at the Boston Museum of Fine Arts—now faces his wife and daughter, in my cousin's home, with a calm, conscious authority. Joyce was an iron merchant in the Quaker City and retired with a fortune at fifty to survive many years in idleness.

Grandma Blakeslee was my best pal. When she came to visit us in New York she would answer my many questions: Who was God, and where did babies come from? In an age when Father Stork had charge of the general delivery I can still see her mouth pucker as she told me. But she never could give away how they were made. Whenever we went out I would repeat after her: "I put my little hand in yours and walk the village streets." As she often read to me, I owe her worlds of adventure and romance. My early summers were spent at Ocean Grove, New Jersey. There I first learned to love the sea, to dash into its waves, to wonder why the long stream of moonlight on it would follow me at night, as I walked along the shore. Its restlessness became a part of me: I have never lost it. Grandma loved the sea, too; I would watch her gaze at it from her porch, as she sat rocking back and forth. I would wonder what she was thinking of. Shortly before her death she wrote me: "It will be your time after a while. Oh, the glorious possibilities of the future for the young."

I recall her black bonnet, with white ruching, its long veil hanging far in back. I got the idea she stooped because of all the troubles she had carried. There was mystery about Grandma: she was a divorced woman!

As she had married against her father's wishes he had cut her off in his will. After her divorce, however, he took care of her; and he called her to his side before he died. "Mallie, I've made it all right with you," Mother said he said. But the new will was never found. Mother believed it had been burned by one of her three aunts. They thus became the witches of my childhood: I saw their caldron and the flames. This will stirred years of family mistrust. There were times when harmony lighted in my mother's family roost; but it seldom lingered. The relatives faced a real moral problem when they found out that some of their income came from a "house of ill fame" (as Mother put it). By some quirk in me this aroused my glee even then; for, while the family argued *what* they should do, they banked the rent. Since Mother always boasted her relatives were "all good Christians and Republicans," I was confused—as I was to be about many things in my boyhood.

Grandma had married Dr. William Riley Blakeslee, soon to serve, not too gloriously, as a major, in the medical corps of the Union Army. He was New England back to 1650. Their marriage was annulled by act of the Pennsylvania State Legislature. The doctor was thus relieved of his obligation to support Grandma and their five children. She had acquiesced. Flouting social opinion in not opposing his action was as unusual as it was courageous, seventy-odd years ago. I never asked her the entire story. Maybe, even as a child, I felt Grandma's need of protection when I took her hand.

A dramatist is initially concerned with "motives for an action." Save in mystery plays, what stage characters do must be made understandable to an audience as they do it. In life, however, motives can seldom be so simplified or conveniently selected. In my mother's elopement, I realize the insecurities of her broken home undoubtedly played a part: by living about, in her teens, she could also have felt the uncertain status of a tolerated relative. Once, as a child, when she was kidnaped like her brother by her father she escaped through the native ingenuity she was never to lose in emergencies. Another brother, a prominent stockbroker associated with Jay Cooke, was as kind to her then as he was socially ambitious for his beautiful sister. That was why he was apparently so shocked by Mother's marriage. How much he knew about Dad's "life," I never heard. When my grandmother Blakeslee died, in 1896, he would not stand beside my father at her grave.

Then in his thirties, Dad must have been a gay blade when he swung along Mother's Philadelphia streets with the swishing cane he always carried. His father, who died before I was born, owned an hotel on Leonard Street in New York, and was prominent in Tammany Hall. I have a handbill of a rally for Samuel Tilden, at which he was a committeeman, in the faction courageously opposing Boss Tweed. He was a commissioner, and was said to have introduced water sprinklers to clean the streets. This is the only record, on either side, of a family interest in any sort of reform.

Dad's mother was a Hall, "from upstate." She was a woman of character, as the firm mouth in her daguerreotype shows. She fiercely loved Dad and her other son, Will. They were her life; she was to be unscrupulous in their defense. This tense bond, my mother was to have her own special reasons for resenting. Somehow I never really loved Grandma Middleton. I enjoyed her most when she told of her youth. She was vivid with minute details about her early married life in New York. One of my first plays—*The Future Mrs. Trot,* mercifully unproduced—was directly inspired by her trips on the canal boats up the Hudson. She was also full of old wives' tales, which she related with high humor and faulty grammar. She was a spiritualist. Amazed, I often read the slates she kept till her death, on which her husband had chalked a celestial message "in his own handwriting." It warned her to move, as her house was to burn down. She did, and it did also—so she said.

A word is due about Will, who aroused my curiosities and added to my confusions. He always lived with her; he was to care for her, too, through her long senility—for she outlived my father and never knew of his death. But Will, who "worked with Dad," was a periodic. When he disappeared for days Dad would hunt for him and place him in a hospital. Will's one distinction was that he was among the first to sample the famous "Keeley Gold Cure." He thus became, as Mother would repeat, "a horrible example of what drink did." To shore up my moral foundations I signed a temperance pledge. In fact, I neither smoked nor drank for some twenty years, till a good woman came along and I said, "Oh, shucks." Will also made me puzzle over what Mother called "moral standards." I wondered how such a mouse-like man could be such a sinner—for he "kept a woman"! What bothered me was that I secretly admired his daring, without knowing why. Though he never spoke of it, I soon found other excitements in his talk. He was the first person I knew who had ever gone to Europe, destined to be so large a part of my life.

Dad himself was tall. He had his father's deep brown eyes and classic profile, which have also disturbed the women my brother has known. His hair, always carefully trimmed, was likewise brown. Until his death, at seventy, it was only slightly grayed, while his face held hardly a wrinkle. His mustache was sandy to the end. I never saw the line of his mouth beneath it; but it must have been firm and full, for he was affectionate and generous to a fault. He had started as a clerk for the New York City Railroad. Probably the following letter he always kept may have helped him to the job. Thomas Hunter, who signed it, became a tradition in New York City education. Until the end Dad valued his contact with the "Hunter Associates," made up of his old pupils. So far as I know it was the only club Dad ever belonged to.

Grammar School 35. May 28/67.

George Clinton Middleton was a pupil of Class 3rd for a period of one year. During this time he always conducted himself as a young man of excellent character. He passed successfully the examination and was admitted as a member of "The New York City College": he is therefore a good scholar in the common branches of an English Education, and will be well fitted to fill a responsible situation. He has always been thoroughly honest as regards his duties in school, and I have no doubt that he will prove himself a young man of thorough integrity. I have not the slightest hesitation in recommending him for any situation that may offer.

GEORGE N. MOORE, *Class Teacher*
THOS. HUNTER, *Principal*

With the undoubted political influence of his father, his own capacity for figures, his organizing skill, his charm and way with people, Dad might have won an outstanding place in almost any commended field. But Chance, on whose caprices he himself was largely to live, switched him to other levels. How that so incredibly happened is of no importance here.

When Mother first saw this "man about town" he must have overwhelmed the virginal reserves of her tight little world. Mother was something he, on his side, had never known. Her great beauty, even at seventy-five, beneath Time's web of tiny lines, still was as delicate as rose leaves—which I always thought of when I looked at her. Her profile was worthy of Despiau's modeling tool. Her blue eyes were honest and clear; her mouth, sensitive beyond an artist's skill to suggest.

They lived together forty years.

My earliest visual recollection is of walking at the age of four or five along Fourth Avenue, by the old Madison Square Garden, in New York City. This rose cater-cornered from our seven-room flat near Twenty-fifth Street, and preceded the Moorish tan-brick structure that was torn down in 1926 for the New York Life. It had been built on the emplacement of the old New York & Harlem Railroad station. The present Fourth Avenue traffic tunnel is all that is left of the feed line into what was then uptown.

As I began early to like "shows," the Garden was my joy. I recall the old-fashioned six-day walking match on a sawdust track as one star of yesterday sped around, holding a feather by way of a spotlight. And there was Professor Gleason "skilled in handling vicious horses" who once, as I sat fascinated, even took on a zebra! But the great thrill was to watch the billposters upon shaky ladders, with dripping brushes, pasting up the fabulous circus lithographs. I once saw P. T. Barnum himself, riding inside the arena in his open victoria, bow to the cheering crowds. Here, in those middle eighties, Buffalo Bill's Wild West Show started its triumphal tours. I saw his first New York performances. How romantic to the gaping lad was the famous scout with his goatee, his long hair rippling beneath a wide-rimmed hat, his leather-fringed coat, his high shiny boots and gauntlets, as he rode his white horse into the arena for the initial salute, before the shooting at glass balls began. In 1929, the same thrill came back to me across four decades, in Cody, Wyoming, where his flashing personality is fixed in Mrs. Whitney's animated statue.

Without the billboards the old Garden seemed green and silent. I hated to see it come down in 1890. I suffered as the crowbars dug into the brick walls and toppled them over in dusty shrouds. An era fell with them. But only age broods over what has gone; soon I was to see the new Garden rise from Stanford White's plans. Years later I was to meet the ruddy-faced, beauty-loving architect at the Players: a short while, in fact, before the very masterpiece he had erected became the scene of his murder.

But its tower, reaching some three hundred feet skyward, fascinated me most. In 1921, I came upon the Giralda Tower in Seville and saw how literally White had adapted the Moorish miracle. But most exciting was to watch Saint-Gaudens' Diana being lifted by tackles into place. There, poised on one foot upon the top, the celebrated Huntress was finally to swirl about in golden nudity. The wind so filled her long scarf that the taut-drawn arrow turned and pointed to its source. In 1938 I found her again in Philadelphia, when I was doing a play with Eva Le Gallienne. She rested in a museum away from heavenly storms, where she seemed as young as when I had first seen her face them as a boy.

The kindly countenance of the old sculptor himself then came back to me as I had last talked with him, his legs extended and shoulders shrugged, writing at a desk in the Players. I had shown him a photograph of that most moving of all American sculptures: the Adams Memorial, in Rock Creek Cemetery, Washington, D.C., which by then had a place in my personal story. "That is one of the loveliest photographs I have ever seen of it," Saint-Gaudens said, as he autographed it. It is on the wall before me. Recently his Admiral Farragut has been restored to public view. Time had worn away Stanford White's delicately designed base, curved like a frigate's quarter-deck, upon which the doughty sailor stood at the busy Fifth Avenue corner of Madison Square Park. Now he has been moved nearer the tranquil flower beds. But the old binoculars are in hand, his eyes are staring straight ahead, and the wind still plucks back his coat edge to show his ship's movement as it sped on through mines. "Damn the torpedoes!" he cried as he sailed into Mobile Bay. "Damn the torpedoes!" we boys would also shout, as we sped round him in our race. For he was pivot in our course.

Under a tree still standing in the Square near by, I had a summer friend whose fabulous tales and personality roused my imagination. George Francis Train, then in his sixties, dark of skin though of best New England blood, would loll theatrically on the park bench, inviting attention by his spectacular appearance. Generally he was dressed in white with a loose red silk belt; his hands were heavy with rings, and he wore a thick watch chain that held in its links odd coins of every country he had seen and told about. What tales he would dress up of being the man who "ordered the building" of the famous *Flying Cloud,* and how *he* had expanded American shipping and planned railroads: and how *he* had gone around the world in eighty days and how *he* had met kings and queens! With his story-telling went peanuts, and candy.

Later I saw him again; but he would no longer shake my hand: "When children grow up it saps my vitality. Children give me life. So long as I can be with children I will not grow old," he said as he turned from me.

Train was the first man I met who was "in the papers," and about whom people talked. Dad and Mother called him a crank. Puzzled, I soon learned every one who was different was a crank. Such a tag offered people the easiest way of disposing of dissenters whom I instinctively liked.

I was never bored in the city streets. My playmates, I see now, were mainly the children of immigrants; but never, as a child, did I sense any important difference in race, religion, or color. Their parents had every manner of making a living, and some of the manners would have brought lifted eyebrows in a world I then did not even dimly perceive. I liked each fellow for what he was, and I am grateful that, when I later moved into strata full of racial and social prejudices, I never came to measure any one except in terms of individual worth.

One of my first and closest friends was a Jew. His grandfather had been private physician and staff surgeon to Kaiser Wilhelm I of Germany. He was the only one of our gang who ever got anywhere. He became an internationally famous otolaryngologist, and recently died in the very house where we had played together.

We boys would suck lemons before the cornetist of each itinerant German band so his mouth would water. How wonderful to follow about the trained bears, with rings in their noses, prancing at the Swiss keeper's command, or those hat-doffing "dagos" with bright-capped "monks" that would climb to heaven for a coin. At Twenty-sixth Street the ambulance from Bellevue would clang for the right of way, as we eagerly dashed towards the accident—secretly hoping the worst! Around that same corner, too, would careen my favorite fire engine, No. 16: its shrieking whistle tore me from anything the moment held, as I rushed after its three dappled, mane-streaming horses, with the leaping black-spotted Dalmatian, who was my friend in quieter moments at the station house. Dead Man's Curve, a half-mile off, was ever worth a gamble. Something *terrible* might happen as the Broadway car, clutching the cable so tightly, swung around with unmeasured force. There was always a ride behind the squat smoke-belching engine on the Third Avenue L, or the great adventure of climbing to the top of the Fifth Avenue bus, to sit beside the driver at that dizzy height as he "gitteapped" his brown steeds.

Every night I would wistfully watch the nimble lamplighter criss-cross through the side streets to each post, poke in his long magic wand, tipped with a tin contraption in which lived a flame, to push open the gas cock, and scamper on, leaving the street light to grow stronger as the twilight deepened. How I should like to have done that! From our windows on rainy days I would gaze for hours at the city's horse-drawn traffic below, looking over the tall wooden "tele-graph poles" on which were strung hundreds of wires. I would stare at the repair men wiggling among them, and wait to see if any would be killed. Once I leaned far out to watch the passing, three blocks away, of the cortège with the body of General Grant.

Often I would "hitch" my way to the old Polo Grounds, where, by cleaning up peanut shells and score cards of the day before, I could see the game free. Baseball was to be my passion for years. I saw many of its great moments. It fed my sense of suspense, I suppose; each pitch or error made a new scene or situation. I was to know by sight every personality in the game; for my idle pennies were also to take me to those tail-cutting board bleachers. There I was to hear American humor at its best. I used to try to remember it: later, it was to go into my notebooks for plays. The interest rode fullfledged until my return from Europe in 1922. George M. Cohan then invited me to the entire World Series. I went and enjoyed, of course: but my long absence abroad had dulled the keen edge of enthusiasm. As I sat there it was only the young lad's thrill I seemed to remember with regret.

I first met George M. Cohan through Dad in those far-away days. We were to be friends to his death in 1944. Dad had, in fact, through his associations, many theatrical contacts—among others, two actors I was to know at the Players: Henry E. Dixey, of *Adonis* fame, and Frazer Coulter, who gave rise then to many legends. None of these is better known than his going through a fortune he inherited at seventy to find himself destitute again, with the remark: "How was I to know I was going to live so long?" Dad had been a friend of Charles Thorne, the popular romantic actor of his day; and once he backed one of Thorne's plays, for he loved the theatre. He and Mother first aroused my interest. He also knew the box-office man in the old Fourteenth Street Theatre. The first play I saw there was *Evangeline*. Even though the house might be sold out, Mr. McGuire would "pass me through," to stand in back. For years I went to every Saturday matinée.

There I saw some of my childhood heroes: W. J. Scanlan, who went insane; J. K. Emmett, another Irish favorite, preceding Chauncey Olcott; James A. Herne, destined to write *Shore Acres;* and even Robert Hilliard, whose only trouble, Cohan once said, "was that he was stage-struck." Yes, and Laura Burt—my first juvenile love, at nine or ten, because she was always saving her man "from the very teeth of death itself," whether the whirling buzz-saw in *Blue Jeans,* or the terrible chasm over which she had to swing on a rope in *In Old Kentucky.* The latter was written by my puckish latter-day friend C. T. Dazey, who, after any first night of a play which got bad notices, would enter the club, rub his hands and gleefully say: "Ah! Another failure!"

Only a decade ago this old theatre housed Eva Le Gallienne's Civic Repertory Group. Once, when I went backstage, I looked for the up-sliding door cut in the proscenium arch itself, which still worked. It was through this that the curtain calls were formerly taken. Many a villian have I hissed, as he came in sight. One winked at me, in my front-row seat. I winked back. We fellows understood. How proud I was to be taken into their make-believe! The theatre is torn down now. But recently, as I passed the yawning space, I fancied *The Still Alarm*, with Harry Lacy, was again on the stage—with a real fire engine, whistling and smoking, with real horses rushing to the blaze to save the plot or maybe the raven-haired Laura herself.

Dimly, too, from my play-going dawn, emerges Edwin Booth, at the old Fifth Avenue Theatre. I saw him twice in November, 1888. The picture lingers of his Iago, killing Roderigo—the white bodice, the striped cloak over arm, and the diabolic smile as the sword slowly pierced; and of his Shylock, groping from the Rialto bridge to learn of his daughter's flight.

Even then Booth was planning his gift of the Players clubhouse to actors and practicers of other arts, where they might meet in fellowship. On its third floor now, beside the room in which he died, stand the glass cases which guard all his costumes. Each time I have passed them, in my more than forty years of membership, I have been happy I saw the great man himself in two of them when I was a child.

Dad loved winter sports, and would sometimes take me away on short trips to Montreal or Saranac; but this was only between "meets." Once he took me to the race track, along with his entourage of "secretaries"—and in a Pullman, too! The races I have seen at Longchamp, Budapest, Tijuana never gave me such a thrill as that afternoon when Dad held court. The memory of that lad sitting on a high stool in one of the picturesque betting rings of the day—watching the odds being posted and changed, the money and white slips of papers being passed and stuffed in large, shoulder-slung leather handbags— came back one morning not long ago. I was in the gallery of the Stock Exchange, watching the quivering quotations, the weavings and hand wavings of the floor brokers and their staffs below. As I thought how respectable it was all considered, I recalled Dad's words: "What is the difference between playing the market and playing the races? Isn't it taking a chance either way? Ponies are often 'pulled,' and the market is 'rigged.' But at the track a fellow at least can *see* the run he is getting for his money." I never did work out the why and the wherefore of much of our moral attitudes.

But the theatre and restaurants were practically the limit of our social life. What an event to discover with Mother and Dad that first little dining room in the Lafayette on University Place, which Martin had just opened, with its popular $1.25 *table d'hôte*. Then to see it expand each year, till I was shown to the balcony table, especially reserved for Dad each Sunday, at Martin's Café, flowering on the site of old Delmonico's at Fifth Avenue and Twenty-sixth Street. Dad would wear his cutaway, and Mother her always exquisite best. Everybody in the sporting or theatrical world, and the ruling politicians, would be there and know him. He pointed them out to me, too, and told about them. With many thus first seen as a youngster, I was afterwards to have some professional association. The stage was being set.

There was, for instance, Peter DeLacy, who usually dined alone. He was owl-like, heavy-set, soft-spoken, and secretive. He was kind to his kind, as I had reason to know. He was one of the most famous bookmakers of his day, with influence and proper "connections." Not cultivated like Richard Canfield—who was to serve Augustus Thomas as a model for his play, *The Witching Hour*—he had no polished surfaces and no Whistlers. He was only interested in "poolrooms," and controlled many in the city. Dad explained to me once that, a short time before, the race tracks in New Jersey had tried to close DeLacy up, so as to force his patrons to place their bets at the tracks. As his sense of justice and his pocketbook were outraged, he rose in his wrath. The gambler himself led a crusade against the tracks, proclaimed they were "a menace to the morals of the young," enlisted even the ministers in his campaign, and finally found legal ways of closing every track in the state! Years later I recalled that delicious tale, and based on it *Hit-the-Trail-Holliday*—which Guy Bolton and I were to write and George Cohan to produce, as we shall see.

Gentleman Jim Corbett would also come there with a blonde, always dressed in black, wearing a diamond sunburst. I had watched him train at Deal Beach for his fight with John L. Sullivan. By what flight of imagination could I have foreseen that nearly a half-century later I was to hear him at our Dutch Treat Club tell of the ring strategy he used, or that I should witness a movie version of that famous battle! But never was I to see Corbett without recalling Dad's home-coming the night of the ring victory itself. For my young eyes popped out at his magic. From his pockets he pulled handfuls of bills and coin, which he scattered on the bed till the white spread was nearly covered. Dad had won it all on Corbett's victory through some mysterious method of hedging I never could understand. When Corbett went on the stage I was to read him one of my first plays.

Among others I saw at Martin's were Marie Tempest (to whom later I was also to read a comedy), the ever beautiful Lillian Russell, and Diamond Jim Brady—before the Dolly sisters held sway, and not a bit like the characters in the film; the enormous Howe, of the notorious firm of Howe and Hummel: and even tiny, bald, wizened-faced Abe Hummel himself, immaculate, always in white tie and tails. I couldn't have dreamed that before Hummel went to jail I was to get him to protect my rights, when my first play was produced, in 1902, by Julia Marlowe.

Martin himself, ruddy, with pointed mustache ends, would come to our table at the dessert, salute my mother, and ceremoniously hand her a tiny colored bottle of cordial. Her eyes would sparkle: she starved for such attentions. Sometimes she would sip claret with Dad, who seldom drank and never smoked. As he lifted his glass to toast her I would look to see if the large diamond he wore were there: for that ring circulated to and from pawnshops at need. A dozen happenings flash into my mind with it. Dad had bought his first diamond from an itinerant peddler. He said it was the first one which Dreicer, the famous jeweler, ever sold. Mother was given diamonds, too, in one of the fifty-thousand-dollar years; she wore them, like her gowns, with unostentatious taste. What emotions were to be aroused about them after Dad's death, and even into the writing of this narrative. How tenaciously she was to guard some of them, through the changing family fortunes. Only when one knows the whole story can one measure how dramatic mere things may be.

It was exciting to go to such places. Dad had a gracious way with him. He had the right word and jest for each casual passer-by. No one could be wittier. He would laugh till his face was scarlet. Everybody liked him. He and Mother were easily the handsomest couple there, and I was proud to be there with them.

That Mother and Father, so different in background if not in blood, should ever have come together and then stayed, spoke of some bond between them as deep as it was often to be devastating. In my own mind I often tried to dramatize her first encounter with his world. I never knew whether she was aware of it before they eloped, or whether she married in spite of instinctive hesitations she may have had. Perhaps not until she began to live in his city did she realize what was the life of a "sporting man," as the vernacular of the day termed it. It was so far removed from the standards of her own conventional upbringing that she could only judge it by them. The cold fact was that she could not help being ashamed of the way he made his living. She knew it put him and her outside a certain pale which she cared about and had a right to by birth. As a result, she lived a life of restricted loneliness, deliberately shunning contacts with his professional friends and their wives, most of whom she felt were "beneath her," and frequently her only outlet was in words. Verbally undisciplined, she automatically was to spill whatever her emotions prompted. And a child with big ears heard all, with interest but ever mounting bewilderment.

Dad had not the excuse of a ruling passion, as I was to learn in time. He did, without a trace of thrill, what his own world never questioned. He had assumed the responsibilities of a family. To him it was right to meet them any way he could; and he did this generously. He never tried to escape from the pattern he had himself made. He was a realist without illusions: but he lived within his own strict code of probity, with one unbreakable bond—his word. It was not cynicism which made him say to me, near the end of his life, "The world is only interested in the winners."

On the other hand Mother's disapproval of everybody in that world puzzled me, since I knew that each individual in it, down and out, would, upon appeal, inspire her sympathy. Her heart was larger than her own narrow social code. Yet I could not understand how she could accept rich bounties of living from the very sources she railed at. I myself was never at ease, accepting my own education, leisures, and enjoyments. I felt an insisting need of loyalty to my parents. They both deeply loved me. Affections and inherent rectitudes kept scrapping with what I knew was social opinion. One thing alone seemed clear. Try as I might to deny Dad to others, I could not deny to myself his many fine qualities. Besides, I loved him. Though he was never to phrase it, it must have been hard for him to realize I was soon to be an alien to him.

It was thus in a strange, twisting environment that I grew up, with the melodramatic paraphernalia and suspense inherent in the risks and rewards of Dad's activities. Though at times I was forced to take part in fantastic happenings I could not, of course, appreciate then how full of sheer theatre stuff that environment was. Not till later did I realize how it must have sharpened my instincts as a playwright, by exciting the selective processes which separate drama from the dry routine of living.

But the writer of plays, trained to deal in situation and climax, often forgets that in reality they happen infrequently. His art heightens the colors of life or arbitrarily rearranges its arabesques. Everyone's days move along amiably on a monotonous, uneventful level. Only the peaks are heart-thumping. So no pall continuously hung over our family. Chance also brought its own contagious excitements; and good luck, even with Mother, softened impeachment. None the less, for me, there was the stark fact under whatever temporary covering we put over it. I went on the defensive if anyone approached or lifted an edge of inquiry about Dad; for Mother's constant effort to hide from everybody "what he did" was inevitably to become my own harsh way. Youth could not protect itself against such maternal impacts nor know how to evaluate them. So, even across the threshold of manhood, I was to live, willy-nilly, in two worlds: with the people who knew Dad or knew about him, and with the people who did not. My technic was to keep them apart. On the whole I succeeded; with radarlike intuition I early learned and practiced every strategy of self-protection against the dreaded questions.

Amid such events and reactions of my formative years there were the intensive interludes I knew of in my parents' intimate personal life. The part Mother had me play on one specific occasion, and what was awakened by it, remain my most vivid childhood recollection. I remember when Mother first began to suspect that Dad was "not true" to her. She determined to get proof, and did. She was to be always timid in ordinary social intercourse; but, as I was often to learn, girded for battle or deeply hurt at real or fancied wrongs, she threw off every restraint. I never knew anything that could halt her; she would surge up to any redoubt without the slightest fear. And words burst from her in blistering, vivid phrases I secretly admired even then. Although they seemed to come from her heart, often they only poured from her wound. Once that was healed, the pain was quickly forgotten. Like a child, she could be gently turned from the subject, soothed with a kiss or kindly act. Then her eyes, as though full of fright at what she had said or done, would fill with tears. Throughout her long life she was to be two women. One of these I deeply loved; the other I pitied, when I was not shocked. But at the time of which I write I was only amazed at what she said and did. I must add, though, that I tingled with excitement as I followed each act in the plot she cunningly worked out "to catch him."

Somehow she found that Dad had a private letter box in a near-by barber shop. This was not then forbidden by law, and all sorts of clandestine correspondence found cover in such places. Mother went to the district post office, filled out a slip in his name, and had all his letters forwarded to our flat, where he never received any mail. One finally came, postmarked "Paterson, N.J." I seem to recall eagerly bringing it up from our letter box. This was the one Mother awaited. In it, she told me, "that woman" made a rendezvous with Dad for a night or so following. Mother resealed the letter, rubbed out the superseding address, and saw he got it.

That night she calmly accepted without protest his usual excuse as to why he would be late. But she did not go herself to confront them, as she had planned. She thought of something more effective. She stayed by my brother's crib and sent her devoted maid, Agnes, with me. She had written a note and read it to me. She told me to give it to my father. I went with Agnes to the place of rendezvous, on the downtown side of the L station at Thirty-third Street and Sixth Avenue. Finally Dad came. I saw him walking up and down, swinging his cane. I went to him and gave him the note, in which Mother had written: "Another proof of your unfaithfulness." Then Agnes and I left him, speechless, and staring at the sheet of paper.

Maupassant himself could not have conceived anything more fiendish. Mother, who would not hurt a soul when she was herself, could do this under the stimulus of pain and outraged pride. She knew, too, what she was doing. She knew how it would affect Dad. What she overlooked was its effect on me.

I did not know *what* it was I felt that night. But it was to be repeated often, as I wrote plays in the time ahead. I had a strange thrill. Something spoke within me, knowing what I did of the situation, as I approached Dad, as he saw me with a startled look, and as I slowly handed him the note. Instinctively I *knew* it was dramatic! For the first time I was conscious of what that meant. I believe now, as I look back, that the dramatist in me was born that night. I was eight years old.

Objectively, I can see how these atmospheric disturbances in my home life deprived me of the settled security to which a child has a right. That was the harm and the good; for like the starfish I began early to grow another radiating arm in its place. Lacking safety, I created a sense of it by the normal psychological formula. A lively imagination first unconsciously summoned the sly, subtle processes of identification. To this was soon added the baser need of projecting my adolescent self-pity. Now, in retrospect, I can easily trace the different directions it took. Naturally, my sympathies went out to the moral outcasts in drama and life. I writhed at all social or racial discriminations meted out to any individual for reasons not of his own making. It was but a step into the common crowds, before whom all the peddlers of political nostrums hawked their wares. I turned to everybody who coddled the underdogs or offered, sincerely or not, programs of reform and social betterment. Perhaps then was born my first impulse toward reforming adventures; but, more immediately important, I gave myself to books and the stage. *There* was a world of imaginings no one could touch. The theatre, I could have on my own terms, for the seeking. Further, I might make and possess another world over which I could run up my own personal flag. This meant doing things and being somebody.

There was nothing odd in any of this. Mine was not the first desire for a place in the world to be born of a compensatory impulse. It gathered strength with time. It was back of the drive and some achievements ahead. For all this I now doff my hat to the skeleton in the family closet, which, I am sure, never meant to kick up any such didos. But the facts about its continuing influence are set down without apology or regret. They might conveniently be concealed had they not been of the essence of my life and of its fashioning. What they did to me, to my work, interests and activities, made them insist on their brief and bony rattle in this narrative.

Now I am through with such matters.

Sarony

IDA VIOLA BLAKESLEE   GEORGE CLINTON MIDDLETON

At the time of their marriage, 1879

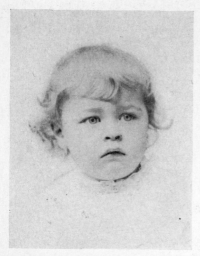

At three years

At fourteen years

Nazareth Hall, '95

Columbia, '02

THE DRAMATIST'S EARLY STAGES

CHAPTER II

PRELIMINARY CANTERS

OF COURSE, there was schooling—week days and Sunday. Dad thought early I ought to take a job; but Mother was determined I should have an education "and a religious upbringing." As a result of my ensuing inquisitive adventures in orthodoxy I confess I was to end up a mere but tolerant skeptic. The youngster went at the same time to four Sunday schools—Methodist, Presbyterian, and two Episcopal—possibly because of the Christmas presents. I was to pass my puberty among the Moravians, while the Unitarians were to top off my college years. Once in my teens I nearly joined up with the Episcopalians, on account of a girl whose father was the minister. As my ardor cooled I told myself it was because her father was "too high-church."

Mother had no Protestant prejudices, though theoretically she hated the Catholics until her sister married Al Dunphy, who had two nuns in his family. He was a crack newspaperman, for years the State Editor of the *Newark Evening News*. In time Mother was to love him more than any of her own blood relatives. To me he remains the most perfect gentleman I ever knew—wise, generous, and tolerant.* I was constantly reminded that Dad was "an atheist." However, he did have one creed, the Golden Rule, which he quoted often and lived up to religiously. Though the signposts pointing the different roads to salvation confused my sense of direction, I was ever susceptible to religious emotion. Never so much so as four decades later, when I was to wander reverently amid the Catholic churches of France and Spain, recognizing the spiritual solace which flowed from their cathedral beauties.

My green summers at Ocean Grove, with its huge Methodist camp-meeting auditorium, were as rich with ministers as with adolescent adorations. All denominations there shared the pulpit-platform: De Witt Talmage set off his gospel fireworks to my delight, and the eloquent Russell Conwell spread out his *Acres of Diamonds,* to

---

*It is in the home of his son, Dr. E. B. Dunphy, Clinical Professor of Ophthalmology at Harvard, that the family portraits live.

make the fortune he gave to the causes dear to him. From my present perspective, however, Minot J. Savage merits a paragraph here anent my spiritual pilgrimage.

His face seemed to lack definite line as he stood in the dimly lighted Church of the Messiah, in New York City, where my latter-day friend, John Haynes Holmes, was to succeed him. But as Dr. Savage spoke, always without manuscript, his soft voice would gather emotion. His face flushed: his eyes became those of a mystic who had looked on universals. He was then a spirit glowing with a deep faith in human progress, in the Christian beauties to be found in the mysteries which science was always unveiling. As the eminent Unitarian talked of the Gods many different people had made, out of their needs, the Devils man had also created, out of his own sin, the Bibles he had written and the Creeds he had lived and killed for, I was to sense for the first time a unity in man's spiritual reach to establish a relationship with the Unknowable and a kinship with all creeds. Dr. Savage—whom I was scarcely to know—did the most to stir my spirit through my mind.

Once, too, while at college, I had gone to hear him with a distracting girl whose spring beauty had stirred a young man's fancy. As I stood by her side, while the organ soared, still under the magic of his voice, I felt a union with everything. It was my first mystic moment: a sense of oneness with the universe. It was to come to me seldom, for always I was to feel Life as conscious conflict: Drama.

But of that Sunday-school era one who touched closest to my theatre world to be was Dr. George H. Houghton of the Church of the Transfiguration, which he founded. The father of E. M. Holland, who in 1907 starred in one of my dramatizations, caused this Church to get its famous name. When George Holland died Joseph Jefferson asked a near-by curate to officiate at his funeral. He refused because Holland "was an actor," but suggested that Dr. Houghton might at his "little church around the corner." Our Sunday school was in a large room above the rectory. But I would wander alone in the low sprawling church, so friendly did it seem to the wondering boy. I met the old Doctor once—he was nearly seventy then—and he smiled. He seemed small, as I look back. I was glad to shake his hand, which I knew had been held out to negro slaves and all the lowly.

Even today I feel a strange presence when I slip into its pews; perhaps it is his, watching with satisfaction the mecca his little church has become to those who have entertained their generation. For here, as a man, I was to be in spirit with others of my theatre world, at the services of my friends, John Drew, Francis Wilson, and Otis Skinner, as they went on to other scenes. In colored patterns, from the world outside they, too, had brightened by their art, the sun filtered through the memorial window we of the Players had placed there to Edwin Booth: the friend of each, I love to think, was waiting for them.

At fourteen Mother shipped me to a church school run by Moravians, to get me away from "bad influences." As she learned about Nazareth Hall from one of them, I couldn't quite figure it out. He had been my schoolmate at Grammar School No. 40, where I had started in the primary classes. Among all the trivia of those New York public-school days, but one episode has significance for this record. It was the first remembered escape route I took, so often to be traveled as I was growing up. Summoned before my class for a forgotten reason, with every eye on me, I had an irrepressible desire to flee. I did not know what to do. So I did the first thing that came to me. I threw my book into the air, dropped to the floor, and lay there motionless. They thought I had fainted. They carried me out. I let them—but recovered when I had lost my audience. What I long remembered, however, was my first thrill at twelve, in feeling the effect on an audience of an *unexpected* action. It was arresting; it focused attention; it was the playwright's method; it was the actor's art. It was something Eva Le Gallienne once was to tell me Ina Claire had helpfully advised her about, when a certain speech in *Rosmersholm* failed to register on the audience: "Make a quick gesture there, Eva, and give a sharp cry *before* you say those important words. The audience will *have* to look at you." But when I later met the fellow my book had hit he was less appreciative than Eva. "I thought you were nuts," he said. Well, maybe.

The cornerstone of Nazareth Hall was laid in 1775. Through the Pennsylvania forests historic figures then trod the trails, for they felt the ravages of the French and Indian War and the impact of the Revolution. The Hall was built in five months, with the substantial proportions of a Silesian manor house. While six nationalities worked on its stone walls they carried guns to ward off lurking Indians. Originally meant to be Count Zinzendorf's manor, it became a Moravian missionary retreat and place of worship, in what was almost a wilderness. With their zeal for communal education, it slowly evolved from an "economy," for boys of the Faith alone, to a colonial boarding school. From then, until only a few years ago, it existed: George B. Cortelyou and George W. Wickersham being among its distinguished students.

Forty-odd years after I had graduated I drove through Nazareth. I stopped by the village church. The square railed-about platform was still at the base of the steeple. Here, when death came, Moravian custom decreed, trombones should announce it. I heard them at our school beyond, hushing laughter with their sudden statement of sorrow. Now the thought of that arresting quality which lay in a horn brought back to mind the story about young Stephen Phillips, reading his poetic play *Herod* to Beerbohm Tree. Suddenly the listless actor leaned forward, all alert. "My boy, you *are* a dramatist," he said. For at a crucial moment the stage direction read: "A horn is heard." Tree knew its electric implication to an audience. My church trombone had similarly signaled to me across the spaces.

Driving onto the "parade grounds" where I had commanded a company as a rather ridiculous captain, I found that, like most things one remembers, it had shrunk. The granite shaft commemorating the school dead in the Civil War seemed puny. But the old building, then a warehouse, stood serene. I looked in the printing office where I had helped edit the *Hall Boy*. Around the brick wall had stood the old "necessary," with its wooden seats, its drafty circular openings of various accommodations, and that ledge of wood in back slanted to prevent dallying and quicken movement. The terraced "garden" below the playground, laid out in 1786, had long ago lost the trim cut of each friendly path I remembered. Near by was what remained from the "summer house" where I had read omnivorously. Here, too, I once acted an alfresco Celia. On the hill beyond, water still oozed from a hidden spring, making a wet place around which we had had to steer our sleds when we coasted down from the flat, grave-stoned cemetery above. Here in Nazareth the city boy had first seen clean country snow, and learned the lesson of the season's turn; here also I heard my first golden oriole singing to its spring mate in the old willow, to be recalled long after when I heard my first nightingale in the poet Mistral's garden in the south of France.

The day of my return, I picked out my classroom window in the old school building. There one Sunday night, Charles Kreider, still alive as I write, was reading us "The Adventure of the Speckled Band." Sherlock Holmes jumped to his feet in the dark, hitting savagely with his cane at something crawling down the bell rope

to the bed, and cried: "Don't you see it, Watson, don't you see it?"
. . . Just at that most thrilling moment in detective fiction, the church
bell rang. Kreider stopped. "Fall in," he said, amid our groans. No
one listened to the sermon: We were all wondering what was crawling down that rope. On our return, at double quick, Kreider finished
the tale. By deftly stopping, and leaving us like the snake itself in
the air, he had given me my first conscious contact with deliberately
contrived suspense. If only a dramatist could always find such "holding" quality from one act to another. The only time I met Conan
Doyle, this experience won the genial author's smile.

Of my teachers Kreider alone stimulated an interest in the stage.
As our play coach, he cast me for parts in the school shows. I there
brightened two Shakespearean comedies. The pink, frilly shepherdess
dress I wore as Celia cramped my style; but I opened a gap for my
betoweled breasts and modestly covered all with a cascade of carnations. I recall my thrill in knowing I could "put lines over." I had
also "stolen a scene," by primping at the brook as Rosalind was having
that endless to-do with Orlando. Early I betrayed another Thespian
tendency by wondering why *I* hadn't been cast for Rosalind.

But any sprouting vanity was squashed when I played the in-
nocuous Julia in *The Two Gentlemen of Verona*. William Lyon
Phelps once told me that was one Shakespearean comedy he had
never seen. Even if Billy had happened around that June night he
would have seen only a cut version. For Kreider, sensing the distress
of the audience at the heat and the acting, dropped the curtain on
my best soliloquy. For weeks I had worked on it. I was properly
furious and stamped it, too. When it came my turn to cut an actor's
lines I recalled how badly I had felt at sixteen when temperament
and I first met.

An adolescent experience common enough in boys' schools was
also stirring up for significant results ahead. I suppose something
about sex should figure in a writer's autobiography though I am less
interested in the subject than I once was. So, except for this preliminary canter, I will wait until it can be bridled to an important
occasion. No roadside pawing need be bothered with. Dad, oddly
enough, was verbally sex-shy: he never "told me a thing" nor retailed
a dirty story. Mother never summoned the bees and flowers; but
what she said about Dad's "women" made a deadly sin of what I
understood about sexual intercourse. I got myself identified with the
early Christians and thought sex was something that should be ex-

pressed only with bad women. I hit the first boy who sneeringly told me my father and mother "had to go together" to have me. Perhaps thoughts of a spastic romance of street mongrels rose before me and of the barber I saw dash cold water on their project. It was years before I got over a sense of shame when normal sex impulses took shape, as it were. For me, initial surrender, when the time came, was to be a triumph over myself more than over the willing woman. Otherwise my early record, I suppose, was about like other fellows' and equally muddled.

I had, of course, futile flirtations in Nazareth. There was one droopy-eyed carpenter's daughter who kept my mind off the church sermons in her near-by pew. I met her years after and ran for my life. But I was hungry for something my time then had a right to. There were two kind, older ladies on whom I often called, but no girls my own age with whom I could healthfully have diffused my sex in games, dancing, or calf companionship. So, undefined feelings were channeled to Ferd. He had charm and played a violin; but he was not especially intelligent—which didn't matter. We had no interests to talk about or share. As I now see, Ferd appealed to my fictive imagination. His mother was French, his father German. Somebody told me French and Germans were traditional enemies. That perked my interest. He liked me but returned none of my innocent attentions, which included vanilla alakumas from the village store. Yet I suffered if he didn't stay with me when we went ice skating. I fell into funks and dark-roomed silences.

About him I soon began to weave plots and build situations. I would talk them out by myself, picture all in fancied scenes, with dialogue pointed for verbal effect, suspense, climax, and "curtain." So here, in fact, was the first marshaling of literary equipment, the groping for and with words to express the emotions of conscious manhood. By inspiring me to *phrase* feeling Ferd was unloosening my creative faculties. Odd, too, that now for the first time my conflicts were about something in which my family situation had no part. The field of feeling was widening, though the furrows were still shallow.

Later Ferd and I cared for the same girl. She died. He killed himself.

Robert Louis Stevenson spoke of "his younger self" as his "little brother." Edmond Rostand's bushy-haired anemic son, I was to know in Paris, wrote a play about an older man who meets and talks with a boy—who is himself as he was. I have the same wistful feeling writing of the lad I then was, and am about to leave. Yet after I came home from Nazareth to prepare for college it was my brother, Scudder, who seemed like my younger self. I recall how proudly parental I had felt when Mother first let me take him on that perilous eight-mile journey to see Grandma Blakeslee in Newark. He was young enough to look up to me.

Even then his large brown eyes and profile—which Ernest Haskell a dozen years later drew in silver point, saying, "It was the loveliest line I ever saw"—predicted *un homme de belles fortunes.* His wit, second only to Dad's, was to bring him a host of friends in his distinguished magazine career ahead; for he was ever to add his share of gay verbal adventure, as the hours warmed and passed. There had been hopes of continued companionship, when I held the hand of the eager outlooking youngster that he was. In time he was to follow the law of his strong nature, as he, too, wove his way through some of the later designs of our home life. But that is not my winter's tale.

Of his poetic gift I can freely write. In his crude copybook era it was first beamed. I recall his annotations on two unfinished bits of verse: "I find it difficult to express myself in words I can spell." Another adolescent lament collapsed into a footnote: "She has come back: no need to finish this." Those early poems revealed a sense of satire which might have tinkled with a librettist's coin. But his three volumes,* to be published in good time, contain little of his rare humor: he seemed to feel it intruded on his unquestioned lyric gift, sensitive perception and beauty of phrase, which were later to win the praise of John Masefield, Alfred Noyes, Witter Bynner, and Charles Hanson Towne. Scudder's *Nation* prize-winning poem *Jezebel,* in 1924, bespoke his growing social feelings and broad sympathies —a garden in which his then emerging rebellions might have borne abundant fruits with an intenser cultivation. The last time I saw Robinson Jeffers, in 1943, he said nice things about "your verse," mistaking a mere dramatist for a real poet. I often wished I had Scudder's gift. There were so many things I was never to say in my own medium, which is a limited one for personal expression.

The theatre, I suspect, was my real reason for selecting Columbia as my college, because it meant I could stay in New York. I could

* *Streets and Faces,* and *The New Day,* Macmillan; *Upper Night,* Henry Holt.

there see every play, and did. It was all "theatre" to me: actors, scenery, lights, costumes, and audience. Such love as I now had for it was no divided dedication. The theatre was a unit. No radio nor movie then claimed the side attentions of actor or author. No audience could desert the footlights that lit the living, as today, to see and hear but speaking shadows. The theatre was self-contained: a total world for those who were in it, or who loved it. It demanded and received total loyalty.

I knew nothing then of the managerial abuses with which it reeked. It only meant great stars, experienced ensembles, frequent productions throughout the long seasons. There were stock companies—the Empire, the Lyceum, and Daly's; and in summer others brought back the plays I loved or had never seen. The theatre had traditions. And it had—to my salvation—top galleries! I knew every "peanut" in town. I mounted them on my pennies to enter the changing world of time and place, completely mine while I was there. Mostly, I went alone. It was to be my deepest love: another of my escapes, if you will.

From these steep angles, with eyes glued to the stage, I watched Joseph Jefferson, Clara Morris, Marie Wainwright, William H. Crane, Cora Tanner, Steele MacKaye (father of Percy), Margaret Mather, Rose Coghlan, Fanny Davenport (the Sardou specialist), Madame Modjeska (an adorable Rosalind even at sixty), with others whose names made the record of that decade. I was to make sacrifices to go more often. And so I never forget the obligation the actor and the audience should have for each other: the actor, to give his best performance; the audience, not to be late to disturb the opening scenes. It amuses me to find that my old feeling lingers even with a film. Nor was bribery beneath me. A quarter slipped into the doorman's hand; a dime to an usher. I early discovered "billboard" or "lithograph" tickets, sold by storekeepers in whose windows the "show" was advertised. I was among the earliest to find the picturesque Leblang and his cut-rate tickets, and was one day to tell him of it when a Broadway play of mine needed his help. So, season after season, I was unconsciously absorbing the art of the theatre. The business side of it was to come later.

But Saturday was all-important. After the matinée I would stroll along the Rialto; Broadway from Fourteenth Street north, already edging beyond Forty-second. Within that magic circle the leading theatres clustered. On Fourth Avenue hunched the Lyceum, designed

by Steele MacKaye, which "Uncle Dan" Frohman (who died the
day I wrote this) made famous. Here I first saw E. H. Sothern and
James K. Hackett, who were to do plays of mine. There was the
Madison Square, with a gallery which would almost pitch one onto
the stage. In these two theatres the names of Frohman, Belasco, and
De Mille first took meaning. At the Fifth Avenue, on Twenty-eighth
Street, I first saw Minnie Maddern Fiske, whom I so admired to her
gallant end: for I was to be at almost her last performance in Cali-
fornia. The Bijou, the Grand Opera House, Palmer's, the Standard, the
Broadway, the Casino, and, of course, Daly's—time jumbles them to-
gether. Besides my favorite Fourteenth Street there had been the old
Star, the Academy of Music, Proctor's Twenty-third Street—and the
Empire, the only one of them all still in harness.

But a few of the personalities who filled their stages have happily survived the brick and mortar I have named: Julia Marlowe,
Maude Adams, Viola Allen, and David Warfield. Otis Skinner, too,
until only a short while ago. The last time I was to see him he was
sitting proudly in the National Theatre, in Washington, at the opening of a new play in which his daughter Cornelia was starring.
It was a long reach from the time I had first met her in Paris, during
the very days she and Miss Kimbrough have written about so amusingly in *Our Hearts Were Young and Gay.* Nothing was to give
Otis such joy as her marching success, stemming, as her high gifts
have done, from a distinguished father and gracious mother, Maud
Durbin, who for many years toured with Otis in a repertoire of the
classics. He was almost the last survivor of those who had played
with Edwin Booth. From my top gallery—where I saw everything he
had acted—I had little thought, of course, I should come to know
and hold in my affections so grand a trouper.

But on those young Saturdays, as the crowd poured out, I would
swing along with my cane, like Dad. How glad I was to catch the
eye of any one I knew. I would stop at Huyler's, or Maillard's, for
hot chocolate, which "every one" then did. Sometimes on Sunday
I walked to the homes of stars for an off-stage glimpse, as they
went airing in their open carriages: Once I had ventured in West
Twenty-third Street, where the Pasteur Institute was later to stand.
But then its high iron-fenced house had guarded mystery and romance.
There Freddie Gebhardt and the "Jersey Lily" Langtry had lived
"openly" together. She was my first idea of a "free woman," since
she practiced "free love." It was this which alone attracted me:

for she was an uninspired actress. I was to hear much of her from Paul Kester, who wrote for her *Mlle. Mars.* He remarked, "She has always taken her experiences like a man." Which recalls later days when, sandwiched in vaudeville next to some trapeze artists, she said she had no fear of having them about as "I've fallen so many times myself." How surprised that youngster would have been to think he would ever meet her!

When I had tea with Lily Langtry on one of her last trips, much of the famous beauty lingered. There were lines, of course; for only a Lillian Russell was never to show them to Time. The classic aloofness of her full, firmly modeled face remained. But as she talked one felt the glow which had warmed a royal heart. She was tall but had grown heavy. It is absurd that I should best remember how tight and bulging her black and white high, buttoned shoes seemed, as she stretched her feet out before her. But I wanted to tell her what mysteries she had stood for in my callow time. I did not. Maybe I thought faded glory might not like to remember so far back.

So now, after Nazareth, I was sixteen, with stage memories and an eagerness for more in the coming school and college years. I had abounding health. I was rich in emotion, enthusiasm, and curiosity. Never were my roving interests to be curbed. I was free as any lark. I read everything, saw any play, lapped up any preacher or politician. This was my parents' most priceless gift. For that freedom I can find no proper words of gratitude.

Though I still have the certificates from the Regents of New York State, testifying my "preliminary education" was sufficient to meet "the requirements for admission to the bar"—Mother thought the law was "so respectable"—I prepared at Dwight School for a "classical education," just in case. It was named after the famous educator, Timothy Dwight, then president of Yale. When I was graduated on April 27, 1898, after two years' cramming, the old man himself gave the talk at Carnegie Lyceum where many of my later one-act plays were initially to be done. What an honor to share the platform with him; for I was class poet! My opus began:

> My friends, I'd have you understand
> That all the laws of poetry grand
> I put away.

No foot nor verse to bother me;
The proof of which you will soon see,
I pity thee.

'Tis true indeed I am no poet,
Luckily for me I know it.
That you'll see.

And so I must apologize
And beg you not to eulogize
My poem.

The publication of this choice morsel in the *Dwight School News* was possible only because I was its editor-in-chief!

I was admitted to Columbia as a "regular student." But I declined to join my class of 1902. I became a "special student." No one but myself knew why. "I just didn't want to take a lot of prescribed courses," I explained. I had a physical horror of class rushes, fights, and the indignities of hazing. But these did not cover the actual reason. Simply, it lay in my continued distorted values about my family situation. As I did not wish others to know about it I always felt most free with strangers. There I could select and control my intimacies. Yet by temperament I was an outgoing chap. I loved to be in things and manage them. This constant conflict had kept me jigging between the front and rear lines: in the arena with a trident, or up in the stadium seat watching and envying.

College, however, now suddenly presented a sharper dilemma than the schools that preceded it; I saw more conspicuous opportunities and, inversely, more demands upon certain qualities in me. I went into a funk and decided to dodge them all, just as I had "pulled a faint" at twelve to escape. When I try to separate the determining occasion from the deeper cause, it seems as if almost anything may have sprung my decision. One strand may serve as well as another.

Before I even entered college some fraternities "sounded me out," and I learned incidentally that Jews were "not wanted" in them. For obvious reasons I resented any such exclusiveness. I myself could never be part of anything so apart; and fear that I might be subject to similar exclusion for other reasons, in which my personal qualities would play no part, also caused me to shy away. I figured I might avoid any such issue by giving the impression of transiency at college: by staying out of the class I could avoid any obligations to the group. Within my inner reserves, at least, safety might lie in a protective separateness. Hence I became a "special." When I was asked to join anything I had my excuse. I alone understood the fancy footwork and alibis that my whole life, in fact, was to hold.

But I could not stay long in any such improvised storm-cellar. My native expansiveness overcame the temporary validity of my withdrawal. Two years later I decided to make up "all my credits," and joined my class. I yelled my head off for Harold Weeks and "Bill" Morley when they hurdled their way to football victory over Yale. I also cheered my friend Ned Bruce, on the same team—until his recent death one of the vital figures in the Federal art world in Washington. I nearly got elected Class President, too, by some dissidents who ganged up against fraternity combinations. Somewhere I picked up a "merit certificate" from King's Crown for "nonathletic activities." Maybe it was for the college plays I mixed in, or for my work on the three college papers. On Class Day I was honored by being Presentation Orator.

I never felt I could join a fraternity, though I kept friends within those which had "rushed" me. In my four college years—in many ways happy ones—there was always something alien in me to my classmates. Like the character in Gene O'Neill's play, then and many other times in life, I felt I didn't "belong." Of such drossy strands was the cockeyed pattern of that young manhood woven. Fortunately I had popped above such troubled waters of my own churning. Perhaps, after all, it was with me as with my close friend Don Marquis, when he had fallen off the water wagon:

"George, I have at last triumphed over my own will power."

At any rate: "Rah! Rah! Rah! C-O-L-U-M-B-I-A! ! !"

CHAPTER III

COLUMBIA WAS "STILL IN POSSESSION OF HER FACULTIES"

COLUMBIA UNIVERSITY moved to Morningside Heights in 1897, the year before I entered. The campus had a few buildings—all brick, and new—though the great Library, with its perfect dome, took your breath with its beauty. Seth Low, who gave it, was then President.

He was in middle age, pudgy, with a round face and twinkly eyes. I vividly recall his suave verbal facility. In my senior year he became Mayor of New York on an anti-Tammany reform wave. "Columbia is losing her President," he said, "but she is still in possession of her Faculties." Nicholas Murray Butler succeeded him in 1901 to retire as President Emeritus, in 1945.

I only had a hat-doffing acquaintance with Dean Van Amringe, then completing forty years of service. "Van Am" was a living tradition: his wide-flowing white mustache, military manner and vigorous phrase stamped his individuality on us all. Frederick Keppel, who followed him as College Dean, was then assistant secretary. He already radiated a confidence in his own future. Laden with world-wide honors when he died in 1943, as head of the Carnegie Corporation, Fred had been only a campus "hi-de-do" at college. We were with time to have many friends in common, as we found out years later when we checked up at a sidewalk café in Tours. I thought with regret how much better we each knew them than we did each other. Some, I shall speak of as they find their way into this narrative.

The History Department was exciting: William R. Shepherd, John William Burgess, William Archibald Dunning, and James Harvey Robinson gave me much. Shepherd and I quickly hit it off and were to be close friends till his death. His General History was a breathless trip across the ages. Will talked at express speed, excelled in thumbnail portraits, and could wrap a treaty in a paragraph. Though he was to make a significant contribution to Spanish-Americana, dug out of the archives in Madrid, he was not so deeply concerned with the philosophy of history as the eminent Professor Burgess. The latter's senior course on Constitutional History, which focused upon man's effort to reconcile liberty with authority, was a bit beyond this freshman—though the future Mayor of New York, John Purroy Mitchel, who sat beside me, obviously ate it up. Both professors had humor, but neither beamed with the Olympian tolerance of a Dunning. When he was seriously expounding successive political theories his eyes asked why the heck I was bothering about them, anyway. Once he autographed his book, on which his lectures were based, "With profound sympathy." He couldn't know how susceptible I should always be to the charms of personality. I would feel that he sympathized with Dean Woodbridge, our famous college wit. When the hour bell rang, indicating the end of the lecture period, he was in the middle of a sentence. The students began to shuffle impatiently. The Dean paused and looked them over. "Just a moment, gentlemen: I still have a few more pearls to cast."

Yet none caught my imagination as James Harvey Robinson, then acting Dean of Barnard, who was to be Professor of History till he resigned, in 1919. So I had him in full vigor. His humor was tower-toppling. A few soft-spoken, hesitant inquiries and a world of preconceptions would crash. He was a skeptic: he tolerantly smiled at human nature's effort to adapt to each age. In his measure of events battles and kings received little emphasis. His was a constant appraisal of true values: as original as broad. It shed light on progress, which the "arid chronicles" had by-passed. It came to me with morning freshness; its exhilaration lingers now as I thumb my notebooks on his History of Culture During the Middle Ages.

What did people like ourselves think and feel? What was their attitude towards the world about and beyond? What was their conception of the universe? What books did they read? What were their tastes? My notes ask. The ideals of the different ages, too, are in strong contrast. "What would Horace have thought of a monk?" Robinson once put to us. He spoke slowly, so that my pages flood with literal transcripts: the portraits of Dante, Gregory, Erasmus, and Petrarch—what letters! There are pages, I find, about heresy, the Inquisition, monasticism, together with the whole interplay of feudalism, the Church and the growth of Protestantism.

He thus unlocked special doors to abiding interests though I could then only peep in with untrained eyes. Not till I lived in Paris, in 1920, was I to enter them with understanding. For then I began to study early Christian art; its iconography became my passion. I had to reach back again to the moral and social backgrounds—back to Robinson. Only then was I to realize how much he had brought me twenty years before.

When I became a reporter on *Spectator,* the college daily, I asked permission to interview professors and write up their activities. I wanted to meet the outstanding figures. Men like Chandler, the chemist, Hyslop, absorbed in psychical research, the psychologists Farrand and Cattell, together with Boas, the anthropologist, were pay dirt. My musical ignorance made me shy off Edward MacDowell, then Professor of Music: one of my college regrets. But two, with whom I took no courses, brought me literary forage: A. V. Williams Jackson and Harry Thurston Peck, of tragic story.

None could have been more unlike than the leading Indo-Iranian scholar and the foremost Latinist. Both were conscious dressers: Jackson with silk hat and high-winged collars; Peck with carnation and strange vests. I never saw Jackson with glasses: Peck could see nothing without them. The former was super-refined and the politest of men: Peck was earthy, relished a rowdy story, and would lick his chops over human frailty. Each satisfied a part of me. The exquisite Jackson would invite me to his office, where Shakespeare was analyzed to a lounging few, with tea and surveying Buddhas. But I would always wait to see Peck alone. Some direct results of my visits to him have their place here.

As editor of the *Bookman* he was my first link to the literary world. He sent me my first professional check: five dollars, for a poem. (Under Arthur Bartlett Maurice, I was to contribute to that literary monthly for years, using three pen names.) When I entered his book-littered office, Peck would look up, squint behind his heavy lenses till recognition would spread into a welcoming smile. He was odd-looking. His sideburns and hair were then scant and graying. His soft words came slowly. To the young man he seemed so much more "a man of the world" than most professors. He suggested intrigue: and women, I later knew, admitted his great charm. His erudition was proverbial: easily tapped, it drenched a listener with astonishment and the oddest of facts.

Though he aroused my interest in the more contemporary writers, we quickly found a common love in Honoré de Balzac. I was then reading the great Frenchman through, and Peck knew every bit of backstairs gossip about him. I soon grew even more interested

in the man than in his novels. During college years I turned out a
sonnet on him, an essay on his dramas, and a graduation thesis. Thirty
years later I wrote my long-planned play, *That Was Balzac*.* During
the years between I was to turn to Balzac in all sorts of weather.
Then I would often recall those talks with Peck, who had awakened
me to the fascination of mastering the minutiae of one man's life.
As I was to write, when my play was published:

> Balzac never conceived a more amazing character than he himself
> was, nor wrote a more spectacular novel than the life he lived. His
> extraordinary capacity for prolonged work, his abounding energy and
> mania for travel: his mysticism and bizarre superstitions: his fantastic
> financial projects, business imbroglios, publicized poverty and fabulous
> extravagances: his frenzied hobbies: his secret intrigues and notorious
> *passades* between coffee cups—even the enduring ladies who lit his life in
> different ways—were all woven into his novels or turned to living myths
> in his own imagination, where real and unreal were constantly confused.

I was glad to have known Professor Peck before scandal touched
his final years, before his suicide while his brilliant mind was un-
dimmed. I was ever grateful for that interest in Balzac it had early
warmed in me.

Even more to affect my career, however, were my mentors in
English and Literature—after a very humiliating début. I had always
scribbled; I had already edited several school papers. At Nazareth
I had earned candy money writing "essays" for my classmates, at so
much per page. I was working up quite a "ghost" trade until I
credited to Robert Burns, "Be it ever so humble, there's no place like
home." Yet at Columbia I now flunked in English Composition! I
was dumped into the "awkward squad," the sub-freshman-subcellar
of literary incompetence. But down there, waiting for me, with sponge
and ammonia, was George Rice Carpenter, the celebrated Professor
of Rhetoric, recognized Dantist, author of many textbooks, short biographies of Longfellow, Whittier, and Whitman, which I had read.
The energy with which, in addition to his crowded courses, he was
devoting his executive skill to the ever expanding University, eventually caused his premature death. But his frank, boyish face never
revealed the strain.

I sidled to him in dismay. My style was "diarrhoetic," he said. But
nobody had ever told me how to build a sentence or a paragraph. He

* Random House, 1936.

gave me a little book called *Dots.* I knew nothing about punctuation. I plugged hard. (When in doubt, even today, I use a semicolon instead of a dash.) Through him and Dr. George Odell, who was sharing the course, I was eased into the steady company of my class. With two exceptions I was to be the only one who took up writing as a profession.

Before I graduated I contributed a dozen stories to the *Literary Monthly* and *Morningside,* over which John Erskine and Melville Cane cast an eye. I also became an editor on one of them. I wrote several "Psychologies," as I dubbed them. They were monologues of frivolous ladies, glittering with artificial epigrams, such as "She caught no engagement rings in her social merry-go-round." But I was already functioning entirely in dialogue, the dramatist's medium—much easier to punctuate. So I'm not sure my fizzle didn't determine me to "show 'em." At any rate it brought me nearer one professor whose friendship, as a fellow Player, has lasted ever since.

George Odell was one of the handsomest of men: and is yet, I may add, at eighty. His head might have been a model for a Roman coin. His hair whitened early: it gave dignity to his high brow, merry, deep-set eyes, and fine full-cut nose. His skin was sallow; I don't think he ever exercised. His personality enhanced his great asset as a teacher: enthusiasm. He aroused many a fellow to an interest in good literature and the theatre; for, like Brander Matthews, his associate during forty years, he had a fund of informing anecdote of great actors or stage tradition.

Back in college days I went every week to his rooms, which he then shared with William Tenney Brewster and Ralph Ringwalt, also in the English Department. By then he was mulling over his *Annals of the New York Stage.** This is a monumental masterpiece of detailed research and measured estimates. Into it has gone the centered interest of his life. Never was I to know a man so dedicated to what could only be a labor of love. The gold medal which the New York Historical Society bestowed on him in 1942, appraises his great achievement. I knew him first as an inveterate theatre and opera goer. He kept no secret of those enjoyments from his students. A few of his words about music were to enrich my future.

Many personal associations, among musicians and interpretative artists, have since come to me: there flashes an evening with Sto-kowski and talks on Chinese music when we went to see *The Yellow*

---

* Columbia University Press. He has now completed fifteen volumes.

Jacket: dinners with Bodanzky, a lover like myself of Balzac; badinage with cherubic Iturbi and genial David Bispham; trips with Arbós, conductor of the Madrid Symphony; Landowska, Elgar, Richard Strauss, the smile of a Sembrich, and the cherished nod of a Paderewski were all ahead; to say nothing of many musician members of the Players and guests at the Dutch Treat Club with whom bread was broken. Memories of this picturesque lunching club bring back the echoes of Jeritza and shortly after Flagstad and her sister, singing the intimate folk songs of their respective lands; Marian Anderson with an unforgettable "Erlkönig," and Heifetz, made up as a hick, playing "Turkey in the Straw" as it was never fiddled before or since. Once, too, the aging Vladimir de Pachmann, greatest of Chopinists, while thrilling us with a series of cadenzas, turned to his spellbound audience and said, "Pretty, isn't it?" *

But, up to college, music had had no part in my life: I could not carry a tune and had no gifts, even of appreciation. I had never heard a symphony nor attended an opera. About the only composer I seem to have known was Sousa—who had a daughter. Yet in a lecture Odell said quite casually:

"You know, gentlemen, you should understand what the opera is, and something about those who create it. Even a slight conversational knowledge of its literature is part of a cultivated man's education."

It struck fire. Here was another new world to look into. From a seat in the top gallery of the Metropolitan, I heard *Faust.* The pygmies I saw far off were Melba and the two de Reszkes. Then I heard Calvé in *Carmen*—with opera glasses this time, though she was large enough then. And so my interest in music was to continue from opera up through symphonies to chamber music, and those wonderful concerts of the recent war years in the Library of Congress, sponsored by Mrs. Coolidge and Mrs. Whittall. No one ever thus brought me a greater gift. For music, with time, was to become a consolation that freed me of immediacies and a stimulus that freed the fancies of creation. Such uncatalogued suggestions were to make my college education really important for the living ahead.

Never, till long after, did I tell George Odell of this.

---

* Will Irwin's delightful history of this weekly luncheon club, now internationally famous, is included in the *38th Anniversary of the Dutch Treat Club* (1943). Men and women prominent in their professions come as its guests, to speak or perform. Its annual "show" is comparable in fame with the Gridiron Club dinner in Washington.

It is hard to write of Brander Matthews, one of the best known literary personalities of that day. Then and for a dozen years after I graduated, I was closer to him than to any other professor. Yet when the First World War came he closed our accounts. He felt that the La Follette family, into which I had married by then, were of the old Civil War breed of "copperheads." Once he even so intimated. It was natural, with his French connections and English-born wife. I understood.

After the war was over, we saw each other again at the Players, where he brought periodic amusement to those at his round table. But I was never again to see him alone. Gone for me were his old "Sunday nights" or the other days I like best to think of—days, when, for example, he asked me to dine with Johnston Forbes-Robertson on his farewell tour in *Hamlet,* at sixty, or first to meet William Archer, Henry Arthur Jones, Bronson Howard, Clyde Fitch, George Arliss, or Hamlin Garland. But even beyond this: the times we would talk alone when I spilled my writing ambitions or sought his advice. He was kind beyond words, and generous beyond the need.

He was proud to be the first Professor of Dramatic Literature in America. He anticipated George Pierce Baker's famous "B47" at Harvard. Though he had students who went into the professional theatre none were to be so spectacular as the Harvard tribe: Eugene O'Neill, Sidney Howard, Philip Barry and Edward Sheldon, destined, aside from his dramatic gifts, to become a legend in fortitude during his bedridden years. But "Brander," as we always spoke of him, was the pioneer, the first to jimmy play construction into a college curriculum. Through his lectures on the technic of the French drama, our generation of playwrights was shamed from its spineless structures. He was the American midwife of the "well made play"— *la pièce bien faite,* as Sarcey put it. By bringing me that French critic and expert technicians like Scribe, Augier, Dumas *fils,* and Hervieu, Brander also inspired me to read their plays in the original. I saw I must know French and learned to speak it, inaccurately but with fluency. This ability, twenty years later, was to be an open sesame to Paris and the enchantments of its theatre world, afforded few American playwrights. So I would not attempt to measure my professional debt to Brander Matthews.

Nobody ever resembled him. The caricatures gave his face a goatish slant. It lay in his light brown, scrawny beard which wandered aimlessly about. He wore glasses, with a cord. His eyes were

quizzical and self-protective. As he hurried to the crowded classroom
there was always a burst of applause. He would brush it aside as he
placed on his desk a large crystal clock, to which he would constantly
refer. After clearing his throat he would begin, easily, from notes.
He would blow his nose frequently, wipe his glasses, look up at them
to see they were clean. That would generally remind him of something. And out of the richest of literary backgrounds he would lift
sharp-barbed, inevitably phrased anecdotes of the great. I have never
heard anybody tell them better. He gathered them assiduously, sorted
them in different envelopes for their predestined place in some long
planned essay. The volumes of these are still rich in pertinent
illustration.

Though I disagreed with his narrow economic and political in-
sularities, I admired sides of his personal character. Born of an
aristocratic family, he shocked the conventions of his world by his
marriage; for Mrs. Matthews was an actress. It was not done in his
day. Socially, things were not made easy for him, I was told; but he
acquiesced in no tactlessly offered discriminations. He lived up to the
concept of a man of letters: the last of a New York literary tradition,
surviving Laurence Hutton, William Dean Howells, Mark Twain, F.
Hopkinson Smith, and Richard Watson Gilder, all his friends at
the Players. He was widely known and had many honors. Yet once
as I sat with him in his book-lined study, confiding my literary
discouragement, all the mask of his habitual gayety dropped.

"You know, George, I wrote some novels when I was young. And
then I noticed, after a while, nobody asked me when my next novel
was coming out."

I could say nothing. It was the most tragic confession I ever heard
from a writer of his reputation.

I thought of Brander's realistic appraisal of his own limited success
in fiction when I came across a letter of Professor George Edward
Woodberry. He wrote to our mutual friend William A. Bradley, poet
and editor of distinction who was then the agent in Paris of many
famous French authors, including Proust, Romain Rolland and Jules
Romains:

Now, without holding myself up as an example, isn't there some encouragement for you in all this to still "follow your star," as Norton
said to me? It may not bring success; it may not even result in such
excellence as you hoped for: that doesn't seem to me to matter. To be
faithful to your instincts and impulses that carry you in the direction of

the excellence you most desire and value—surely that is to lead the noble life. I can't show you any worldly success or any excellence acknowledged by others, as a result of my half-broken career; but I am content to have followed it, and it is the literary career, which we well know is often a tragic one.*

Of Woodberry, Joel Spingarn has said that "as a teacher he deserves to rank with the most inspiring the country has ever produced." Though I was never in the inner circle of his intimate student friends —they were mainly several years ahead of me—yet I took his courses in English Literature and Shakespeare. Woodberry's verse stands in all anthologies; his biographies of Poe, Hawthorne, and Whitman are standards; his critical essays and lectures are alive today; † his collected letters ‡ reveal the spirit of the lonely man that he was. I had soon felt the hovering aura: he had worked in Lowell's library, had been a favorite pupil of Charles Eliot Norton, and had come under the influence of George Herbert Palmer and Henry Adams. Some of the keenest fellows at college were his devoted disciples, and admitted his inspirational force: Hans Zinsser, Ferris Greenslet, John Erskine, Joel Spingarn, Melville Cane, Louis Ledoux, Harold Kellock, George B. Hellman, and William A. Bradley, each to make a literary name for himself and several, happily, to become my close friends.

I eagerly awaited his lectures. He was slow of movement and speech: I never saw him hurry. Though he was only middle-aged he had little physical energy. Wistful and reticent, he looked shyly over the class. He nearly always stood as he talked. His full mustache was lighter than his hair: his eyes were lustrous, as though wet with constant tears. His humor was quiet but glowing over even his most serious words. When in repose his face wore a gentle smile.

I still have my notes of his lectures. As I reread them—especially his analysis of Shakespeare and the epic forces in drama—I realize I did not appreciate him to the full. He was a greater person than I sensed. I was too young to evaluate him. I was not entirely unmindful of his high idealism and his wish to inspire youth to the beauty of living. Years after his sudden and unexplained resignation from

* George Woodberry to W. A. Bradley: Apr. 17, 1919.

† In a letter dated Jan. 15, 1941, John Erskine wrote me: "I quite agree with you about Woodberry. In spite of his sticking to the Ivory Tower, he had an immense intellectual grasp of life. I have been reading his essay on democracy in *Heart of Man* and once more got the old thrill."

‡ *Selected Letters*, published by Harcourt, Brace & Co. The entire collection is deposited at Amherst.

Columbia I sent him a play, just published: *Nowadays*.* His answer, written where he was to spend most of his final years, tells
something of the man:

                                    Beverly [Mass.], Aug. 20, 1915

DEAR MIDDLETON:

Thank you much for your "souvenir." I must read it at my leisure,
however, and beg you to excuse my delay. You see I have been rather ill,
and not allowed to read, for about nine months; but I was in Italy four
of them, and though ill had my compensations. I got home in June.

But I can be glad and happy to have your book to put with my
mementos of those young years, of which I have a good store now—
two shelves—full of books by my students! And I am still more glad of
the success of your career for your own sake. It is a great thing to do so
well as you have done in these days,—or, as I might say, "Nowadays,"—
and you may well be a bit proud yourself.

Do you remember when you told me about your buying as much
Balzac as you could,—a long row of volumes!—Well, they don't let me
write much of a letter, so I must not begin one; but I recall our days
together with much happiness, and watch your progress with as much
eagerness and hope as of old.

                    Sincerely yours
                            G. E. WOODBERRY

President Butler once said, "What society needs is broad men
sharpened to a point." I am grateful for those who enlarged my
interests, and it was Matthews, Odell, Woodberry, Peck, and Jackson
who helped shape me for my special work. But Columbia's drama
courses afforded none of the practical stage experience students at
Harvard were soon to have under Professor Baker. My genial fellow
Player recognized from the start of his famous B47 that *doing* was
more important than being told. Columbia had no experimental stage
in which to teach technical production details, where lessons in directing, scene building, or designing, as well as acting, might be available to one who wished to make the theatre his profession. This hiatus,
between theory or analysis of play writing and its practice, kept Brander's fine pioneer offering from the greater influence. To me, for
instance, such opportunities were not to come except in the professional theatre itself.

But there were "shows" and musical contraptions at Columbia, of
no pretension, in which I did take part. Here was my unrecorded

* Henry Holt & Co., 1915.

metropolitan début as an actor. It was in Augustin Daly's old farce *A Night Off*. Henry Sydnor Harrison was in it, too, and his droll personality gave his role the peculiar flavor which later characterized his own novels. His early death ended a most assured literary career; even at Columbia, perhaps, *Queed, V. V.'s Eyes,* and *Angela's Business* (to sell, together, about five hundred thousand copies) were in the forming. Two others of that tiny cast were to make a dent: S. John Block, who became a perennial Socialist candidate, charter expert, and the adoring husband of Anita Block—lecturer, critic, and long-time foreign play reader for the Theatre Guild—and made with her the most aggressively theatre-loving couple I ever knew. The other was Henry Kiralfy, the lawyer, son of the great spectacle impresario. Through him I first gained some insight into a family with a long theatrical tradition.

I also tried my initial "stage direction" in two college musicals. Here future theatre personalities were likewise in the bud. One production was fathered by Roi Cooper Megrue and mothered by Crosby Gaige, as it were. Roi was to become a play agent and successful playwright, while Crosby soon produced plays, owned theatres galore, and became an outstanding book collector. One other was to achieve play and film fame: Ralph Wupperman, of the Angostura Bitters clan. On the screen, however, he is Ralph Morgan, brother of Frank. Each time I see him I recall our common dressing room at Carnegie Lyceum, as he was squeezing into a pink corset. Next him, doing the same, was Edward Tinker, now known as an author and a special book reviewer on the *New York Times*. Our greatest college skirt and toe dancer à la Loie Fuller was Philip Moeller, dramatist and director of the Theatre Guild to be. One never knows, in youth, where fame may be lurking!

In my junior year I also stepped onto my first professional stage. I "suped" with Sir Henry Irving and Ellen Terry, in the old Harlem Opera House. It was Friday—they were sailing the next morning. I was a knight. I wore armor. I was planted by the bar in the Court-room scene and was told not to move. I watched Irving tastily arrange the flowers on the stage before the curtain rose. Then I felt his hate as he sharpened his knife and eyed Antonio. I heard his grunts, through which the lightning of genius would flash on his famous exit. I stood within five feet of the first lady of the English stage. I was moved by the velvety beauty of Terry's lovely voice. But she remembered nothing. Every line was "given her" by the other actors.

The audience only heard the poet's words: what I heard, amid these, were her own additions:

> "The quality of mercy is not strained;
>   (We're going home tomorrow, boys)
> It droppeth as the gentle rain from heaven
>   (We're going home tomorrow, boys)
> Upon the place beneath.
>   (Home, sweet home-um.)"

When the curtain fell to thunderous applause, the entire company took the call, including the knights. Then the "principals"—including the knights. We had been told not to move. Then Irving and Terry —plus the knights. But this time, as the curtain fell, the stage manager gave me a shove. We knights went clattering, like dominoes, into the wings, while Terry and Irving took the call, alone. Then I heard him say farewell. It was a real farewell, for it was the last time they played together in America.

As my senior year drew to a close Franz Boas, who died recently at eighty-four and was a professor at Columbia for forty-three years, saved my degree for me; but he did it with diabolical humor. Though not then the best known living anthropologist, Boas was already an outstanding personality. He lacked the style of Sir James Frazer, author of *The Golden Bough,* who, when I heard him lecture in Paris, was elegance itself. Boas never could escape his native accent; I felt he had also picked up odd tonal rhythms from "our contemporary ancestors" he had lived with. Besides my difficulty in following him, my outside theatre interests were by now far from his world. So I remained blissfully ignorant of everything except how one might recognize whether some primitive woman had been a virgin by the way she wove her basket. I remember nothing else about the course, except its dénouement. One best remembers the event in which one centers.

I was assigned to write an essay on Totemism. I forgot it. A sharp note reminded me. Not knowing even what totemism was, I went to the encyclopedia. Skipping about the box heads, I turned in what a Frenchman would call a *feuilleton.* Professor Boas sent for me. I did not go: I feared the worst but thought he might forget. Then came another sharp note, reminding me, "Your degree is in jeopardy." I needed the credits. Boas was then also Curator of Anthropology at the American Museum of Natural History. I went with trepidation, through the wonder-filled halls of my boyhood. His office was packed with spears, shields, and other weapons near at hand. He sat at the desk grimly eyeing me, like some warrior waiting to pass and execute sentence. He was a small man, with piercing eyes and a fringe of hair about a bald space. He waved me to a seat with a short jerk of his hand. He eyed me and said nothing in words. I decided to take the bull by the horns. That about describes it.

"It was pretty terrible, wasn't it?" I ventured.

"What do you expect to do, when you graduate?" he barked back.

"I don't know now whether I'm going to graduate. It depends on you, you reminded me."

"Well, *if* you graduate?" he corrected sarcastically.

"I think I'll write."

"What? Fiction?"

"Yes, and plays."

"They both require imagination," he snapped back. "Lord knows, you have more imagination than facts—judging by this essay." He fingered it. "It is full of surprises and suspense. I don't mind telling you I haven't the slightest idea what could possibly be coming next. You said things about totemism no one ever knew." Again something told me to keep still. "I got you here because I thought it would be a shame to keep a fellow with your imagination hanging around college. I was afraid you might want to. You've got your right profession picked. You stick to fiction and drama. I sent your credits in this morning."

And so I was graduated.

Five months after that talk, I was part-author of a play at the Criterion Theatre, New York City. It was acted by the most popular star of her day: Julia Marlowe. Only a short while before I had seen her, for fifty cents, in another play from the top gallery of that same theatre!

I now began my professional life.

CHAPTER IV

I BREAK INTO THE THEATRE
WITH JULIA MARLOWE

I WAS TWENTY-TWO, with fifteen years of excited interest in the theatre. I have, as yet, only hinted at my desire to act. Where that came from is another mystery. My mother's prejudice alone kept me "from going on the stage." Such a career had even been predicted by my class prophet at Dwight.

The hallway had been my theatre as a lad. While Agnes peeled potatoes, I would make her watch my toy theatre, where I acted all the parts. I pulled the little cardboard characters by threads along the grooves, the way Edward Sheldon admitted later that he had also done, as a youngster. I made up scenes and cut new grooves, which would resist as new paths do. I would use candles and lanterns for footlights. To make my voice blend to my feeling I had practiced elocution. In the mirror I tried to register my emotion by facial contortions. I had herded my playmates and acted for, at, or with them, "making it up" as we went along.

In 1921, at Charles Dullin's Paris apartment, I was to see his students do a similar type of improvising: an episode was chosen (starving girl finds pocketbook another woman claims she has lost). They acted and dialogued the scene without rehearsal. I then realized the possibility of this method of instruction and subscribed a negligible sum to help start his theatre, the Atelier, which soon became the rage of Paris.

My own youthful solo masterpiece, however, was the transformation scene I arranged of Dr. Jekyll into Mr. Hyde. A black thread tied to an Argand burner created my light effect. When I hit it, in my drug-churning frenzy, the blaze would mysteriously go out. No lighting that Belasco put into the plays we did together ever pleased me more.

Yet I was learning the *feel* of dialogue, the phrasing for effect, the fact that some words will not marry on the tongue, that declaratives carry while subjunctives confuse. I was feeling out "laughs," their timing, pauses, or the potency of pantomime. Of course I didn't analyze it all then; but this kind of practice, and my already alert observation of how great actors obtained their effects, were sharpening a natural instinct for my time to come. Thus I first wrote my dialogue not on paper but on a living audience. Stage dialogue, I learned, must be written to be said, not to be read.

To complete these short chronicles of my acting, I will call up the Players' revival of *Henry IV*—in which I literally supported our beloved Otis Skinner as Falstaff—and James K. Hackett's spectacular performance of *Macbeth* (described later) at the Odéon in Paris, in 1921, before President Millerand and one Crown Prince Hirohito, who has recently been somewhat in the news. Manager Al Woods also offered me a part in one of my own plays because he liked the way I read it. The final opportunity came from Greta Garbo. In 1929, she lived near us in Santa Monica. Once at her own postbox, as the lovely lady stroked my enviable little terrier, Skippy, she suddenly asked me whether I wouldn't "like to go into pictures" with her. She might swear she never meant it: but there was something attractive about the idea.

There has slept in my files a remnant of my first play effort, *Minnie Dale*—an echo, no doubt, of some Fourteenth Street Theatre favorite. As a reward Grandmother gave me a set of Shakespeare, expecting me to go and do likewise. I was eleven. My first produced play was really a one-acter: *Gloves and a Woman*. A summer girl inspired it in my teens—I wrote the play to kiss her. I acted in it myself, of course. I kissed her. Stage business is business. But everybody said the comedy was too short. So I put in another kiss. Ditto for the third performance, as the play had by now also made a hit with me. Then the girl, with an eye to the future, asked what she might expect if the play were "in for a run."

But I had literally tasted make-up and the effect of my own lines on an audience. The playwright in me was coming up for air. In college, I even began to write long plays, collaborations mostly. None was produced; but, in 1901, a melodrama I did with Leonidas Westervelt was accepted by Augustus Cook, a famous Napoleon. It dealt with "T. R." and was called *The Rough Riders*. The star, however, dropped dead "after rereading it," his manager sarcastically explained. He had not even supplied the promised advance payment. It was my first contact with the theatre's uncertainties. I needed that money to stick at play writing; for now I saw I was to be in the theatre to the hilt.

Minnie Dale

in 3 Acts   by Geo Middleton.

Minnie Dale	Al. Race
Capt Cl. Hall	Peter Race
Mrs. Race	John Wend
John, a friend of Hall.	Jack, a friend of Race.
Kitty Bell	Chas. Smith
People, Police, and Prisoners — &c.

Scenes. ACT 1 SCENE I.

Country Scene = A tree - Road - Mountains in rear
bench, and etc

SCENE II = A mountain scene = bushes, rocks, &c.
The scene should be laid at evening.

SCENE III = Lockup - with room adjoining cells on top

ACT II SCENE I.

Peter Race's house in London = at 8, oclock

After I graduated in June I asked my parents to keep me "till Xmas." Then, I cockily added, I would be "supporting myself." And so I lived at home and wrote on the oak dining table, whose grain and varnish I can still see. Imagine my surprise, at ten o'clock on the night of October 15, 1902, to receive the telegram which I have before me:

Can you come to Boston immediately as my guest on a very important matter in which I want your aid? Please answer Hotel Touraine.

PAUL KESTER

I caught the midnight sleeper. Mother cried—her boy was leaving home; but I was aglow. I suspected Julia Marlowe might be in the offing.

When Paul Kester died, in 1933, his obituary filled a column of the New York Times. Yet in college drama courses his name is seldom mentioned; nor do academic critics even give him a place in the American theatre. Paul Wilstach, his intimate friend, told me that once, as they were about to go through a revolving door, a man ahead recognized Kester and stopped. It was Walter Prichard Eaton, the drama critic.

"After you, Mr. Kester," he said.

"Yes, you critics always have been," Paul replied, with his impish smile.

Paul, however, deserved some of their harsh words because he symbolized a phase of the theatre, as the century turned, which has seldom been appraised. He wrote in an era of stars, when fashioning parts for them appeared to be the dramatist's job rather than making good plays. This garmenting of actors was an enduring tradition as old as Burbage. Many hits were made by such mutual accommodation between author and artist. Any dramatist well knows that the plausibility of his plot or scene may depend entirely on some actor's peculiar personality or method. Comedy lines, too, will remain without the point the author intended until spoken by a special "type." Much of a playwright's so-called "characterization" is thus merely good casting.

The permanent stock companies, like Daly's, chose plays, or had hack writers arrange them, to exploit favorites under contract. "Show pieces" have always been devised to make an actor's holiday. Sarah Bernhardt had her Sardou who, in unimportant plays, tricked every situation to bring out, in studied rotation, each facet of her glittering art. "Sardoudeldom," it was called.

Today, however, the absorption of stage stars by the movies and the infrequent development of new ones has changed everything. Only an author in vogue can afford to write a play for one of the few remaining stars. If rejected by the inevitable one, it has practically no market. On her last visit here, Duse asked me why she had such difficulty having plays written for her. I asked who would do them if she did not. "It *is* also hard for an old woman," she commented. Writing today thus tends to plays with small casts, inexpensive companies—plays which, nevertheless, may be important. But many a script, useless without the cohesive contribution of a commanding personality, now sleeps in the author's portfolio.

Paul Kester, however, flourished in an era of different proportions. By them he should be measured. He could and did write only for stars —good or limited. He deliberately restricted his skill to their exploitation. He was a stage tailor: he skillfully cut his cloth to the figure which was to wear it. He took the blame for technical deficiencies he was aware of, rather than ask the star to do what he knew was beyond her power. He thus helped many an actress to a higher professional rating. In *Mlle. Mars,* his play for Lily Langtry, I suggested how the climax might be built up. "She couldn't reach it," he said. "This way she can get away with it." So he got little credit from critics; but his stars scored. No other American playwright had then gathered such a galaxy to his name.

Beginning with his first play, which, at twenty-two, he wrote in 1892 for Minnie Maddern Fiske, and which was produced by Madame Modjeska, the list included the electric younger Salvini, Mlle. Rhea, a "circuit" favorite in her day, Bertha Galland, Laurette Taylor, then in the bud, Lily Langtry, Margaret Anglin, E. H. Sothern, Julia Marlowe, and Ada Rehan. For it was Paul's *Sweet Nell of Old Drury,* to be played around the world, which brought Rehan back to the stage after Augustin Daly's death. (And what a first night reception we gave her!) Since many of these were dramatizations of best-selling historical novels, such as *When Knighthood Was in Flower,* there remains no printed record of Paul's uncanny part-building technic.

That he was a sensitive craftsman is shown in his poems, closely observed gypsy stories, and later novels: one, *His Own Country,* had a strange publishing history and is, in my judgment, the most tragic story of the colored problem any American author has penned. That he had a part in theatrical history is told in seventeen thousand unexplored "items," covering over fifty years, which he deposited in the New York Public Library. While traveling Paul always had in his valise bundles of such unanswered letters, from distinguished correspondents here and abroad. When he carried them about, he told me, his "conscience felt better."

I met Paul Kester while I was at college. He was the first professional dramatist I ever knew. I told him I was writing plays, and he asked to see a script. He liked the one-acter I ventured. He had me meet Margaret Anglin, who was later to produce one of my long plays and now promised to do this short one.* He introduced me to Mrs. Eugenie Woodward, an experienced actress, close friend of Julia Marlowe and the Otis Skinners. I took over some work Paul was to do with her. She was a tolerant mentor and taught me much of stage mechanics. None of our three plays ever got on. But Paul liked what I had done.

Paul made other associations possible—one with his cousin, William Dean Howells. That distinguished figure was kindness itself, interested in the little bark I was sending out in new waters to unknown ports. A delicious humor hovered over Paul's relation with people: he saw through the weaknesses of those he loved best. When he later wrote about my published play, *Nowadays,* which I had dedicated to him, he said I would understand "that it takes some time to recover from the excitement, and to rest up from showing it to your friends and leading up to it casually in conversation." My friendship with Paul deepened. He was to be my best man when I married. To no one do I owe more in my career, for he gave me encouragement when I needed it, and opportunity when I could take it. The telegram to come to Boston was the passport.

Paul loved the country, with an abiding passion for old houses. Historic Gunston Hall, home of George Mason, and Woodlawn, home of Nellie Custis, both were his. He lived there, on the Potomac, with his remarkable mother. Paul Wilstach, who, besides being a playwright himself, was close friend and biographer of Richard Mansfield, made his home near by; and there he wrote his authoritative books on tidewater Virginia. Vaughan Kester, Paul's brother, there wrote his successful novels, one of which, *The Prodigal Judge,* I was to dramatize. Wandering about the historic halls were dozens of cats, which Paul named satirically after the characters in his various plays: *Dorothy Vernon, Mlle. Mars,* and so on. He was a predestined country gentleman. He would buy these houses but never could afford to restore them. Gunston kept its ugly unbelonging tower, and Woodlawn needed its old wing back. Yet I have found his name in old churches thereabouts he had helped to restore. He loved Virginia. He is buried in its soil, beside his mother, in historic Pohick Churchyard. Paul Wilstach, with some friends, made the memorial slabs possible. I go there often. I loved Paul Kester. The moment is dearer when I think of him.

---

* *The Enemy.* Long after, this was produced in vaudeville by Herbert Kelcey and Effie Shannon. One week was enough for everybody.

One passes Woodlawn on the way to Pohick Church. I am only a few miles away as I write. Today the old brick house stands on the hill, restored as Paul dreamed it. It was there I came with Julia Marlowe, in October, 1902, when I was just twenty-two. There we worked on *The Cavalier*. Years afterward, when I wrote that my wife and I were now living in Washington, she answered in her firm familiar hand:

That territory is so full of remembrances to you both, of our dear Paul Kester. What an inspiration he was to us all! When I return to America I shall go there again and I shall hope that you and Fola will go with me—for a few moments near our dear friends . . . and say a little prayer of thanksgiving that all is well with them and "nothing can touch them further."

That may not be; but I saw Julia again in November, 1943, for the first time in twenty years. In her New York apartment, full of souvenirs of her career, hung the Irving Wiles portrait of her. As we stood looking at it together, there flashed back to mind the day in 1902 when she, with Paul and me, had gone to see it after it was first publicly exhibited. Seldom is it given to the autobiographer to see so juxtaposed, after forty years, the record of a past with a living present. Yet few friends I know could have stood such a visual test with time, as did this distinguished lady of the theatre, long now in retirement, yet full of vitality and still beautiful. Beside me, too, hovered the eager lad of twenty-two that I then was, on whom lit Paul's tolerant smile at my ignorance of so much in the world I was now to enter.

When I arrived in Boston that October day, Paul explained that Marlowe's play, *Queen Fiametta,* by Catulle Mendès, was a "bust." Her public objected to her playing a role of questionable morals, or, more accurately, "Julia is uncomfortable in the part." It must not get out that she was to shelve it for Paul's dramatization of *The Cavalier,* by George W. Cable, whose nostalgic Creole tales are a part of Southern literature.

But Paul had not begun the play; to help, I was drafted into the theatrical profession. After Boston and Providence we had a first act. *Fiametta* was booked in Baltimore next. Stopping over Sunday in New York, however, I read Miss Marlowe had had a "nervous breakdown." She had been ordered to Hot Springs "to recuperate." Then Paul wired me to meet him at the Twenty-third Street ferry, "with

MARGARET ANGLIN IN "A WIFE'S STRATEGY"

PAUL KESTER

In remembrance of
Charlotte Durand

Julia Marlowe

To the Middleton
Jan. 3 1907.

Byron

JULIA MARLOWE IN "THE CAVALIER"

two weeks' clothing for a stay in the country." I packed, anxious about the contract he had given me.

The star, heavily veiled, was helped from her cab by Paul and her sartorial manager, Charles B. Dillingham. As she was leaning heavily on their arms, I rushed to assist. "Keep the reporters away," she murmured weakly. I did not see any. She huddled in the waiting room, a pathetic figure. I sat beside her. I saw the telegrams her manager offered for her approval. One, dated from Philadelphia, read about as follows:

Miss Marlowe, in charge of her physician, passed through here at noon. Her condition is slightly improved. She has been ordered to take a month's rest.

There were other wires to be serialized en route. Then I helped her to her stateroom. As soon as the train pulled out, she threw back the veils, ate a hefty meal, and was discussing Walt Whitman with us. We were going to Paul's home, Woodlawn, not Hot Springs, to finish *The Cavalier. Queen Fiametta,* "beloved of Boccaccio," was off her throne. But the public must be made to feel it was illness and not bad business which forced the abdication! Such were the theatrical deceptions of the era; which is why I tell this yarn. Now nobody bothers to deceive—or could. Ah! the good old days!

We kept at it like Trojans. How excited I was under the same roof, working on a play for the most popular star of her day. I kept thinking of every role I had seen her in. Nor had I missed one when she and her first husband, Robert Taber, played together. At night Paul and I would go to her room to discuss the day's work. Then she would read us poetry. Others may retain the memory of Julia Marlowe as Rosalind or Juliet or what not. I prefer mine: the loose black hair enfolding her pale face, the rich full mouth and large wise eyes that looked out provocatively at me, when I was twenty-two, as she lay propped up in bed, with a crimson coverlet pulled to the book of verse she was reading, in that priceless voice of hers.

Once I ventured to read her a rough draft of the final act. She smiled. When Paul read it he threw up his hands. I had dared to give a scene to somebody else when "she was on." It wasn't done then with stars. This recalls Paul's tailoring skill. On his revised script I had penciled some verbal rearrangements. His lines seemed jerky and without flow. He also smiled. Then he explained why he had written such fluctuating phrases. The abrupt transitions and hesitations not only made the dialogue more natural but were little tricks of speech in which Julia excelled. Paul was writing the dialogue she could best make natural and spontaneous.

At night I would walk out alone to register all I was learning. Once, I heard her singing. She was trying the scene we had written: she, a Confederate woman, was singing to a dying Union prisoner who loved her "The Star Spangled Banner." In the darkness I heard Marlowe's voice thrilling with the song and the emotion of the scene. When it was over I rushed to her room with tears in my eyes. I kissed her hand. As I said, I was twenty-two. She didn't mind. Forty years later I heard that voice again as I stood outside Woodlawn alone.

While the New York papers began to carry announcements of her "great improvement" and "possible" return to the stage, I helped her "get her lines," by reading our text, since she learned a part by writing it down. (Recently Julia told me that when first studying her Shakespearean roles she would read the entire play through every day for a month or so. At rehearsal she knew every role.) Sometimes we would go into the warm Virginia autumn sun and I would "cue" her. It was quite "As-You-Like-It-ish." But as soon as we came to New York the idyll was over. They plunged immediately into all the confusions of hurried rehearsals. Except for Paul I almost ceased to exist. When the play was announced in the press my name was left off! But I had a contract.

Perhaps I wouldn't have thought of it if Dad hadn't said, "Get something in writing." He didn't know Paul; but he did know some managers. So I asked Paul. And this is what he wrote:

My dear George,
   In the event of the production of our dramatization of Mr. Cable's Cavalier I agree to divide with you equally all royalties recieved [*sic*] on my contract—2 percent of the gross receipts—made with Mr. Dillingham, and your name to figure as co-author of the dramatization.

                                                              PAUL KESTER
   PROVIDENCE, RHODE ISLAND
      20th October, 1902

   I found it recently in my safe-deposit box folded in a fading envelope on which Dad himself had written: "Matter of Paul Kester & Geo. Middleton." It was my shortest and sweetest contract: none ever could have meant more.

Charles Dillingham, Julia's nominal manager, probably thought he was doing Paul a favor by ignoring me. Yet I knew what it would mean to have my name tied up with Julia Marlowe. Even though I learned Charles Frohman had an interest in the play and was directing rehearsals, I was determined to get my rights. My ignorance of possible reprisals from the Theatrical Trust was naïve. I was too virgin even to be afraid of consequences.

It was then that I boldly went to see the notorious Abe Hummel, Dad's friend. There were two small men already involved in *The Cavalier:* Kester and Cable. But Abe Hummel was the smallest. He was under five feet. I had seen him often at Martin's and on the sidewalks outside "first nights." Just as, later, it was said the opera season did not start till Otto Kahn went to his seat, so it was essential for Abe Hummel, Theodore Kremer (author of *The Fatal Wedding* and fifty other such melodramas), Diamond Jim Brady, and misshapen Marshall P. Wilder to christen each opening. What was most important to me, Hummel knew not only everybody in the theatre but all its cupboards. What I had in mind, I can't recall. Possibly only the thought of Dad's own code: "Influence should always be tried before going to law." But my name must be on the program.

At that time Howe and Hummel's office was in the New York Life Building. I went downtown so seldom that I recall it vividly. I sent my name in. Perhaps I was mistaken for my father: but, if so, Hummel couldn't have been kinder. That passionate, determined young playwright must have amused him. From the very chair in which I sat, Hummel had probably heard, by contrast, some of New York's juiciest scandals. The facts were simple. I had a contractual letter from Paul. But it was only binding on him. He couldn't compel the management to carry it out.

"What shall I do, Mr. Hummel?" I asked.

He reached over, patted my arm reassuringly, and whispered, with a knowing smile:

"Leave it to me."

Which was exactly what I intended.

The next day Dillingham wired me to come to his office. I had twisted my ankle, and so I limped in, on my cane. It added to the scene. Charlie was indignant. How dared I "even suspect" that my name wasn't going to appear? Had I seen the announcement *just* going out? Here, he would show it to me. (Business of thrusting it at me.) And there it was: Paul Kester and George Middleton! What did I mean, anyway, going to a lawyer—a busy "celebrated lawyer like Abe Hummel?" I didn't crow out loud or even smile. I learned early to give people a chance to escape from embarrassing situations if they are trying to. It was "all a mistake," of course. An oversight. Everything would be all right. Sure.

I sneaked in at a side door of the theatre and sat hidden at rehearsals. I wanted to learn. Charles Frohman was putting on the finishing touches—which always means making cuts. He never saw me to speak to, and nobody introduced me. I learned by accident, for they didn't tell me, that the play was to open at New Haven. As soon as I could, I rushed to Parson's Theatre. I fingered a program with trepidation. I wondered whether they had been stalling me along. My name was there! Paul Kester *and* George Middleton! Nothing else mattered.

I never knew what Abe Hummel said to Dillingham. I never asked, either. Shortly after, Hummel went to jail. When he got out he went abroad. It was said that he was supported there by contributions from his clients. He had suggested he might write his memoirs.

The Cavalier opened in New York on December 8, 1902. It ran "one hundred nights" at the Criterion and filled out the season on the road. Six months out of college, I had made $1,960 in that time. The world was mine. The rest would be easy. I was a success. I was to be an important person in the theatre. The next season, however, I made exactly $72 out of it. It was six years, in fact, before I had another success!

What was this theatre about which I had had so many illusions— from the top gallery?

CHAPTER V

FROM THE TOP GALLERY
IT WAS DIFFERENT

THE THEATRE was dominated by a vicious Trust. The charming chaos was gone: its managerial end was now controlled by a few autocrats. The business trend towards centralization had caught up with it. There, too, as with similar combines, the method of correcting obvious operating waste was also breeding the abuses of authority. Actors and authors still were unorganized. I was soon to see they were exploited without redress and had little power to determine their contractual conditions. My resentment against such arbitrary power was to grow slowly. When the time came to improve the author's position, I was determined to do my part. The necessary unifying occasion did not come until some twenty years later.

Formerly the manager booked his play directly with each theatre into key cities and some fifteen hundred one-night stands. The trick was to arrange consecutive stops between important cities. Only thus could travel costs be kept down, enabling the company to stay in the black. Four managers, who controlled theatre chains, had now united to correct hit-and-miss methods. The Syndicate was born. Its secret was simple: it sucked into its system not only the theatres it controlled but others that would comply with its demands. It refused to book in its theatres any production which played an opposition house: nor would it supply plays to a theatre which performed a rival attraction. While thus guaranteeing protection and profits to some, it stifled the competition of others.

Practically no producer could operate without Klaw and Erlanger's say-so. As they were the booking agents of the Trust, every route had to go through their office. They could punish a manager by jumping his attraction back and forth so that all profit was eaten up by railroad fares. They could pull out of their hats New York openings or holiday weeks where heavy business was sure. They had, indeed, become dictators. By their ability to promise long runs or economical routes they also practically controlled the foreign market. This closed the

53

door to many an American author. The Syndicate also aimed to kill
off any American producer who was too independent.

This almost life and death power was held by Abe Erlanger, an
organizing genius. With his swarthy figure, and his Napoleonic complex and memorabilia, he was the personification of arrogance. When
I went to his office I looked to see if the tricorne were hanging on the
hatrack. No theatre man was so feared, because no one had so much
to give. I heard him once at rehearsal remark that the scene didn't
"add up." This was his way of dismissing any project he disliked.
I had only one experience with him. My letters show I refused to write
a play for a friend, in whose career he was interested. I asked a contract with a money advance before embarking on a labor of love. I was
too unimportant to believe he ever held it against me, though I heard
he did not like me. But he was only a phase in the theatre that can't
happen again. The managerial presumption that he symbolized is
dead, and no one was more pleased at its passing than many of those
he ruled over.

The other powers in the Syndicate were negligible as play producers, except Charles Frohman with whom I had only some polite
meetings. He merited his important standing: he had an undoubted
flair for the theatre. Unlike his genial brother Dan, my friend and
critic through many years, C. F. was always inaccessible to me. There
are legends about this inaccessibility. I remember one, told me by
Louise Closser Hale (the engaging creator of "Prossy" in *Candida*
when it was first performed, in 1903, by Arnold Daly).

Some years before, she had called at the Empire Theatre for a job.

"I want to see Mr. Frohman," she said to the office boy.

"Mr. Frohman is not here," he replied curtly.

"I'll wait till he returns," she answered, and sat down.

The office boy was silent.

After two hours she ventured: "When will Mr. Frohman be back?"

"I don't know. He sailed for Europe this morning."

The office boy was Arnold Daly.

C. F. was squat, sallow-faced, large-eyed and imperative. Some
swore by him, and others at him; but he knew exactly what direction
he wished the theatre to take. Though he controlled the Empire
Theatre Stock Company, he, more than anybody, expanded the "star
system." He intensified the exploitation of personalities. He broke with
the Daly and Palmer tradition, which put ensembles first. He plucked
John Drew from Daly's and stereotyped a man who, as Ada Rehan

told Fola La Follette, was "one of the great character actors of his generation."

Frohman's productions were thought of in terms of a "John Drew part" or a "Maude Adams or Annie Russell part." The stage annals record the stars he created—some without validity. Except for the already established Clyde Fitch and Augustus Thomas, C. F. encouraged no American dramatist, as he became successful. He was only interested in the tested foreign product. None of us youngsters ever thought of submitting him a script. His play reader, Theodore Burt Sayre, admitted to me that C. F. had never produced an American play by an unknown dramatist, even though he had recommended it.

Frohman's word was his bond. Often he had no contracts with stars or foreign authors other than a memorandum; for he was the channel through which most European plays and actors poured. It was told on him that he cabled an elusive English star asking how much she wanted for coming over and she demanded a thousand dollars a week. He cabled, "Accept thousand with pleasure." She replied, "Thousand for acting, pleasure extra."

Every English and French dramatist wrote with an eye on his American market: most made their fortunes here. Even in 1928, when I represented the Dramatists' Guild in Paris, French authors told of the large royalty advances Frohman had given. They could not understand why they no longer had that automatic preference over the American author. Personally I did not object to Frohman's support of foreign plays: the theatre should have the best, nationality aside. I was also glad to see personalities like Marie Tempest, Charles Hawtrey, Sir John Hare, Sir Charles Wyndham, and the amazing Irene Vanbrugh, favorite actress of Sir Arthur Pinero, one of the superb artists of her generation.

However, there were cooperating with the Syndicate some intelligent and independent men whose productions were needed to keep open such a large string of theatres. Among them were Henry Savage, George C. Tyler, Daniel Frohman, Cohan and Harris, Henry Miller, and young budding producers who secretly shied from the dictates of the Trust, as the oncoming Shuberts began to sniff prospects. Some popular stars, too, refused at first to be tied down and barnstormed with sympathetic publicity in tent and lecture hall, when theatres were denied them; but in time they were forced to give in. Only the courageous Minnie Maddern Fiske held out.

The theatre was at one of its most picturesque moments, though the young playwright's course was full of shoals. While there were some open channels the water was so muddied that he had to navigate carefully amid capricious winds. Nor was enterprise entirely free: there were overlords on the ramparts.

Paul Kester phrased the uncertainties when the royalties from *The Cavalier* began:

"George, never forget, play writing averages up. You are gambling on the most capricious of things: public approval. When you get a big success you earn more than you deserve: with a failure you never get enough. A few months' work may set you up for several years: several years' work may not bring you enough to keep you a few weeks. In other words, don't change your scale of living. Don't live up to your successes."

I was never to forget his advice in all my changing fortunes ahead —from $75,000 a year to nothing. The good years bridged the bad: the road of play writing has only averaged up. But I have always had my freedom, swinging along it!

When I found how difficult the portals were to enter I accepted it. I knew the odds on each script were against production. I decided the opportunities could be improved by getting to the "right people." Outlet alone could bring income. So I systematically set out to open my oyster. I knew nobody was as interested in my success as I was myself. So I tried to meet everybody who might know anybody I might also need to meet. I lived in the New York axis about which the whole theatre world then turned. I determined to be known personally. My name and face must be married in people's minds.

I took all my daily rebuffs, broken dates, and other crudities of the theatre world as part of the game. I hung on till I met those I had gone gunning for. I would always get my man. I was young. I was tireless. The unsuspected doors of opportunity often swung open by themselves. This was the case with the Players.

On May 21, 1903, I received the following note:

DEAR MIDDLETON:
I'm in town for one day and I've put your name on the book here. Get your seconder to endorse you at once.
Yours truly
BRANDER MATTHEWS

Paul Kester seconded me. In due time I was admitted. The Players became and has remained an enduring part of my life.

Today only a few are alive who knew Edwin Booth or even saw him act, as I did at eight. When I joined the club only ten years had passed since our greatest actor had murmured his last words in the room upstairs. Yet a few years ago I heard, in that same room, the voice I had heard on the stage as a lad.

Wandering about Harvard one day, I walked by chance into a classroom where Professor Frederick Packard was running voice recordings of stage personalities. I told him that Booth's daughter owned a wax impression of her father's voice, but the cylinder was imperfect and would not reproduce. He borrowed it, and in time the recording engineers transferred it to a flat disk. On the next "Founder's Night"— dedicated to Booth's memory—some of us, with ear phones, listened to the faint but clear voice across the years. Side by side, deeply moved, stood Otis Skinner and our president, Walter Hampden, who himself had so often spoken the lines he now listened to, "To be or not to be" and Othello's story. How natural Booth's method was! How colloquial! How rich! How mysterious to hear the words a few feet from the very bed in which he had died—some forty years before! And Walter recently told me that Booth had made those recordings after he retired, in that same room—now used for our Directors' meetings, where I once served.

When I first became a member, Booth's friends and associates in establishing the club were still active. Brander Matthews was one of these; and venturing through its rooms, I got glimpses of Mark Twain, Dr. S. Weir Mitchell, Augustus Saint-Gaudens, Richard Watson Gilder, Edmund Clarence Stedman, and Stanford White. There were not many dramatists; but Langdon Mitchell, Louis Evan Shipman, Paul Wilstach, Booth Tarkington, Clyde Fitch, Victor Mapes, and Augustus Thomas were kind to this ambitious writer. Actors galore, of course. How I reveled in "being taken in" by Francis Wilson, John Drew, Richard Mansfield, John Barrymore, David Warfield, Nat C. Goodwin, Otis Skinner, James T. Powers, Frederic De Belleville, James K. Hackett, Henry Miller, William Faversham, Leo Ditrichstein, and E. H. Sothern. They were then making theatrical history. About them, in goodly fellowship and equality, before bar and table, were the myriad of "supporting actors" without whom even the stars would not shine: A. G. ("Bogey") Andrews, still active many years later—"at 87," as he whispered to me only the other day after his big hit in *The Cherry Orchard;* Étienne Girardot, who made *Charley's Aunt* famous; Howard Kyle, Russ Whytal, and so on.

There were others—actors, writers, and artists—who from time to time, will come into these pages. For the old clubhouse—the only one standing today of those which flourished then—has been part of my life's rhythm: always, in its brown serenity, waiting my return, however long my absences. Here laughter was to meet the wit that flowed from men who have gone on—some only too recently, as the sweet-spirited Ray Stannard Baker. Here, among magazine men, long talks with David Munro, of old *North American* fame, quizzical Lincoln Steffens, wise John S. Phillips and Albert Bigelow Paine, to be biographer of Mark Twain. Here, too, art took on fresher interest with keen-humored Royal Cortissoz, expansive eye-filling Robert Reid, the cosmopolitan Gari Melchers and the sardonic Thomas W. Dewing, who first introduced me to the suave loveliness of Vermeer and whose granddaughter, Elizabeth Dewing, was to be my brother's second wife. Here was the lounge and reading room, where one skimmed the daily news and magazine beneath the famous Sargent portrait of Edwin Booth:

> That face which no man ever saw
> And from his memory banished quite.

Here, on lower levels (of the clubhouse), my many hours trying to master the pool table and the mysteries of "Kelly," the only game I ever played there till I stumbled on bridge—which just describes it. Here I was to receive and render congratulations or the silent hand-shake as, with time, the shuttle made its pattern of success or failure, life or death. Here was to be harborage when my little barks, sent out so hopefully, failed to arrive, or returned tattered and empty of cargo—more rarely, with unexpected treasure. Here in the quiet of the memento-filled library—one of the loveliest rooms in the world—I was to write scenes for the theatre or letters, out of my deep personal self, to the woman I loved.

It is strange how much of life these rooms could hold; and yet how little. For we members seldom have really known much of one another. Perhaps the impersonal accepting friendship of men for men has been its charm. Often I was surprised to find who were married or divorced, how men had steered their lives, and from whence. I realize now how few ever really knew me; how few, in turn, I knew. Yet I found there a valued, selfless friend, who after my marriage also became my wife's close friend. He listened to my outpourings of plots, plans, and later my personal problems and had a profound influence on my life and work. Ralph Curtis Ringwalt's fine editorial and legal mind—as evidenced in his *Briefs for Debate,* a classic of its kind—gave the corrective criticism I needed on the scripts I always sent or read to him. I dedicated to him my *Possession* volume. Nothing the Players ever brought me meant more than our friendship, which began there and deepened through forty years of intimate association. At his recent funeral, in the little Ohio town where he was benefactor and first citizen, I thought, of course, of many things. Something he said, not long ago, came back that also echoes my own feelings: "I shall always remember what the Players meant to me in those young days." *

I also followed every outside literary trail: footloose to no matter what tea, reception, or party. Nothing equaled the whirligig to be found at "Flora Mai" Holly's Friday Nights. Then an authors' agent, she had been at the *Bookman* when Harry Thurston Peck was editor and had lingered into the long regime of Arthur Bartlett Maurice. A mite of a woman, radiating wit and warmth, her successive flats were all as big as a minute: but somehow everybody managed to find a place, even on the icebox.

If Brian Hooker, Charles Hanson Towne, "Hal" Witter Bynner, Ridgely Torrence, and Richard Le Gallienne were there poetically quintetting, Gertrude Atherton might be cushioned on the floor, dogmatically giving all the answers to the aggressive Mary Austin or the gentle but profounder Zona Gale. Clayton Hamilton would probably be in his blue flannel shirt and flowing red tie, shouting above everybody: "Hi, George, I'm walking tomorrow to Camden to salute Walt Whitman's cottage. Come along." The looming lecturer would not be outstepped by our friend the poet and redoubtable pedestrian, John Finley, then president of the College of the City of New York. And calmly watching us, like some impersonal tapestry against the wall, was George Casamajor—a Spanish count in his own right and an El Greco in modern dress—admittedly the most cultivated of us all. To George I owe one of my persistent aspirations, phrased by his favorite philosopher, Paul Gaultier: "Life should be looked at esthetically and not morally." But I was to achieve it only by flashes: I always had too many indignations.

---

* To celebrate our fiftieth anniversary, in 1938, *The Players Book,* edited by Henry Wysham Lanier, was published, being "a half century of Fact, Fancy, Fun and Folklore."

No bloodhound, however, kept the scent more than I on the work side; for I frankly sought hack jobs, adaptations, rewrites, dramatizations—anything to get material, anybody who would help me sell plays. I tried to read them to stars or managers, for a play should be taken in at a sitting, not eye-nibbled at odd times amid telephone calls and catnaps.

Listening to a play, however, is not easy: many readers have no knack of making the scenes live. The reader's personality may also blur the characterization or trick the listener's judgment. Dion Boucicault, Willard Mack, Clyde Fitch, among others, read so magnetically that it was difficult to refuse them a contract, and all accounts agree Bernard Shaw is a wonder. I learned to individualize each character and to suggest the stage business without interrupting the dialogue. Even the tempo or the emotion of the scene might be made persuasive. But if listeners have suffered—so have I. To read to "dead pans" or the bored was no ordinary ordeal; yet other hearers made it a joy through helpful appreciation.

Before my long association with David Belasco, he was liable to get a convenient neuralgia when the given hour for the reading arrived. Others just didn't show up. But one had always to be gallant: to accept the excuses without question and keep at it. "I suppose I'll have to listen to you," Al Woods once conceded. My method of approach was determined by the individual; it was catch-as-catch-can, with no holds barred. Woods would get set, with a box of cigars, hat on back of head and feet on his expensive desk. With him I would walk about, double up on the curses, clutch his arm for the love scene, and make him feel, like the gal, that he had gone through something. Belasco always had smelling salts handy; though he also liked to have things acted out, as he himself always did. I once read a play to Henry Harris after twenty-four broken dates. He bought it for Elsie Ferguson, but it never went on. The producer of *The Lion and the Mouse* would always close his eyes—"to visualize it," he said. The poor author could never be sure that he was awake. Of others there was no doubt. Lee Shubert started to sleep peacefully on the sixth page of one opus. I mumbled on a few minutes, skipped to the last page, and banged the table. Lee woke and said: "Very good, Middleton; but it lacks feminine interest." Yet Shaw himself has confessed that William Archer fell asleep on him. When he told Henry Arthur Jones about it, the latter remarked that "sleep is a form of criticism." Perhaps what George Ade suggested is best: bring a loaded pistol and lay it by the manuscript, murmuring casually to the manager: "You're going to like this play."

When Weber and Fields decided to produce "legitimate" drama I told Fields I had two. I read him the one I felt he would like best. At the end he bought the other; but he never asked me to read him the script. I judge he gave me $500 rather than listen. I tried to catch stars when they were on the road and lonely. I nailed the distinguished English actor, E. S. Willard, in Rochester. Later, he sent me a charmingly inscribed photograph, which has smiled at me ever since with a sort of oh-how-could-you-Middleton! look.

So it would go with other stars to be. There were bright-eyed Laura Hope Crews, then a slim ingénue in stock, the first to whom I ever read a play; eager Elsie Janis with quick risibilities and a hovering mother; Arnold Daly, in violent pajamas that bothered my eyes; considerate and sympathetic George Arliss; gracious, queenly Viola Allen, in her heyday, who made you feel you were doing her a favor; chirpy, entrancing Billie Burke, who gurgled enthusiastically and embraced me two decades later in Hollywood, as young as ever; keen-eyed, alert, ever "kidding" Robert Edeson, to whom, in 1930, I was to give almost his last film role in Hollywood; and George M. Cohan, of whom more anon. With the passing of time others were to move into the picture: Katharine Cornell and Eva Le Gallienne, both for parts with David Belasco that they did not accept; Alla Nazimova and one other actress in two of my plays whose careers were to be stopped, under strange circumstances, within a few weeks of each other. E. H. Sothern, Noel Coward, Sybil Thorndike, Fay Bainter, Ina Claire, Peggy Wood, and Margaret Anglin were among those who were to speak my lines. There was reading also to a young woman whose mother was long kind enough to remember the play: for early I was devoted to the art of Helen Hayes; but it was always to be in the other fellow's play.

My files tell of many failures to read direct: as those charming letters from Mrs. Fiske, who would always take up the scripts herself "in the order of receipt." Stacks of letters record rejections and broken hopes. So often their reasons for not producing were sound. Fewer letters showed bad guessing about my plays which did manage to get over.

One reading experience demands a place here because I was honored by a great lady of the English stage: Dame Marie Tempest, the last of her genre, who was to die at seventy-eight while preparing for another tour. I am sure a bit of sentiment made my reading possible; for on our family doctor's desk I had long noticed her photograph, though a ribbon tactfully hid the dedication. Suspecting his devotion dating from the misty days of her first American appearance, in her *Red Hussar* comic opera epoch, I boldly asked him if he could arrange the reading. I can see her now sitting erect, her back not touching the chair, listening with quiet encouraging patience though probably quite wisely thinking of other things. When I was staging the London production of *Polly with a Past,* in 1921, I thanked her for her kindness to "that promising playwright." As I mentioned the doctor's name, she smiled. Her eyes puckered up the way I had seen them so often on the stage. But she said nothing. After all, it was so far away and . . .

In 1937, John Gielgud, the distinguished English actor of the Terry clan, told me a charming tale about her. It was when he was appearing as *Hamlet* at the Empire Theatre, and I was chairman of a dinner the Players gave him, with Walter Hampden and Otis Skinner present in their official capacities. On Gielgud's "party call" at luncheon, I happened to mention I had once read a play to Marie Tempest.

He had stage-managed her golden jubilee, in 1935. As the dress rehearsal was over and he was dismissing the host of stars who were paying tribute, she halted everybody. "Wait," she said. "I must now rehearse my speech to Their Majesties." And everyone waited till she did, for King and Queen must have a perfect performance. The speech, according to the press, began: "After having, I suppose, taken calls for fifty years, I ought to be able to face this; but I confess I am rather shattered." The care with which she rehearsed her confusion revealed the way she had always served her art, whose comedy was her own, like those provocative eyes which had focused on mine for a little while, a long while ago.

The thought of Marie Tempest brings back from vanished theatre wings, waiting for their little bows, a host of others I was now to know: Otis Skinner, flamboyant and scene-filling, like rich claret running over everything; William Gillette of the scarce gesture and staccato sentence; the tumultuous Zaza of Mrs. Leslie Carter; lovely Eleanor Robson, destined to leave the stage too soon and become Mrs. August Belmont; and slim, beautiful Ethel Barrymore, with the husky voice and worldly smile, who would outlast them all in active harness and remain with *The Corn Is Green* in her middle sixties, as commandingly expert and bewitching to me as ever. How I have always yearned to have her do a play of mine! Yes, even yet.

And there was Lotta Crabtree. She had left the stage a decade before. While the henna-dyed hair did not disguise the years, her black, darting eyes still announced the tiny parcel of dynamite which had set off our granddaddies before the Civil War. I was always tempted to ask her to take a curtain call for me alone—with her ankle; for the wiggle of her tiny foot, as she stuck it out from the wings, was famous. As a child, Fola La Follette, seeing her first play, had wept at the suffering of the little girl on the stage. To console her, Fola's mother revealed that Lotta was a grown woman. For the first time Fola doubted her mother's veracity. Years later she told Lotta of this incident when I introduced them at the Players on an April Ladies' Day. Lotta smiled.

"That was why I never wanted to meet children, my dear," she said. "They were always disillusioned to find I was a grown-up."

I went occasionally to her heavily junked apartment on Fifty-ninth Street, near William Dean Howells'. Her mother was then alive; Lotta had never married, and they had been inseparable, from the fifties, when they toured the mining camps on muleback or in wooden wagons. Two odd characters with amazing stage backgrounds! Through her mother's keen real estate instinct Lotta was then worth several millions. Yet she once explained: "You know, my dear, every time I've given any money, it has always brought them hard luck." Who could have thought up a better reason for keeping it? Years later, in 1931, I hunted out those old border theatres—where Lotta had told me her shows had been interrupted by gunplay or to let her pick up the gold nuggets thrown as pay onto the crude stages; and I seemed to see, cavorting there, this sprite taught to dance by Lola Montez, who had brought such joy to those who built and shot that county up. Meredith says somewhere that we must always "hold the coming generation in hail." I'm glad I could always wistfully salute the one which was passing.

I have seen finer technical actors than Richard Mansfield, though to me none was ever more arresting. One's eyes had to follow him wherever he moved. Here is personified that strange mystery which makes the stage appeal of one so much more compelling than another's polished art. The latter perhaps can be perfected or made to enhance the former: but personality, that compels attention, is God-given. Mansfield was intermittently the artist: he was always a person. So long as I could enjoy what special flavor an actor might bring, I early resolved not to dull it by easy cavilings. I was grateful whenever an actor led me, even falteringly, into his chosen world. I made every allowance for variation: I knew none could etch with repetitious accuracy the same high lights of his nightly creation.

Mansfield's curious swaying stride, fist on his hip with arm parallel to body, fascinated me; as did his open gesture, with two fingers held close to palm, like a Latin benediction reversed to a petition. In spite of make-up and costume he was always Mansfield. He made little effort to conceal what was the actor's essence, his palette if you will, as personal and recognizable as that of a Renoir. There was the same tonal modulation, within the selected color emphasis he gave each character. Yet his voice could be young as in *Old Heidelberg,* or old as with the Baron Chevrial, in *The Parisian Romance,* which made him a star. It was a vibrant baritone: neither Hampden nor Coquelin excelled his Cyrano in the battle scene: he could top the cannons with the stirring "Les Cadets de Gascogne." He could exude a suave, worldly charm: I was once to see a Christmas Eve performance of *Prince Karl,* when to an almost empty house he improvised with song and fable for his company and me. It was then one remembered he had once played KoKo in *The Mikado.* No one could so sting with the sarcastic impertinences of a Bernard Shaw, whose *Arms and the Man* and *The Devil's Disciple* he introduced to America. His tricky *Dr. Jekyll and Mr. Hyde* held no such moment of freezing terror for me as did his *Richard the Third* when, torn from his nightmare in the tent scene, he rushed hysterically across the stage to murder Catsby, only to find his bodyguard was not another phantom of his guilty dream. A dozen such moments spring back faster than I can write: for I saw every play in his repertoire many times.

There are also words which live again at his own table, where I sat entranced as he talked to me, who had so often gazed at him from my top gallery: his description of having Sarah Bernhardt lunch in his private car when she wrapped a leopard skin tightly about her legs, "to protect her virtue, I assume"—as he put it—and the story in which he acted and characterized each person who peopled it.

The story had to do with a famous dandy in Paris who was broke. Nothing was left but suicide or a debtors' prison. He decided on the latter—and to go there with a flourish. He entered a well known restaurant and was, as usual, effusively greeted while being shown to his favorite table. He ordered the best dinner—and how Mansfield rolled out the dishes and the wines! When the bill came he called the *maître d'hôtel*.

"I cannot pay this. I haven't a sou in the world, except the *pourboire*"—which he threw with a sweeping gesture on the table. "There is only one thing for you to do. Call the *gendarmes* and have me arrested."

But, instead, the *propriétaire* came, with a hand-washing gesture, and begged *Monsieur* to accept the dinner *avec les compliments de la maison*. They bowed him out ceremoniously. He was baffled and thwarted. He walked along the boulevard disconsolate. But the needs of nature suddenly spoke. He hurried into a street toilet—and was arrested for theft because he didn't have a sou to give to the woman in charge, for the toilet paper!

During these years I scarcely ever missed a first night. I bought general admissions and stood through most plays. There, in back, I could more easily meet the world I was determined to make mine, like one Monte Cristo. Now—now, I felt part of this theatre world: a small part, to be sure, as in those earlier days when I had flowed anonymously with the matinée crowds along the Rialto. But *now* I had had a play produced: the popular Julia Marlowe's name could be mentioned modestly, though frequently. Oh, yes, there would be "some announcement soon." Things were pending. "Nothing official." I wasn't sure yet; but there would soon be a new production. Of course there would be, I kept saying to myself, if I had anything to do with it. Getting produced was what was important. That was the job in hand. Let's keep trying.

Of six plays I wrote at the time, in whole or in part, three were to fail. The first play I did alone, which saw the footlights after *The Cavalier*, was *A Wife's Strategy*. It was all very mysterious. On December 7, 1904, in New York, I received the following wire:

Can you possibly come Chicago immediately bring original manuscript important keep matter confidential even from Marbury.

MARGARET ANGLIN

I knew this meant that her play was a failure. After my experience with Julia Marlowe's "nervous breakdown" I was getting wise. I had read the script to the brilliant rising actress a while before. She was desperate for a new play, and I was equally desperate to supply it.

The combination seemed irresistible. I went to Chicago. She bought the play.

On the photograph, which I asked Margaret Anglin to sign when *A Wife's Strategy* closed only two weeks after its opening she added with characteristic wit, "In kindest remembrance of *A Wife's Tragedy*." The italics were hers.

It was almost that to me!

CHAPTER VI

A TOY TRAGEDY, A THOUSAND CANDLES
AND A GREAT LADY

I LINGER with *A Wife's Strategy* not for any merit of its political story but because it brings into my narrative a gifted actress and a subject of concern to all playwrights. I had first sold the play to Amelia Bingham, whose heart was as big as her waistline. Her malapropisms were famous, and one sentence quite overwhelmed me: "George, your play is full of incidences but that scene is *assical*." Having limited gifts herself, she sensibly surrounded herself with talented actors. Amelia probably did more than any one to raise salaries. She made Clyde Fitch's *The Climbers* a landmark in ensemble casting. She promised me the same. Frank Worthing, an Englishman, who had made a hit in *The Cavalier*, was now under contract to her. Frank, a splendid, high-tensioned actor, could suggest a well bred Confederate officer; but he carried his handkerchief in his cuff and dabbed his nose like no American politician. He himself felt miscast. With vicious humor he burlesqued the text at rehearsals. There was a stage direction to go to his wife "like a tired child." What he did to Mother was as cruel as it was funny. It taught me to omit figurative directions. Amelia soon decided to let the play go. I had trouble collecting the money due me, for her husband, Lloyd Bingham, claimed I had "read the play so damn well" that I had misrepresented it.

Margaret Anglin now took it on. Its production was among her first independent ventures after her outstanding success as Roxane and as leading lady with the Empire Theatre Stock Company. I had followed her rapid rise to stardom and was happy to hitch my go-cart to her.

While she lacked that ultimate lure of a warm entrancing personality, her training from young womanhood, touring the provinces in Canada, had made her a fluent mistress of stage mechanics. "You go where you want, and I'll find you," I heard her once tell an actor. Her memory, like Huey Long's, was photographic. She could read a page and know it. An extremely cultivated woman, with social

67

background and personal charm, she knew how to "protect" herself and even held her own with Richard Mansfield. Her wit matched his. When he sarcastically asked her whether she could make herself up "beautifully enough to play Roxane," she retorted she could if he could make himself up "ugly enough to play Cyrano."

She was equally at ease in high comedy and agitated emotion; but Belasco thought her greatest asset was a "vocal quiver" which brought your tears. Its effect was automatic; no one could sob as she, nor better portray a scene, as in *Mrs. Dane's Defence,* where, cornered, she would try to lie her way out. Her capacity to project "inner states" had inspired me with the hope that the sort of plays I wished to write might lead to a permanent collaboration. But she always had to have her own way, and that included scripts. Nothing was said before our contract was signed; at rehearsal, however, the question of "changes" arose—one of the most trying of our trade problems.

Perhaps I refused to do the altering she wished because I was inexperienced. Managers complain that first-play fellows are the most unreasonable: for to them their words are pearls. Yet all plays of a workaday theatre, in rehearsal or before they are "set" by audience reaction, need at least currying; often even a plastic operation. Here the "play doctor" may be summoned with forceps and bandages. Such revisions have slapped many a newborn infant to life, though its cries and those of the helpless dramatist may often be hard to distinguish. How we dreaded the coming of "rewrite men," then systematically sicked on by certain firms.

More often changes are suggested by the stage director. The color he imparts takes on his special slant. Woe be if the scripts are not up his alley. Gradually I became house-broken; and when I come to analyze the directing genius of David Belasco I will detail how he improved my scripts. Casting often compels plot changes: sometimes the audience dictates them. In *The Big Pond,* which Al Thomas and I wrote years later, our Frenchman was so attractively played by Kenneth MacKenna that the audience demanded he get the girl though it was originally arranged otherwise. When Richard Mansfield spoke the opening lines of his serious drama, *Castle Sombras,* the audience laughed. He instantly threw the whole part for satire and turned the play into a comedy.

The playwright, with a gift for "putting a play on," may often anticipate effects which lie beyond dialogue. How otherwise would an audience be convulsed when a character said "Yes," after rocking in her chair three times, yet would hardly smile if she only rocked twice—as George Kelly told me happened in his *Show Off?* Why should the guffaw in the last act of *It Pays to Advertise* "die" until it was discovered a "plant" word in the first act had been muffed? Thus every play offers a myriad of such little changes increasing the ripple which gives life to the line. The "click" of a scene may often be sprung only after weeks of verbal manipulations.

In Anderson's *Valley Forge,* one line—"This liberty will look easy by and by when nobody dies to get it"—proved to be so striking that Max had to move it from its modest place in the text to become the talked-of "tag" of the play. Harold Moulton, who owns all the Pinero scripts, told me that he had shown the typed copy of *The Second Mrs. Tanqueray* to Mrs. Pat Campbell, creator of the part in 1893. She glanced at the last page and said: "Yes, that's the final script, before Pin sent it off to the printer. I know because it has some of the changes *I* suggested!" Don Marquis once wrote a tale showing how the practical playwright always had functioned: for the actor, Burbage, while rehearsing *Macbeth,* felt the need of some lines "to space it." So Bill sat down and scribbled off "Out, out brief candle . . ." These unrelated examples reveal that production is fusion. Many collaborate on it; changes are part of getting a play across. An experienced writer welcomes any life-line, if he can't supply his own preserver. For the right "curtain line" to the second act of my *Blood Money,* produced in 1927, I would have given half my royalties— maybe.

But the issue was not whether changes ought to be made: it was *who* should make them. While the author himself was then supposed to have the right, there was no authority to enforce it. As a result of my experience with *A Wife's Strategy* I made up my mind to do what I could to help establish the author's control over his text, with power to make his own changes or prevent changes by others. It was twenty years before the Dramatists' Guild was strong enough to bring this about. Incidentally, we authors now have approval of cast, and a veto over the director. The old idea that a manager in leasing the script could massage it out of shape seems to have been lost.

But at the time my play was produced a young dramatist was more or less at the mercy of star and manager. I hold no brief for *A Wife's Strategy.* I have never reread it, nor was it ever published; yet it was persuasive enough at the time for two stars to buy it. However, the changes, which Margaret Anglin wanted, so violated whatever integrity the idea had that I simply couldn't agree. So she put down the script, and I put down my foot. She put on her Persian lamb and walked out; I put on mine (Dad's) and boiled. But in those days actors were not paid for rehearsals. If they were stopped the actors would be out of pocket and jobs. I had a sneaking idea that if the play were done at all it would be on the star's terms. There was no organization to which I might appeal. So I gave in.

But I felt as Ibsen must have felt when everybody wanted Nora to stay and not bang the door on her doll's house; though Ibsen did consent to write his own happy ending for those countries where he was helpless to control the copyright, because he preferred doing the mayhem himself to leaving it to the local hacks. Instead of my altering the script, however, an acquiescent rewrite woman was ready with the changes. I had used the device of having my star remain silent throughout the third act, sitting tense as the results of her previous action whirled about her. I thought it rather good, especially since Strindberg had used the same device in *The Stranger*. At any rate I learned Acts III and IV were to be telescoped with a big scene to climax in a blaze of Anglinonics!

I had heard the story about Al Woods, who told an author that his play was to open in Atlantic City. When the author arrived he found it was opening that night in Buffalo. Meantime Al had called in a play doctor, who supplied a new act.

We were to open in Albany. But my star wasn't on the company train. Neither were the two leading men; in fact I found, to avoid me, they, plus the lady playwright, had tiptoed up the day before and put in the "new ending" I had not even seen at the dress rehearsal. In fact, I seem to recall a headache came on that afternoon in New York just as she had reached it because she "hadn't felt equal to doing it." She probably saw me on the side lines making manicure gestures.

Margaret Anglin's close friends called her "Mary." Mary was also the name of the character in my play. On the opening night, when I arrived in Albany, I sent some roses and wrote, with not unbecoming sarcasm: "To both Marys." I was still praying she might be right. I was even reconciled to accepting any royalties which should happen along. But, to my horror, I saw the program did not mention the reduction in acts! The stage manager was sent before the curtain, and tactfully stated: "We hope you will enjoy the play in three acts as much as you would have in four." The next day, of course, the press wires said, "The author desperately tried to save his play by hastily condensing it from four acts to three."

I sat with the astonished manager. When the new "big scene" came I said: "From now on I know nothing." In my version it was the husband who asked the wife's forgiveness. But not in my other Mary's version. She went into the finest ground-groveling, please-for-give-me scene I ever saw. Amid strange disjointed words, she sobbed and sobbed, and, behind her handkerchief, prompted the poor bewildered actor in his responses. Like Coquelin, Mary never felt anything she acted: she had perfect control over every nuance of expression. She begged Hubby's forgiveness so well that I almost forgave her myself. It was acting; but it wasn't my play.

It closed in two weeks. I was never so crushed before or since. There is nothing harder than the first failure unless it be the last. This was my first-born, all on my own. I had felt sure, after *The Cavalier,* the future would be milk and honey. It was wormwood. Odd how an author at such times loses proportion; he feels the world is aware of his failure when it didn't even know he had a production.

Francis Wilson, in his autobiography, tells about sidling, ashamed, into the Players after his second play had failed following a success. I rushed up to him cheerfully. "Ah, Frank, now you are one of us." Perhaps that day I recalled what Bronson Howard had once told me. He had had three successes in a row. The fourth was a dire failure. He, too, felt terribly because he had agreed to write a comedy for W. H. Crane and Stuart Robson, then the most popular starring team. But when Howard went to see them on tour he was greeted at the station by a band. "We knew if your last play had been a hit the new one for us would surely be a flop," Crane explained. The cheers were justified; for their comedy was to be *The Henrietta,* their greatest success.

But I had none of these consolations after *A Wife's Strategy.* I hugged the Players. While I was buried deep in a library chair and my own gloom, Oliver Herford was showing a stranger about the house. Near me, as I sat, was our collection of death masks. I had apparently chosen an appropriate place. Oliver pointed to one, in his slow, shy way:

"That is Richard Brinsley Sheridan."

"The dramatist?" the guest asked in surprise. "The author of *The School for Scandal* and *The Rivals?*"

"Yes."

The guest surveyed it a moment: "He doesn't look like a gay and witty man."

"He wasn't feeling at his best when that was made," Oliver drawled.

(This recalls what he once said to Al Thomas, who had come upon him glaring down at his feet. "You seem to be brooding about something, Oliver." "As a matter of fact I am, old chap. You know I'm frightfully indignant about something, and I can't seem to remember what it is.")

I thought my career over. I had had a disastrous failure with a rising star. No alibi explained that away. I did sell it later to Paramount for $3,000; but the picture was never made. Another comic episode floats back from that tryout. We played two nights in Rochester. One critic had said my play "lacked comedy." So I wrote a new scene, which went in the second night. The same critic reported: "The author was present last night to hear some new comedy he had written. He enjoyed it."

In 1928, when I was an executive in Hollywood, Mary asked me to supper. She was good enough to speak of some of my successes. Then she recalled how she had "produced almost your first play. You must never forget, George, how I once held you on my lap." I nodded. But I also remembered my position there.

Shortly after this, however, Anglin had discovered William Vaughn Moody's *The Great Divide*. The Moodys later lived down our street, and I've heard the story. Trying it out, after only a few rehearsals, she would not go on for the last act, at that first performance, until Moody signed the contract she wanted. After holding the curtain a half-hour she got it. She and Henry Miller produced it on a memorable night in New York. She thus brought to light one of the finest American plays; this contribution will glow in stage annals amid her superb presentations of the Greek tragedies.

Moody's masterpiece emphasized that the American theatre had already begun to shake off foreign inspiration. No longer apt was the sneer of Ambrose Bierce that a dramatist was "one who adapts plays from the French." Vivid, graphic pictures of our own life, in fact, were crowding the stages to my delight. New playwrights were pushing through with strong social themes; though already, for a decade, the "state" dramas of Augustus Thomas (*Alabama, Arizona, and In Mizzoura*) with other native studies, such as *Shore Acres*, by

James A. Herne, had focused on our varied local backgrounds. Nor can even this necessarily hasty comment overlook those penetrating satires which Edward Harrigan and Charles Hoyt had turned out. And Charles Klein was pounding away on his topical melodramas. Of different quality, but likewise essentially American, were the minutely observed social comedies of real but often shallow people, by Clyde Fitch the most successful playwright of his day.

Somebody has said it was a shame Fitch did men so badly and Thomas only did men well. While this is not entirely true Augustus Thomas did tend to a more virile type of portraiture and story. In my many personal contacts with him he seemed to be essentially a man's man. Though a superb after-dinner talker he had a wit, in play and life, more caustic than genial. When he went before the western legislatures, with Percy MacKaye, Josephine Preston Peabody, Fola La Follette and others, on behalf of the stage child, his sophisticated statements were considered too "citified." It was odd, for Gus came from the Middle West and his training had been in the newspaper and theatrical world.

He had been amateur actor, and the first to press-agent Julia Marlowe, as she reminded me the other day. He had taken tickets, managed shows, understudied; in fact, had a more varied theatrical background than Fitch, who jumped from Amherst to play writing. Gus was also to be active throughout in the politics of the theatre and in the battles slowly to take shape between the managers and actors and authors. Fitch never was. Gus equaled Fitch in technical skill; his plays were well carpentered and fluid. I studied them carefully. Further, they deepened in time until *The Witching Hour* became his finest contribution. Like Fitch, he was a skillful director. During a rehearsal he made a remark which has gone into theatrical history; all playwrights have used versions of it ever since. Jo Brooks, his manager then, stopped a scene.

"What's the trouble, Jo?" Thomas asked.

"Gus, there are a whole lot of funny things that could be said right here."

"What are they?"

Fitch was not a large man but suggested high-voltage energy as he rushed along Broadway with scripts sticking out of his pocket. Yet he was the essence of Continental courtesy and culture. I was amazed to find in the Metropolitan Museum a painting attributed to Roger van der Weyden, "the gift of Clyde Fitch and Ferdinand

Gottschalk," who was later to appear in two of my plays. He and Fitch had found this obvious studio piece in a junk shop at Calais. Fitch had a special flavor; even a casual note could delicately suggest the time allotted me: "If you will come in Saturday at 6 I will be delighted to see you for a word, a puff, and a sip." No one could have been a more gracious host.

About this time Brander Matthews asked me to lunch with Fitch, who was full of his play, *The Truth*. In spite of Clara Bloodgood's moving performance, it was to close. His analysis of the reason throws another sidelight on the Syndicate. Its "booking department" got 5 per cent of the receipts for each play routed. As it wholly or in part controlled about 90 per cent of the theatres, it favored those attractions in which it had a financial interest. At the Criterion Theatre the "stop" was $9,000 a week. If receipts fell below that it had to get out: the theatre's rent being based on a percentage of box-office receipts. As Fitch volubly explained, *The Truth* was playing to $5,000 a week. The rent was $2,500. The company, which received the other $2,500, had a running expense of $2,000. The play was thus profiting the manager $500. Yet *The Truth* was put out for a "musical," which drew $12,000 and netted $6,000 rent. So Fitch's most brilliant play— later done successfully by Marie Tempest, Grace George, and nearly every Continental star actress—could not survive in a theatre set-up where the Syndicate was not only the booking agent but also an "inside" speculator.

Though Clyde Fitch's plays are now seldom performed, his early death at forty-four, in 1909, took a cultivated man of letters who, with time, might have broken from the trivial people whose surface concerns most often filled his interest to become a vital playwright as well as the most popular one. In the height of that success, won by the hardest drudgery, he could take time to be helpful to one who, like myself, was still knocking at the door. It was to open again for me with another resounding failure which was to swing into as resounding a hit. Its story was considered unique.

The Shuberts had now begun to break the Syndicate's stranglehold on the stage. Whatever the motives, their skillful, aggressive campaign to open up the theatre was salutary. The fight was not refined. It used the methods of other "independents" in breaking into monopoly's feeding ground. To live, the Shuberts saw they must themselves produce or tie up with independent producers; to book those plays, they must lure theatres from the Syndicate or build new ones. Both happened.

Managers weary of Erlanger's domination gladly took a chance and left him. New producers were encouraged by subsidies and "open booking." Stars, too, were enticed. With the increase in theatres more new plays were sought, and more actors got jobs in the extra companies now needed to fill what soon became the overseated communities. For, as so often happens, the reform carried its own germs of destruction. Of this anon. At the moment fresh air blew in, giving a new vitality to the American theatre. This must not be forgotten in any appraisal of the Shuberts. James K. Hackett, the actor-producer, became one of their affiliates; my dramatization of *The House of a Thousand Candles,* which he controlled, was booked through the Independents. This melodrama was admittedly to have one of the strangest of stage histories: and, for me, a host of new faces.

Elisabeth Marbury gave me Meredith Nicholson's best seller to see if I saw "a play in it." It had a sure-fire stage butler and a trick situation. What more did a dramatist need? Marbury, Alice Kauser, and Mrs. Henry C. De Mille—mother of Cecil and Will—were then the best known "lady play-agents." Clyde Fitch was devoted to "Bessie," and she was closest to Charles Frohman. She had offices in Paris and, in London, with Golding Bright, the agent of Barrie and Pinero. She had social connections through Anne Morgan, "sister of," and Elsie de Wolfe, the actress, now Lady Mendl, with whom she made her home for years. She was stumpy, round-faced, with owl-like cheeks and a bland expression. Her figure was a caricature of Gertrude Stein though she lacked Gertrude's outgoing vitality and quick movement. She was more of a cynic, though both found equal amusement in human weakness. With me she was always more interested in talking about ward politics than in my scripts.

I dramatized the *Candles* while at a camp in Maine, near Kennebunk, where the novelist was summering. I found Meredith Nicholson full of racy humor and charm, but did not then know that Professor Woodberry was one of his intimates and wrote him some of his choicest letters. When I read my version to Meredith he liked it. So we became friends. In my tattered work-copy of his novel he wrote, "Youth alone of beautiful things is lovelier than light." It was a line from his story.

In those days such plays were often tried out in "stock." With certain broad types one might learn at small expense the "audience values" of a script. Mine was thus given in Worcester, Massachusetts, with Malcolm Williams and the talented Florence Reed (later to star in *The Shanghai Gesture*). The *Candles* scored, but legitimate production was held up. I spoke of it to James K. Hackett, who bought it sight unseen, as he had made money out of several "big sellers," like *The Crisis,* "no matter how bad the versions." Some questions arose about my treatment. From this grew a closer association with Bronson Howard, which lasted till his death. Though his playwriting days were over he had been the first American dramatist who had earned his fortune exclusively in the theatre.

In a theatre full of foreign adaptations he had turned towards our social scene with American character against its own background. For their time his dramas were courageous. Though not bound by the rigidities of the "well made play"—soon to be the model of his British contemporaries—his technic did lean toward a tightening of treatment. He thus had influenced our own writers in the selection of subject. He had talked with me of the tricks of the trade, in which he gave helpful advice. I recall one instance, concerning the opening performance of his *Shenandoah,* in 1888, which marked Charles Frohman's initial independent production.

The first act was in Charleston, South Carolina. It ended with Fort Sumter being fired upon. By that shot the southern girl and her northern lover were separated. A wide window in back was arranged so that the shot could be seen arching slowly across the sky. It burst over the fort. The audience gasped. But the shot that blew up the fort blew up the play. The audience was so keen on *how* the stunt was done that it was not interested in the effect on the lovers. Howard, however, by shutting out the view, turned it into a thrilling climax, which "made the play"; the audience and the lovers merely heard the *boom* of that fatal cannon. The look on their two faces told what it meant to their love. Nothing visual can ever equal what one can imagine.

So when my handling of a situation in the *Candles* was questioned I said I would leave it to Bronson Howard. To fool or not to fool an audience was the question. Howard agreed with my treatment: "Not to deceive the audience." So it stayed as I wrote it; and, in this case, it happened to be proper. Yet though this was long a basic rule of play making it was soon to be violated by Megrue with *Under Cover* and by Cohan with *The Seven Keys to Baldpate*—where the technic of the mystery novel was for the first time transferred to the stage. Which shows how the stage itself ever adapts to daring and novel concepts of entertainment.

My melodrama, however, "got over." After the first performance in Springfield, Ohio, it had twenty-two curtain calls—which I counted, of course. It then opened in the novelist's home town, Indianapolis, with George Ade, Booth Tarkington, and all the other pomp that the publishers of the book could pump up. Meredith's close friend, James Whitcomb Riley, was hidden somewhere though I never met him. E. M. Holland, an actor in the fine tradition, gave dignity and importance to our production. There was the usual script work to be done. Almost everybody, my letter files reveal, wrote me despairingly about needed changes. I never thought it could be made a "New York show." Imagine my horror when I learned it was booked to open at Daly's Theatre, of all places, on January 6, 1908. This was desecration. But the Shuberts, who had gained control of that famous New York house, needed a play to keep it open. Its great days were over soon after Daly's death; but rich memories remained for me.

I shall never forget walking through the stage door on Twenty-ninth Street off Broadway for the first time, as our trick scenery was being taken in past the dressing rooms, onto the stage itself where greatness had trod. I looked beyond the footlights, up to my top gallery from which I had seen every play Augustin Daly had produced during the last years of his life. I closed my eyes. And about me there seemed to hover my deepest devotion in the theatre: the incomparable Ada Rehan.

Rehan had entered Daly's celebrated stock company in 1879. I was too immature, of course, to appreciate her even as the young woman Sargent later painted, in that portrait which hung in Daly's foyer till, after the theatre's sale, she went herself one day, as she told Fola La Follette, and carried it off in a cab. Though she played two hundred parts in her twenty years at Daly's, she was only turning into her forties when I saw her that first afternoon, as Beatrice, in *Much Ado About Nothing*.

> Then felt I like some watcher of the skies
> When a new planet swims into his ken.

Why hadn't I known of Rehan earlier? I asked myself. From that time I shamelessly confess I was her slave. She could do no wrong. Her *bravura* comedy was above the personal. It was Comedy itself. Rehan was epic to me. Didn't James Huneker once say, at a late revival, "She is still the Goddess in the cloud?" When we talked of her I told him that was exactly how I felt about her. I do now in remembering.

Sir Arthur Pinero had rehearsed her in his comedy *The Magistrate,* back in the nineties: the only time he came to America. But he had seen her often during her six triumphal tours in London— when it, with Paris, was hers. I once asked him for an appraisal of the many actresses who had done his plays. "Ada Rehan," said he, without hesitation, "was the finest comédienne I have ever seen." Later, I heard David Belasco second that estimate. And Ellen Terry once wrote of her: "Never have I seen such superb high comedy. . . . I can only exclaim not explain. . . . I wish I could just once have played with her." I'm sure she was thinking of *The Merry Wives of Windsor.**

Rehan's imperial carriage that kept its dignity in the most hoydenish of situations, the droop of her mouth, her rich voice that held an overtone of poetry or brittle artifice, her capacity to cancel with a look the literal word: the manner and the style of it all! Moments of Rosalind, Lady Teazel, Viola, Portia, and Peggy in *The Country Girl* have remained for me unsurpassed, as was that entrance of Katharina, the Shrew. The cry of rage, the sweep aside of the portière, the rush to the center of the stage, the abrupt halt, with arms folded high and the scorn—never did anger so blaze across the footlights. My eyes still hold the color of that flashing terra-cotta gown, with its hanging sleeves, designed by Hamilton Bell. Pinero first brought him to this country as an actor; but when I last saw him he was curator of the Johnson Collection of paintings in Philadelphia. Though he graciously showed me through it himself, we spoke most of Rehan and that gown.

Perhaps all this sounds rhapsodic. But why not? So it sings in my memory. As Lawrence Barrett said: "An actor sculptures in snow." Nothing remains after a performance but the living memory itself of those who saw, or some feeble effort, like this, to make a verbal record. And I saw Ada Rehan!

Yet I never met her. I heard much of her from Fola La Follette. When she first went on the stage she was offered the understudy of a star in New York or a small bit with Miss Rehan, during her last

---

* In response to my inquiry Shaw sent me one of his famous postcards, dated Apr. 30, 1946, in which he said: "Ada Rehan was the greatest English speaking actress of his time, unrivalled in Shakespear."

tour. Fola chose the latter. She wrote in the *Bookman* (June, 1916) of the kindness of this great lady towards a youngster. One episode, I may repeat:

Two weeks before we were to appear in Madison, Wisconsin, Miss Rehan sent for me and offered to let me play one of the more important women roles in my home town. Though I preferred not to do anything different there than elsewhere I have always held very dear this memory of her generous thoughtfulness.

Of the many times I watched Miss Rehan's Katharine, her performance the night we played in Madison stands out above all others. Those of the company who had been with her at Daly's said it was like the most brilliant of the old days. . . . The audience gave Miss Rehan an ovation and she rose to their loving appreciation with the elemental fire and winged comedy that has rendered all other Katharines like babbling brooks to the memory of Niagara.

She had invited my father and mother to come back after the performance. When they expressed their deep gratitude for all the happiness she had given them that night and in the years past, her eyes filled with tears and she said this was to be her last season. My father protested and said she had no right to withdraw her magic from people's lives. Her face lighted for a moment in appreciation of the sincerity and intensity of my father's feeling and then she sighed:

"Oh, Mr. La Follette, I am an old woman."

"Your gift of comedy is eternal youth, Miss Rehan."

A wistful smile shadowed the quivering corners of her wonderful mouth before she answered: "Oh, I didn't mean these white hairs, but here." And her hand rested on her heart.

I used to watch Ada Rehan walking along our street with her dog. Her hair was prematurely gray. Like Duse she did nothing to touch it up. When I went to college I would often saunter past her Ninety-third Street house in the hope of seeing her. Mrs. Brander Matthews would often tell of talking to her on Riverside; Paul Kester too, her devoted friend, would feed my interest. And I remembered many of these things that day on the stage of Daly's Theatre itself, where greatness trod, as they brought in the trick scenery of the *Candles*.

Though then living in close retirement Ada Rehan had appeared at Modjeska's benefit, May 2, 1905. It was at the Metropolitan Opera House. The audience rose to her as the curtain rose on her. It was a famous scene in *The Country Girl*. She wore her well known green silk boy's costume, and golden wig. Of all the remembrances she received that day, she chose to carry a little old-fashioned bunch of flowers, frilled with paper, which Fola had lovingly selected and sent to her. I like to think of this now, for that was Ada Rehan's last appearance on any stage! Merely dwelling on it here has made me forget my own reactions to the quick passing of my melodrama at Daly's—remembering the glory that was Rehan's.*

The House of a Thousand Candles was deservedly a dire New York failure, but it blossomed a year later on the road into a spectacular success, as we shall see. The Thursday after, another play of mine, written with Leonidas Westervelt, also failed in Philadelphia. Even the then popular Robert Edeson, as star, and a fine company which included Frank McIntyre, Beverly Sitgreaves, Marjorie Wood, and Wallace Eddinger, one of the original Little Lord Fauntleroys, couldn't bring *The Sinner* to life; one critic epitaphing his review: "Hic Jacet: a play."

Neither of these failures within two days seemed important. I was in the midst of an emotional experience so self-absorbing there was no room for such minor incidents. I borrowed some money and went abroad to keep a rendezvous.

I went directly to Paris: first of many visits. The train puffed in at daybreak, in a fog. The fog still stays over those weeks. I was looking in too much to look out. I wanted the luxury of aloneness: the loyalty of complete uninterrupted surrender to the situation. It

---

* A bit of theatrical history and some evidence of Ada Rehan's mood may be found in an unpublished letter she wrote to the critic William Winter, from Holmrock August 7, 1906, after the Modjeska benefit:

"It was delightful to hear from you from so far away and to find one is not forgotten. Your sweet flowers touched me so much and your kind message. It was unfortunate my illness in May, so discouraging. I began to hope I was strong enough and that I might play again. . . . Only stopped a few days in London. I was not permitted to see anyone nor go anywhere but I stole off to see E. Terry in *Brassbound*. She was very happy in the part and you know her well enough to know that brings out the best in her. She was quite charming and looked remarkably well. Much better than when I last saw her. She had reason to be bright. She has just received over $6,000 from her wonderful London public. I suppose some of it came from America but I am not sure. There is some talk of her renting the Lyceum and starting her boy as Manager. But I doubt that she would be so unwise. Mr. Shaw wrote me asking if I would play *Brassbound* next October. If not that he thought he would consider some wonderful terms that C. Fro[h]man had offered for a jubilee season in America for E. T. I at once gave up all claim I had. And I think now all that world is much pleased. That is all the news I have of myself. I see poor Toole is gone. Very few left now. Only Wyndham & Bancroft & you & I. Well I am willing at any moment. I don't feel as if I am much use any more. But one must wait till one's wanted . . ." (From Harold Moulton's collection.)

FOLA LA FOLLETTE, IN PERCY MACKAYE'S "THE SCARECROW," AND GEORGE MIDDLETON

At the time of their marriage

ADA REHAN

RICHARD MANSFIELD

held a problem: my creative energies burrowed about in a dozen directions for a personal solution. Never before had I really lived an emotion through; always I had been inhibited where more than casual male experiences were concerned. This one demanded complete abandon and got it. That was the good of it to the writer, before feelings became rationalized and proportions calmly assayed. So I squeezed the juice, sucked the rind, and then phrased its taste. These authors!

Yet it is the nature of the writing animal so to function: he can't help it. It is not a vice: it belongs to him as cold and heat belong to the air. Again, as in my school days at Nazareth, emotion, now supercharged, sought its enclosing words; again the intimate problem was to be transmuted into literary forms. Not actual transcripts of my personal situation, but expressions inspired by it, were to come a half-dozen little plays and one long domestic drama, *The Road Together,* which was itself to have almost as strenuous a history, as I shall relate. Only because of such fruit and seedlings scattered for other sproutings, must this momentary tribute here be made to so enriching an experience.

It is easy to give a delayed, cynical shrug at our emotions after they have made us dance our little jigs, like the Punch-and-Judy-stringed figures we became. But we need not throw them back too roughly into their boxes: they were alive, like dreams, while they lasted. It is what one feels at the time which counts at the time. And every young man should have at least one "Tschaikovsky song" in his life, as Safonoff, the conductor, called her: to hurt him and to teach. But the timing is important. Mine came and later passed when the moment for each was propitious; so I have never ceased to be grateful.

I stayed for a while at a little hotel in the Cité de Rétiro. Then followed weeks at a *pension,* in the Rue des Écoles, on the top floor, with a balcony and wise Madame Thieffry, who kept it—one of those substantial middle-aged women of France I was so to admire. Though I recall seeing Coquelin in *L'Abbé Constantin,* Mounet-Sully, and Féraudy, I was in no mood for such make-believe. I went once to the Sorbonne to hear Émile Faguet. I sat alone for hours in the Café d'Harcourt; a strange way in the Latin Quarter for a healthy fellow of twenty-eight to be seeing Paris for the first time. Yet I always tried to be loyal to what I felt a situation required, with inner rectitudes time may so often have found amusing.

There were also long walks with Booth Tarkington as guide through old Paris, which first opened its heart to me; there was Harry Leon Wilson; a dodging of Owen Johnson, the novelist, for reasons he will never know; and solitary visits to cathedrals and galleries, of course, to kill time. For I was awaiting the lady—which is the deadliest of all bores in an intrigue.

So no first impression of any place clearly remains or my inner reactions to all I was seeing. There was a week's visit, though, with Nancy Houston Banks, author of *Oldfield,* at her Bloomsbury lodgings, in London, where the novelist was to hear my story—dear tolerant friend that she was to be to that bewildered young fellow, way out of his depth. The first sight of Bernard Shaw, his hair still reddish, at Pinero's *Thunderbolt;* the first meeting with Sir Arthur himself; the beginning of a treasured friendship. Then Paris again, where the rendezvous was kept.

Some weeks later I came back on a twelve-day boat to Philadelphia. I arrived on the first of June, 1908. When the papers were thrown aboard I grabbed them with my usual thirst for news. On the front page, right column, I read that Senator Robert M. La Follette had spoken eighteen hours and twenty-three minutes against the Aldrich-Vreeland Currency Bill. It was, and still is, the longest filibuster on record. The paper added that in the gallery, "encouraging him through the night, was his daughter, Fola."

It was thus Fola La Follette came back again into my life. Three years later we were married. There has been no one since. So much for the mutations of emotion.

CHAPTER VII

ENTER FOLA LA FOLLETTE

LINCOLN STEFFENS inscribed the copy of his Autobiography which he gave us: "To George and Fola: who know all this and all the rest, too, about Steff." I had seen something of him before I met Fola; but it was through their deep affection for each other that Steff and I were also to become friends.

At the time he was working on his book he wrote her: "Old friends become not only very dear, they become necessities. They are the only people one doesn't have to talk with: they understand all about it by just being together." That was how it was to be with us, as we three would meet amid our varied activities and friends at home and abroad or at his final home in Carmel. In that same letter he said: "Wherever two or three of my old friends are gathered together there I shall be also, . . . Life grows better and better as I live it. Every chapter is an improvement upon its predecessor. I am sure that old age is the best of Life, mismanaged though it usually is. I mean to manage mine and save it, as I used to food, for the last."

Steff had been an intimate in Fola's home ever since the days when he was sent out to Madison by the *American Magazine* to write up her father. Though Governor La Follette was then already known through his previous activities in the House and his extensive lecture tours—he and Bryan were the most popular Chautauqua speakers—the Steffens article gave the country at large some sense of his legislative program and the basic meaning of the "Wisconsin idea." It also aroused my interest in a man who had so dramatically fought the Republican bosses then controlling Wisconsin. This was why I always told Steff that he was responsible for my marriage: when I was presented to a Miss La Follette three years later, at a tea, the name brought back the article. I had hesitated to go that day, but something had compelled me. In fact, I laughingly said to my brother, "I may meet my Fate," which shows how narrowly one might miss it.

As I started to talk to her, there came back to mind newspaper items I had read, from time to time, about "the Governor's daughter, recently graduated from Wisconsin University with Phi Beta Kappa honors, etc.," who "had given up the social life of the Executive Residence to go on the stage." La Follette himself was now in the Senate and . . .

"Are you the daughter of—" I started to ask her.

"Yes," a bit wearily.

"Let's sit down," I said. She couldn't help herself. We discussed the theatre. "I'd like to come see you sometime," I suggested, after a second look at the charming young woman.

"Oh, yes: it would be nice, sometime," she politely countered.

And, as Fola relates it, I said: "In New York sometime is no time. How about tomorrow?"

She had a rented room in a small apartment, with the Ninth Avenue L rumbling overhead. She said afterwards she was sure I would not come; she had borrowed the sitting room on the chance. But I did. That began it.

Fola was now to be one of my "theatre folks." As our personal stories begin to move along together, her own adventures become part of the picture of the stage I am seeking to give throughout this narrative. Fola's decision to "go on the stage" naturally attracted attention. She was immediately to find out how strange were the ways of theatrical press agents.

Channing Pollock, then head of the Shubert press department, confessed all in his colorful autobiography *The Harvest of My Years,* which came out a few years before his death. Today the fantastic "press story" has shifted from theatre to movie realm. But at this period the technic was to make up a lie, get it "carried," and then, if possible, make the lie come true. It was the heyday of Anna Held's milk bath for her over-all complexion and Mrs. Pat Campbell's demand to have tan-bark spread on the street before the theatre so that street noises would not disturb Pinero or Ibsen. Even Channing's good-natured deprecation of those methods doesn't excuse its one rule: get anything into the papers—to hell with truth or anyone's feelings.

As her father was then stepping into the national spotlight Fola had been a ready-made victim. Months of harassing press exploitation culminated in a trying experience when the company manager sent Fola what she thought was a call to appear for an understudy rehearsal. Instead she found the place filled with newspapermen and cartoonists waiting for an interview. Questions were shot at her, as to whether her father would resign as Governor and accept election to the United States Senate by the Wisconsin legislature, then in session. She sought to turn the interview to the theatre while refusing to comment on the political situation. But this did not faze them. The papers carried illustrated interviews, and one made her predict in vulgar idiom what her father would "do to them when he arrived in the Senate." The day these stories were published her father telegraphed: "How could you give out such an interview?" But he understood what had happened when she wired back: "How could you ever think I did?"

Some months after her father had been elected to the Senate Fola went with her mother in Washington to call at the home of a cabinet member. His daughter sought Fola out.

"I don't approve of your being on the stage, Miss La Follette," she said. "You ought to be here in Washington."

"Doing what?" Fola asked.

"Assisting your mother, making calls, arranging the flowers for her receptions, and entering into the social life of Washington, as Miss Elkins does."

Fola smiled. "Has it ever occurred to you that it might be necessary for me to earn my own living, if anything happened to my father?"

"Oh, but things will be different now. Your father is in the United States Senate and will soon be wealthy."

Reminded that a Senator's salary was only five thousand a year, and doubtless also answering a challenging gleam in Fola's eye, the ingenuous young hostess hastily added:

"Of course, I don't mean anything wrong; but you know nothing succeeds like success."

In New York Fola had found her values did not prevail in Broadway theatrical offices. In making the rounds "to get a job" clothes, not talent or a dedicated love of the art of the theatre, often seemed to be the most effective opening wedge to opportunity. Arrogant office boys ignored an unknown actress in a tailored suit, whereas elaborate, expensive clothes opened doors. To impress certain managers, agents frequently advised an actress to "dress" a particular part she was seeking. Before the days of Actors' Equity, in the organization of which Fola was to have a part, women had to supply their own stage clothes in modern plays. Cash, too, was needed for collateral work with voice, dance, and the like. The tools could thus be polished a bit in the intervals when the actor was looking for work.

The actor can only learn his art by acting. That means a job; for it is a living audience alone that brings acting to life. The painter's canvas can be hung for posterity to take to itself, as it did Vermeer after two centuries of neglect: the phrases of a novelist or poet may some day warm a far-away stranger's heart, as a rediscovered Sapphic ode; but the actor without his audience has only a wall mirror into which he may reflect but not fix a playwright's lines. Since all that the actor has is his personal medium—face, voice, and body—he can never have the same detachment towards his creation as the writer or artist, who places his creation on page or canvas, to rest forever apart from himself. Out of the ugliest or most unworthy of such human instruments beauty may still be born; but, no matter how great the soul of an actor, physical limitations may keep it boxed from an audience. Paradoxically, the lovely externals the stage and motion pictures so prize may conceal a vacuous soul. Many actors are trapped by their own personalities: they can only play themselves. Others can only act characters which are unlike themselves. Some grasp of these variables, as we go along, may help us better to appraise the actor and his art.

In waiting for the necessary chance to act, Fola had the usual ups and downs of a young actress seeking a foothold. Her parents were generous; but she did not wish to take money from home, since the margin was limited. A governor's salary was small: there were three younger children; while the lecture platform was profitable there were many obligations. Once, when Fola knew the family funds were very low, without saying anything to her parents, she took a job as nursemaid, "living in" and taking care of a young baby. In telling me of this she said she had "learned a lot about Central Park policemen." She ate in the kitchen with the cook—to the delight of both, I am sure—until a telephone message came requesting her to call Senator La Follette. The temporary confusion of her employer on learning "who she was" amused Fola, who accepted, when her job permitted, a place at the family table.

In her own home such artificial social standards did not exist. No work well done was ever looked down upon. During childhood summers on her grandfather's farm the "hired girl" was usually the daughter of a neighbor. Helping with the housework had been no barrier to the family table. It was a dignified job, and she, like her

mother, knew how to do every phase of it. Fola was older than her
brothers and sister, and took care of them when occasion required,
helped with their lessons and shared their plans and dreams. Her
father had no political secrets from them: the children listened to all
discussions and had their say at the family table. From her parents'
democratic pioneer background and from her father's turbulent public
life, as I was early to find, Fola had acquired a sense of values she
was never to lose in the political storms ahead.

But the theatre was her abiding love. It was in the art of acting
rather than in public life, for which she was so qualified, that she
found her most direct personal expression. As she herself phrased it
—and it went into my play, *Tradition,* which touched on aspects of
stage life—"I don't care whether I play a leading lady or a scrub-
woman, if I can do it with truth and beauty."

College theatricals afforded the first acting experience. During
the summers of her junior and senior years she played with companies
touring Wisconsin and Michigan, taking some of her final "exams"
on the road. Once in Appleton she was interviewed for the local
paper by a slim young woman with dark eyes, named Edna Ferber.
Telegrams offered Fola professional engagements. With her parents'
approval she signed a contract with the Shuberts. On her arrival in
New York she chose to play tiny parts in Ada Rehan's company
rather than a more important role combined with understudy to a
star then playing on Broadway.

Though the repertory theatre of Rehan's earlier days had vanished, there were then opportunities in different mediums for young
actresses to learn their profession. Fola made the most of these. Vaudeville welcomed one-act sketches on its programs. The diversified
audiences—three or four shows a day, with every week in a different
stand—were splendid experience in timing, or squeezing values out of
lines and situations: for acting reacts both upon and from an audience.
Several hundred stock houses of all degrees of competence were also
outlets. Weekly "bits," "extra" work, or "jobbing" paid little; but
they gave her a chance to observe expert actors, coming up through
stock to stardom or vice versa. Such had been the training ground
for Henrietta Crosman, Rose Stahl, Frances Starr, and other leading
actresses. There were also road companies of metropolitan hits; best
of all, a season, with a small role and understudy, supporting some
star. That was how Margaret Anglin stepped into the leading part
of *The Adventures of Lady Ursula,* when Virginia Harned, then E.

H. Sothern's wife, fell ill on the road. Anglin's notices were rap-
turous. She sent them to every manager and agent in New York.
Miss Harned recovered "sooner than was expected."

From Fola's tours with Leo Ditrichstein, Alice Fischer, Henry
Kolker, Frank Reicher, and Edwin Arden, I learned more of "road"
conditions. There has been no greater change than in the attitude
towards the actress. In small towns, when the hotels were full Fola
was frequently refused lodgings because of her profession. The effort
to find a room with a gas burner, where the small-salaried members
of the company might cook a chop together or brew their own tea,
was often a daily necessity. Yet who would not accept such chances
to follow what his heart desired?

How much such opportunities could mean to Fola is revealed in
something she wrote of Ada Rehan. When Fola was not on stage
she would stand in the "first entrance" each performance to watch
Rehan's famous scenes. But after some off-stage disturbances the stage
manager had forbidden any actors to stand there.

One evening after the second act of *The School for Scandal* the stage
manager rapped on my door with a summons for me to go to Miss Rehan
at once. I went in trepidation, wondering in what way I had brought
Miss Rehan's displeasure upon me. . . . She turned from her dressing table:
"Child, why don't I see you any more in the first entrance during the
second act of *The School* or the fourth act of *The Shrew*?"

I stood for an instant in dumb amazement, as I did not know she
had ever noticed me there. . . . Then I explained. The stage manager
was summoned at once. To my inexpressible joy I heard Miss Rehan
direct him to admit me to the first entrance and to see that a chair
was provided for me whenever I wished to watch the play. Then she
added to me:

"If there is anybody in my company who cares enough about acting
to wish to watch and learn, they are to have the opportunity. How else
are the young people to grow?"

So Fola and I had both done a little in the theatre we loved. There
was much we hoped to do. We soon shared in its uncertainties and
rewards: she read my scripts and advised me; I followed her stage
jobs, lectures, and reading programs, as they came. With our many
common interests our friendship began. On that broad basis, in time,
our love was to rest. She spontaneously liked my father, and there
was always to be a strong bond of understanding between them. She
was the first with whom I ever discussed my family matters. It was

like her to be astonished at my twisted values. She knew no other measure of an individual than what he himself was. This, too, was her parents' code. The rest was merely explanation.

I must have seemed strange to Senator La Follette when we first met at Fola's apartment: a New York "clubman," with glasses on a cord and immature political ideas. However, sensing my interest, he asked why I hadn't gone into politics. I knew he always urged young men to enter "the service of the state." I had been reading Boissier's *Cicero and His Friends,* a study of why the literary man so often fails in politics: Cicero, himself, saw too many sides of a question to be a man of action. Only the one-track man, the author contended, could be effective, except in forensic conflict. But the Senator had little sympathy with my literary point of view. In fact, I didn't make much of an impression.

Some months later, when my *House of a Thousand Candles* played Washington, I sent him a box. He had always followed the theatre closely. He spoke of Ada Rehan, Modjeska, Mary Anderson, Tommaso Salvini, W. J. Florence, Joseph Jefferson, and the giants of his day. Though he had had to watch every penny when a Congressman, he and his wife would save up till Edwin Booth played a week in Baltimore—the great actor never came to Washington after Lincoln's assassination—and go every night. When he learned I was a member of the Players, he told me of sending to Booth his college prize-winning lecture on Iago, in 1879. I later found the autographed copy in Booth's personal library he left the club. The Senator always regretted he had never visited the clubhouse with its mementoes of his favorite actor. Afterwards, when my other plays were in Washington or Baltimore, he would write me his reactions. On that common love of the theatre we were first to find a bond.

At dinner that evening, after the box party, the children—Bob, Jr., Phil, and "little Mary," aged twelve, ten, and eight—did special theatrical stunts for the visiting dramatist, using items from their father's formal wear, mother's shawls, and sister Fola's wigs. I've often recalled how Phil mysteriously kept a monocle in his eye, while himself roaring at brother Bob's uncanny sense of burlesque. Even more, I remember their mother's gay laughter—the loveliest of laughs, ever.

One thing the Senator said has stayed. He was then still being "punished" by the Senate, where he had dared break precedent by speaking during his first year. It was admittedly a "rich man's club," controlled by one man, Aldrich, and his "old guard," who ruled with a tight hand. But while La Follette did speak his mind he could effect little legislation. So I asked: "Do you think you'll be able to accomplish here what you did in Wisconsin against similar reactionary forces?"

He smiled. "It will be hard. But if I get one or two fellows to agree with me in committee I *may* be able to get a bill reported out." In a few short years his single vote on the floor often held the balance of power.

How personal our relationship was to be, I no more knew than he knew that, months before, I had asked his daughter to marry me. Fola hadn't seen it my way. I needed seasoning, I suspect. After that I went abroad, where I got it.

It was at the New York home of Frederic C. Howe and his wife, Marie Jenney Howe, with whom Fola was then staying, that we had "planned to do something about it." Marie, author of a vivid biography of George Sand, was Fola's most intimate friend. Fred, who was also author of numerous books—including *Wisconsin: An Experiment in Democracy,* which dealt largely with the program of Fola's father—was then head of the People's Institute, at Cooper Union. He had formerly been associated with Newton Baker, Peter Witt, and that Cleveland group who, under the leadership of its famous mayor, Tom Johnson, made municipal history. When Fola had played Cleveland in stock she and Mayor Johnson became the close friends they were to be until his death.

Only once was I to meet him; and as Marie arranged it I suspected that he wanted to look me over. She was his close friend. Keen, eloquent, of deep feeling and rare beauty, she had, before her marriage to Fred, been a well known Unitarian minister. It was she who married my brother and Lucille Davidson. Their son David, who is now a brilliant mathematician, went often to the Howe home as a lad. Others who had long been Fola's intimate friends soon became mine. Among those who came nearest were Netha and Gilbert Roe. (John Ernest Roe, their son, during the Second World War was to be general counsel to the Alien Property Custodian, with an office on the floor below mine.)

As Senator La Follette's former law partner, Gilbert Roe was his most trusted confidant. The data in Gilbert's book, *Our Judicial Oligarchy,* were to supply ammunition in the Senator's effort to curb the courts' tendency, in their decisions, to assume legislative function. Though Gilbert had wealthy clients, many a threadbare radical turned to him with Netha's sympathetic encouragement. Thus I ran into that strange exciting crew to whom, with plenty of humor, he gave free legal dosage. Even as I went a-wooing, the threads were being woven into rich patterns of future friendship and associations.

I was then living at the Columbia University Club, next to the Players, in Gramercy Park. Each morning as I looked out, I would feel happy at its sheer friendliness, even before Edmond Quinn's serene statue of Edwin Booth stood meditatively gazing towards the clubhouse he had so loved. I was dashing off book reviews or articles, for I had come back from Europe broke. I had no material to sell. I thought I should have to take a salaried job for the first time. Suddenly I was offered $1,500 for my share of the "stock rights" in *The House of a Thousand Candles,* which I had thought was a dead duck. It came winging with bank notes in its bill.

"Stock," meant a resident company which would do a different play each week. Success there, however, was capricious. Many a Broadway hit died on its feet while the occasional Broadway flop would run for years. Special agents released these. Royalties—$100 to $1,000 a week—would be split evenly between author and manager. But many abuses had grown up, and I was now to profit by one of them: the "inside speculation" of the leasing agents.*

I accidentally learned that James K. Hackett, being hard pressed, had sold out his managerial interest (50 per cent) in the *Candles* to our agent. It made me wary. "Block booking" was then a common practice in stock; under it agents would lease strong brothers only if weak sisters were also dated for subsequent weeks. And the latter were frequently owned *outright* by the agent. The agent, with his ownership of Jim's interest in addition to his commission, I figured, would push my play all the more. I decided not to sell. It was my best gamble.

The first year, the *Candles* broke all stock records. The second year, reversing the usual order, four little road companies toured the "sticks." Meantime my stock rentals kept up. In fact, the melodrama was repeated for years: I don't know how many thousand perform-

* The agency agreement in which the Dramatists' Guild regulated the relations of its members, was published in the *Authors' League Bulletin* (hereafter called *Bulletin*), July, 1928. Beginning with its first issue, Apr., 1913, this official paper has continued to be a source record of business matters of interest to all authors. I wrote a full account of agency abuses in the *Bulletin,* Aug., 1928.

ances. I was always meeting English, Australian, and South African actors who would tell me of having done it, though nothing from many of them ever got into my bank book.

At any rate my Broadway flop was soon bringing me a small yet steady income. I was free to finish my first book of one-act plays, *Embers,* and to do several dramatic concoctions aimed at a popular low-priced audience. There was something in promise and a few thousands in the bank.

Fola, too, was earning from her writing, as well as the theatre. she had scored a personal success in Percy MacKaye's play, *The Scarecrow.* After seeing the performance one night with Percy, from the balcony of the Garrick Theatre in New York, Lincoln Steffens had written to a friend:

It is beautiful; that play. It is a rare combination of whimsical humor & profound philosophy. And Fola has the key to the whole conception: simple, pure, young, curious, honest & no part at all of the world of wonder and mystery. It was a perfect play of a lovely part. I was delighted with her, & proud—I was as proud as if she were a relative, a very near relative. And Percy feels the same way about her. She plays it as he wished to have that part played. He is an author perfectly satisfied for once with an actress.

A road tour was in prospect. So the path ahead seemed clear. A simple engagement announcement was sent out, on October 5, 1911, by John Hannan, long the Senator's devoted secretary. I asked Paul Kester to be my best man. He wrote from Gunston Hall:

It is a great compliment and a great privilege to be asked to come up for your marriage. I'd love to come—stand by you and Miss Fola as you put it—but what on earth does one wear? I'm too poor to order clothes just now. I possess a frock coat, but whether I could wear it or not I don't know. And I think there is a hole in my silk hat, but it came from Bond Street—once! You know I love you both and I wish I could array myself in a manner suitable to an occasion which will be so memorable for us all. We simply swear by Fola down here.

On October 25, reversing custom, some twenty-odd friends at the Players gave me a bachelor dinner, in the old private dining room. The autographed menu, which I prize, was headed by Benedick's famous line:

When I said I would die a bachelor, I did not think I should live till I were married.

I notice the grapefruit was "à la Whitehouse," the salad "à La Follette," and the "Fola pudding" was served with "no sauce." I may also say the impending 1912 Presidential campaign inspired the kingfish course to be "Prince Imperial."

We were married on Sunday October 29 by the Senate Chaplain, Reverend U. G. B. Pierce. We exchanged rings, following an old medieval custom. Little Mary "stood by" her sister. No guests had been formally invited. Some who happened to be in Washington were asked to "drop in." We went directly to a little three-room flat we had rented and furnished in West Twelfth Street, New York. It was a "walk-up" on the fifth floor and cost $42. A reporter who once puffed his way up to interview us was heard to remark: "They live here because Middleton is too proud to take money from her dad."

Some months later, while we were attending the Chicago national Republican convention, where the Senator was a Presidential candidate, word came that Fola's grandfather Case had died. We left at once for Baraboo, Wisconsin. There where she had played as a girl, I had my earliest glimpse of her "folks" and their neighbors, so different from my city people. Outside the old farmhouse, I watched the passing line of men and women, whose forefathers had pioneered from different countries to escape poverty or religious persecution. Here near Devils Lake, the oldest of exposed geological formations, her mother's people had built their lives. These men and women had been the grass roots from which sprang the liberal movement her father led, to make Wisconsin a laboratory of political experiment and social reform. I felt I was looking at the living pages of history.

We spent our first summer at the La Follette "farm," outside Madison, with the gentle slope down to Lake Mendota, and the Capitol dome itself across the waters. Twenty years later, after our exhilarating times in Europe and Hollywood, I lived there quietly for two winters writing my *Hiss! Boom!! Blah!!!* and *That Was Balzac*. Then I had an even closer view of those "grass roots," rarely afforded the academic student of American politics. For there the weeds and flowers of our democratic system are best observed; there personal rancors and interests vie with dedication and unselfish service. In 1932 I was, in fact, to listen to "leaders" and "advisers" discussing with Bob and Phil, then respectively Senator and Governor of Wisconsin, a third party's possibilities.

On that last stay in Wisconsin I would sit on that porch, under the famed wild grapevine—the largest in the state—and gaze over that lake, as during the first summer after our marriage. It is by such return to familiar scenes one can often measure the changes within oneself. But that appraisal is not for now. The life immediately ahead of me, in 1912, was to be rich and full. Besides, Fola was henceforth to be my daily partner in all its adventures.

As the seasons turned once again, there comes the recollection of another summer afternoon, at Siasconset on Nantucket Island, twenty miles out in the ocean. We set forth alone, over the dunes and moors. For no one had the need of "elemental earth," as Fola. Always it was to bring refreshment and revival to her, just as in the darkest of the world's moments in the two wars ahead she was to seek the song of birds. Something the little feathered fellows seemed to say always brought her peace. Through knowing her I was for the first time to enter truly into such mysteries as had lain hidden in the poetry of George Meredith, we both loved.

In the spirit of that renewal, which Nature always brought that writer, after the hard realities of our own work disappointments, hand and hand we swung one day over the trail which started at the village line. It wound along the snake-lined curves made by the wagon wheels, up and down the hillocks, when meadow larks greeted us through rough scrub oaks, long eel grass until . . . the sea! *Ta Thalatta!* The Xenophonic cry of my fading school days came back.

We rushed up its dunes as they bulged like altars towards it. The sun was hot. The water called. In the solitude we stripped. Naked we stood at the wavering edge. Then Fola dashed in. I stood for a while and watched, as the sun caught her golden hair. Never had I seen a woman's nakedness lined by green water. Then I, too, plunged into the sea I had loved from boyhood—along whose shores I had so often wandered in adolescent fancy. But now I was in full manhood, swimming free, freer than ever before. Yet I was nearer to the sea, since never before had I been naked in it. I saw her then on the shore waiting, with the blue above and the green of the grass beyond. I swam to her. We both stood dripping on the sands.

We held our hands high to the sun. Exultant. And life was good. For, in its strange ways, we had found each other, out of such different pasts.

CHAPTER VIII

THE WASHINGTON SCENE

THE GREATEST FUN in being a dramatist wasn't merely in writing plays. It lay in the peculiar slant through which I could often detect and appreciate, for my own satisfaction, at least, the unending suspense and drama of the passing show. Often I was to be an onlooker, absorbed in the play of each unfolding day. And in new scenes, personalities, or the freshening of old attractions, which my marriage now brought, I was even more zestfully to enjoy the spectacle. They are all, of course, integral parts of a writer's story.

As I tell my tale many may judge it full of wasted hours. Yet I could never become a *flâneur,* lingering idly, as I passed, nor for long enjoy a dilettante's sips and savors. Too quick an imagination embroiled me: always, in fact, I have felt the "emanations of emotion." I sensed the painter behind his picture, the builders back of their cathedral, the man apart from the deed. Most surfaces would thus develop fictive if not real depths when I looked upon them long enough. It was often engrossing enough merely to be aware of them, without conscious thought of them as "copy"; though later I would find spare parts had somehow slipped into my literary baggage. Willynilly, nothing is waste to an author.

I might have got in more cash and into more anthologies, by a more sleeve-shining application to my desk. What if Fola and I often had less financial margin than people knew? Was it better to live as we went, to amass our treasure of enhancing interests, scenes, and friends? I pose the rhetorical question while wondering if I am trussing up a philosophy of life to rationalize and excuse it in the home stretch. I never forgot, however, what Santayana once said: "Man is not made to understand life but to live it."

We were in a most uncertain game, as the unexpected closing of Fola's *The Scarecrow* proved, while my Broadway ventures stuck unprofitably in port. But driblets leaked in from the *Candles,* and my two "hack" dramatizations, *Barriers Burned Away* and *Rosalind at Red Gate,* which I never saw. Cigarette money came from our articles and reviews, one of which first brought an irate and unknown author named Sinclair Lewis, who has sputtered at and with us ever since. Though our combined revenue was small we did not have to punch a time clock. By adjusting work hours we were free to partake in our widening interests. The dividends from these I have kept. They alone have escaped the hounds of March, panics, and the financial advice of experts.

The pictures of Greenwich Village days immediately ahead hang quietly now only in memory; but to this hour, as I write in the Capitol itself, the Washington scene was to be and continue my own special theatre de luxe.

I was to know Mrs. Belle Case La Follette better—"Mater," as I was soon to call her. Those who had that privilege could understand her husband's words: "She has been my wisest and best counselor." Only the intimate family letters in Fola's biography of her father will reveal how encompassing a marriage was theirs; except John Adams with his Abigail, no man in public life was to have so equal a mate. In the same class at Wisconsin ('79), the first woman admitted to the state bar, mother of four children, constant companion on campaign trips and ever present in the councils of his Progressive groups, Mater was carrying in 1912, besides the demands of motherhood, her own world of social and platform activities, her part-editorship of *La Follette's Weekly* as well as the official obligations of a Senator's wife.

Her abundant brown hair was to become only slightly gray, even towards the end of her life. Her blue eyes were steady and never wandered from you when she talked. Her words did not always form quickly into fluid sentences; seeking accuracy and precision, she often hesitated slightly in selection. She was wise: perhaps that says it all. I was to feel closer to her as the years passed: I know she held me dear. We could talk together.

In Washington their home was near the Rock Creek Park, along whose lovely trails I was to tramp with her. A favorite walk led to Saint-Gaudens' Adams Memorial. I had never seen it before that afternoon Fola and I walked there with her and sat facing it, as we had settled our simple wedding plans. I thought of that special day when Fola and I went back again to it alone, in 1940, and remembered what it had always meant to Mater. For about that time she wrote her interpretation of the famous statue which, I believe, is also a self-revelation:

The Adams Memorial in Rock Creek Cemetery is Washington's greatest work of art. The big cone pine tree and the high encircling evergreens give seclusion to the spot, and no matter how many may go and come, you seem to be alone with the wonderful draped figure, trying to fathom its meaning. To me it brings repose like the thought of my mother; and I have observed that while those who see it first usually speak of its sorrow, as they contemplate it, they grow thoughtful and uplifted—not depressed. Saint-Gaudens was himself reluctant to interpret his masterpiece with a name, and once said in answer that it was about all there is in life.

One day it came to me quite suddenly, that after all there was no mystery in this great work of art, that like all fundamental truth it was simple. It is not grief, nor resignation, nor peace, nor satisfaction. It is all of life, not a phase. It is—Experience—Life's composite. One has lived all and felt all—has known happiness and has suffered so much that there is nothing more to fear; yet is not bowed down, but is strengthened —a soul—prepared to live, ready for eternity.

Have you not seen this all-knowing, unquestioning, peace-inspiring look on many a dear woman's face, perhaps your mother's? Jane Addams has it, and so, too, have some old Italian peasant women she befriends. It is not peculiar to any class, race, or occupation. It is the strengthened, glorified, chastened look of those who live with courage, conviction, faith, hope, readiness for all things: those who understand and accept life as a part of the infinite plan. There is no beauty in the world like it.*

Washington's formal social life, save official obligations, little concerned the La Follettes, though to their open house, aside from political associates, came Liberals with letters from all over the world. With a standing invitation, every Sunday morning at breakfast Andrew Furuseth, the Viking head of the Seamen's Union, joined the family circle. Once he told me the unwritten story back of Hawaii's admission into the Union. A remarkable man whose every hour was dedicated to freeing the sailor from serfdom. Nothing could be more moving than Pater's own story of what happened when he went with "Andy" to see President Wilson sign the "La Follette Seamen's Act." There is no finer summary to such a life than something he himself once said, when he learned the police were threatening to arrest him:

"They can't put me in a room smaller than the room I always have; they can't give me food simpler than the food I always eat; they can't make me lonelier than I have always been. Let them come."

* *La Follette's Magazine,* Memorial Number, Nov. 7, 1931, edited by Fola La Follette and Fred Holmes.

Years later, Bob, Jr., spoke at Andy's funeral.

I especially enjoyed the evenings when the Senator would read to us. A master of dialect, he could turn without effort from the poetry of Robert Burns to the delightful Irish folk tales of Darby O'Gill, sharply defining each character with every color of his resonant voice. He would sit in a special chair, with a high carved back which framed a vivid stretch of kis khelim. The reflected light from his book was enough to suffuse his face, bring out his high brow, thick hair—iron-gray in later years but never snow-white—and his firm but mobile mouth. Often he read Shakespeare. Much of *Hamlet* he knew by heart, although he always held in his delicate fingers a leather-bound copy of Edwin Booth's acting version. He considered John Barrymore the finest Hamlet since Booth. Once he had a talk with Jack after the performance and, at the latter's request, sent him a copy of his lecture on Hamlet which he had often delivered at universities and chautauquas. Among the La Follette papers is Jack's penetrating letter expressing complete accord with the Senator's analysis of the Danish prince.

But, all visual recollections aside, there best lingers the man's warmth. Though there were periods of thunderous silence, he was by nature outgoing. How I have since missed the patient explanations with which he would feed my hunger about his work, the Senate set-up on each subject under debate, parliamentary maneuvers or legislative tactics, at which he himself was skilled. His estimate, too, of what could or could not be done was later to help me in our organizing problems with the Dramatists' Guild. "Never try to put over two things at once, Mid," he said. "You unite the opposition, and both your wishes will be defeated." "Don't fight on too many fronts at once." And again: "Never start anything you are not prepared to see through to the end."

I don't know where came my interest in politics. I never desired to run for office, though a henchman of Boss Platt once urged me, at a meeting, to move into a "safe Republican district and work up." Perhaps Grandfather Middleton's Tammany blood restrained me. But as a lad I halted at every street meeting, where I did my own share of spouting and heckling. I suppose the dramatist-author relation got me; the give-and-take of curb retort; or, at the big Madison Square Garden rallies—where I first heard Bryan in 1896—the thrill of one man pitted against a crowd. In my schoolday letters to Dad, I find I was worried by his planning to vote for "the peerless orator." I won him over to

McKinley. Casual contacts with the Nebraskan were later to alter my estimate. Henry George, who supported Bryan in 1896, became my idol. The dramatic nature of his Independent campaign for Mayor of New York, battling both Tammany and the Republican machine, together with his sudden death in its midst, stirred me deeply. I was one of 100,000 who passed his bier at the Grand Central Palace. I can still see his fine, high brow, reddish beard, and gentle smile. Henry George was a good man, with broad human sympathies. I am glad I picked him for my first public hero.

Public questions, in fact, had always absorbed me. I was the only boy at Nazareth Hall who took a newspaper. My scrapbook betrays what invited my scissors: from the Treaty of Shimonoseki to Grover Cleveland's intervention between Venezuela and England in his Monroe Doctrine message to Congress, now conveniently forgotten. When "Teddy" came back from San Juan I was in the crowd. What a glamorous appeal his broad teeth-peeling smile and terse exclamations had to my youth! I shook his hand. I too had been deeply stirred by our Spanish War, with what effects we shall see.

It was a preacher, however, who earlier had fed my too, too easy emotions over public events: Thomas Dixon, Jr., to be best remembered as the author of *The Birth of a Nation,* Griffith's epoch-making film of 1915. His urge to write surged from moral indignations, tied with a shrewd sense of what might sell. His novels, in fact, sold over five million copies; though he died at eighty-two in 1946, penniless, he once admitted he had earned over $1,300,000! *The Leopard's Spots,* from which the play *The Clansman* was made, came out of his Southern roots and Ku Klux Klan family memories. He was to ask me to dramatize it with him; but his views on the negro question were not my porridge. I was, however, to give him some suggestions on his first draft. It was little enough for what he did for me in my tender years.

He had been the youngest legislator ever elected in South Carolina. Though a lawyer he soon followed his Baptist father into the ministry. But he was unhappy in orthodox restrictions. Coming to New York in 1889, a successful lecturer, he started a "nonpartisan" church. Later I followed his spectacular attacks on Tammany. When he held forth at the old Academy of Music I had a reserved front-row seat. I followed him to the Grand Opera House, where he preached till 1899. Each Sunday eleven o'clock became a red-letter hour. It was there he touched my life.

He seemed then to be the most moving of orators. Over six feet, with deep-set ferretlike black eyes, he would snap his mouth shut after an impassioned phrase, fold his long arms, clutch each elbow, slouch to the side, cock his head, and await the reaction of his capacity audience. For he was ever an actor. But what was most important: he talked about subjects which interested me. He used public questions as his battlefield. "Politics is religion in action," he once declared.

Thus I first met the dramatic concept—which like most simplifications does not stand analysis—that every political conflict is basically an ethical one and that a good candidate is always arraigned against the powers of evil. But, like most reformers, Tom Dixon picked his own gods, devils and abuses. The news was his stuff: the biblical text, only the pretext. I didn't care. He came when I was thirsty: he gave to my need out of his own rich dramatic emotion. Tom shook me up: he gave me an urge. He made me think of plays and scenes, even before I wrote. Always, when he got through at twelve-thirty, I would want to gird a sword. He was, as I have said, the first to make public questions and personalities dramatic to me.

Now, close after our marriage, I was to have a ring-side seat during that tumultuous 1912 Presidential primary fight, with Senator La Follette a candidate for nomination against President Taft, while "T. R." anxiously fingered his hat beside the ring. I was also to have a small listening part in many of the Progressive councils, as one of the clan; for Pater gave every confidence to his own. From the start, as ever afterwards, he made me feel I "belonged."

To me, this baptismal campaign soon took on the elements of a stage play: suspense, unpredictable "twists," and an unexpected climax. I also had a hero. As I came to know my father-in-law through the slow unfolding of occasions—which is the playwright's way of revealing character—my affections became engaged. The first requisite to arouse audience interest and sympathy in a stage hero's course, is to create such attachment, identification with his ventures, and desire to cheer for him whatever the fortunes of battle. This I now had. Quickly, too, I saw a plot: the struggle for delegates, the warm loyalties of self-sacrificing workers clashing with the calculating intriguers behind the scenes, where even treachery was thought to be at work. Shot through these personalized dramatic formulas were surrounding ambitions and the bias of allegiances.

All of which was part of an historic episode I saw from the inside, as it was enacted scene by scene, to include the much publicized dinner of the Periodical Publishers' Association, in Philadelphia, on February 2, 1912. I was the only member of the family who was present and had consecutive knowledge of what took place when Fola's father made the speech which failed so badly with his audience. The subsequent false reports and misrepresentations of that occasion made me aware as never before how drama lives to the fullest only when the background of the situation is known. It seemed a far cry, that midnight hour, from the street-corner meetings of my boyhood to the glittering banquet hall of the Bellevue-Stratford Hotel, on which a country's press was centered, as I suffered through his inopportune failure and joined him afterwards and walked alone with him from the speakers' table to his room.

To submit, as I had done from boyhood, to the temporary influence of each passing public man I admired had been a repetitive stimulus. But thereafter it was a far richer experience to have but one figure in continuing focus. Behind his official position, lighted by constant publicity, there was always to be the individual himself. When personal problems are thought of in relation to acts, the human drama itself takes on a deeper significance, as in the theatre, where the audience has knowledge about a leading character which others in the play do not possess.

My marriage was to bring me that close identification with a man I had admired at a distance, who now was completely to win my devotion through the knowing. From those days till I stood with his family at his deathbed he was to have my ceaseless admiration. I was to be with him in some of his happiest moments ahead and some of the most tragic. "Pater," as he became and shall be here, and all his family, were to be dear to me.

I was also to learn now something I had never known: what it was to *have* a family, where all were for one another—no matter what.

Though I was to live in Washington as well as visit it many times I can only stop off infrequently in this book. So perhaps I had better tarry while I am there. If, as Bergson says, we trail our past behind us, it is equally true an autobiographer already knows, as he writes, the relative importance each passing event had and was to have for him. "The future has to be lived before it can be written about," as Nehru put it. So there need be no beading recollections in strict sequence; I will depart from chronological narrative, here or elsewhere, as subject matter at times may prompt.

Of course, much that follows was to find its way into pen if not billfold; for I still have unproduced scripts with Washington backgrounds—and a new one in the hopper. Mater early wrote me not to let "your interest in politics belittle your own art. The larger experience and wide knowledge though may help you to dramatize the big movement." Another play, as it happens—*Hiss! Boom!! Blah!!!* —when published in 1933, was commented on as undoubtedly "having been lived through." It was, intently, as I am trying to show.

The windows of Capitol Hill, in 1912, soon opened to me. Through them I observed its leading actors, who were to come and pass. Soon I realized that most Congressmen equal in probity and ability and application any similar cross-section group in America. The sense of their common humanity, in fact, was intensified as I learned the demands, obligations, and personal problems faced by an elected official. I have often wondered since what would result if columnists, commentators, and armchair critics of Congress were required to assume the responsibilities of public office before being hired to retail their easy estimates of men and votes.

Consider the alternatives constantly facing the representatives of the people. Suppose, for example, that a man is dedicated to some deeply felt reform or moral issue. Should he impair his usefulness to it by refusing to support cheap vote-catching bills when, by judicious jigging, he can retain his seat and so accomplish his major program? What can Ibsen's all-or-nothing Brands achieve in a democracy based on compromises and checks and balances? Must dreams for a betterment be satisfied with half-loaves? Are "expediencies" and "doing right" inevitably in opposition? Should a man in politics let himself be tripped while eyeing a star, because he wasn't careful to watch his step?

To acquire some understanding of the atmosphere of so-called "practical politics," in which any elected public servant breathes, is not to end in cynicism. I remember, though, how shocked I was years later in Paris when dear old Professor Seignobos of the Sorbonne said to me: "There is only one rule in politics, monsieur: get into power and stay there." Yet in time this axiom helped me to understand that the faults and virtues of our democratic system, as well as the officials themselves, are of the "nature of things."

In my judgment there is no better place to size up the quality of such men than in intimate, informal committee meetings. And I haunted those which the Senate so frequently afforded, from the start.

They held peculiar attractions to one dramatist: the row of Senators, the side tables of bored reporters, the messengers taking copy to various wire services, the waiting witness seat, loud-speakers, experts, departmental observers perhaps under attack, mysterious spectators taking notes, habitual "fans" and those marvelous impersonal men and women machines who "take it down." Even when hearings proved to be only fishing expeditions damaging facts might be hooked if not ethically landed. There was generally present the detective element of a play: the air of expectancy in the search for facts. Thus, as in a court trial, a hearing is inherent theatre, though it offers more structural freedom of scene, character, and dialogue, since the rules of evidence and cross-examination do not hold.

Testimony, like stage dialogue, embraces revelation, evasion, thrust and parry, together with the same audience reaction to retort. Never in a theatre did I hear a more spontaneous laugh than when Senator Pepper, settled for an hour's advertised blistering of Lindbergh, carelessly began: "Now, Colonel, when did you first go to Europe?" "On May 21, 1927," was the quiet reply. The precise date of his famous flight brought to cheers an audience full of hostile elements. The drone of his motor over those unflown seas dulled the aggressive Senator. Like the actor who fell on his face upon his first entrance, he never got into his role again.

Then, too, no stage cast could equal this in the revolving episodes that came in view: Herbert Hoover or our personal friend, Norman Thomas, Willkie or Earl Browder; J. P. Morgan, the Du Pont brothers or Cabinet officers (for only Congressional committees can put the Executive branch to question); General Marshall, Pinkertons, share-croppers, Wall Street operators, college presidents, radio chain presidents, too, and wire tappers, cartel experts, oil men, gamblers (one the owner of a famous Florida resort), high-powered lawyers (whispering confidentially to their clients), keen committee investigators, lobbyists galore, experts of every economic persuasion to color any cause, and many a nobody who might jump out of the news or into it.

Much interest lay in linking name and face, knowing the looks, voices, and "feel" of those coming and going on the national and business stage: history makers or symbols of economic and social creeds. Only thus can one get next to such men for the asking. To receive this impression brings vitality thereafter to running events. A newspaper, too, takes on new life with the reading, just as the

Congressional Record can then be better sampled selectively. And what play material—all!

Every conceivable trade and profession, with its hair down or netted, can be seen there through the fissures of investigation. Besides, the Senators themselves are on show. Those who swing in broad strokes upon the floor, here betray their thin thoroughness or flounderings amid cold facts, while those who seldom make front pages, colorless in the Chamber, would surprise me by sly humor, skill at probing, or grasp of the technical subjects under scrutiny. No more conspicuous example need be recalled than that of a recent Senator from Missouri, who, never showy or self-impelling in the Senate, won the enthusiasm of those of us who followed the hearings of his war-delving committee. Several times I walked with him to his offices to feel, in response to my inquiries, his capacity to cut quickly to the essence of the subject—a quality admitted by reporters who now cover his press conferences in the White House.

The Senators, and the diverse witnesses who face them, go to make up America. Never was I so to sense the broad aspects of one phase of our national life as in the hearings on "Little Steel," in 1939. There my brother-in-law, Bob, Jr., marshaled an unbelievable array of witnesses—from Tom Girdler to a miner's wife, unwrapping a shirt stained with the blood of her son, whom a strikebreaker had shot. Here was personalized the conflict of classes living before committeemen who themselves, too, were rooted in similar contrasting backgrounds and points of view. No wonder three novels stemmed from nearly fifty volumes of those Civil Liberties hearings. As I listened day after day to such living drama while waiting for a play of mine to go into rehearsal with Eva Le Gallienne, its story of a dead French Queen faded to insignificance.

Why has the Senate gallery likewise held me? Is it some recall of my theatre gallery days? Is it the same looking down upon a show—not always so selective in material nor so economically wrapped? Yet the Senate, when it wishes, can outdo any fictive contraptions.

The seasoned spectator soon learns who possess floor privileges: the "exes" of both Houses, the personal secretaries, the majority and minority clerks (who arrange the pairs and come to intense activity getting their sides out as a vote approaches), the committee experts when bills are up, the calm parliamentarian (nearly always sustained as he whispers his answers to the presiding officer), the Senate clerks, led by the Sergeant-at-Arms, who also shepherds the darting, blue-

trousered pages. I have always watched, too, the amazing official reporters taking the words down, in twenty-minute shifts, and came to
know some of them. Even the most routine session may hold much of
interest.

It is fun, also, to study the Senate cast itself, the cut of their jibs,
and their cruising habits. Nothing has more amused the writer in me
than to try to phrase their little mannerisms and ways of speech.
You can bet your nickel on those who will always "vote right," or the
congenital non-hitchers always unpredictable. I came to recognize the
ponderous cannonaders—swamped by sectional concern, political tie-
ups, economic prejudice, or other obligations—who shoot their bolt
without a rim of brightness; the snipers who dart in and out with
their verbal popguns: bird-shot men who never hit a bull's-eye but
riddle their colleagues by irrelevant interruptions and daily speeches
to help their reelection campaigns. Others command most attention by
never wasting lead on inconsequental game—always compelling immediate attention by their known integrity and intelligence. Among
these, too, may be the inspired sprinters, magnificent for twenty
minutes. And the charmers—how beguiling and persuasive if one
didn't know, with some, shallow sunlit waters may also conceal lack
of depth.

Senate debate, being unlimited except by unanimous consent, often
meanders with much extraneous matter in its current. But, once a
filibuster is suspected or obvious, every parliamentary technicality spits
and crackles. The marauder himself will be first to refuse conventional
amenities: he can delay by a dozen devices which only sharpen in turn
the gleam of the opposing group, waiting with their own tomahawks,
to ambush the filibusterer at his slightest slip. To one aware of these
floor maneuvers the action becomes real theatre. It was these clashing
tactics which made so enthralling to me Huey Long's notorious six-
teen-hour filibuster. I still consider it one of the most amazing and
amusing if futile exhibitions I ever sat through; for in selling his
specious line of goods—which had bits of truth wrapped about political
nostrums—he was a showman then without a peer in public life.

I could launch an argosy of other recalls—none to compare with
the simple pageantry of a joint session in the House, and that moving
moment when President Roosevelt, in his steel harness, would drag
slowly up the railed gangway to speak. In the miniature setting of the
Senate Chamber, there stand out the state funeral to the eloquent
Borah, the first appearance of Winston Churchill, and the final uncer-

tain hours and votes of many important debates. Most personal in First World War days was to hear my father-in-law deliver on October 6, 1917, what history may consider his profoundest speech— proclaiming his constitutional right to criticize the government in time of war. Never was I so entranced. My imagination—fearful of what might happen amid war intensities—as well as my affections were focused on that cool-speaking, relentlessly indicting man, who faced an almost completely hostile Senate, which in spite of itself was held to the end, when the galleries broke the spell with unpermitted applause as he sat down.

No play could have enclosed such implicit drama. I was not ashamed of the tears I did not even try to hold back before such courage.

In those 1912 days, too, I first met Louis D. Brandeis. He was already famous, of course, as the "people's lawyer." Cooperating with Pater in many legislative fights, he was then supporting him in his Presidential primary campaign. So close, indeed, had the two families become that to each of the La Follette children he and Mrs. Brandeis were "Uncle Louis" and "Aunt Alice."

During the thirty-odd years since, Fola's father and mother have both gone; and only a short time ago she and I were to attend the simple service of the great Justice himself, in the California Street apartment where he had passed his last busy years. There was no religious ceremony; but a few words were spoken by Justice Felix Frankfurter, an intimate friend, and Dean Acheson, one of his former law clerks at the Supreme Court, now Under Secretary of State. Strains of a Beethoven quartet he loved filled the rooms, where Chief Justice Stone and former Chief Justice Hughes sat, with the members of the Supreme Court amid family, close friends and associates, before the simple rose-banked coffin. He had been ready for a long while when the hour should come to go.

Almost five years previously Fola had spoken at Ford Hall, Boston, on the occasion of his eightieth birthday. And in the same room where his funeral service had been held, Fola, with Justice Frankfurter, again in the presence of the Supreme Court and intimate friends, was, on October 15, 1945, to say the final words for Alice Brandeis. Nothing could more ultimately phrase the inner serenity and beauty of their fifty years together than some words Fola quoted which the Justice himself once said, during difficult days, when his appointment to the Court was under such scurrilous attack:

"I could not have lived my life without Alice. If my wife had been hurt, how could I have had the strength to go on?"

Not the first time, as at the La Follette table when I met Brandeis, but one last day, moving in those rooms, he now walks into these pages. He lingers here for a moment, with the same kindly smile he would always have for me. I feel the same gentle pressure on my arm he would always give, as he strolled towards the door in courteous farewell.

How vivid he will always be: something of Lincoln, with high cheekbones, the abundant aureole of iron-gray hair and his deep-set eyes, where calmly rested the wisdom of his race, of which he was so proud. Though his interest in even the least important person reached out at once and one spoke to him with perfect ease—for he was a perfect listener—always when I left, after the allotted time each perforce had, I would know I had indeed been with a noble man, in all that word conveys.

The biographers will analyze why Brandeis was unquestionably one of the great legal minds: his briefs before he went on the Supreme Court, and his opinions there handed down, are admitted classics in form and social implication. He was content they should remain his final statement, for he told me that when he went on the bench he resolved "to write nothing further for the public." In these opinions "I could and would freely express my social philosophy." Of course Fola and I heard him discuss the Ballinger case and other similar affairs of national concern; but most I would love to have him speak of Zionism. All that was done there in Palestine was measured in his judgment; but it never lost the glow of a firm faith in its inherent rightness and possibilities of full attainment. He would also send me material concerning the progress of the movement. He told me, too, how he first happened to become interested. Had I his extraordinary memory for literal detail I might venture to retail it here.

Only once did I ever take notes, after I left, of what he said; so content had I always been just to savor his humor and wisdom, as he spoke, with anecdotal lore and comment, or to succumb to the quiet exaltation of spirit his talk awakened in me.

Often when he spoke of people or experiences, so comprehensive were they, I would anxiously ask if he had ever written them down. His talks with Wilson and Balfour, of Russia and Palestine, for example. But he would only smile. Some of it perhaps, he intimated, might remain in his letters; but I am afraid most will imperfectly move, with edges rough, in the uncertain memory of those who heard.

He never hesitated for word, fact, or precise date, as he spoke in his quiet, unhurried way. Humor, like some tolerant mentor, would hover over his perfectly phrased expression. How simply he once said: "I don't want power. I've never wanted public office." Nor could one forget a sentence which held so final a distillation of observation: "The man to put over an idea is the one who is in love with it." While speaking of his reading, during early fighting days, he told me he had found relaxation in books "on exploration and colonization." Did it ever come in useful? I asked. And he recalled one lawsuit won because he "happened to read" about an out-of-the-way locality and remembered a contradicting evidential item. Then he added: "Everything a lawyer reads may be of value to him."

Incidentally, he disliked the new Supreme Court Building. "One couldn't see nor hear." He loved the old Chambers, where the Senate originally met, tucked away in the Capitol itself. Never did he use his new offices. Rising very early, he preferred to work in a little apartment on another floor of the house in which he lived. He enjoyed the freedom of questioning practiced before our Supreme Court. He said he had never liked to plead before the High Court in Massachusetts, because "I could never get a line on what the judges were thinking, since they seldom asked questions." One always seemed to follow—"he looked intently at you, but I knew he was hard of hearing."

In response to my inquiry, he felt "life in the last analysis is determined by the moral law: a few simple precepts, such as the Golden Rule." It was these which represented the "wisdom of the race." There were other guiding principles of conduct which each individual finds for himself. He spoke of one such, when I asked him whether he had ever regretted giving up his law practice and crusading efforts in order to go on the highest bench. He admitted few judges had previously been so involved in as many controversial questions as he. But he knew the time had come to put all that aside. "The fifties are the best time," he added. He felt at sixty "I could no longer give it what I had—the long hours and the hard work." So, henceforth, he made it his sole business "to give decisions."

Did he regret resigning? No. There, too, when he felt the time had come to leave he told his brother and the President. That was all.

He wanted to leave while he was in the best of health. He felt there "would be no particular problem created by my leaving." In fact, he was pleased with the President's choice of his successor, Justice Douglas. After he had resigned he did not follow court proceedings closely. He believed it wise not to. He didn't need to have opinions "which might be subject to construction." Back of all this lay a motivating philosophy of conduct I spoke of. He put it in two sentences:

"Too many people make it hard on themselves and on others by being undecided after they have once made a decision. I was always able to decide and then go on."

I mentioned Nehru's celebrated autobiography *Towards Freedom*. He agreed it was a great book. He himself happened to be reading it. He called our attention to a sentence which Nehru quoted from the *Bhagavad-Gita* as having been "recited every evening in Gandhi's prayers which say what a man should be like." The Justice found the passage for Fola when next she saw him, and she copied it. It now stands before her dressing table where she can read it each morning. It is a reminder, if such were needed, of a generous friend she and all her family held very dear for himself, all the countless associations— and for the thought itself:

A man should be *"calm of purpose, serene and unmoved, doing his job and not caring overmuch for the result of his action."*

Such was the living background of the Washington scene which was continually to be mine: to give and to help me keep proportion amid the personal happenings ahead and the make-believes of a writer's fictive fashionings.

CHAPTER IX

TWO NAMES ON OUR GREENWICH VILLAGE DOOR

AFTER TWO YEARS of stair-climbing in West Twelfth Street, Fola wanted more space and "a room of her own," as Virginia Woolf put it. So she found 158 Waverly Place.

Opposite the Northern Dispensary, founded in 1831, our apartment was in the heart of Greenwich Village. Although nationally publicized, the Village was not yet commercialized. Rents were low; one romantically accepted its inconveniences. The oldest houses still gallantly bore their colored window frames, flower boxes, or ivory-white doors. Dormer windows perked out of patched, slanting roofs, as such houses seemed to agree to hold their neighbors up. Now high apartments have largely supplanted these as steady incomes have moved in to make higher rents possible. The Village with its hide-aways may still attract aspiring youth, but its spirit has been killed by exploiting realtors. The ghost of its personality blinks nightly in the neon signs of oddly named restaurants: but the Village of our early married years is dead. It was not merely a local entity—it was a state of mind; and, like a gentleman, it was hard to define, but recognizable.

Only a block away spread Washington Square, the meeting place of all America. On the north, looking towards Stanford White's stately Memorial Arch, lingered the remainders of aristocratic old New York, with the city's most gracious row of houses. The south side expressed the new America with its foreign strains sprawling over paths and benches. The University building, on the east, gazed down on the melting pot, where frilled nurses pushed well groomed baby carriages amid the ragamuffin groups. I never was to tire of wandering there.

I would stop before Madame Catherine Branchard's, 60 and 61 South. There so many friends and acquaintances of ours had had rooms, one time or another (not, of course, back to Adelina Patti, almost Madame's first *pensionnaire*); David Graham Phillips,* whom I was later to see stretched out on the street near the Players, shot by a madman; John Dos Passos, at the start of his brilliant career; Theodore Dreiser, slow of speech, ill at ease with small talk, hulky, with an odd smile, who couldn't speak or listen without pleating his napkin or handkerchief; Gelett Burgess, active in the Authors' League, traces of whom we were years later to run upon when he lived near the ruins of lovely Les Baux, in France, where his unsuspected passion had been to dig for Roman relics; and there were "Bill" and Inez Irwin, Jack Reed, Charles Norris, husband of Kathleen . . .

The Square holds more intimate memories, too. The house where a long bachelor affair was finished: the hotel, on the west side, from which my mother used to look in her wistful widowed days, and the door through which, as she stepped forth, she was fatally stricken: and in the years between, the nights when I talked over my work problems with Fola, amid its arc lights and shadows.

de Fola La Follette   et   George Middleton

Jeanne de Lanux

"158," as we always called it, was built on what had been the Sedan farm. The McLaughlins, who owned the house, were all born in it. There were only four apartments, one on each story. We had the ground floor. Our three front rooms, which had fourteen-foot ceilings, could accommodate a hundred guests at a reception. When we leased it there were Franklin stoves and fireplaces, gas in the fussy old chandeliers, with a water heater for our baths. Fola soon turned it

* Oddly enough, the bust of the novelist, which Henry Hering had ready for casting when the war plane crashed into the Empire State Building, July 25, 1945, was smashed to bits by the engine which went entirely through the Tower and crashed into Henry's studio in the next block!

into a lovely home. Just to sit in the deep couch and look at the long, gilt-encircled pier glass, which had watched the generations grow, the real mahogany doors, with carved ivory tinted pilasters, lit with the golden lamp glow always brought us a sense of peace. On the floor above lived Anne O'Hagan Shinn, the writer, with her husband. The Walter Hampdens were to stay for years on the top floor, but when we moved in Mr. and Mrs. George Arliss had it.

When finances permitted Fola and I had our own secret retreats outside, where neither would intrude on the other. We soon established our own rhythm of life. This left luncheon free for our individual concerns. So we did not have to emulate a friend and her husband, each of whom did what the other wanted on alternate days. On Sunday they did what neither wanted.

Of course, our problem of adjustment was somewhat unique. Each had work which was basically complementary to the other's. When the theatre's unpredictable delays gave either a hiatus, other interests would move into the foreground. Time never lolled on our hands: we had too much to share to be bored. Varied activities surged about or through our village door—our door which was always to bear our two names. For Fola was never to take mine. The theatre, of course, remained our underlying concern.

One rather unique happening anticipated a professional cooperation soon to be realized in the organization of the Authors' League. Several of us writers had seen Margaret Illington's moving performance in Charles Kenyon's play, *Kindling,* produced by a new manager. Opening against established stars, it had received but a scanty first night press. Business did not take hold. We felt we should try to save so fine a work. Each agreed to take five well known authors to see it within three days. We then sent out a circular letter, with thirty names, calling it to the public's attention. It became news. Editors opened their columns: we wrote Sunday articles. The enterprising young manager put our endorsements on flaring billboards.

Kindling was saved by our disinterested support (for none of us knew either author or manager). We were, I believe, the first group ever so to get together. The play was to run seventy-two weeks on the road. Margaret later gave a watch chain to each of us, and I wore mine for years.

To confirm some dates, I recently wrote to the manager, who, besides being the producer of the play, was also her husband. He replied:

ROBERT MARION LA FOLLETTE

Glander

BELLE CASE LA FOLLETTE

De Longe

EUGENE O'NEILL

GEORGE M. COHAN

Author and star of "Ah! Wilderness"

I finally found the article . . . that seems to give the history of the "Kindling Boosters"—of which you were one of the most enthusiastic and effective.

You were so kind that Margaret always remembered you with grati- tude and affection—as I do and always shall.

Margaret's untimely death was a hard blow to him.

He and I became friends. He grew wealthy and famous. A few years ago, I had stopped on the corner of Twenty-second Street and Fourth Avenue, in New York, to admire a high building. I realized he was standing beside me.

"Ed," I asked, "have you ever noticed what a swell job the architect of this office building did? I think it is one of the best in the city."

"Yes, George, I know. You see I happen to own it."

The world called him "Major Bowes." He was "Major" to every- body, in fact; but I'm afraid I shall always remember him as "Ed"— his name to me in those other days.

Most villagers were radicals—especially about sex and marriage. Conventions were flouted: couples lived openly together. But such free relationships amused me since the most notorious were often more adhesive and tyrannical than the legal unions. Other well known personalities were keen on economic problems: brilliant misshapen Randolph Bourne, Walter Weyl, Jack Reed, fresh from Harvard, Max Eastman, and "Hutch" Hapgood, a top-notch reporter and friend of everybody. Max had quit as Associate in Philosophy at Columbia to edit the *Masses,* which was to have a wild time trying to express the insurgent spirit. What personal charm Max had, with his lazy drawl, languid movement, sly humor, and limpid eyes. He was the pictorial model of a newspaperman in my play, *Nowadays,* though he never knew it. (Maybe he will get around to reading the play now.) With him on the *Masses* was associated, among others, eager, vocative, con- tinuously self-confessing, kindly Floyd Dell, straight from the literary pages of the *Chicago Evening Post,* with a novelist's career ahead.

Tall, handsome, debonair Jack Reed was to become a tradition. An emotional Don Quixote with a God-given eye to see, he would run off to a revolution in Mexico or a labor massacre, like Ludlow, to report them brilliantly, as he later went to Russia to tell its story. Unlike Lincoln Steffens, he escaped detachment, though to both revolution was the raw birth pains of a new hoped-for order. Jack was an odd sport from a respectable family tree. Walter Lippmann had been a college classmate, and their friendship deepened during the columnist's more radical days. Walter has told how difficult it was even to get Jack to join the Socialist Club, at Harvard. Yet how different their later directions! For Jack was to be buried in the walls of the Kremlin, the Pantheon of Communism. There were rumors at the time, however, that he had looked out on his Russian deathbed with disillusion.

No. 23 Fifth Avenue, which wealthy, luscious, black-banged Mabel Dodge presided over, was then the rendezvous of many picturesque Villagers who kept bouncing in and out the headlines. I recall one-eyed Bill Haywood, fierce to look upon, who shocked the conservatives as leader of the I.W.W. but in reality was big-hearted and tender; he was to die a lonely exile in Russia. Also Emma Goldman, the anarchist, who when deported to Russia was bitterly disillusioned on discovering it wasn't her revolution. But what a *pot au feu* she could cook! In fact, Emma's best culinary rival, as I can attest, was the fiery Carlo Tresca.

Banished, I believe, from his own sunny Italy, hated here for his attacks on our capitalistic set-up, Tresca was to achieve editorial accolades years later, after his self-predicted assassination, because of his equally violent attacks on both fascism and communism. Nothing could better illustrate what ironies smirk in our changing attitudes towards the rebels of another day. His friend, when I first knew him, was the beautiful, dark-haired, blue-eyed, eloquent Elizabeth Gurley Flynn, who had first wooed my interest with her contagious oratory during the Paterson textile strike where I, too, gave my bit in protest against work conditions and the free-speech gag. Incidentally, Edward McNamara, who became actor, member of the Players and one of the wits of his time, was a cop during this strike and kept our picket line moving along.

About Mabel Dodge's well foddered tables, in fact, one might find anybody with everybody, talking: genial, lovable Art Young, who took his bitterness out in his pencil; the effervescent likable-in-spite-of-all Harry Kemp; moody, flamboyant Jig Cook, whose unique story was to be written by his wife, Susan Glaspell (with a literary career of her own ahead and a Pulitzer Prize); Jo Davidson, destined to sculpt many men in public eye, including Fola's father; Lee Simonson, art director of the Theatre Guild—the catalogue of those who mingled and munched would include most of the Liberal Club or all the contributors to the *Masses*. They quarreled among themselves but never with Mabel; though she missed little and silently enjoyed watching the animals perform. It was all a show till her own susceptible emotions took her into the cage. There she captured what she wanted, and Jack Reed was heroically then in the picture.

Mabel has confessed everything in four volumes. Come to think of it, almost everybody who went there has gone autobiographical: Lincoln Steffens, Hutchins Hapgood, Floyd Dell, Max Eastman, Art Young, and Emma Goldman, among others. I also seem to recollect the visits at No. 23, in his decline, of the entertaining, unreliable English editor Frank Harris, who was part of the literary history of several decades. He lived in the same Ninth Street flat I had visited as a boy, when my Sunday-school teacher lived there! Harris, too, for years strip-teased his inner life. Greenwich Village has been scratched bare of even its skimpiest kernels—and many of the glittering morsels were only that.

I knew I was never received as a "real Villager." I could not hide my reserves. Truth was, the "causes" were often more sympathetic to me than their advocates, though Fola and I, from time to time, did take part in any organized protest where civil liberties or free speech was involved. Yet, otherwise, I enjoyed merely gabbing with them. I loved my ring-side seat from which I encouraged the fighters. They all passionately, if only temporarily, believed in something. What's more, they went down the line for it. It was their caring and enthusiasm that got me. Many an item I picked up went into my notebooks to stimulate scene, theme or merely to point a phrase. The writer's mill was welcoming any grist.

One particular bit of fodder comes to mind. Huxley said that Darwin's "idea of a tragedy was a deduction slain by a fact." In those days I was tending to consider all of those who were not in sympathy with my own groping liberal ideas as horny monsters devoid of feeling. So-called "capitalists," as a class, aroused their own particular prejudices. A writer, however, learns in strange ways; often the concrete human instance awakens him with a start to greater fairness in his social appraisals. Hence, an experience growing out of Fola's activity in the notorious "White Goods Workers' Strike" deserves a motto for one's morals.

The Women's Trade Union League had asked her to read poetry to the girls when they were off the picket lines. I went with her. As she stood before them, she suddenly felt poetry was not enough for hungry eyes.

"I only wish there was something I could *do*," she said, as she stopped.

A girl in back called out: "There is, Miss La Follette. You can go with us on the picket line. If there's a lady with us the police won't beat us up." Then she poured out how they had been "beaten up" by strikebreakers, hired "to break up the line."

So Fola joined them. On the picket line she saw the brutal handling repeated upon another girl. When Fola protested the plain-clothes deputy showed his badge and carted the girl off to the Police Court. She was released to appear for trial that night, and Fola brought her to our flat. She was a Jew, and so Fola herself carefully prepared what she thought was a Kosher meal. But the girl was so orthodox that she couldn't eat off our plates.

We went that night to court. Fola testified as to what had happened, and was supported by Edna Kenton, the novelist, and Walter Weyl, whose books were then in vogue. But the Magistrate, who had an antilabor record, took the unsupported word of the detective. I could hardly restrain myself. It was the first time I had realized how much temperament and an economic slant may influence a court decision.

The girl said to Fola afterwards: "I didn't do anything, and I got sentenced. I wish I had done something."

So are radicals made.

The next day the papers all carried the story about Fola on the line. Frank O'Malley's front-page lead in the *New York Sun* was surprisingly sympathetic. Years later, he told us that he had been sent to write one of his celebrated flip stories about a "publicity-seeking actress." But he was himself indignant at what he had seen.

Josephine Preston Peabody, the poet, author of the successful *The Piper*, was stopping with her friends, the Thomas Chadbournes. He was a wealthy corporation lawyer. They asked us to dinner. There Fola told of the court happening and how the girl had asked:

"Miss La Follette, when the Judge made me hold up my hand with his and mumbled something, was he saying a prayer for me?"

That night Mrs. Chadbourne and Josephine volunteered to join the picket line and to bring their friends. Socially prominent names made front-page publicity. Mrs. J. Borden Harriman became interested. She took to court the President's two daughters, Margaret and Eleanor, whom Lenore Riley referred to in her speeches as "the Wilson girls." At the night-court sessions my blood boiled at the change in manner with which the strikers were now treated—for the benefit of such select company.

On the following Saturday Fola spoke before the Wrapper and Kimono Union. The employers believed that, because rents were then due and the girls were in danger of eviction, they could not hold out. As Fola was explaining how desperate the situation was, she noticed in back a tall, handsome, well dressed man. Tears were slipping down his face. When she stopped he took her aside:

"Miss La Follette, would a thousand dollars help? If so I'll give it in my wife's name."

Fola was bowled over. But the money "would have to be given that day to meet those rents," and it was Saturday afternoon. I went with the man in his limousine to the Metropolitan Club, where he got the money in small bills. We raced to strike headquarters with the cash. It was Thomas L. Chadbourne, the capitalist lawyer, who had saved the girls. Incidentally, it broke the opposition. The strikers won. "It was that damn publicity that beat us," one employer was quoted as saying.

Later, when I read of Chadbourne as counsel for "big business," I would recall this unrecorded episode, when he was so stirred by Fola's simple story. I shall always remember him—with tears slipping down his face. It was in such ways that one writer learned.

But other implications radiated from the ideas which the Liberal Club agitated. Here Henrietta Rodman was literally a moving figure. From her, newspapermen found explosive copy to shock the small-town back-door gossips. It was all symptomatic of the new values the war was to hasten. The club aimed to harness together the various brands of insurgency. But nothing is harder. Conservatives stick together by mass gravitation: inertia is their protective strategy. To me life was more exciting in the freer ferment.

The Liberal Club put on steam when the radicals got control. It moved to Macdougal Street. Polly's, where Fola and I often ate, was in the basement under the clubrooms. Here the so-called intellectual rebels had their powwows. They were all equally amusing to outsiders and to one another, for most had a keen sense of humor. They fertilized every sort of project. Out of the Washington Square Bookshop, run by the Boni brothers, came the Washington Square Players. And from them came the Theatre Guild.

I was to submit to the Washington Square group, *Collusion,* a one-act play, a length in which they then specialized. They rejected it.

When that play was professionally produced it became the subject of much controversy. I never heard why they didn't accept it; but I had already had several plays "uptown," and was thus merely a Broadway playwright. Later they, in fact, went uptown also and I became a very modest bondholder in the new Guild Theatre they ultimately built. At any rate, I followed all they did but made no further effort to be a part. This was a mistake, for the Theatre Guild, as it evolved, became a vital factor in stage history; and I might have found a place in it. Today Theresa Helburn and Lawrence Langner, the last active survivors, are among the foremost figures in the contemporary theatre.

At the start the Washington Square Players were strictly an amateur movement—like the Provincetown Players, with whom they cooperated. The story of that experimental theatre on Macdougal Street, founded to give the American playwright "a chance to work out his ideas in freedom," has often been told: the dream of Jig Cook, who was to die in Greece—with a stone from the Temple of Apollo to mark his grave. At the Provincetown Playhouse Paul Green, now our leading writer of folk drama, was to have his first professional production: *In Abraham's Bosom,* which won the 1927 Pulitzer Prize.

On its initial bill in 1916, I had one premonitory emotion of which I am proud. I had gone into the narrow, darkened playhouse, converted from a stable, without noticing the program. The curtain rose on a play about sailors. I did not know who wrote it. When the curtain fell I eagerly turned to Fola. "There is a real playwright. Who is he?" It was Eugene O'Neill. I had never met him.

I still had never met him some years later when I wrote impulsively, so thrilled was I by the beauty and power of his first long play, which Richard Bennett produced at a matinée. It swept me quite off my feet. He replied:

PROVINCETOWN, MASS., March 12, 1920

MY DEAR MR. MIDDLETON:

. . . Your letter is one of the most gratifying things the production of *Beyond the Horizon* has brought to me and I am very deeply grateful for your thoughtfulness in writing it. Real appreciation from one who knows is a rarity to cheer about—especially when one is deafened by ballyhooing.

You and St. John Ervine are the only playwrights who have given me a brotherly word of encouragement—and you can bet your letters are going into the old oak chest as heirlooms in embryo! And your letters have taught me, I hope—if ever I get the authority for it—to do likewise and write to the first author whose play I respect—especially if I don't know him—to tell him so; for, through you, I have learned the things that count most of all.

Cordially

EUGENE O'NEILL

This play won the 1920 Pulitzer Prize, and he wrote two other plays that won it in later years. Up to 1946 he is the only American dramatist to receive the Nobel Prize for Literature (1936), an honor among dramatists shared with Pirandello, Benevente, Hauptmann, Echegaray and Shaw.

I am naturally happy over my early salute.

The last time I was to see George Arliss, he and his wife invited me to dine. He asked me where I was living. "I am still at 158," I replied. "Now I tell everybody that George Arliss once lived there, on the top floor." He smiled in that quaint way he had, "Have they put up a tablet yet?"

Perhaps when they do we might be included; for Fola and I, in spite of long absences, were to keep it as our home for twenty-six years.

CHAPTER X

I GO INTO THE WOMAN
QUESTION

When my dramatization of Vaughan Kester's *The Prodigal Judge* opened at Atlantic City, in 1913, I asked at the hotel for a room "with twin beds and bath." I signed "Fola La Follette and George Middleton." The clerk hesitated.

"Don't you want two rooms, Mr. Middleton?"

"If we *weren't* married, would I have signed it that way?" I asked.

He puzzled a moment; for clerks, like travelers, must be content. Then as he worked it out he smiled slowly, ceremoniously handing over the key with a you-win gesture. Except possibly in Europe, I never signed ourselves otherwise. Over there the male puts, after his name, "et Madame." "Madame," on the Continent, covers a multitude of sins. When Fola had asked how I felt about her keeping her own name I couldn't see why any woman, professional or otherwise, should give up her identification tag. I wouldn't have changed mine, though men have done so in some European countries.

When I defended Fola's right to do as she wished, a teapot tempest spilled over. Editorials, interviews, and what not followed, for we were accused of starting another of those "feminists' demands" which were "breaking up the home." We had to phrase publicly what had merely been a personal matter. My bulk, and Fola's obvious femininity didn't suggest a henpecked ménage. But what about the children? We suggested the only point was that they should keep whichever name they started with, it being more practical, perhaps, that Dad get the call to help out the genealogists. We asked a few questions ourselves for the fun of it: What about second or third marriages where the first crop of children still wore the first husband's name? Our prize exhibit, however, was a friend who had worn the names of four husbands, two pen names, plus the in-and-out maiden one she started with!

We had no aggressive feeling about it. Fola never corrected any one who called her "Mrs. Middleton." I called her "Miss La Follette" or "Fola La Follette." Most people accepted our wish. I disliked having her called "Mrs. La Follette," since that implied it was also my name. The only time in France I was embarrassed was when I forgot and literally translated the phrase I generally used at home: "Ma femme: Mademoiselle La Follette." It seemed like a sort of marital mishap; but it always pleased the French. Fola's bank account was in her own name. Our visiting cards were separate, though we always had one card which carried both names. It really was very simple, though odd things occurred. Maxwell Anderson, the dramatist, who knew us both, didn't for years know we were married.

Along came Ruth Hale. She was to start the Lucy Stone League (named after the pioneer feminist, then dead only some twenty years). "Lucy Stoner," as a name for a married woman who keeps her maiden name, has since gone into the English language. In a brief made by the National Woman's Party, the married woman's common-law rights are set forth. I never knew she had so many. Ruth herself publicly confessed what a "raking down" she had given Fola La Follette for not taking my name; but later, as Ruth walked down the church aisle, when she and Heywood Broun were married, somebody said, "Congratulations, Mrs. Broun." She shot back: "I'm not Mrs. Broun—I'm Ruth Hale." She suddenly felt that to change her name was to give up the "symbol of her own personality." Heywood aided and abetted.

Ruth never did things by halves: nothing fazed her. About this time she was doing press work for John Barrymore, who was playing in *The Jest*. One scorching matinée he refused to go on because of the heat. He stripped to the buff in his dressing room, and no one could get him to put on a stitch. The curtain was already being held on a packed house. Ruth was called. She rushed to his door, knocked, and was told diabolically to "come in." She did. He rose, still without his stitch. But she wasn't fazed. She shook her finger at him. "Now listen, Jack. I see big Heywood and little Heywood like that every day. This is no treat to me. You stop being foolish, and get into your costume." He did.

Ruth was as imperative about keeping her name. She would not answer to "Mrs. Broun." She fought the Secretary of State over pass-port regulations, and forced the copyright office to change its rule that "a married woman's registration of a claim of copyright should be made in the given name of the wife followed by that of her husband." Having her own name incorporated in a real-estate deed was Ruth's unique victory. She thus let no challenge go unanswered. To her drive and organization should largely go the credit in bringing to the general public this interesting phase of feminism; for under that broad word now huddled the social, economic, and political relations of men and women. And Fola and I were to become closely identified with its general objectives. My early interest was to become an activity.

George Meredith had first harrowed the soil for me. His novels were the most plastic influence on my young manhood. He had not opened to me, like Balzac, the broad reaches of human nature; but his ideal of the reciprocal attitudes of the sexes had struck responsive cords. I found Meredith's valiant ladies, with their insisting integrities and rebellions against masculine orientalism, strangely sympathetic. At times I even flattered myself I understood them.

That I had never met a real Meredithian until I married one, had not kept me from believing she might exist. Amid the other adventures of a normal male, I had thus a yardstick at hand in times of danger: though on occasions I could, of course, manlike, conveniently tuck it away. Failure to live up to the standards of any such unique woman offers a committed male many opportunities for self-abasement, though the dividends, over the years, are otherwise cumulative and preferred.

Besides, high plateaux hold ravines as well as peaks; the typical Meredithian herself happily retains her special tolerance for the weaknesses of others and admits her own. No one was better to understand this than the English novelist who exposed her humanity yet asserted her right to a spiritual equality. Few writers, in fact, were more responsible for the changes in the position of woman. My interest was axiomatic in the demands of woman for equality, symbolized in the so-called Feminist Movement.

Havelock Ellis and Edward Carpenter, the poet, both stretched my horizons in the early twenties; but it was George Meredith I had always been more eager to meet. The witty American-born Mrs. "Tay Pay" O'Connor, once my fellow traveler on the high seas to France, promised to take me down to Box Hill when next I was in England. "Please tell Meredith I have no claim on his time except that I have read him through," I added in parting, "and that I would only want to press his hand in gratitude for all he has meant to me."

It was a year after his death, however, before I saw her again. "I have a photograph for you," she said at once. "And I shall will you the original letter Meredith sent me about it." She gave me a copy she had typed out for me.

Box Hill, Dorking, April 29th, 1908

Dear Mrs. O'Connor:

Here is a Bluebeard's answer to you! No! The permission for Hollyer
to sell is not to be granted. It might lead to the appearance of a singularly
modest man in shop windows between a bishop and a specimen of
tarnished silver, having the charm of the metal and its tarnished dis-
figurement.

But I will send to Hollyer for copies, and beg you, with your young
enthusiast, to accept them. Is it fair of a grandmother to give her beautiful
eyes to male infants? Women bearing the darts in their hearts complain
of treachery. We will hope the younger Howard will be more conscientious in the use he makes of his grandmother's gift.

Most truly yours

George Meredith

The "male infant" (as he described me) has always treasured it
and the Hollyer photograph he had autographed for me in his wiry
hand.

On January 2, 1916, Fola and I rode on the train from Washington
with William Jennings Bryan. He graciously asked us to dine with
him. He talked about his suffrage tour and the arguments, or rather
the one argument, he had used: There were more men in jail than
women; ergo, women were better than men; and double ergo, their
vote would improve the electorate. Which I thought a lot of bosh,
though he generously offered Fola the argument for use.

I was secretly amused, for Fola herself had already done sixty-five
consecutive speaking dates for suffrage in as many days in ten different
states. I had a long play under contract for fall production. We were
hard up. To carry me without further borrowing, she went on this
grueling summer trip, under chautauqua tents where the temperature
was often a hundred. I had had the usual male reactions about being
"kept," and so, for the first time, grasped how some women have also
felt. But, being a feminist, what could I do? In fact, I think I got a
little play out of my own conflict.

Whenever Fola and I were separated no day went by without a letter. Many such diaries of our activities have been kept; those of her trip
pictured the strata of the Middle West, and its social attitudes. Under
the title "Suffragetting on the Chautauqua Circuit," Fola wrote up
her experiences in the *Ladies' Home Journal* (January, 1916). These
were all to help me when I dealt with types outside my immediate
contacts; the atmosphere of my little playlet *The Groove,* for example,

and, later, scenes in *Hiss! Boom!! Blah!!!* They also told of the many
listeners who came up to say, "We are friends of your father." Pater
had backtracked for years over the very routes Fola was then on. He,
too, had spoken for Woman Suffrage: there was no time when he and
Mater were not for it.

On May 6, 1911, I had marched in the first Suffrage Parade down
Fifth Avenue in New York. Some five thousand women donned white,
when possible; under banners of thirty professions they marched four
abreast, and Fola headed the actresses' division. Leading the College
Equal Suffrage League, in cap and gown, was the orator of the cause,
Reverend Anna Howard Shaw, who had been battling all her life;
also the redoubtable Harriot Stanton Blatch, daughter of the pioneer
Elizabeth Cady Stanton, already a grandmother herself (who had no
sympathy with any sentimental appeal for suffrage which she wisely
knew was a political issue). There was Florence Kelley, lawyer, secretary of the National Consumers' League, as eloquent as either, and the
extraordinary Charlotte Perkins Gilman. One who knew the background of their long fight could sense their pride in what they had
here inspired. The beautiful Inez Milholland, destined to live only a
few more radiant years, rode a prancing horse, with her banner high.

There were exactly eighty-seven of us male "charter members."
(Our next parade, in 1913, was no fun: we had over a thousand men!)
Among those I knew I single out Professor John Dewey, leading as
marshal, Oswald Garrison Villard (his venerable mother, Mrs. Henry
Villard, was also in the parade), James L. Laidlaw, Max Eastman, and
two poets—Richard Le Gallienne, father of Eva, and "Hal" Witter
Bynner. When we came to Union Square wild cheers and a rush of
disbanded women greeted us. I even believe spring flowers were scattered. An old clipping gives the picture of us men, marching at the
end of the long procession:

They displayed a hardihood and dauntlessness beyond even that of
the women, to whom public parading was a terror: for while the women
were gazed upon with respect and frequent applause, the men every
step of the two mile walk had to submit to jeers, whistles, "me-a-ows,"
and such cries as "Take that handkerchief out of your cuff," "Oh, you
gay deceiver," "You forgot to shave this morning," etc., etc. Not one of
them deserted the ranks.

I once asked Emma Goldman what value there could possibly be
in throwing bombs. "The theory," she replied, "is that *that* is some-

times the only way to call attention to an abuse." Visual bombs were thrown that day, all right. Men and women marching together for what they cared about had dramatized the issue. But in other ways must suffrage be kept before the people. Amid unposted clippings in our files I thumb picturesque reminders of those days: among those that received national attention were a mock trial as to a wife's earnings, in which Fola acted the wife, and "living advertisements"—Fola and others carrying large placards in the subway with the notice that the company had refused to permit suffrage advertising.

But speaking demands were most incessant. Aside from a twenty-four-hour marathon in which we all did our verbal stint, Fola took many short trips in which I sometimes joined. Often I would speak alone, at street corners and "store" meetings on Fifth Avenue, during the lunch hour; but it was considered more pictorially persuasive for husband (if tall) and wife (if shorter) to appear together. However, Fola drew the crowds. Her gift of verbal exposition clarified any proposition. Her stage training enabled her to "put it over." Long experience in a political family used to dealing with the "folks" made her equally at home with some audiences on which speakers with more sophisticated backgrounds could make no impression. I recall preceding her in Catskill, New York. After fifteen minutes I died on my feet: never have I felt so lifeless an audience. Like a coward, I cut my allotted half-hour short and Fola took on. When I came back from the alley all the ice I left had been warmed out of them.

But the really exciting gathering was at the Metropolitan Temple in New York City. It was the most widely publicized suffrage meeting ever held in America. Its sheer audacity sprang from the fertile brain of Marie Jenney Howe, who was also the chairwoman: a most efficient one.

It was called "Twenty-five Answers to Antis." Each speaker took a trite objection to suffrage and had five minutes to mop it up. Thirty seconds before the end of the allotted time Marie rang a bell: On the sentence her gavel would drop. Fola's assignment was the political objection, "Women would take the offices from the men." After stating that all the interests had representatives in Congress to protect them, she asked: "Don't you think it would be a good thing to have representatives of the children's interests in the United States Senate? Don't you think a Jane Addams would be a good substitute for a William Lorimer?" When she sat down somebody called out, "You're a chip from the old block." So thrilled was I by her dramatic delivery,

I whispered something appropriate to my bride who kept her own name. A friend of ours in the audience heard a stranger remark: "You see those two? I think there's something doing between them."

A letter Fola wrote her brother, Bob, Jr., gives a picture of our hectic days:

Mid and I have to speak Saturday. Monday night we read in Troy, New York. Tuesday we speak in Yonkers [4,000 attended]. Thursday I am speaking in Pelham and Friday we read at Century Theatre [club] and Saturday the suffrage parade. The following week we've given to the New York State Campaign.

At various times she also conducted a speaking class for the campaigners. On Election Day she was in charge of the district watchers. I ferried lunch. That night we knew before midnight that suffrage had lost by less than 200,000. We heard the returns down in Printing House Square. We immediately started a new campaign: Fola made the first speech. There were only a few of us, but we soon had a crowd. Among others Will Irwin and Mrs. Whitehouse spoke. I am reported to have said that we intended "to give the upper cut to every prejudice that stands in the way," which I suppose was my idea of a fighting speech. Later we went up to Herald Square and Columbus Circle.

But I was absorbing material in which to dip my pen. The mite of interpretation I contributed was nothing to what I got out of the suffrage cause. My instinctive sympathies were now reinforced by facts and feeling which stemmed from the group of wonderful women with whom it was my privilege to be closely associated. Some gallant ladies I have already named. Others brought the prestige of their special fields. Frances Perkins, already a factor in labor, lived around our corner near Mary Simkhovitch, who had even then made Greenwich House famous. Some came through the La Follette doorway: Jane Addams—whom I was myself to meet only in several passings, though enough to hold the valued impression of her serenity —and Lillian D. Wald, another great woman of our time. In these fighting suffrage days Fola and I often visited her in her Henry Street Settlement. (Never was she wiser, in all that touched the common humanity she loved, nor herself more beautiful than in the last years, when we were to see her in her enforced retirement at Westport. The world made a track to her garden, as she sat surrounded by the flowers which framed her graciousness.)

But there was one who was, with time, to grow deeply into my affections: a gentlewoman from Boston, intimate friend of the Brandeises, the William Jameses, and the Felix Frankfurters. She was also to be close to each one in my wife's family to her end. Disliking her Massachusetts Senator, Cabot Lodge, because of his reactionary views, she began after 1910 to look upon La Follette as "my Senator." I've always remembered what she said to President Wilson when she was heading a suffrage delegation at the White House. He told the women who crowded his office that he could not speak for his party.

She broke in:

"Mr. President, we don't ask you to speak *for* your party. We ask you to speak *to* your party."

It was one of the few times, I heard, that the President was at a loss for a reply. That was the caliber of Mrs. Glendower Evans.

Unlike many who have given their lives to social service, she had not come up the hard way. She went abroad, after her young husband's untimely death, with a letter from Louis Brandeis to Ramsay MacDonald; and this visit stirred her interest in the labor movement. On her return to America, she used her stocks and bonds as passports to the board meetings of her various corporations. There she criticized the managements on their labor policies. What she discovered inspired her to join the picket line in Lawrence, during one of its famous strikes. Boston's Back Bay was horrified. She served on the Massachusetts Minimum Wage Commission and interested herself in prison reforms. She and Fola's mother campaigned together on the chautauquas for woman suffrage. She financially backed papers and causes without end—none with more passion than the defense of Sacco and Vanzetti.

Never was she to lose her interest. When Fola and I went to visit her in Brookline during her last long illness,* "Bunkie," as Fola called her, asked me to tell her "all that was happening in Washington." She lay in silence, pale as the sheets about her, her pure white hair smoothed tightly back, accentuating the delicate line of her sensitive features, her marvelous black eyes kindling with the old flame as I talked. Often I have thought how poor a man must be who does not possess the memory of some such valiant woman as this.

Between speaking, banner carrying, and general factotum work I

* Her memorial service was held at Ford Hall, Boston, Jan. 28, 1938, presided over by Felix Frankfurter. Fola spoke, reading some letters her mother had written to "Bunkie." The list of those who spoke and their subjects will be the best record of her many interests and great service when it is ultimately published.

soon sat at the feet of one of the brainiest and most stimulating of nationally known leaders, who for years had pioneered in the more radical and economic aspects of the woman question. In the tranquil parlor of the Hotel Astor, Charlotte Perkins Gilman was giving her series of lectures on feminism. The *New York Times,* an "anti" paper, published long extracts which caused wide comment. It was almost the first time any serious publicity had been given.

Charlotte not only turned out books, verse, novels, and articles, but published each month the *Forerunner,* a *tour de force,* since she wrote every line herself. To me it was a monthly record of one brilliant woman's specialized survey of the passing scene. We came to know her well, Fola mainly in the remarkable lunch club, Heterodoxy, which Marie Howe had founded. In fact, we were both to have her valued friendship until the war separated us. Charlotte had little tolerance for those who had opposed our entrance into it. Slim and erect, with a narrow face and sparkling eyes, she spoke incisively, without notes, never hesitating for a word. She presented her facts in chiseled phrase but, like all feminists I knew, with devastating humor. Indeed, it was through humor they knew they would accomplish most. She herself was a mistress of sarcasm, amusing juxtaposition, peppered with ridicule and irony. She disliked the narrow word "feminism"; her philosophy was rather based on what she called "Humanism." No wonder I was stimulated.

I was one of the few men who went to those lectures: which, no doubt, prompted an early columnist to comment that I should be added to the list of "Prominent Feminists—because he not only stands for his wife's visiting cards, but because he constitutes so large a portion of the masculine element at feminist meetings."

I felt I was lucky being there.

It seems strange that this whole feminist front should have aroused such intense feeling. I was glad I could follow its inner political strategies and alarms. Every law has its own particular birth pains, and all birth takes time; but woman suffrage faced both sex prejudice and centuries of courtly tradition. Since the struggle for the vote was not exclusively a conflict between men and women, the sincere opposition of many vigorous females tied up the tactics. The old leaders, who had gallantly gone down the line exclusively for suffrage, and had long been its shock troops, were scared of the newer and more skittish recruits; for these were vocatively not after the vote alone, and were

WHAT IS FEMINISM?
COME AND FIND OUT

FIRST FEMINIST MASS MEETING
at the PEOPLE'S INSTITUTE, Cooper Union

Tuesday Evening, February 17th, 1914, at 8 o'clock, P. M.

Subject: "WHAT FEMINISM MEANS TO ME."

Ten-Minute Speeches by

ROSE YOUNG	GEORGE CREEL
JESSE LYNCH WILLIAMS	MRS. FRANK COTHREN
HENRIETTA RODMAN	FLOYD DELL
GEORGE MIDDLETON	CRYSTAL EASTMAN BENEDICT
FRANCES PERKINS	EDWIN BJORKMAN
WILL IRWIN	MAX EASTMAN

Chairman, MARIE JENNEY HOWE.

SECOND FEMINIST MASS MEETING
at the PEOPLES' INSTITUTE, Cooper Union

Friday, February 20th, 1914, at 8 o'clock, P. M.

Subject: "BREAKING INTO THE HUMAN RACE."

The Right to Work.—
    RHETA CHILDE DORR

The Right of the Mother to Her Profession.—
    BEATRICE FORBES-ROBERTSON-HALE.

The Right to Her Convictions.—
    MARY SHAW.

The Right to Her Name.—
    FOLA LA FOLLETTE.

The Right to Organize.—
    ROSE SCHNEIDERMAN.

The Right to Ignore Fashion.—
    NINA WILCOX PUTNAM.

The Right to Specialize in Home Industries.—
    CHARLOTTE PERKINS GILMAN.

Chairman, MARIE JENNEY HOWE.

ADMISSION FREE.   **NO COLLECTION.**

slashing picturesquely at every sex discrimination and still are. This was feminism in the broad sense, suffrage being merely its political face.

Thus conservatives of both sexes, who might be willing to grant the ballot, trembled over its more radical implications. Eyebrows were lifted, for example, when Fola stoutly defended Henrietta Rodman and gave a two-column interview in the *New York Tribune* upholding a married teacher's right to motherhood, without losing her job. English militants and hunger-striking Pankhursts were bugaboos to the old guard, though we knew them personally to be quite housebroken. By them other women were inspired to go to jail to dramatize their cause. Of these, Julia Emory, now one of Senator La Follette's secretaries, was arrested thirty-four times for picketing and jailed six times! But some of us preferred the more comfortable way: we held meetings. Yet one speech Fola made on "a woman's right to her own name" caused such a rumpus that Mrs. Carrie Chapman Catt was greatly annoyed. A friend of that great leader solemnly told Fola, "Your speech has put suffrage back twenty-five years." She overestimated Fola's influence; for suffrage came along in only six.

Distributed all over New York was a small blue circular of that meeting and the one before it, held at the People's Institute, Cooper Union, in February, 1914.

Marie Jenney Howe was the genius who had the idea for the two unique gatherings and presided over them. She was aided by our intimate friend Edna Kenton, one of the keenest authorities on Henry James, who had written the initial sympathetic study of the English Militant Movement, published in America.

The general subject of the first meeting was "What Feminism Means to Me." The speeches were limited to ten minutes. The second was under the general title "Breaking into the Human Race." The admission was free. They were admittedly two remarkable meetings —with more men than women present. The speakers represented no organizations: it was all an individual expression.

For my talk at the first meeting I assumed a staccato method to give contrast to any possible solemnities. (Boardman Robinson amusingly caricatured my statement that feminism was not "an assault on trousers.") One of my choicest epigrams was quoted and also caricatured from coast to coast: "Marriage is a link and not a handcuff." It was greeted with "loud laughter and applause." I insist on this laudatory record because, through an error in transmission, it was credited in the press to Minerva-like Crystal Eastman, sister of Max. She tried to pass the brat back to me so futilely that I finally admitted it was hers by adoption. I believe it was even quoted in Crystal's obituary.

George Middleton said Feminism is not an assault upon—

But the flamboyant Beatrice Forbes-Robertson let drop a classic sentence which only those who knew her could entirely appreciate. She had just had twins. In fact, I believe this was her first platform appearance after the double-header. As Beatrice was surging along, as only she could, on "The Right of the Mother to Her Profession," she suddenly stopped to interject:

"I generally get what I go after. I keep at it until I do. Now I wanted twins—"

But she never finished the sentence. The audience got the picture. Time was taken out till it recovered. I thought from the cheers that possibly her husband, Swinburne Hale, would be called on for a bow. But there was ample evidence he had already had continual compensations.

So many of the things we passionately proclaimed at that Cooper Union rally have become tired truisms now. Yet my play writing during this period was naturally reflecting the feminist theme. As my Preface to *Nowadays,* which was then in the press, phrased it, this play sought "to reflect some spirit of the moment as expressed in the shifting standards of man and woman in relation to each other."

I did put together one straight suffrage propaganda play: *Back of the Ballot.** I never saw it acted; but I was told it went well enough. I was more interested in writing about the particular personal problems feminism created. Of course I was called a propagandist, as is any author who dips into such passing controversies. Artistic detachment is difficult, because the mere selection of a theme or subject betrays a predisposition. It is also easy to load the dice so that the characters

* Published by Samuel French.

make their points as they roll out: any workaday dramatist knows the tricks of presentation; for an audience will surrender momentarily to almost any idea, once its sympathies are engaged. The unbiased detachment I then sought largely explains why some of my plays were seldom professionally produced. I knew the penalties; but I was then concerned more with interpretation than with persuasion.

I never could see that either sex was responsible for the inequalities and discriminations which feminists wished to change. There were no villains involved. The tragic or comic material for the writer lay in the individual adjustments a new economic age had forced on both men and women, not equally evolved in their respective attitudes towards it, yet bound together by family ties or deep emotions. I never thought of either sex as better or stronger than the other: they were individuals first. It was these individuals I sought to bring together in the conflict I saw developing amid shifting conventions and new claims for self-expression outside the home. How I sometimes failed is evidenced by what a bellboy said about my Margaret Anglin play: "Gee, Mr. Middleton, they was all villains!"

One of these, with a sequel, was the title comedy of my *Tradition* * volume of six one-act plays, just then published. It was produced by the Woman Suffrage Party, at Berkeley Lyceum, New York, January 23, 1913. I was fortunate in having a professional cast. Fola, whose performance pleased both press and playwright, had two splendid foils in Alice Leigh and old George Wilson, of the Boston Museum. The play dealt with a girl's desire to pursue a profession and not be economically dominated by her father. It was later to be widely acted by amateur groups, but this was its only professional production. Though the press was kind I was no end set up with one letter from Cleveland Moffett, the magazine man, whose play shared the bill:

It is a very impressive piece of work, and interested Mrs. Moffett and myself so that we discussed it for about an hour after we returned home. The thought that you set forth has really influenced us in deciding certain points in the career of my little daughter, Eunice. You had a fine cast and the whole thing was splendidly done.

Such audience response had encouraged me to enlarge the theme, even before I received the following letter from the distinguished English critic:

* *Tradition* (Henry Holt & Co., 1913), including *On Bail, Waiting, Their Wife, Mothers,* and *The Cheat of Pity.*

My dear Middleton,   27, Fitzroy Square, W., January 21, 1914

I have used you abominably in never so much as thanking you for your two volumes of plays [*Embers* and *Tradition*]. It is not that they did not interest me, for they did, very much; but I am morbidly dilatory with regard to all letter-writing that is not absolutely imperative at the moment. Please forgive me.

Both books seem to me full of good work. I have only one fundamental criticism to offer—why stick so obstinately to one act? You have certainly the power for larger work. Of the whole lot, I think I like *Tradition* best; and it suggests an idea to me—why not make a trilogy of one-act plays, with this for the second of the three?

The first might show Mary's early struggles_in New York, and the last her ultimate success. It would be a trilogy rather than a three act play because each scene would be complete in itself, and Mary would be the only character common to all the scenes. So think of this. It seems to me it would be novelty in point of form and might be very attractive. Of course, it would be possible to make the existing piece the first of the three; but the other order seems to me better.

In a word, go on and prosper—and take a larger canvas.

Please present my compliments to Mrs. Middleton and believe me

Yours very truly,

William Archer

Perhaps Henry Arthur Jones' word had had weight; for he asked why I wasted "such good ideas on short plays." At any rate, *Tradition* finally evolved into my three-act comedy *Nowadays*. It was destined to bring me many satisfactions and one of the bitterest of all my experiences in the theatre.

The theme, as Charlotte Perkins Gilman wrote of it in the *Forerunner,* when the play was eventually published,

is the great main line of the feminist advance—the demand for a full personal life in some form of work. This is the real crux of the whole change in the position of woman. We have the daughter, insisitng upon her economic freedom, the wife who has been denied it, the mother furtively returning to the old beloved work—too late. We have the husband and the father, not so much unwilling as unable, physically unable, it would seem, to see why any woman should ask more than to be "kept," as well as possible. And we have the son and brother, ruthlessly stripped of every shred of virtue or decency in the effort to "find himself"—while the girl is refused the privilege.

In creating Diana, my heroine, I projected Fola's spirit. I read the script to George Cohan, and a family letter records that "he was delighted with it." Cohan and Harris bought it for fall production. It was booked to open in Washington on December 8, 1913, and Mater planned a reception for the company. George, who had seen Fola in *The Scarecrow*, had signed her to play Diana. While waiting rehearsals she naturally put aside other parts offered her. As I was staging my dramatization of *The Prodigal Judge*, however, Sam Harris postponed the production of *Nowadays*. So *The Prodigal Judge* opened in Washington the very week *Nowadays* had been booked. Mater wrote young Bob:

Cohan told Mid last night that they would produce his *Nowadays*. He is playing at the National Theatre and it is the first opportunity Mid has had to talk to him since Harris so peremptorily postponed the performance. Cohan said it was an unwarranted proceeding and that he would see the right thing was done.

But Sam evidently prevailed. I was told he felt it "was not a commercial proposition." I have before me a faded note which Fola wrote to her mother: "The verdict of C and H is tough. It's a nasty deal on their part to have waited so late after they had advertised it and everything. But don't worry. It will come out OK in the end." She added, "Anyway we're some Irish and have humor and good fighting blood."

But, as all playwrights know, in our game the hoped-for compensating success does not always come at the wished-for hour. *The Prodigal Judge* failed miserably.

As the theme of *Nowadays* was timely and I wanted some record of what I had tried to paint, I decided to publish it. The success of my one-act plays, which Henry Holt and Company had brought out, made them take a chance on the long play. The question of play publication before production, with which I became identified—I was later to publish four long plays, in all—will be discussed later. Here, let me add that *Nowadays* * went through four editions.

* After publication, the Fine Arts Theatre of Chicago planned to produce it and (Benjamin) Butler Davenport also sought it for a theatre he was then building. Nothing came of either. Close association, during our early married years, with Ben, brought to us one of the most cultivated of men, to whom the theatre was a ruling passion. A sincere individualist, who functioned best by being himself and following his own uncompromising flair, Ben has for years pursued his inevitably lonely way at his own Davenport Free Theatre, at 138 East Twenty-seventh Street, New York. Here he produces many standard plays, as well as his own, tinted with his strong convictions on social questions. He also acts in them with his students. A collection is taken between the acts.

What I valued even more than the generous press and comments of literary critics, on its publication, were the reactions of suffragists and feminists, in their group papers, as well as the personal letters from those identified with the movement. I have read enough autobiographies to discover that they all seem designed to keep fresh the bouquets one has long since been handed. So I shall not violate a delightful literary tradition by quoting a few comments concerning the validity of *Nowadays* as a documentary record.

The Woman's Political Union, representing Mrs. Blatch's militant group, wrote:

One finds one of the most sympathetic and understanding presentations of the new spirit among women which has yet been given the public . . . it seems to have been written from the heart out, by one who belongs in the inner circle.

The *Woman Voter*—the paper of the large Woman Suffrage party of New York City—stated:

Nowadays is the first attempt by an American author to treat radically the economic phase of the woman question . . . it speaks for women in no uncertain terms.

There is also part of a personal letter from Alice Stone Blackwell, the daughter of Lucy Stone. Now over eighty, she was the editor, after her famous mother's death, of the *Woman's Journal*—long the only recording tablet of the suffrage movement. Though I have never met her I have guarded this penciled note which she enclosed with proofs of a long review of the play. She wished

to take this opportunity of telling you that the play really brought tears to my eyes. I also want to say that when so many "problem plays" dealing with the woman question have an atmosphere full of bad smells, it is refreshing to come across one that is full of fresh air and sunlight. More power to your elbow.

I dig up also, with some glee what my valued friend Clayton Hamilton wrote in the *Little Review,* about my females in general.

Scarcely any of Mr. Middleton's women would be pleasant to have around the house. . . . Fortunately it is not at all necessary to like Mr. Middleton's women in order to like his plays. One may admire Ibsen's *Hedda Gabler* without wishing to be married to the heroine: and the pleasant thing about Mr. Middleton's women is that, while the reader is permitted to observe and study them, he is also allowed to realize with hearty thankfulness that he will never have to live with any of them.

The world in which his women move is a world of discontent. This discontent is truly representative of the present transitional period in the evolution of society: but it is not representative of that perennial reality of life that remains oblivious of periods and dates. At all times, the really womanly woman has been a lover of her life and has not found it difficult to feel at home.

Jesse Lynch Williams was more sympathetic to the mood and subject matter which then held me. I have always kept the inscribed copy of his comedy *Why Marry?* which, besides being the first Pulitzer Prize play, contained matter he knew was close to Fola and myself, when he wrote "with humble recognition of all they are doing to advance ideas touched on here." Another writer, equally sympathetic, in many ways had a touch of genius we all felt. No man was more admired by his fellow dramatists for his sincerity and artistic integrity. All he wrote was uncompromising in its truth to the vision which was his. In addition Fola and I were to have his confidence and that of Marion, his wife, from the days when his *The Scarecrow* was produced.

From one who was also to be identified in *Tomorrow* with this same question, I reprint the following because it reveals, what was ever a fact, his own generous attitude towards all his contemporaries:

MY DEAR GEORGE:

Nowadays seems to me the most significant contribution in drama to the interpretation of the Woman's movement in America. Its simplicity, insight and sane daring are exhilarating and big with promise of the prime which still lies ahead of you. No one else is ploughing in your dramatic furrow, and you will soon have a field distinctly yours. God speed to your tilling and sowing.

Yours always,

PERCY MACKAYE

While similar appraisals in my files by other feminists will perhaps attest to the play's measure as an interpretation, they did not have any bearing (whose opinion could?) on what success the play might have had outside the library, before an audience. But Fola and I gave it a modified and convincing test, reading it throughout the country. She interpreted the women of the play and I the men, giving the effect of a performance. Here we had proof—to our own satisfaction at least—that the play had audience appeal, had any one in the professional theatre been willing to give *Nowadays* a chance.

But no one would.

CHAPTER XI

I LEAD A DOUBLE LIFE

I was also a journeyman playwright. The commercial theatre was where I had to work. Yet I wanted to say things—important to me, at least. How to do that and eat was the rub. So it is time to go into my busy workshop, rummage a bit among the tools and materials, dust off what I tried to do or did.

Concerning *Masks,** the title comedy in my fourth volume of one-act plays, James Huneker wrote me: "It is an original theme, artfully handled. Is it an apologia?" Other critics dubbed it a dramatization of my problem as a playwright struggling between art and making money—"with George Middleton playing both leading roles," as the *New Republic* put it.

Masks dealt with a dramatist who, to suit the manager, has revised a drama first written *con amore*. The new version is a hit; but the characters, as originally conceived, return to reproach the author for the changes he has made in them and the plot for commercial reasons. The author answers their reproaches by saying he must live.

Through this device I merely offered a nut almost any dramatist sometimes has to crack: should he write only what he believes will make money? How otherwise can he get an audience? How can he deal with themes which set him ticking, but which his own commercial sense warns him will ring no bell? The answer is no answer, of course, for no one can be sure of what may make money. But thinking he knows what might make it has ruined many a dramatist before he started a scamper over the pages. I had myself already found a sort of solution. I published certain plays. This, with Broadway productions more or less successful, led to what several critics called "my double life."

Our medium handicaps us. The novelist is host to the solitary mind, which may adjust its mood to the page, ruminate over reasons, or skip waste matter: the dramatist must instantly organize his group

---

* *Masks* (Henry Holt and Co., 1920), including *Jim's Beast, Tides, Among the Lions, The Reason,* and *The House.*

audience, dash ahead through words alone, without footnotes, to finish within time limits. A dozen uncontrolled incidents can, in one performance, wreck his product beyond repair—a star, for instance, incapacitated on his opening night. But once the novelist has finished, his job is done. He only needs a printer. He addresses himself totally and directly to his reader, who has but to turn the pages as he may wish. The dramatist must be produced and must address himself through actors on a stage to a living audience. Every play, in fact, should only be written to be acted: the "closet drama" is a mere literary exercise. "Water-closet drama," Brander Matthews called it.

Play publication therefore is no substitute for production; it can only be an alternative. Publication may be and certainly will become the author's only accessible record. A stage production may at any time fire it with life. Since drama is a visual art a trained reader may also find pleasure by using imagination to that end. All of which, *faute de mieux,* is why I preached and practiced play publication before as well as after production.

Before my own time the American playwright was never thought of as "a literary man." He had never had the standing of the Continental dramatist, nearly all of whose plays were in print.* I recall how bitterly Clyde Fitch once spoke of this to me. With four other hits, his *Major André,* on the second night, because of bad notices, played to less than a hundred dollars.

"Every book a successful novelist turns out has *some* sale and *some* public. Here I am," he said, "with all these other plays on Broadway, and there isn't the slightest interest in what this one may be like."

But, as Dad said: "People are only interested in the winners." That goes for plays, too. The standing of the American dramatist, in contrast to American authors, in other fields, was partly due to the fact that his scripts could seldom be exploited as literature. Only a few contemporary plays—unless considered literary or poetic—were

---

* As I have always been interested in the attitude of authors towards their trade I was struck with a letter I came across, written in 1877 by Ibsen (*Letters,* Fox, Duffield & Co., 1905, p. 306), claiming "it was injurious to a dramatic work that it should be made accessible to the public in the first instance by means of a stage performance . . . a new play can never be considered and judged apart from its surroundings, purely and simply as a literary work. The judgment will always comprehend both the play and its performance . . . the public is, as a rule, attracted more by the acting and the actor than by the play itself." It should be pointed out that Ibsen was primarily concerned with his plays as printed matter in his own country where he made more money from them than from his stage performances. Besides in those days the copyright law gave him little protection.

decently brought out. Many were printed: but as Barrett H. Clark has authoritatively said they were set up for the use of actors: exits and entrances, with technical stage directions, alone were indicated. Nothing was done to make them easily visualized by the reader.

The fear of piracy was the main factor in keeping our plays from the library. By not publishing, the text was protected under common law. Once it was accessible, however, there was no way of keeping a record of its use. Stock companies and independent producers got the scripts from unauthorized agents. Many plays which have survived were those bootlegged.* In all cases they varied greatly with the rewriting which actors, producers, or "house authors" freely made. Into my own day one Chicago firm had a set of stenographic copies it would rent for performance, without royalty to the author. Titles were scrambled. Indeed, it was not until the gay nineties that any play began to have protection. But the risks through publication still persisted, since prosecution for infringement was difficult. Yet even during my lecturing tours I found my published one-act plays had often been given without let or leave. The Drama League subsequently conducted educational campaigns on the necessity of paying royalties; in addition, certain agents specialized in the exploitation of amateur groups and spent many thousands a year on check-ups of performances through clipping bureaus.

From the way a few plays were beginning to be read I figured some needling might work. Experiments I suggested, with special "drama counters" in department stores, had helped sales. I spoke everywhere I could before drama groups and women's clubs. I wrote about the drama, too. Of course I was anxious to "give a shot" to my own small but growing output. I felt it might aid their production. Two of my associates got their comedies on, three years after publication: *Why Marry?* by Jesse Lynch Williams, with the much married and otherwise greatly gifted Nat Goodwin as star, and Percy Mac-Kaye's delightful *The Scarecrow*.

Curious as to why Bernard Shaw had also first published in America before production, I wrote him. His gracious answer is of biographical interest and indicates the only way rights in a play at one time could be protected.

* There is much collateral information in the prefaces of *America's Lost Plays*. This is a series in twenty volumes of hitherto unpublished plays collected with the aid of the Rockefeller Foundation, under the auspices of the Dramatists' Guild and the general editorship of Barrett H. Clark (Princeton University Press).

20th March 1941

Dear Mr. Middleton,

. . . When I began playwriting 50 years ago, I was a professional critic in the theatre, and therefore could not offer my plays to the managers in the usual way, as they would have at once purchased "an option" on them for, say, £50, and put them on the shelf without the slightest intention of performing them. In short, they would have taken me to be asking for a bribe to join their press retinue. That was how theatre critics were bribed in those days.* Mostly the play offered did not exist and was only a proposal to translate some foreign play. Actor-managers sometimes made the proposal themselves: Irving, Alexander and Wyndham initiated me by trying to buy me in this way.

Accordingly, there was nothing for it but to publish the plays and thus put them in the market for anyone who wanted them. But no publisher would touch plays. When I approached Heinemann, he told me that there were two subjects on which books were unsaleable. One was political economy: the other was drama. He had experimented with the plays of Pinero, and he shewed me the ledger account, which proved that the only copies sold were in the groups needed for rehearsal. There were no sales to the general public: absolutely none at all.

Fortunately Grant Richards, whom I knew through his relationship to Grant Allen, started just then as a publisher, and was willing to publish my plays with literary prefaces and stage directions which were so entirely non-technical in their wording that they never mentioned the stage nor its right, left, centre, upper entries, lower entries etc etc etc, though they were none the less quite practicable.

The books sold quite well enough; and Mansfield came to me for *Arms and the Man* through reading them, though he was very doubtful about the second act, as he appeared in it for a few minutes only.

Heinemann saw that he should have accepted my proposal, and plunged into play publishing with Ibsen, who carried everything before him. Plays came into the book-market, and have remained there ever since.† So, by the way, has political economy.

You know, perhaps, that in those days there were serious legal difficulties in the way of publishing plays. The American performing rights were lost to the author unless his play was publicly performed before publication. Anybody could obtain the theatre rights in the story of a novel unless the author had a dramatic version made and performed. Copyrighting performances in which the charge for admission was a guinea and the publicity was secured by a written notice stuck on the theatre door a few minutes before the play was read by the author and his friends without scenery or costumes as fast as they could gabble

* This practice was not unknown to one of our leading producers.
† Henry Arthur Jones was one of the most persistent advocates of play publication.

through it to a paying audience of one confederate who had actually paid a guinea at the door (theatre kept the guinea as rent) were part of the routine of authorship.* The Copyright Act of 1914 made an end of all that; and it is now forgotten; but you should bear it in mind, as it explains the reluctance of authors to have their plays published while it lasted.

I did not pay for the printing of *Plays Pleasant and Unpleasant:* or of *Widowers' Houses,* which was my first publication as a playwright. They were published on the usual royalty system. But when I wrote *Man and Superman* and had to find a new publisher, I had capital of my own, and manufactured the books at my own cost, the publisher taking a commission only. The American editions were on the usual basis.

I think this covers all your questions.

Glad to hear from you again.

G. Bernard Shaw

This then was the way of my "double life." I wrote the plays I wanted the way I wanted. Henry Holt found merit enough to lend his distinguished imprint. I protected the firm against loss, though, fortunately, there was none: my books all went into three or four editions. While doing this I wrote, in collaboration mostly, the comedies which aimed solely at Broadway success. I mean, in no way, to deprecate the highly successful plays—like *Polly with a Past* or *Adam and Eva*—with which I was fortunately associated. The commercial theatre, indeed, with David Belasco and others, was also being good to me. I merely separated the Broadway hits and misses from those whose immediate aim, I knew, promised little professional stage exploitation. As I wrote in the Preface to the third volume of one-act plays, *Possession:*†

If the author frankly recognizes the many reasons why many plays cannot be produced or cannot succeed, he will pursue his work with a joy it will bring him: he will not compromise with what vision and art he may possess.

By doing this he will at least achieve his own self-expression—which

---

* My early plays were copyrighted in London the same way; otherwise it was believed English performing rights would be lost. There were special companies organized for this; a poster was printed to be pasted outside the theatre, and a program struck off. In asking an actress friend to come and read a part in one of his long plays, Shaw added: "Cutting is permissible provided enough is performed to leave unperformed parts useless to pirates."

† *Possession* (Henry Holt & Co., 1915), including *The Groove, A Good Woman, The Black Tie, Circles,* and *The Unborn.*

should be of prime importance to him: and he will not lose his proportion by coddling himself with self-pity over the neglect of the larger public.

How my efforts may then have stimulated play publication is unimportant; but today every produced play is attractively brought out. Each college now has its own drama courses; our writers are known as never before. These and other amateur groups are our dramatic museums. Through such production the theatre's best is kept alive. Assaulted by radio and movie, without a repertoire or stock system, the professional theatre as an institution is a sick stalk, as we shall later see; though still putting forth an occasional and surprising flower. It is only the amateur who now revives a play after its initial run, though revised revivals may become a vogue.

Yet a great change has come about in the status of the American playwright: he has acquired a new dignity, enhanced, as this story will reveal, by what the Dramatists' Guild did to protect the integrity of his scripts. Today his best plays are not excelled by any in the world: he is, in fact, as much a literary figure as the American novelist. Through publication I can read, as never before, those plays of my associates which I may miss in the theatre, or those of merit which may not have there survived public taste. Aside from making an author's plays more accessible to the translator and thus to the foreign producer, publication has also added comfortably to his income. To cite but one example: Gene O'Neill recently told me that his volumes of one-act plays averaged 15,000 copies each, while *Mourning Becomes Electra* and *Strange Interlude* have sold, between them, over 200,000 copies. *The Iceman Cometh* will outsell both.

I have been told that *Embers,** my book of six one-act plays (1911), was the first collection brought together by an American author. A series followed. In all, I was to publish twenty-six one-acters. The time I could give to such unremunerative efforts was limited. I was to lecture extensively on the "art" of the one-act play and read a varying program, frequently with Fola, throughout the country. How I may have helped in its revival, I cannot say. Clayton Hamilton, in the *Bookman,* later wrote that I "was a pioneer in the general cause of the one-act play." The question, anyway, is academic.

It has always been a favorite form. Certain stars of yesterday, like Rosina Vokes and Mrs. Fiske, succeeded in a bill of three. A few

---

* *Embers* (Henry Holt and Co., 1911), including *The Failures, The Gargoyle, In His House, Madonna,* and *The Man Masterful.*

seasons ago, Noel Coward and Gertrude Lawrence gave samples of their acting skill in Noel's playlets. Nothing he has written excelled them in variety and penetration. "The Blush and Thrill," Grand Guignol type, has had its trials here, but without sustained success. It remained for the amateur to find through them new roads into a new theatre. But in Grandfather's day it sought refuge only as a "curtain raiser." They wanted long hours for their money, until the dinner hour grew later. But managers came to think that in adding a short play they admitted the long play was weak. Hence, today a play which merits only to be a one-acter, may be blown up into a tenuous three-acter, by slow tempos and long French intermissions.

Louis De Foe, dramatic critic on the New York *World,* wrote me that many English managers had told him their greatest difficulty was to get curtain raisers "bad enough to please the pit and gallery crowds." In the French boulevard theatres the short play had disappeared when I lived in Paris. The author of the long play protested, since his *société* ruled that the net royalty should be divided by the total number of "acts" on the bill.

Truth was, vaudeville alone then sheltered the American one-act play. Yet only "sketches" especially adapted to its broken moods, acrobats, and Maggie Clines could succeed. George Kelly, whose *Craig's Wife* won the 1926 Pulitzer prize, had this special "knack." He came up to prominence through the rough road of vaudeville. There, as he told me, he learned his craft through the quick reactions of its alert and democratic audience. My published plays were never good for vaudeville. The exception was *Collusion,* later called *The Unknown Lady.* In it Alla Nazimova made a sensational success everywhere she played it. How and why it was stopped, in both London and New York, is for a later chapter on censorship.

In spite of such limited productive outlets I kept on writing one-acters. The magazines gave some openings: H. L. Mencken and George Jean Nathan, who have probably forgotten it, among the first, when they accepted several for the *Smart Set.* Frederic Taber Cooper, editor of the *Forum,* used several; and there were others. Then I thought of publishing the first collection. Perhaps I hoped it might contribute material for a revaluation of the form, or make its tiny challenge to other American playwrights. For while there were fine short plays, I realized how few of our own authors cared to experiment because of its restricted opportunities. I was inspired also by the high place the form had abroad.

In searching for lecture material on the one-act play I dug into European literature. This form included some of the finest writings of Schnitzler, Sudermann, Strindberg, Bahr, Bracco, Synge, Yeats, Lady Gregory, Shaw, and, of course, Barrie. Both the Austrian, Arthur Schnitzler, and the German, Hermann Sudermann, were to develop the one-act play cycle—one with *Reigen* and *Anatol,* and the other with *Rosen* and *Morituri.* When I called upon them in 1928, each told me how fascinated he had been in thus presenting different facets of a character or concept with a unifying idea. This was somewhat the idea William Archer had suggested for my *Tradition.* There is an obvious cousinship between the play cycle, with its necklace-like structure, and *Victoria Regina* and *Harriet,* with their episodic scene construction.

(Such famous personalities, incidentally, have always had a great allure for actors and playwrights. The dramatist has two possible approaches in a biographical play: he may revolve his hero, as in *Disraeli,* about a plot centering on one specific episode; or he may choose a series of events in an individual's life and stretch them in a panorama across the years. Here the trick is selection of striking episodes which reveal character, rather than setting up a suspensive plot. This freer method I was to use when I wrote my Balzac play. Then I saw what my apprenticeship in the one-act-play technic had meant: it sharpened the internal effectiveness of each episode. Yet the total script must not become a sausage string of one-acters. It must be cumulative; it must blend, and also build in interest towards completion or climax. In that sense, each completed episode itself must have suspense in relation to the whole, as in conventional play structure. The play cycle with its episodic technic thus unquestionably helped to break up the formal acts of another period, where a play was always cramped into three or four tight corsets.)

Today numerous anthologies of one-acters have been printed. One-act magazines have even been set up. Nearly every drama course at college encourages practice in this friendly, if exacting, form. One-act flights are intense but short. There is no structural drudgery such as the longer form exacts of the beginner. Walter Eaton wrote me he had suggested to Professor Baker that my little plays "be used to teach exposition," and I was glad when Gene O'Neill recently told that he recalls this had been done at Harvard.

The one-act play itself has also made an important contribution to the independent theatrical movements. Antoine's Théâtre Libre began in Paris, with amateurs and a bill of four one-act plays. In our Manhattan, the Washington Square Players were first dedicated to the short form alone. One should also register the fact that the Provincetown Players used this type exclusively at its start. From these varied experimental doors in New York stepped Katharine Cornell, Ann Harding, Miriam Hopkins, Helen Westley; Robert Edmond Jones, scenic artist *par excellence*. Here Edna St. Vincent Millay, who wanted only to be an actress, tried her first poetic wings— in the short play medium. *Bound East for Cardiff* was the moving drama I saw that first night when I sensed the genius of O'Neill. It was a short one.

When I first went to the conservative firm headed by the oaklike Henry Holt, to submit my slender manuscript of *Embers,* the idea of any one publishing it seemed fantastic. At the mere suggestion, protective protests arose at once. It had never been done before. But I left the script, politely assured of a speedy answer. I got it. The next morning the Fifth Avenue Coach Company rang me up. They had found on a seat an unopened manuscript, with my name on the cover. It contained my little waifs!

I went to the publishers and asked whether it was their custom to reject via a bus. Bewilderment, apologies, and the promise of another hasty decision, as I drew forth the manuscript from under my coat like a bowl of goldfish. The readers' reports were excellent, I was told; but I believe it was Roland Holt's sense of guilt in losing the script that tipped the scales.*

The timidity with which I offered that first collection—dedicated to my father and mother—still lingers in my Preface, written according to Brander Matthews' advice: "Remember, George, the preface is important. Prepare it carefully so that it will give the reviewer the proper slant on what you are aiming at. It may be all he will ever read or want to."

Here is a bit of it:

These little plays are written for acting, but arranged for reading. Knowing how small an opportunity the professional stage in this country gives for the serious one-act play, so common on the Continent, they are modestly offered to those who see some dignity in the form, and who realize that certain dramatic ideas find their best expression in the concentrated episode. . . .

* On the editorial board at the time were my college mates, Alfred Harcourt and Donald Brace, to leave shortly and launch out upon their own publishing enterprise.

They are studies in consequences and readjustments, being, in fact, a further expression of some preceding situation. Each play is, therefore, the epitome of a larger drama which is suggested in the background.

The one-act play is a distinct art form. It has its own technic: quick exposition, rigid economy, with a single situation to create one impression. It allowed me the sharp projection of ideas, the clash of social attitudes or of individuals, in some revealing moment. I sought to make each play illuminate a vista. When Paul Kester said about *Possession,* "I wish it might have been used as the central knob of a three-act play—it makes you want the rest," or when Walter Prichard Eaton wrote me of *On Bail* that "there is a kind of desolate prospect opened out before and behind the action which I think is very fine and very touching," I felt I had achieved my technical intention. Anticipating a detailed review of all my plays that he was later to write for the *Freeman* (July 21, 1920), Walter added a penetrating comment:

But I am driven to wonder a little if you aren't pushing this moment of experience a little too far—that is, aren't you so interested in opening up the vistas that you don't sufficiently close in the special episode you have selected? I don't want to advocate the "punch," but personally I could stand a little more of the excitement, or briskness, of action which goes into the traditional one-act play. I suppose, though, the special mood that you are after would more or less vanish under the new emphasis.

Though what is dramatic is not always transferable to the stage, much that I thought or lived through had by now found its way there. *Masks,* I have specified; the feminist group certainly speak for themselves. In one study of an author, *The Gargoyle*—which James Huneker admired "for its psychological insight"—I did some personal probing. I had my author say: "My characters are only my different attitudes towards life." That hit home: the pros and cons in my own mind would come out like measle spots. Those plays which dealt with divorce, for example, were mainly the literary surplusage from the premarital dilemmas my own agitations caused. Two of these marital playlets, *Their Wife* and *The Man Masterful,* however, were ambitious technical experiments. Brander Matthews, in his *Yale Review* article *"Hamlet* with Hamlet Left Out" (October, 1915), best explains this intention:

In a volume of one-act plays composed by a young American playwright, Mr. George Middleton, there is a piece called *Their Wife,* in which the most significant figure is that of a woman who has been the wife of one man and who is now the wife of another. The two characters who are seen and heard by the audience are these two husbands. Their wife does not appear; and yet she is the heroine of the play.

It is solely because she is what she is that the action of the piece is possible. It is her character which is the core of the situation wherein the two men find themselves entangled. We do not see her in the flesh, but the dramatist has made us see her in the spirit. He has interpreted her through the mouths of the two men who have loved her and whom she has loved in turn. She is the most clearly depicted person in the play, so clearly depicted indeed that the spectator realizes her for what she is.

Quite possibly an average unobservant playgoer, recalling the play after an interval of a month or two, could discuss its heroine, so oblivious of the fact that he has not actually seen her, that he might find himself endeavouring vainly to remember the name of the actress who played the part.*

In the earlier *The Man Masterful* I had tried this same device to project the man who did not appear. But this play, I may add, was more worth my while, for, through it, years later, I was to have an unforgettable personal experience with Eleonora Duse, while the great actress was on her last tour in America.

Truth and reminiscent satisfaction urge me to say the plays won unexpected space in the book sections and literary reviews—Professors Archibald Henderson and Richard Burton being among my best rooters. My harping on the form, almost alone then, was a bit unusual. With few exceptions the dramatic critics ignored me; but the plays were given publicly by many "readers," like the gifted Bertha Kunz Baker, who also introduced most foreign dramatists to chautauqua audiences. I smile as I thumb my records to note that my work was the subject of lectures from the New York Ethical Culture Society's pulpit and in Emma Goldman's popular itinerant Labor Forum. Emma, because she read into my plays a questioning of conventional morality, was a friendly advocate. I even find a letter from her in 1924, after her deportation (for conspiracy against the draft law), asking permission to handle my plays in Germany. She was broke, and turned for a livelihood to her deep love of the theatre: "You see,

* No more expert craftsman is writing today than John van Druten, who is partial to small casts "as they give me more room in which to develop character." Though twenty characters seem to have life in his *The Voice of the Turtle,* there are only three which actually appear. Incidentally, he told me that he had written this most successful of comedies in six weeks. "All I had to begin with, was Act 1: soldier sleeps on a couch; Act 2: soldier sleeps in a bed; Act 3—I didn't know what was to happen."

as I am now situated, the platform is out of the question and my pen as a medium of support seems to be as useless."

One critic, however, thus appraised my over-all effort:

George Middleton played his part in popularizing the reading play and in giving the stamp of serious interest to the practice of American playwriting. In considering Middleton's work it is well not to underestimate the craft with which he made his little dissertations on the new morality. On the other hand, it is well to recognize that as contributions to thought they were quite without significance. . . . And yet they served their purpose. And Middleton himself must be granted respect beyond that paid to anything he has done, for the reason that he had the vision of a serious play appealing to the minds of serious men and women and clung to this vision until it gained currency.*

Since another comment happily raises a question needed to fill out the one-act picture, I add another note from Louis De Foe:

DEAR GEORGE:

The matter in hand is to tell you how much I enjoyed *Masks* and how grateful I am to you for sending me the book. I had a review to-day in my column in the *World*.

They are the best one-act plays—they and the ones that have preceded them—that are to be found. Strangely I have never seen *even one* acted. I should think you would take steps to have them done.

Considering the amount of rot that gets to the stage it is a crime for the managers to leave such little gems unutilized. But that's a way managers have. Congratulations.

The point was, I had taken steps, thousands of them. I had even knuckled every door for professional production. But Mrs. Fiske, to whom George Arliss first introduced me, put to me the reason why she, at least, couldn't do some of mine that she generously liked:

The trouble with the one-act play is that it is so difficult to find a place in one's repertoire. Few plays are short enough to permit of the adding of a one-act play.

Two of the most beautiful plays I ever produced (Mr. L[uther] Long's *Dolce* and *Little Italy*)—wonderful little plays and extraordinarily successful—I have been able to play only a few times—on special occasions —because there never seemed a place for them.

My one-act adventure, however, had certain compensations. All the short plays were done by amateurs: some in England, France, and

* Thomas H. Dickinson, *Playwrights of the New American Theatre* (Macmillan, 1925).

Germany. Even the Greeks took a hand in *A Good Woman,* to judge by the published translation sent me from Athens. But only one or two had the popularity of Lord Dunsany's little masterpieces, for example, which afforded a field day to the scenic artist, who was so often the most striking factor in the little theatre groups. Mine were all drab interiors—and that went for both parlor and brain. My themes were controversial and often intimate. The chaperons automatically kept them from contaminating the average amateur. My characters were not rough, where the very awkwardness of the unskilled actor would seem in character, as with so many of Gene O'Neill's elemental types. Mine, in fact, were hard to act.

Professor William Lyon Phelps wrote me, of *Embers,* that "the little dramas are full of cerebration." Billy gave his friendly pat to each succeeding volume: * but his first comment hits on their real difficulty for amateurs and indicates why such plays can never be widely played. My action was mental; the dialogue, necessarily so. It needs a highly trained actor's skill to make ideas appear to hop out spontaneously from the character's mind rather than from the actor's memory. The meaning back of the phrase has to be sensed and then suggested, or its drama is lost. The condensation, required by the one-act form, could only be freed by radiating implications. Mine was often the drama of "second intention."

By way of example, when *The Reason* was done professionally in London February 15, 1925, at the Prince of Wales, the *Telegraph* said, "It was as cynical a piece as ever put upon the stage, and also proved a most effective vehicle for a fine display of restrained but forcible emotion." Some further indication of its peculiar flavor, for the point I am making, is revealed in a personal letter from James Huneker, which he dated "Now":

It is Strindbergian—tense, horrid, masterly in analysis. It would play, but I think the title inadequate. It doesn't cut to the bone, as does the piece . . . something poignant yet masked as to meaning.

Imagine then my reaction when I saw a rehearsal of this play done by semi-amateurs in Paris, with the old sighing sentimental approach, that asked the audience to be sorry for someone. As I

---

* The obituary columns were to give ample testimony of such encouragement he extended to many authors. I never knew him well, though I visited his home and we had a first-name calling contact for many years. I was therefore honored when not long before his death, in 1943, he asked me to serve, under his chairmanship, on the Pulitzer Prize Play Committee. I was forced to decline for personal reasons.

hastily tried to correct the readings to the ironic mood the English director shooed me away and begged me "not to upset the actors." He did not know that a playwright's dialogue must not always be interpreted literally. Its drama is often only determined by the mood with which the author floods it, as the color in a spotlight changes the object on which it is turned.

No amateur group, however, ever did my *Criminals*,* which I saw expertly produced by professionals March 3, 1915, at the Fine Arts Theatre in Chicago. The audience took it better than the press. The experience my cousin had on her wedding trip, knowing nothing of what was scheduled, had inspired it. I suppose the case was exceptional even thirty years ago; yet after production and publication of the play at least twelve similar experiences were brought voluntarily to my attention. I would not mention the play at all except for the criticisms it inspired. Burton Rascoe, for example, in the *Chicago Tribune* said it "was uproariously funny." Nothing was funnier, I thought, than the notices.

While I was called "an American Brieux" by one, and all admitted I had handled the theme "with dexterity" and even "delicacy," the *Louisville Courier* sagely remarked: "It may be said that her parents should have taught her something of that emotion and its expressions, but it is rather a complicated job to teach a girl exactly what thrills she may permit herself from the kisses of her lover in order to prepare herself for the embraces of the husband."

Another reviewer objected to so much of my dialogue being "represented by dashes that the imagination has to work overtime," which is exactly what I was after. H. L. Mencken outdid himself. Always kind to my books, he was generous to the technical aspects of this; but added that my argument, after all, was chiefly of academic interest,

for innocence is no longer the function of virginity. . . . The sex hygienists have saved the flapper from her old ignorance, and she now goes to the altar with a learned and even cynical glitter in her eye. Worse, she spends a good deal more time discussing and disseminating her information. All this, of course, is highly embarrassing to the romantic and ingenuous sort of man, of whom I have the honor to be one.

But the comment which now gives me many inward chuckles was by Percy Hammond, with whom I was to have many happy hours after he became dramatic critic of the *New York Tribune*. He tossed

* Published by B. W. Huebsch, 1914.

off this verbal concoction immediately after suffering through the actual performance, as critic on the *Chicago Tribune:*

Poor Janet Merwyn, née York!

We left her barricaded in her room at the Fine Arts theater hysterically hating her new husband because of his odious ardors upon their honeymoon. What should be done with a case like Janet's? Mr. George Middleton, who is all wrought up about it, thinks that parents should tell their daughters that there is no Santa Claus, and he announces as "Criminals" those who do not.

Well, I suspect that Mr. Middleton errs in the especial instance of Janet. Mere knowledge of the brutal facts, one fears, would not have mitigated their shamefulness to so modest a maid. Apprised of the repugnant details of matrimony, she would have jilted her panting suitor and embraced the more conservative joys of spinsterhood. *Her husband seemed a decent sort of gander, expeditious, perhaps, but well meaning.* It was his ignorance rather than the lady's *which caused the debacle.*

· I am inclined to think that the husband's parents, too, should come under Mr. Middleton's indictment for not instructing him as to *the disadvantages of celerity. He knocked the icicle off Diana's temple instead of thawing it.* At any rate Janet is not an object of public distress, though Mr. Middleton, in "Criminals," is overwhelmed by her plight. Ere this, no doubt, she has hearkened to her husband's *modified strophonade* and they are now en route to Niagara Falls with the vexatious circumstance forgot. Mr. Middleton tried to make a tragedy out of a contretemps.*

One can get a lot of fun out of being serious—afterwards.

For ten years I was to do my share to try to establish the one-act play. Then I stopped cold. I never wrote another. I was no longer interested. I put the blue-gold volumes on a shelf in my workshop. Others have taken them down: I have—to write this chapter. But I am glad I did them. On rereading them, I see that they represented something of myself and my attitude towards certain problems of those shifting days. Perhaps, too, they may have some value as their silhouette.

But mine was a busy workshop with other jobs, even while these were being chiseled and polished *con amore,* before I let them forth. For other pleasant hours in a playwright's life were also passing: those spent in the gentle art of collaboration. They, too, were to bring rich associations, new personalities and engrossing experiences.

"Never collaborate," Sacha Guitry, the French dramatist, once admonished me when— But that is the next chapter.

* Italics mine.

CHAPTER XII

THE GENTLE ART OF
COLLABORATION

"Collaborez jamais."

That was what Sacha Guitry, the French actor and author, told me Octave Mirbeau had whispered to him as the old cynic lay dying. The admonition was repeated in Paris when I mentioned how happy I had been with my various collaborators. Sacha was astonished that they and I were still friends, for he knew he couldn't work with anybody. But then I am sure nobody could have worked with him.

In the French theatre, however, many of the dramatists were congenital collaborators. Scribe wrote alone only six or seven of the hundred plays to which his name was signed. Meilhac and Halévy did about fifty together; when I first went to Paris, Flers and Caillavet had been turning out yearly hits. There is an authentic case of a Frenchman collaborating with his mother-in-law. By contrast, Brander Matthews recalled a one-act play which had thirty-six authors.

In America the coupled copyright lists are lengthy—including George S. Kaufman, our most collaborated of contemporaries, who worked with Edna Ferber, Moss Hart and Marc Connelly. It inspired Louis Bromfield to call him a literary Don Juan, since "he seemed able to marry happily with almost anyone." I once asked George why. He wrote:

The reason I collaborate is that I have been so fortunate, in the course of the years, as to find an assortment of gifted dramatic writers who were willing to collaborate with me. In those circumstances I would have been pretty foolish not to collaborate, and pretty hungry if I hadn't.

He might have added that of all literary forms commercial play writing lends itself most easily to collaboration. Besides plot, a play requires structure, dialogue, and characterization. One author may have ideas or the plot sense; another, a strong selective or critical instinct. One may turn out dialogue yet not have another's talent for "building a scene." An amalgamation may make a better whole than either could deliver apart. Some vocative writers produce best through verbal friction; they find their ideas as they talk; they need another upon whom they can strike fire.

But to other writers collaboration is anathema. They lose what they think if they share it. Ibsen tore his hair if any one peeked at his unfinished script. Even his wife never knew the subject. Pinero would slip off into the country for months, see no one and answer no letters. His secretary would say, "Sir Arthur is in retirement." I never could get him even to discuss his plays technically, though he did tell me he always had first to work out the "architecture" of his scenes.

The capacity to collaborate depends chiefly on gifts and temperament. Like marriage between any two persons, collaboration might succeed with somebody else. But to those who can work together it may be just what they need. I doff my hat to Paul Kester and all the others from whom I have learned. It is also a delightful way to avoid the solitudes of composition. Guy Bolton would say, as we started each of our plays: "My, George, what an awful lot of paper has to be covered with words!"

Yet collaboration carries its own death sting, and the field is strewn with victims. No matter how adapted two may be in a work relationship, personal harmony can be hard to maintain. Nothing seems to erupt such varied reactions. Jealousy, egotism, even conflicting codes of business or literary ethics, may coil, rattle, and then strike. A growing belief by the individual in his own importance is the fever sign of coming crisis. This betrays an overstuffed vanity about his contribution or a frustration concerning it.

Because of all this, when I became president of the Dramatists' Guild in 1927, I had Arthur Garfield Hays, then our counsel, draw up an ironclad-inescapable-arbitration-compelling collaborator's agreement,* "on the basis that the two friends would end up bitter enemies or that either might turn out a rotter." Not only did it include each legal and financial contingency, but it tried to anticipate every picayune pinprick, down to "whose name should go first on the program." Since every restriction could be changed "by mutual consent" its teeth were shown only if friendship ceased. It has been the Guild's most popular document.

As A. E. Thomas, himself the author or co-author of many hits, once put it: "Collaborators are like cats; no two are alike." Being

* See *Bulletin*, Mar., 1928.

one of the fortunate felines, I speak first of *The Big Pond*,* our one collaboration. It was originally bought by William Harris, Jr., one of the most intelligent of producers; but he decided not to do it because he felt he couldn't "work with you boys" (Bill just couldn't help wanting changes in a script). While not a hit when produced at the Bijou Theatre in New York, it made Tommy and myself about $10,000 each. Maurice Chevalier did it in the films; but it is probably remembered in stage chronology more because Katharine Hepburn played the lead for the opening performance at Great Neck only. As she gleefully and rightly herself has stated, she was "let out" for incompetence.

Her personality was arresting: she had spurts of flame. We should have capitalized on those moments which took her performance out of routine—as was later to be evidenced in her outstanding film creations. But on the stage she was then too inexperienced to sustain her part, especially when not in movement: she couldn't "hold the scenes together." Yet, though we were booked into New York in a week, I am sorry I failed to insist, so far as I could, on giving her an extra performance or two to flap her young wings more freely. The one man who did see her importance to the play was Jake Shubert. He insisted unavailingly on her return to the cast.

"Tommy" had taken on several collaborators, including Clayton Hamilton, before we did *The Big Pond*. Of course we were asked, "How do authors ever work out a play together?" George Arliss told me that he and Brander Matthews would "chat the play through," talking the dialogue as they went. Edna Ferber and George Kaufman write all the lines together, I'm told; other rapports are amusingly chronicled in Edna's autobiography, *A Peculiar Treasure*. The most popular team today, now crowned with the 1946 Pulitzer Prize for their *State of the Union*, is Howard Lindsay and Russell Crouse. They have harmoniously collaborated even about their methods in appropriate press releases; but beneath the persiflage one senses the many months of hard work on the plot, characterizations, and scene sequence. Each admits that it is a perfectly articulated collaboration where no special line or idea could be tagged with ownership. Their dramatization of Clarence Day's *Life with Father* was planned for two years and actually put on paper in seventeen days. Other collaborators have each written separate acts or scenes, as Nordhoff and

* Produced by Edwin Knopf and William Farnsworth. Published by Samuel French.

Hall do separate chapters of their novels, which are then dovetailed into some unity. Sometimes the collaborator named on the program is only the "rewrite man," or play doctor, who is called in with the oxygen. From some confessions, however, you would think all the other fellow did was act as amanuensis. I never learned much about the mysteries of how lyricist and composer work out their product. I do know that Oscar Hammerstein devised his lyrics one way in the *Show Boat* with Jerome Kern and another in *Oklahoma* and *Carousel* with Richard Rodgers. With Jerry the music came first, and Oscar fitted words to it; with Dick the music fits what Oscar had first so felicitously phrased—which was how Gilbert and Sullivan put together their famous songs. But, as with marriage technic, every couple finds its own way. They do or they don't, as in the historic case of Shaw and Archer, who didn't, over *Widowers' Houses*.

Such hectic sessions, which I am sure happen, like children, in the best regulated collaborations, must seem mad to any bystander listening in. I heard Molnár say such an instance had inspired his comedy *The Play's the Thing*. It was about an eavesdropper who thought the dramatist-hero meant it when he shouted in the next room, "I'll kill you if you don't marry me"—or some such play-writing cliché.

Tommy and I first plotted the entire play act by act; the details in each successive scene were noted—with what pain to him he himself has told. In an unpublished penciled article that I have always treasured, he wrote:

> If I am due at his shop at 9:30 and have not arrived at 9:35, Middleton telephones my house. The moment I poke my nose in his place his boiler is full of steam, he is sitting on the safety valve and smoke is coming out of his nose. Everything we've done the day before is typed, and a lot more that he has thought up in the meantime. He is reading it to me and acting it, too, before I've got my hat off. I hardly have time to say "Rotten" before he's off on a new tangent.
>
> For three or four hours I'm shelled with ideas, notions, phrases, situations, developments, motivations, motifs, and characters. Now and then the barrage lifts long enough for me to stick my head out of the dugout and say "Terrible" or "Fine" or "Not bad" or something equally epigrammatic. But mostly it's a bombardment.
>
> You may gather from this that my job in the making of *The Big Pond* was mostly selection. Right the first time. There's enough that we threw in the garbage can to make ten plays. And considering the large public there seems to be for garbage, I'm going down the alley some dark night to investigate that ash can. There must be money in it.

But Tommy didn't add that, after we propped up its bones, it was he who covered it with his smooth-flowing dialogue. Hardly a pleat was changed or a ruffle altered. What amazed me was how he had woven into it the best lines which had popped out as we were plotting: not one was lost in the basting. But I remembered for years—until his early hits, *The Rainbow* and *Her Husband's Wife* came along— he had been the star reporter on the *New York Sun*, assigned to many a celebrated case.

Even before he and I collaborated, Fola and Ethel Thomas, herself a gifted writer, were equally close. Every summer, we were to visit their home in South County, Rhode Island, which our mutual friend Leonard Bacon has so poetically defined. Ethel's garden suggested in its charm and radiance her own personality. In her home, where each ornament or bit of furniture was selected with care and taste, we learned there was an art of living which these two, as no others we knew, would solve anew with each new day. Their friendship, through the shifting seasons, is an abiding undercurrent in my story.

Our yearly summer collaboration was to cover even a wider field of activity than play writing; in fact, Tommy taught me all I know of golf: the mere reminder of which, however, long made him writhe. I recall, for its almost immortal depth of self-reproach, one classic moment when he was poised for a well thought-out putt: "God, George, think of being two down to a player like you!" This brings to mind another aspect of his wit: When Clayton Hamilton was proudly presenting Tommy to his newborn son, who lay naked on the bed, the little fellow gave one look at the playwright and started to urinate. "Ah," Tommy ventured, "a dramatic critic, like his father!"

My most financially successful tie-up, however, was with Guy Bolton. During European war years we did five plays: two comedies were Broadway and country-wide hits, and were done in London and on the Continent; two others made some money; but the last, a serious play, was a flop. Our individual gifts made an efficient alliance; but geography, among other things, prevented its continuance. When we saw each other recently, after Guy's return from years in England, we drank a toast to happy work days. After all, the mutually divorced may have much to remember with pleasure.

Our collaboration began after his generous note about my *Nowadays* in 1914. With social ease, ready humor, and wide cultivation,

Guy was a delightful companion. His large, fixed dark eyes hid everything in their apparent frankness, saw everything, and forgot nothing. Originally an architect by profession, he was an art connoisseur and had scoured old English houses to pick up and market family portraits. He had English blood, and always felt its pull. At the time we began collaborating Guy was also to do the "books" of such comic-opera classics as *Very Good Eddie* and *Oh! Boy!* with P. G. Wodehouse and Jerome Kern.

Jerry Kern was still to make the Mississippi famous with his immortal song in the *Show Boat* and to build his enduring place in American music. He was a fine business man. In our Dramatists' Guild fight ten years later he, along with George Gershwin, Richard Rodgers, Sigmund Romberg, and Irving Berlin, was to represent the musical comedy composers.* And now nearly all have been or will be subject of "film biographies." Guy, as it happens, has just done Jerome Kern. This is a happy Hollywood device to bring into one movie all the most popular compositions of each composer.

Wodehouse ("P. G.," or "Plum," to his intimates) and I were to cross paths in many places here and abroad. A writing creature of habit, he might automatically glance up at the Grand Canyon and then go back to two-fingering his fantastic tales. After receiving $2,000 a week in Hollywood for thirty weeks, during which he was rarely called to the studio, he naïvely murmured that he didn't "see why they pay me so much for doing nothing at all." An earthquake shook the film city when this made every front page in America. Fola and I were wandering in British Columbia at the time, and even we saw it. As he later explained: "Why, George, I only said a few words to make conversation to a nice newspaper girl, as I walked from her car to our drawing room." It was in that Jeeves-like world that he lived, unreal and Wodehousish, when I first met him with Guy. Nothing he ever wrote or said later indicated an awareness of consuming conflagrations or planet-shaking events. I always found him completely devoid of political sense or obligation. This, I am sure, is the explanation of his broadcasting from Berlin, while a prisoner of war.

I was to learn much about comic opera structure, hearing Plum,

* In 1942, when Irving's *This Is the Army* was playing in Washington, I went back to see him. We spoke of these early days. Then he led me to the stage, where a rehearsal had been called. He slipped his arm in mine and pointed to the huge soldier company, made up entirely of stage actors. His face lit, as he said with deep emotion: "Isn't it wonderful, George? Think. *All* this came out of our theatre! It is *our* theatre that's done it!"

Jerry, and Guy talk. Mechanics are necessarily the concern of all dramatists—musical shows must include "black-outs," "breathing spells," and other spacings, to allow time for dancers, singers, and chorus girls to get their breaths or change to their next costumes. Essential "belly laughs" of line or situation result from studied preparation. This is also true in the higher plane of light comedy, where such laugh pinnacles must suddenly surge up through ripples of running laughter. Whatever may be the type of the laugh-conveying medium, the basic mechanics of achieving the effect are the same. The materials used by all playwrights, in fact, really boil down to the same few ingredients of plot, scene, and joke. It is the cook and the seasoning that make the dish served tasty and palatable. Guy's own instinctive broad understanding of audience reactions, his recognized ingenuity in putting new shine on old shoes he always kept in his closet for dark days, added greatly to the commercial value of his many joint ventures.

Before I leave comic opera, however, I might speak of my only plunge into that strange world. Arthur Hammerstein, who made $3,000,000 out of *Rose-Marie,* commissioned Guy to do a version of our *Polly with a Past.* My pleasant task was to bank some of the expected royalties. As the script got worse and worse and further from the original, I kept shaving my share because new collaborators were called in. I got on Arthur's nerves, hanging about rehearsals, asking questions. The *Elks' Magazine,* however, had offered me $1,000 to write a biological thesis on "How Comic Operas Are Made" (February, 1929). As it turned out, I was the only one who got any money out of the complete failure *Polly* became. I mention it only because of the now famous radio personality who dominated the version. Fred Allen was then known as a "writing comedian"; that is, he supplied his own "gags." In my article I quoted him:

"We funny men have got to be careful. There's a certain firm here who engages us and then, after they've got all our best gags in their script, they give us the gate and put a cheaper man in with our stuff.

"I once had a graveyard painted on a curtain back of my act: it was so arranged that every time I cracked an old joke it would turn over in its grave. When I quit the show those managers kept my drop. It cost me $200 to get back the tombstones I'd paid for myself."

In our method of collaboration it is futile to say whether Guy supplied the cartridge or I pulled the trigger. The aim was everything.

Though it happened that the initial idea was mine for our *Polly with a Past* and *Adam and Eva,* what evolved from the bare ideas is best illustrated by the evolution of the titles themselves. One of us had named the girl Molly. The other thought of "with a past." So Molly was rechristened Polly, for euphony. The biblical tie-up of the phrase "Adam and Eve" equally gained piquancy by changing Eve to Eva. Our popular titles, like the plays, didn't spring full-born from either brow: we merely put our heads together and they bred. So, throughout, in any similar real collaboration one might thus comb each idea, scene, structure, and characterization. Collaborators should be generous rather than appraising of what each may contribute. Silence about the wedding closet is best.

In general, we first developed the entire plot and scene sequence, until we had a complete scenario. We did not dialogue, except in endless notes that we guarded "for that rainy day." These discarded ideas or lines might suddenly take on value; for, if we got stuck, I would dig them out to find new "leads." I first dialogued this scenario through. My draft, with no pretense of finality, was designed to test our structure. Even the scanty sheets I threw over the form would indicate distortions, or wide weaknesses. Story holes would show up, or a character would develop such vitality that it needed more room. Suddenly, too, scenes might ask to be transferred, or they might be found to be duplicated later. If I got stuck, and could find Guy, I would call for him. Our hardest scraps would come at this stage. We usually discovered we both were wrong. Out of criticism came the opening through which a better development would suddenly rush. This process would also occur when I took what Guy had redialogued; only then would the play put on its street clothes and sally forth.

In these final hours no one could work more intensively than Guy. Some of Fola's family letters at the time we were finishing *Polly,* in our little cottage back of Croton, tell of fifteen-hour sessions when she cooked our meals. My incapacity for any let-up on such a drive has been the admiration of some and the despair of most of my friends. I admired Guy's concentration and capacity, when he wished, to shut out other collaborators. Then he never let anything interfere with his work; he took everything in his stride, eating only one layer of his cake at a time. I state this quality, for the stage historian, to explain how Guy Bolton produced some fifty plays over the years and is still going strong.

I thought there was a good comedy in Dad's gambler friend, Peter DeLacy, who had closed all the New Jersey race tracks on a moral issue, because they objected to his operating poolrooms in New York. Guy agreed; but suggested to make it more timely, that we change the background to prohibition. A barkeeper becomes a "Billy" Sunday temperance leader. We named it *What'll You Have?* When it was produced at the Astor Theatre, in New York, it was called *Hit-the-Trail-Holliday,* by George M. Cohan. Even that can happen in the theatre!

George and I had been friends from his vaudeville days, and we have had many companionable hours together from ball parks to Paris. I saw him last in the spring of 1940, at lunch in Washington, where he was trying out what was to be his last role. "If this doesn't go, George, I'll hang up the mitts," he told me—as it turned out, prophetically. Fragments of so vivid a personality will come frequently into these pages. His memory rests in my affections: he reaches back to Dad and my youth.

When *The Cavalier* was produced in 1902, he came before the curtain of his own comedy, then playing on the road, and said: "I want you all to go see the play that's opening here Monday—it's written by a pal of mine." About the era of *Holliday* he seemed blue: "What else has the theatre to give me, George?" he asked. "Here I am, a star in my own play, in my own theatre." The first time, I believe, this had happened in our theatrical history. Yet some of his richest years, as an actor, were ahead; for, while his technical dexterity was recognized, it was not until Gene O'Neill's *Ah! Wilderness* that his art completely broke through. I enjoyed play and performance so much that I wrote to both author and actor. The play's nostalgic mood and tenderness, as it reflected Gene's own childhood, is seldom found in his other dramas. He answered:

It's grand that *Electra* interested you so much—but I'm particularly pleased *Ah! W.* hit in a soft spot. I have a deep personal affection for that play—a feeling towards it that is quite apart from any consideration of it as a piece of dramatic writing by me as a playwright.

It was the first play George had acted since childhood that he had not himself authored. His interpretation of a role he had not tailored to suit his peculiar gifts was a revelation. A long letter came back to me which began:

Guess you thought to yourself "That guy Cohan never answers letters." I'll be honest kid. This is about the sixth letter I've written in five years. *Thanks* for your fine encouraging message to me. I'm sending you a photo of the homeliest man in the American theatre.

As this letter of January 10, 1934, bespeaks our closeness and something little known of the man a few more paragraphs warrant quotation here.

Yes, George, we all have to mellow a little as we go along. My whole back ground was rough and tumble as you know but I never got "hard boiled" as they call it. Always tried—Did the best I could with the Equipment alloted me. I've been fortunate however in having a full life—Plenty of money—Plenty of fun—Plenty of Everything except a certain classification I never achieved.

I have always been proud of your friendship George and always a big rooter for your work and so you can understand what your fine letter to me meant and how I appreciated it. I hope when you return we can have lunch and a good old time chat about our boyhood days. You were a peach to sit down and write me such a damn fine letter.

Well, old pal, I'll close this up now and run to the theatre and put on the old chin whiskers and make believe I'm Old Jed Prouty again. I'm getting so I look like the guy O'Neill wrote . . .

Always yours
GEORGE M.

In 1922 we went together in Paris to watch Lucien Guitry, whom George thought "the greatest actor I ever saw." Guitry's enormous economy of effort impressed him: for the French actor was a master of pause and implication, as I shall show later. George tried, in fact, to bring Guitry to the States "to show the Lambs Club a real actor." But Guitry was afraid of being seasick; his son, Sacha, explained his own failure to go by the pun, "à cause du père et de la mer [mère]."

A man of restless activities, George Cohan had always been interested in play production. In control of many theatres, he had early teamed up with Sam Harris, a likable little man, with a punch when necessary, who took each turn of his varied fortunes with a come-what-may shrug. Though their long partnership had been broken, Sam on his deathbed said to George, "We had lots of fun, didn't we, George?" It expressed what best lingered after their many storms and windfalls, only faintly suggested in the biographical film, *Yankee Doodle Dandy,** in which James Cagney played George. The unfortunate

* An interesting side light on the profits which may come for the use of the life of a composer or dramatist in a film, mentioned before, is revealed in the appraisal of

fight which George made against Actors' Equity was probably his most bitter experience. As he knew I did not sympathize with his position, we never discussed it. Several years later, after I had shown him through my favorite old churches in Paris, he said as we parted: "George, this is the first time I haven't thought of Equity in two years." But when Guy and I took him our play in 1917 all this was still ahead. We hoped he would produce it, possibly act it himself.

When I told him our title he said: "That's funny—I'm working on a play with that same title. My leading character is a barkeeper. What's yours?" It seemed an incredible coincidence. He felt he should not hear the play; I, nevertheless, insisted.

I had read him and was to read him many plays—often merely for his criticism; some, he bought. My latest two he would have produced if we could have cast them. He seldom moved as he listened. He followed and gave no suggestion of sleep. But he was not otherwise responsive. I had seen him listen all through without a smile; but at the end he said, "That play is full of laughs." He was appraising it in terms of its holding interest to him and also in its "audience reaction."

After the reading of *What'll You Have?* Guy and I were sure George found little in it. But I was mistaken: he had found an idea he badly needed himself. As he told me later: "All a playwright needs is an idea."

The next morning he tried to get me at the Players. Many messages reached me some days later, after I came to town. When I rang him he greeted me: "Say, George, how much do you want for your play?" I was flabbergasted. Before I could find speech—and that means something for me—he went on: "I want to combine your bartender story with mine. I can't get beyond the first act; but I see a way to use you boys' idea." I said I should have to ask Guy. He and I both needed money, and so we accepted. Our names were to go on the program as supplying the idea. He gave us $2,500 and a percentage. It was fairly successful, had two companies, sold for Australia, and was made into a picture, in all of which we shared. Afterwards, George told me that while trying to reach me he had nearly finished the play!

Our *Polly with a Past* and *Adam and Eva* * followed quickly. The former was first tried out by Comstock and Gest in Cleveland stock,

---

the estate George left. Of a net of $827,384, the film accounted for $421,766; and it will continue to earn profits for years.

* Published together by Henry Holt, 1923; separately by Samuel French.

on June 26, 1916, as *A Happy Thought*. Morrie Gest was picturesque, black-tie-flowing and imaginative. He thought of the theatre in circus terms and waved huge spectacles into life. David Belasco, his father-in-law, went to see it and refused $15,000 to stage it but arranged to take it over himself. He was the most spectacular theatre personality I ever knew. I was to work on six scripts with him. I shall analyze his methods in a separate chapter.

Polly, with Ina Claire, produced at the Belasco Theatre in New York, September 6, 1917, ran 326 performances and toured all the following season. The visit of President Wilson, at the height of his war popularity, gave it national publicity, through one widely quoted line from the play, which proclaimed that Polly's escapade was so notorious that "it pushed the President's message off the front page of the Evening Post." Gilbert Miller produced it in London in 1921; even to this day *Polly* is played in the English provinces. It and *Adam and Eva* have been lasting stock and amateur favorites. The two together brought $100,000 in the silent pictures. But the talking rights of neither have yet been sold, because of a peculiar facet of the relations between stage and screen.

When *Adam and Eva,* produced and splendidly cast by Comstock and Gest, staged by Robert Milton, after a successful spring tryout, was about to open at the Longacre Theatre, in New York, the Actors' Equity strike was suddenly called. Of course I favored Equity. From Fola's own experiences I well knew how some actors had been exploited. Once, on tour, neither she nor the other actors were paid for a performance missed because the property man got drunk and the costume trunks were put on the wrong train. Fola protested, as a matter of principle, since the stage hands got their pay. One told her, "You see *we've* got a union." Fola related this experience when she spoke at the first public organization meeting for Equity, at the Little Theatre, New York, November 16, 1913. I could see some resented what they thought was her implication, that actors were laborers; though they worked for a salary, they thought they should be classed as artists. Yet, to win, the actors had to join the American Federation of Labor.

Adam and Eva, which opened September 13, 1919, ran 301 performances, with two road companies the following season. It failed at the Little Theatre, in London, with an English background, as its production had been unfortunately delayed until after the release in England of a very bad silent picture film, which even Marion Davies could not save. Of our two other plays, *The Cave Girl* * was a rewrite of my own play of the same title which had been produced by Cohan and Harris, with the beautiful Lola Fisher. At the Longacre Theatre our new version proved far below our two previous comedies though it staggered along and fell into a picture sale. Guy and I netted about $10,000 each on the venture.

But no play with which I was ever associated was so dogged with might-have-beens as *The Light of the World* † a drama about the Oberammergau Passion Players. From time to time large-scale religious dramas, written around some aspect of the Christ legend, had had a wide audience appeal. Ours had a novel treatment and approach to the eternal problem of applying Christianity to a transgressor of a man-made code. It was fantastic to feel, and some others did who first saw the play, that a fortune may have slipped through our fingers.

This had long been Guy's pet idea, and its tryout gave every indication of a success. The notices in Buffalo and Detroit were splendid. I find Pater wrote Bob, Jr., that it was also "made the subject of a leading editorial in the Detroit *Free Press.* This is an unusual distinction and argues well for its permanent value." The editorial (May 17, 1919) began:

> A drama of singular power and beauty, and of striking ethical significance, is being presented in Detroit this week. It is a work of such import that it demands recognition beyond the ordinary critical review.

At Baltimore, the management tried to extend the engagement. The family went to see the play, and Pater wrote:

> The audience displayed great enthusiasm. The laughter and applause were plentiful and there were numerous curtain calls. The play strikes deeper notes than *Polly* and I should think might even be a more popular play. It is a very clever piece of work . . . everyone in our party predicts a great future for the play.

As in the case of *Adam and Eva,* I had not only my royalty interest but a small "piece of the show." With a success that meant a cut-in on all the profits and on the manager's share of film and other rights. A failure, on the other hand, meant sharing in the losses. My first venture had been profitable. But when Guy and I came to talk over *The Light of the World,* with its expensive cast and production, we

---

* Published by Samuel French.
† Published by Henry Holt, 1920, and by Samuel French.

agreed that an author, if he had to keep his eye on the expenses of a production, might not think of what was most advantageous to the play. For instance, he might be so sensitive to the heavy drain of a star's salary on the weekly profits that he would be less insistent on having one than if the manager carried the entire risk of financial loss. It is mentioned here since this "inside interest" was more and more to become a factor in play production. At any rate, before we opened I asked the management if I might withdraw. Subsequently Guy changed his mind and not only retained his own interest but took over mine. Though I wondered, in the face of the out-of-town notices, whether I had made a mistake, my instinct this time proved sound.

When *The Light of the World* opened with a "special invitation performance in honor of the clergymen of New York and other prominent city and state officials" at the Lyric Theatre, January 5, 1920, it was such a failure that we could not get anybody in on a transfer. Whatever the good intentions of the management plus the lavish money spent at a total loss, its Manhattan birth was a midwife's butchery. Over my protests the New York program credited the authorship to a Pierre Sasson. Though one of the leading critics stated that he had known its original foreign text, others who knew we had written it were offended at what promised to be a press-agent trick to get a news story when our authorship was revealed. But what operated more than anything else against the venture was that the same managers, who were exploiting the Christ story at the Lyric, had another play at the Century Theatre called *Aphrodite.* This was based on the lurid, sexy Pierre Louÿs's novel, with a much publicized scene where a naked lady got up from her couch just too fast for the waiting police to focus on her with a summons. The sincerity of the whole set-up was quite naturally questioned. Though alibis are always in bad taste they may suggest, what I shall emphasize frequently, that outside factors can often tip the scales in a play's fate.

If the production had been delayed so that it could have been eased into the quieter emotion of a postwar mood, if a Belasco had brought it forth with the magic of his name and with all the atmosphere he would have thrown about it, if a compelling star had played the role of Christus, and above all if it had been produced with the utmost simplicity of the real Oberammergau play (which I was soon to see, shocked at the recollection of the contrasting overelaborateness of our own production), if—if—

The play must have had some inherent merit, for in Paris, when I had it translated, Gémier, the distinguished director of the Odéon, accepted it. It never went on. In 1936, Armand Vecsey, to whom Guy had originally given the script, sent me a letter Fritz Wreede,* the leading German play agent, had addressed to him from Berlin, August 28, 1921. I quote from it, as it is the greatest self-explaining might-have-been of all:

. . . Now, about *The Light of the World* by Guy Bolton and George Middleton. Prof. [Max] Reinhardt has read the book and he liked it immensely. He, of course, would like to produce it, but, owing to his many other activities, he wouldn't know exactly when.

So I tried to make others interested in it, showing the book around. A few days after Reinhardt told me his opinion about the book, he again called me up and asked me what I did with it. The reason for this was that he had met Richard Strauss, who had asked him whether he knew of a book suitable for a libretto of a grand opera. So Reinhardt immediately thought of this book.

I immediately got in contact with Dr. Richard Strauss and took the book to him. He had read the book, and I just come from him, after a long discussion. Strauss is crazy about the book. Hofmannsthal, his librettist [who did *Electra* and *Der Rosenkavalier*], also read it and also found it excellent. I ask you to talk with the authors immediately to learn their terms. Of an advance against the royalties, there cannot be even a talk: you know very well the economic situation here. But for the authors, I think, it would be a great honor to have their script used by such a master.

Will you kindly notify me immediately by cable?

Though I was in Europe in 1921, I did not know of this letter till fifteen years later! As it happened, Fola and I later spent some hours with Reinhardt, in a little café by the swift-flowing Salzach, in Salzburg, where we had gone to the Mozart Festival and to see the famous director's production of Calderon's *The Great World Theatre,* with the popular Alexander Moissi.† But Reinhardt failed to make the connection with my name. I knew nothing of these transactions.

In sending me the letter, Armand wrote saying that Fritz had committed suicide—a victim of the Nazi regime. Strauss was prais-

* By an odd twist of circumstances a statement of money due to his estate, on his interest in music and plays in America, crossed my desk for examination at the Office of the Alien Property Custodian, in 1943.

† The *New York Times,* Sept. 3, 1922, contains my report on this.

ing it. Hofmannsthal was dead. Reinhardt died in exile. So much for all the imps, which might have been angels, hovering over a play.

So much, too, for the satisfactions and disappointments of my "double life" of play publication and collaboration, with the interesting personalities who thereby entered my busy workshop; the ebb and flow normal to theatre life. Yet even many of those days were being colored by an unforgettable experience. It was to broaden and enrich my life and writing. It was not something I should have deliberately sought.

On the March day of 1917 when Senator La Follette led the famous filibuster against the Armed Ship bill, because he thought it would lead America into the war, his name was called out to me as I entered one of my clubs, and I was hissed.

That day I did not sit at my usual place. As I hesitated a man who was alone at another table spoke. It was George P. Brett, head of the Macmillan Company. To many he had seemed cold and distant, though always the quintessence of a calm courtesy. He was slight of figure and bore himself stiffly. I had up to then known him only casually, but he had seen what had happened.

"Won't you sit with me, Middleton?" he asked.

CHAPTER XIII

MANY EMOTIONS

In 1933, when I published *Hiss! Boom!! Blah!!!* * with a dedication to Bob and Phil La Follette, I tried to pack into it the outstanding crises during 1919–1923 through which individuals in various groups of one community passed. The wide swing of reactions we all went through caused me, as Percy Hammond put it in the *New York Tribune,* to "eye this wayward era critically," turn it "across my knee," and "trounce it more in irony than in anger." Professor John Dewey noted that "it is remarkable how much of the essence of the last few years" I had got into it. Sam Behrman, our best social commentator through his own comedies, wrote: "It is, of course, the most important play you've ever done. And one of the few that deal with contemporary problems, social and economic, that aren't stiff and solemn with propaganda."

I venture some "quotes" since professional production was, as frequently, denied me. So vinegared a salad, of course, would offend the public palate, always weak on the ironies. But Eugene O'Neill, ever sympathetic with technical experiments, called it "a fine piece of work"; and when Martin Flavin wrote that it was "an extremely interesting cross-section of American manners and morals in a technic quite new in the theatre" he touched on what was to be my only satisfaction, aside from getting things off my own chest. For it was—the reader will shudder to learn—in fifty scenes with fifty-odd characters: "a fast moving kaleidoscope," as the *New York Telegram* summed it up. These many-scened plays usually show progressive snapshots of one individual's life. I was seeking, though, to use "news" and to dramatize "actualities," interrupted by cynical comments from a disembodied voice. So, perhaps, the stage historian may find the pages worth a glance. It interested me to observe how effectively the same devices were later employed by the young WPA writers in *The Living Newspaper.*

I was also pleased that my fellow craftsmen recognized elements of

* Published by Samuel French.

168

technical novelty, for, aside from social implications, it was an effort to experiment with the looser movie technic. In one of his last letters to me Sir Arthur Pinero wrote: "I am fully alive to the earnestness of purpose and extraordinary skill with which you have built up this work." And John Drinkwater liked "its attack and fine indignation . . . if you can get it adequately produced it ought to make an exciting effect on the stage." Other English friends writing to me nearly all quaked over its production difficulties, though I personally felt it could be put on suggestively. St. John Ervine wrote: "I have just read it with immense interest and even greater consternation, for I kept asking myself how on earth I'd put this piece on the stage if I were a producer. It will test the quality of the finest director in America." Harley Granville-Barker, who at the Court Theatre had for years been England's outstanding director-dramatist, volunteered: "I wondered when we last met under the shadow of Hollywood what would result from your sojourn there. Well, this has—with a vengeance: an artistic vengeance on them. You show the movies how they can be out-movied by the despised theatre. And you have—you in America—had the courage to tackle and prove your technical case. . . . But you will have had or will have great fun staging it, seeing it come to abundant and overwhelming life. And your tribute to the *Senator*— that strikes another note. I appreciate that to the full."

I speak of the play at this place in my narrative because the first act, "Hiss," deals with the 1917-1919 war. Each scene of it, in fact, reaches back to the stirring days that lie just ahead in the story of my life. The act has sometimes been done separately, and I have seen one effective production at the Playhouse of the Henry Street Settlement, New York City. The *Wall Street Journal* called it "a vast rough canvas of America at war." Other critics, however, felt it suggested "the undercurrents" which whirled so relentlessly about one who had "refused to float to easy safety on them." For it was stated the Senator was really La Follette, who had opposed our entrance into the first European conflict. This is true.*

My father-in-law's course personalized a theme which always has sparked the dramatic instinct: one man against an organized ma-

---

* I was too near La Follette to write of his personal experience until this time, some fifteen years later. The only play I wrote about the war while it lasted was *Tides.* This was suggested by Charles Edward Russell and other radical friends, whose course in wishing our participation inspired one psychological explanation: having fought a whole lifetime in the minority they were finally to find comfort in being with the crowd.

jority, whether the hero be a tragic or a comic figure, obviously wrong or to be ultimately proved right. In his case it was not merely that a public character should become the most excoriated man in America. Piquancy was added since, on his heels, were those who, barking patriotic phrases, were really after his economic and political heresies. I marveled that Fola, though deeply feeling the personal abuse that questioned her father's motives, could pass by in her stride all this verbal vomit. Since childhood, however, she has been trained to accept abuse as part of a public man's lot, while I had no such background. Up to then I had enjoyed only the advantages of being related to a conspicuous figure. I was now to share in some of its penalties. So, while shuttling between such realities on the national scene and the little cardboard make-believes of a Belasco production, I naturally carried with me my father-in-law's personal drama. I wondered then what my own ultimate measure of a public man would be. Perhaps Lord Morley in his *Recollections* may have offered about the most satisfactory answer, in a question:

"What arms did your man carry in the serried conflicts of his time? Did he let them rust, and trust for safety to his shield?" *

My closeness to Pater during the enforced isolation of those days, when numerous intimate friends deserted him, I soon came to realize as a privilege, and an expanding experience to a writer interested in the human reactions his disputed course created. Beyond the inspiration of a courageous individual, I was to see a side of war itself that was shown to few. Yet I too had once thrilled to the arousing emotions of war; as a youth I had wanted the Spanish-American War "to free Cuba."

But I knew nothing in 1897 of the forces which pushed us into that ridiculous adventure, or of what a circulation build-up for yellow journalism that war really was. I never had heard of imperialistic dreams in high places nor of the part played by sugar interests. I believed all the slogans then ladled up in the headlines to make men want to kill—for "justice," "freedom," and "democracy." The "yoke of

---

* I had occasion to send this to President Roosevelt and was interested in his terse comment on a writer who greatly influenced my own political thinking:

January 4, 1938

MY DEAR MR. MIDDLETON:

Please accept my thanks for your thoughtfulness in sending me the quotation from John Morley's Recollections. It expresses an ideal of courage with robustness characteristic of that fine old English Liberal.

Mrs. Roosevelt joins me in wishing you and Miss La Follette a Happy New Year.

Very sincerely yours

FRANKLIN D. ROOSEVELT

tyranny" must be thrown off! But since I did, as usual, a lot of talking I felt I should fight for what I believed. The only decent and logical thing I could do was to volunteer. So I decided to enlist in a regiment Chandler was forming. I was under legal age; but I lied about that. I didn't tell my parents.

The recruiting station was on Sixth Avenue, near Eighth Street. I went in, signed, and joined the line for medical examination. The exalted emotion with which I entered caused me to remember vividly the scene and my reaction to it. About the huge room were men more or less naked, dirty, unshaven—the sweepings of the streets, they seemed. Aesthetically my democracy shriveled. Nor could I feel they were inspired, as I was, by a dedicated impulse. I noticed their patched pants and soiled underlinen on the long low benches. The thought flashed that they were joining the army simply because they had no jobs. They were helping to free a people though they had no economic freedom themselves. It was necessity, not sacrifice to serve others. I felt strangely superior and sick—this was not my idea of how the white-mantled army of righteousness saving the downtrodden should be made up. I wanted to run; but I hung onto myself and my place in the line.

It moved nearer the doctor. I started to strip. An officer stopped me: Better wait till my eyes were examined. I fought back my revulsion at the growing smell of unwashed flesh. Finally, my turn came. I was determined to go through with it, for I now felt it was a crucial moral test as well. I would meet it. But I was rejected: eyesight. And I hurried out into the fresh air greatly relieved.

Yet, in one respect, I did feel right with myself. I had made my gesture to boyish ideals. I had at least shown I was willing to fight for what I then also wanted others to be sent out to die for. Somehow, at seventeen, I had stumbled upon a fairly good code of conduct: to certify by action what one believes or preaches. At thirty-seven, however, not only my connections but my own reasoned opposition to our entrance into that First World War brought me up against the inevitable intolerances of war itself. In metropolitan circles I was even to have a place on its receiving line. But in the bitter disillusion that was to follow Versailles, with its making for the Second World War, I recognized that history may often hide its own meanings even from those who make it. What those ultimate meanings may be will only be found in the long reaches of time. My own bitterness was softened by the thought I once expressed in my play *The Road Together*: "Who ever knows what is right? The answer always lies so many years ahead."

But it sounds melodramatic now to recall that our telephone was tapped, or that Fola and I discovered some old suffrage friends were in secret service. I naturally felt indignant that the lecture and reading dates for my plays, which we were building up, were stopped; it was part of the picture, of course, that no patriotic club program maker should venture the La Follette name upon a program. Though there was also a fair share of more painful personal episodes I see no reason to retail them here. All went to the making of me, as I evolved through the war experience, or as some other happier happenings—two, I may mention—kept alive my instinctive faith in the essential goodness of people.

The peripheral patriotism of certain chairwarmers—with club petitions, for instance, to expel those who didn't hold with their own views—paled by contrast before one hour I then had shared with Allan Pollock, the English actor. That very day he had signed a contract to be the leading man to Billie Burke, then at the height of her popularity. Walking down Broadway, he was happily telling me how it would mean fine roles ahead. We paused at Herald Square as the bulletin board suddenly flashed the news of Belgium's invasion. I watched Allan's thin, lovely, sensitive face, change under emotion: pure, steady, and white-flamed. He was silent: I said nothing. Then he spoke very quietly: "George, I'm going back home." I put my arm through his as we walked along. He sailed a few weeks later.*

Near the end of the war Fola and I had a telephone call from Inez and Will Irwin, asking us to dine with some friends. While we had found generous islands in the great city, we had not received many such invitations. Will was just back from the front, and was shocked at the club talk of the home-stayers. "I guess hate is furthest from the trenches, George," he remarked.

When Fola and I arrived for dinner we found the room full. They were all old friends: some we had not seen since war broke. All of them had differed with us. But no word of the war was spoken. It was a happy evening. Afterwards Inez told us that as she phoned she said to each one: "Fola and George are coming." She gave each a chance to

* Though grievously wounded, Allan survived the war and produced *A Bill of Divorcement* in the United States. This was largely through the suggestion of Ethel and Al Thomas, who brought the play to his attention. Katharine Cornell scored in it. John Barrymore starred in the film version; and of all his late films this one best suggests the great gifts Jack had. In it Katharine Hepburn made her first film success.

decline. None did. Nothing ever touched us more than the Irwins' thoughtful act. People are good.

"I know it's been hard on you children," Pater said to me during those war days.

Fola and I were sitting on the porch with him in Washington, and I had just opened several of his telegrams. He asked me whether they were the "usual sort" he was so constantly receiving. These both suggested he go hang himself. Several times he had been sent a rope; once he had even faced a man with a dagger. But he knew no such thing as physical fear.

"I may never live to see my own vindication: but you will," he said quietly.

When in 1920 he had been reelected Senator, by the largest majority ever given to a man in Wisconsin, I recalled this prophecy. He smiled.

"Yes, Mid. The circle is complete: all the rest is velvet."

It was during war days that Bob, Jr., then in his twenties, had a recurrent streptococcus infection that became a medical case. Only by building up his resistance might it be permanently beaten. Fola went to Washington. For months she aided her mother, with two nurses, caring for him and preparing food to tempt his appetite. Day and night the family did all that love and faith could do; but it was his own strong will that sustained his weakened body through the long ordeal.

Finally, it was decided to move him out of Washington heat. Fola scouted and went, among other places, to Mary Johnston's home in the Appalachians. The author of such big sellers as *Audrey, Prisoners of Hope,* and *To Have and to Hold* (which has had over a hundred editions), had become Fola's friend, and later mine, during suffrage days, when Fola spoke in Richmond. She and her sister Eloise had opened her home, Three Hills, at Warm Springs, Virginia, for paying guests. In 1936, Fola and I were to spend our twenty-fifth wedding anniversary in its protective quiet and beauty. But Mary was no longer there. She had died at sixty-five, only the spring before. It remained for Arthur Goodrich, who wrote in her home many of his novels and plays, including *So This Is London!* to pen a tribute to her who once had said that death is "just going from one room to another." And now my fellow clubmate has himself passed over its sill.

Mary was always delicate: it was hard work which went into some twenty-odd novels. Their themes ranged from her beloved Virginia, through feminism, into her later mysticism. Though the latter went to a narrower market, as Arthur knew, "she was happier in them than in the success which she deliberately put aside in order to write them." She did one play, *The Goddess of Reason,* for Julia Marlowe. No one could be more interesting to sit with, as her sensitive mind played tolerantly over human problems.

When Fola asked Mary to advise where the sick lad and his parents might go, she at once offered her own home, in spite of possible local reactions. With the nurses, however, and the fact that Fola and I were to stay with them, a whole house was required. The only one obtainable at near-by Hot Springs had been operated by a professional gambler. It was large, with a spacious porch. The living room opening on it was turned over to Bob, Jr. Off this was a well-like room in which the circular white-lined poker table humped.

One night late I found the Senator there alone. He was taking the place of one of the nurses. He asked me in to "powwow." I can see him now, in his dark dressing gown which toned into the soft reddish glow of the overhead lamp, and with his whitening hair. His face was tranquil—like a Buddha—save for the marks of his long anxiety over Bob's illness.

"Pater," I suddenly asked, "if you had known all they would put you through, would you have done the same?"

He was silent a long while. I seemed to see him measuring what he had been through. Never, in all his life, was he to blame the people for what they did, aware as he was of all the pressures they were opened to. But he took nothing harder than that certain lifelong friends should have attacked him or impugned his integrity. Then he pierced me with his eyes, and his jaw shut firm for a moment, as tears slowly came. And, out of the deepest conviction I ever expect to hear of any man, he said:

"Mid, I just couldn't vote for this war."

I have often thought of that night since his statue, by Jo Davidson, was unveiled in Statuary Hall, in the national Capitol, on April 25, 1929, only four years after his death. Then, indeed, for him the circle was complete.

Perhaps it is fitting here to publish one letter which its author told me "some day to put into the record." I reread it, for the first time after it reached me, on the day after Irvin's death. His last letter, so widely published, brought back the inherent bigness of spirit which also lives in these lines.

830 PARK AVENUE, NEW YORK CITY
August 25, 1933

MY DEAR GEORGE MIDDLETON:

I hear that the members of his family have in preparation an authentic biography of your father-in-law, the late U.S. Senator Robert La Follette. If this be true, I'm asking you to convey to them this belated word of contrition from me.

Away back yonder in the War Time, when anybody with a foreign-sounding name was a potential spy and every man who dared to disagree with the majority of us was a suspect traitor, I too succumbed to the prevalent hysteria. Under the spell of that madness—which we mistook for patriotism—I wrote in the guise of a short story a certain piece of propaganda wherein by suggestion, at least, Senator La Follette was the villain of the piece, and at the finish the fictional victim of his own misguided and un-American doctrines.*

For years I have deeply regretted that I wrote that story, because more and more I have come to realize that the policies which he so courageously advocated, in the face of a then almost nation-wide condemnation, were in the main right policies. We-all were blind, not he. We ran with the herd; he, almost alone, risked his political future and for the moment sacrificed his political popularity, to stand fast by his honest opinions.

I am sorry that I never had an opportunity to tender to him, while he lived, my heartfelt apology for the injustice I did him. I am glad to make these tardy amends to his own household, and incidentally to pay a small personal tribute to the memory of a far-seeing statesman, a most gallant gentleman and a very great American.

Yours very truly,

IRVIN S. COBB

At Hot Springs, I daily watched Bob, Jr., begin his climb back to health. Yet it was nearly a year before he could return to his father's office. There he was to serve as "clerk" and secretary, in an over-all apprenticeship for his own Senatorship which began seven years later. In those bedridden months, sharing intimately his father's daily experiences, Bob gained the sense of proportions with which to face what lay ahead. I have felt that nothing which his own, then unforeseen, public life could ever bring him, would be more difficult to face, or would so test his fortitude as those war years. And the younger

---

* "The Thunders of Silence," published in the *Saturday Evening Post*, Feb. 9, 1918.

Phil, seeing the effigy of his father burned in the streets of his home town while he was still at Wisconsin University, and later serving in the armed forces of his country, was tested by experience as few have been who entered public office.*

It was during this period that death came to my father. The doctor had told us he had little longer to go. Too much had been asked of even his stout heart. By putting him to bed his life might be prolonged. But we all knew he would have been miserable away from the open air, the green trees, the sunshine, the streets and, above all, people. The old friends were gone: "The hardest thing about growing old, George, is to see them all drop off," he said. Yet he made new ones on the byways. He would often linger, with my devoted mother or his nurse, by the Hudson River he had swum in as a boy. He read, too, his beloved Dickens. He cut many hundreds of clippings for me of odd happenings he thought might be useful in my plays. One of my first nights, he could not attend. Mother told me he imagined himself in the audience. "Now the first act must be over," and he applauded.

I was alone with Dad when he died. At the end there came into his eyes an extraordinary light, as though in astonishment he suddenly beheld an answer to all the questions of his troubled life. Then his eyes closed slowly, while he sighed in full contentment. I saw that same last light in Chaliapin's eyes, as Boris Godounoff. Perhaps the great artist sought to show, as Boris looked into the unknown, that the first glimpse might reveal a reality beyond, which the dying alone could ever be sure of.

Only a few of the myriad Dad had known or helped remained to follow him to his grave. It was a February day after a blizzard. Dad had always loved the winter best. His last letter spoke of it. The avenues were filled with snow and rough with ice. As we went bumping along through a narrow East Side street I saw a man lift his hat in Continental fashion, and salute the dead who passed. Now, twenty-odd years later, I salute Dad, too—for all he was and all I came to know he meant in my life.

But salutes at the end are not enough; no, not enough.

* Though one of the most prominent speakers in "America First" when the Second World War broke, Phil volunteered again. He later became a colonel under General MacArthur.

FOLA LA FOLLETTE AND GEORGE MIDDLETON
In the Maine woods

Monsieur Middleton
confraternel hommage
Anatole France

In constructing the successive scenes of a play, an author has to reckon with what Aristotle called the "ground swell of emotion." This is the interval the playwright must skillfully handle so that both actor and audience can be imperceptibly led out of one situation and its attending emotion into another. Life brings these less formally handled transitions also from each period of a man's development into those which follow. Perhaps almost unconsciously, the war was also then playing that part for me. But in the crises which individuals face as well as nations, the answers are seldom found in any sheer logic of events: it is chance and the unpredictable which most generally affect the sequences of our lives. The dramatist, though, must be more careful how he calls upon them in his fictive solutions. That is where life and the stage so infrequently meet. I was often to think of that difference through those emotion-laden days as themes and plots tried in vain to find their way to paper.

Two deep autumns Fola and I were to spend at Kineo on Moosehead Lake, with Marice and Gardner Hale. Upon the shifting background of life and husbands, which had taken her from Tuxedo to Rumania, Egypt to Berlin and through the odd strata of New York and Parisian society, colorful Marice Hale had based her cosmopolitan stories and books. Gardner looked like a pagan Christ with his long slim body, tan pointed beard, full tousled hair, and wide wise eyes. He was the son of the Latinist, Professor William Gardner Hale, about whom and whose wife I was to write a little play, *The House,* which George Arliss once planned to do. Early, Gardner came upon a forgotten study on the technic of fresco painting by Cennini, and he made it his life work. His own authoritative book, *Fresco Painting,* with an introduction by Orozco, was published posthumously.

Ten miles from a railroad, with only a little boat to bring mail and supplies, Fola and I were to live in our first forest abandon together. Here was a moment's naked morning plunge with lake mists rising: campfire and smoked-up coffee pot; green canoes and untrodden paths, rich with late berries, food for the partridges I hated to kill and large vicious trout. Nor can I now forget the deep green of that buck's eyes Gardner once shot. They seemed to stare increduously at what had happened: Did his destiny, his fight for life during the young years, mean nothing before a man with a gun? Here were long weeks of spiritual healing; weeks of work on *The Cave Girl* and my *Masks* volume—and much reading, too. Yet I forgot afterwards which books they were till I was strangely reminded of one of them when Fola and I dined at the White House in 1940.

The occasion was a dinner to give the National Achievement Award to Katharine Cornell.* Kit never looked lovelier than she did in her white Hattie Carnegie gown. She was quite overcome, too, when Mrs. Roosevelt herself gave the gold medal, after Mrs. Belmont had graciously spoken and Alec Woollcott had outdone himself in pointed theatrical anecdote. But though the dinner had been planned in her honor the Governor-General of Canada and Lady Tweedsmuir were White House guests: so protocol demanded a more formal set-up.

I confess my stage manager's instinct bowed in admiration of the way it was handled. Only once before—at a high mass in Lourdes, which I watched from behind the choir—had I been so fascinated by the smooth machinery with which each move was coordinated. On entering, for example, I was shown the table plan and given a card with two crosses where my dinner companion and I were to sit, in relation to the President. My responsibility was to find my partner (as Fola was to be found by hers) and escort her at the given moment to her place; and I had no trouble, for she was Eleanor Robson Belmont, whom I had known since her early stage days.

As Fola and I went to the Blue Room—Fola on the arm of an enviable bachelor navy aide, who announced her, with me following —we were stationed in line, with the other arrivals, against the wall. I learned afterwards we were grouped in some sort of planned order. When the President and Mrs. Roosevelt were announced with Lord and Lady Tweedsmuir, we went to be received: married men ahead of their wives. When a woman was attended by a man not her husband, it was she who went first. As we approached the President the aide called our names. He and Mrs. Roosevelt shook hands with each guest. Then each man immediately sought out his dinner companion. As soon as the President was seated we sat down, not waiting for Mrs. Roosevelt. Her brother took Fola in—Alec sat on her other side—and told her that this was his sister's innovation.

After dinner, when the men were alone, I found myself at the President's elbow near Lord Tweedsmuir—or John Buchan, if you will. I contribute my mite as to the late President's social charm,

* Two years later I was also present when this award was given to Rachel Crothers: the second time a woman of the theatre was so honored. On this occasion John Mason Brown made one of his characteristically happy addresses, with some words from Lucile Watson and John Golden, who had produced many of Rachel's plays.

voluble humor and robust capacity for hearty enjoyment. Recently returned from his trip to South America he was full of it. Apropos a book on the Spanish Main, just published, he remarked that he had read the writings of all the early explorers and adventurers in the original, as he "got along" well enough in Spanish. He thought Buenos Aires was the best laid-out city he had ever seen. Arriving in Uruguay for the reception he said its President had whispered as they got into the automobile together: "If anybody jumps on the running board with a pistol don't be worried. He's going to shoot at me, not you. That's what happened to Vargas last week." As Lord Tweedsmuir told how greatly touched the French Canadians had been when the President addressed them in their own tongue, the President asked if we knew where the best French was spoken—and answered himself by saying it was among two thousand colored Haitians, one of whom had written a great book on international law. The day he arrived at Trinidad, England was changing Kings. On account of the difference in time no one was sure who might be on the throne. A possible breach in international etiquette was avoided by an agreement with the Governor that no one should look at a watch before they drank the anonymous toast to "His Majesty the King." "No one ever knew whether it was the last toast to King Edward or the first toast to King George," the President added with obvious relish and a contented chuckle.

In 1921, when I was staging *Polly with a Past* in London, some plans had been broached for me to dramatize one of John Buchan's popular novels. Though it had fallen through, and I had missed meeting him then, I ventured now to recall the episode to him. He was a small man and somehow reminded me of Paul Kester. His nose was sharp and gave a pointed direction to his face, which seemed to focus intently on you. With all his ineffable charm, he made me instantly at home; almost confidentially, he said, "I like to talk with my fellow writers." In the course of our talk I told him that his *Prester John* was one of my favorite mystery novels. His face brightened at my remembering one of his almost forgotten books.

"I'm glad you like it. It is one of my favorites, too. When did you read it?"

Suddenly I remembered what I had completely forgotten until that very moment: I had read it in our little one-roomed shack at Kineo, with the wind roaring across Moosehead Lake and the rain pelting against our windows so that every board squirmed. There, glued to the uncertain kerosene light, I read that hair-curling African adventure straight through.

As I told the author, he smiled approvingly and admitted it was an "ideal background."

By such strange chances are memories revived. Little had I thought when I read that story that, twenty-odd years afterward, I should be speaking of it to its author—where I did!

We left Kineo on Armistice Day. I felt sorry for the New Englanders along the route. It is so hard for them to meet an occasion like this with what needed a Mardi Gras abandon. Yet all along the single track, at the little stations, groups had their horns and banners. Peace had come! The war to end war and to make the world safe for democracy was over! Never again could such things be!

Fola and I came back to more productions, more plays, another book and fervid social activity. Every one felt relieved and released. There was plenty of money, too. Even my bank account from plays began to bulge. Prosperity! New prospects were opening up, more chances for Broadway productions, more money to be made. Success! Suddenly I gave it all up. It was Fola who thought of it.

One day, before our fireplace, she took my hand:

"Mid, do you realize what is happening to you? You're getting back in the old rut before we went to Kineo. You talk of nothing but box-office receipts, press stories, publicity and what's in *Variety*. You used to care so much for other things."

"What's the answer?" I asked.

"Don't you think we ought to make a break? A *real* break?"

She was right. On such big decisions Fola always has been: and her average is more than good on the others. We made our break. We sailed on the *Aquitania,* in August, 1920, planning to stay abroad two months.

We stayed two years!

CHAPTER XIV

FROM OUR PARIS BALCONY

As THE *Aquitania* pulled out of New York harbor the distinguished gentleman who greeted us on deck proved an old friend: William Archer, who, as Barrie once wrote, "had done more for the English stage than any man living." I had enjoyed his *Play-Making,* a most helpful book about the technics of the craft. Though he himself had felt there were "no rules for writing a play," there might be profit in stressing "its problems and its possibilities." And now, in the article he was writing for *Harper's,* he measured my fellow authors by the way in which each had lived up to his capacities. Years of professional criticism thus bore out Pinero's estimate: "His aim was to get the best out of a writer that was in him and not to be satisfied till he got it."

Archer was verging on his own success, *The Green Goddess,* about production of which, with George Arliss, he had just seen Winthrop Ames. His first play to be produced, written at sixty-five, had been accepted when Granville-Barker brought it over. Archer was shy in speaking of it though he told us he had dreamed its plot; in fact, because he lacked confidence in his own dialogue, he had offered the unfinished script to both Shaw and Pinero, who urged him to complete it himself. He was sure the critics would be astonished to find the "high-brow" essayist and translator of Ibsen had dipped into straight melodrama—for which, however, he "always had a weak spot."

Slowly, with smooth sailing days, we discovered Archer's varied interests. In spite of initial diffidence and a cloaking, Scottish reserve, we relished this humor, as it played through honest eyes and trenchant phrase. Yearning to be an explorer, he had twice gone around the world, with long stays in India, background of *The Green Goddess.* Telepathy, too, fascinated him; he matched Fola's strange psychic experiences with his own, which he knew "could not be explained along physical lines." There were anecdotes, too, of literary figures: Ibsen and their first meeting; his long friendship with Shaw and their one amusing attempt at collaboration—*Widowers' Houses.*

As we neared Plymouth, after six days as his table companions, we had quite lost our hearts. His fine integrity dominates my memory of that crossing. Happily, we were to see something more of him, though only four years were left him. I am sure, as his time came, the last words in his diary summed up much of his feeling about life: "If the worst comes to the worst, I've had my innings."

When I came to London the following November to arrange to produce *Polly with a Past,* Archer invited me to a "housewarming" at H. G. Wells's new apartment, for "Shaw and Gilbert Chesterton and some others will probably be there."

To a question as to what either Shaw or Wells would be interested in hearing about, he replied: "About money matters. They are both intensely interested in American business, you know," he added, with one of his wise smiles.

I only had a portly, profile impression of Chesterton, with a hurried handclasp and a quick twist of his large head and his long-corded glasses. When I could speak to Shaw, he explained how his weekly article contract with Hearst made the publisher pay the American income tax. Wells felt how much better his *Outline of History* might have been exploited.

Archer had slyly remarked both Shaw and Wells were socialists.

From Cherbourg Fola and I had gone direct to Paris. We were received at 20 rue Jacob, in the heart of the Latin Quarter, by the Hales, who had come back from a fresco job in Florence to install us in their studio—of our dreams. It was up five flights, like our first walk-up in New York, though the stairway's contortions made it seem seven. The house was two hundred years old, with a carriage driveway into the long court past the *loge* of the concierge. Here, Madame Mulot sat guard day and night. Though we grew in her good graces I was not "established" until Douglas Fairbanks left me a note and she herself spoke to the great "Dou-glass'." After that the world of the quarter was ours.

In the rear lolled a *pavillon,* in which had lived the famous actor Talma, and an eighteenth century *temple d'amitié* was hidden beyond. In the *pavillon,* Natalie Barney—the American *amazone* to whom Rémy de Gourmont wrote some literary letters—held sway over an odd world of her own. Her Fridays were famous: here I was to meet many of my theatre world, including the dramatists Paul Géraldy and Georges de Porto-Riche. Fola and I had known Natalie's inde-

pendent mother in suffrage days. When we arrived we found her bid
to tea and a watermelon!

Beyond 20 rue Jacob had stretched Racine's garden; through it
Marshal Saxe had stolen to the kisses of Adrienne Lecouvreur; and
the actress had lived but a step from the later Hôtel d'Alsace, in which
Oscar Wilde died. Near by, almost intact, stood the printing house
which Balzac had bought, running up his impossible debts, and held
rendezvous with the guardian angel of his young manhood, the
already aging Madame de Berny. It was this I had in mind when I
dedicated to Fola my play, *That Was Balzac:*

Souvenir of Paris years—where the material of this was collected—
and of our little balcony *au cinquième,* which Balzac himself probably
saw when he looked from his own window in the rue des Marais, a century
ago.

We had three rooms, with a *cabinet* tucked in one corner as an
after thought. Fola bathed in a circular tin tub, dragged from under
the bed, which she mastered in attitudes worthy of a Degas's pencil.
For me the sponge was safer. Inconveniences, including a stove of
uncertain ardor, won easy tolerance. The studio opened on the balcony. The sun set behind Saint-Sulpice on Montmartre. At night,
through the glass strips above, one saw the moon and the bolder stars.
Here, except when touring, we were to spend two years; here, also,
when alone or with Fola on later visits, I was to stay. It meant Paris:
for we never knew its hotels.

We soon decided to live the life of the French people if possible—
not to impose our habits upon a different milieu. From the first we
kept house. We had a cuisine not five feet wide. It was so tiny I almost
forgot it. Here, on two gas burners, mysteries of French cooking were
summoned, *alouettes sans têtes, mousse chocolat,* or what not; for Fola
found magic and devotion in two French maids, through her appreciation of their qualities and an interest in their personal lives. Since
each, in her time with us, gave an insight into the subtle relationships
of French life, they first suggest the picture of our living. They were
more dear than some of those "people of importance" who occasionally
climbed our stairs.

Maria, a peasant from Picardy, squat, sixty, hard of hearing but
wise with life, had worked for the "best people," without losing her
independence. Out of another epoch, she recognized only its inner
standards of what made a lady and a gentleman. To those who fell

outside she stood aloof and silent; to the others she permitted a warm but reserved relation. Fola felt that the greatest compliment she ever had was Natalie Barney's saying, "When you are away, Maria dusts a little for me and waits your return."

Gabrielle was from the South, young, with mischievous eyes, saucy tongue and a brain. In another century she might have been a king's mistress and run her world. She had style; she dramatized each day and her part in it. She had quick loyalties and defenses. No one could get the better of her. She seemed to have read everything our friends had written. Sometimes, when she was serving, I would turn to her; and to the astonishment of our guests she would answer my literary question with quiet authority. One writer Gabrielle admired was Johan Bojer, the Norwegian novelist. She was happy when we asked the author of *The Great Hunger* and his wife to a seven-thirty dinner.

By a coincidence, we were having tea that afternoon with Giselle Bunau-Varilla, the sculptress. Her father was the spectacular Philippe Bunau-Varilla, formerly engineer-in-chief of the Panama Company and the first Minister of the Republic of Panama, in Washington. He was about sixty years old, but vigorous in spite of his leg recently crippled at Verdun. His face, with close-clipped mustache, and his baldish head were strong as Malvina Hoffman's bust of him. He told us his "inside story" of how, through him, the "revolution" was brought about, the Republic recognized by "T. R.," so that the canal could be built. He gave me his book, *The Great Adventure of Panama*, and the inscription suggested there might be a play in it. While we were there Fola was called from tea to the telephone. It was Gabrielle.

Bojer, it seemed, finding we had no phone, had come to ask us to advance the dinner to six-thirty. He told Gabrielle he and his wife had been asked to a box party by Philippe Bunau-Varilla's brother, who was the editor of *Le Matin*. Bojer felt it "important" to go. Gabrielle was furious, though she politely told him that she was sure "Monsieur and Madame will be happy to accommodate him." She assured him dinner would be at six-thirty. Oh, yes; she would see he would not be late for the theatre. She phoned us to be there. Her sense of drama took command.

When Bojer and his cultivated wife came—expecting, of course, a homey *pot-au-feu*—they had one of Gabrielle's magics, *canard à l'orange,* with appropriate wines in honor of the distinguished novelist. But as she served and the Bojers quickly realized what had happened the gleam in her eye was worthy of a Bette Davis. Further, Bojer, planning a lecture tour in America, found, with the liqueurs, that there was no one better qualified to give him pointers than his hosts. Then began a visible struggle; but our maid's gentle reminders they must not be late gave our guests no retreat. I had expected the brilliant Johan Bojer to be the center of my attention; but it was Gabrielle.

To know her and Maria is a hint of how rich and colorful were our Paris days. Maria died before the Second World War; but Gabrielle has again written us in 1946 from her little town in the South of France where a room awaits "Monsieur et Madame."

To read French fluently as we both did, was one thing; to converse was another; but to understand it at the theatre was something else again. As any interruption would break our hold on the meaning, we always sat in the first row. Fola, being thorough, also studied systematically: I went walking and found more words. Somehow I mastered how to duck a troublesome idiom and to use *chose* or *machin* —which could stand for any noun I forgot. At any rate the French preferred my high-geared inaccurate fluency to pedestrian perfection. Yvonne Printemps, the too, too fascinating actress, later told me she enjoyed my French: *"Ça marche toujours."* Well, it did keep going; but when I conceded that I got my genders mixed she murmured, with open-eyed innocence, "But, monsieur, what's a little gender between friends?" Which was also something else again.

I also went to the Sorbonne. Geoffrey Parsons (who twenty years later was to be awarded a Pulitzer prize for his *New York Tribune* editorials) and I found it together. The newspaperman was at work on his book, *The Stream of History*. Though we had often said hello since Columbia days, Fola and I now daily enjoyed his impish humor. Each morning for four months we went, like schoolboys, to the Amphithéâtre Michelet. The fee was negligible, the *salle* uncomfortable, the seats hard, the ventilation ghastly, of course: the classes were a layer cake of the world's races, frosted with every conceivable accent. But the lectures were enthralling in content and construction. My notes still breathe with their stimulus: French art, ideas, science, history and its great literature. I had the privilege I had wished as a young man; to go to college at forty! Now what I took in was sifted through some experience of life and a selective judgment that the young fellow had lacked.

During the war this *Cours de la Civilisation française* had become famous. Its object was to show foreigners, who were to teach French,

what France herself had contributed. Twice a week the professors in
turn took us across the pages of France, and its spirit spoke: the
scientific impersonality of Rey, the Midi romanticism of Le Breton,
the skepticism of Guignebert, successor to Renan, and the eighteenth
century grace of Reynier, who seemed to wear satin breeches and flit
a lacy kerchief before the salon ladies he evoked. I also sampled the
many free courses: Aulard, the great authority on the French Revolution; precise phrasing Emile Mâle, the iconographer, whose books
became my guides among the churches; Bédier, who dated medieval
manuscripts before your very eye.* When Fola was away, I even
reported:

Three fine lectures today: Ariosto, geography of Mesopotamia, and
a Latin poet on Alexander the Great! *Une salade.*

One afternoon Geoffrey and I hunted up a small amphitheatre
back of the Sorbonne. Only a dozen frozen-browed listeners were
following while a soft-voiced woman chalked deep-dipping surds on
the blackboard and explained the equations with charm and affection,
dusting the chalk from her hands as she did so. All the time, a
machine was breaking up molecules or something in steady bombard-
ment, terrible with future implications.

The woman's face was hauntingly familiar. Not until I saw Duse
in Sacha Guitry's dressing room did I realize how much Madame
Curie had suggested the Italian actress. Geoffrey and I had sat spellbound while such figures poured from a human brain into words. We
both knew we were in the presence of genius. I wonder now whether
we were seeing the first hints of the atomic bomb.

But the academic was not enough for my conversational needs. So
I wandered about Paris with a shy fellow from Roanne, who had a
sense of humor, and sympathetic cultural interests. Bertrand had been
introduced to us by Jeanne de Lanux, the artist, and a pupil of Dal-
croze, who had kept his celebrated school of eurythmics going for him
during the war. While Jeanne and Fola would go forth on their own
quests, I would point out to Bertrand everything I didn't know the
word for, from the tints in a Titian to the entrails in the butcher
shops. Each morning when he whistled from the courtyard I would
hurry down with my *Rochegude,* which held the street-by-street story

---

* Some years later, when Professors Bédier and Paul Hazard dined with us in
New York and I talked too much (in French), Bédier wrote in my copy of his
famous *Tristan,* "Souvenir d'une maison New-Yorkaise, que je n'oublierai jamais."
Which might mean several things.

of every old house in Paris. Soon I was showing him his city. He, too, would lead me through the museums: Carnavalet, Cluny, and, on a rainy day, Louvre. His selective appreciation inspired me to grub up on everything from Coptic tissues to medieval ivories.

We would also linger by the kiosks, which held the different-colored theatre posters (*affiches*), telling of plays and casts. He explained *reprise* (revival), *relâche* (no performance), and *remise* (postponed). We searched for the old theatres; most were faded then: some to base cinema uses now returned. But others, like the Comédie-Française itself, must have changed little. The Vaudeville was still vigorous: here Camille had started her unending coughing tour on every stage; here Bartet had made her début to become a tradition of sensitive characterization and refined charm; through its doors, Réjane, incomparable comédienne, in her grand days, brought the world. Farther on, the Variétés, where Offenbach had ruled for twenty years; the Gymnase, of the early Sardou, and the Palais-Royal, tucked discreetly away from the palace itself, as though its gay obscenities could tickle best off beaten tracks.

It was thus by seeking that I found the Paris I was to love and make mine to remember. Seven years later, in Hollywood, thousands of feet of film of the French city came to the Fox studio, without titles to indicate locations. For days I had it run off: the streets, the churches, the railroad stations, the parks and markets. My task was to identify and index them for the "library," to be "cut in" as background for French stories. Odd to have been paid for such an enjoyable recall!

As the story ran, I knew Paris. My own Broadway world soon began to come to me. Gladly I led my friends about; Julia Marlowe and E. H. Sothern, who had a near-by apartment, once went with me. I thought the best of D'Artagnans would like to see where the gasconading hero had walked and fought—shown to me fifteen years before by Booth Tarkington. Old Paris, however, must be seen in a fiacre. The *cocher* I asked to show me about said it wouldn't "amuse" him; but, knowing the first law with the French was to make everything personal, I made a bet that I could show him more of old Paris than he could me. He grinned, and we three got in. I think even the old nag perked up. It became a game. I would surprise him with some hidden court, to have his whip point above to a moss-covered Revolutionary street sign. The two distinguished stars got in and out, stood on tiptoe, or bent under some low-ceilinged room. Finally the odor that floated up my favorite sixteenth century *escalier*—one of the few left—was too much for the lady who had spoken some of my first lines on the stage. So we called it a day: I admitted, of course, that I was beaten, and paid the *cocher*.

Many a time after, I heard the *clump-clump* of a horse on the wooden blocks and a guttural voice calling: "Hé, monsieur! Voudriez-vous voir le vieux Paris?" It was my *cocher*.

But in spite of such diversified lures the theatre itself was our constant quarry. Its intrigues (*cuisine*) and cliques (*petites chapelles*)* unfolded slowly—though I did not study its business mechanics, or even go "back stage" until I had a better command of the language. At the start, going to the theatre was adventure enough.

Of course we had seen Bernhardt, Réjane, Simone, and Coquelin, who had toured America; but now we were on the home ground of Parisian favorites: the three Guitrys, Féraudy, Le Bargy, Jeanne Granier, Piérat, Suzanne Desprès, Gémier, Gaby Morlay, and a cluster of brilliant comedians like Victor Bucher, Max Dearly, and three who became international film stars, unsurpassed—Raimu, Jouvet, and Harry Baur. Though Gallic emotion was seldom to move me—only Bernhardt and the plaintive Piérat ever drew a tributary tear—Fola and I succumbed at once to the joys of French comedians. Never anywhere were we to see the comedy of line better projected.

If we had been at a hotel, I should have asked the concierge to get tickets "for a good show" and ended up at the Folies Bergères. If we had asked for the Comédie-Française he would have dropped dead. But when I ventured after our seats myself, I learned how exasperating French theatrical customs were. The box office (*bureau*) leisurely opened around eleven and might close at noon for lunch. The line would make its own laws: I saw a stately dame wave every one aside, march to the *guichet,* demand two seats, and get them. When a man ahead blustered, she crushed him with an "I'm older than you." Once as I neared the *buraliste*—all ticket sellers were ladies, so to speak— a "decorated" official sidled past, and brushed aside my protest by haughtily hissing that he was "a friend of the manager." I was reminded of the dialogue in *Le Roi,* where the servant announced to Raimu that somebody wished to see him. He did not recognize the name until the servant added, "He is not decorated." "Oh, I know him," Raimu replied.

* So much of French theatrical language is picturesque that I add some examples.

I held the line up myself by asking what held the line up. I learned tickets were never printed with seat-numbered stubs. I was advised, from a concealed plan, which seats I might have. Repeating the numbers, when I could remember them, I would look in the lobby for the little model theatre to see whether I liked them. Meantime the line would wait. The tickets then had to be written on, stamped, and dated. No wonder six people might take a half-hour. Many seats, too, were never for sale: First, the author got some for each performance. These *billets de faveur* ("Annie Oakleys," or passes, as you will) were generally handed over to one agency which sold them at half-price—for the author's account. The Lord only knew who besides doctors, police, public officials, special *concessionnaires* and other official parasites had free reservations.

Since the tax differed on tickets sold in advance (*location*) from those sold at the performance, the box offices closed at six o'clock to reopen later. If I waited till night I was given a blank admission which passed me to the *contrôle*. This throned triumvirate represented the *assistance publique* (which kept an eye on the taxes), the *Société* (which looked after its authors' royalties, to post each night the receipts of every theatre in Paris), and the management (*direction*). When I gave my blank ticket one would write my seat number in. But as I couldn't tell what I might draw I would tip some one to see first whether there were any front seats. All this because I wanted to do things like the French!

Fola and I never solved when a Paris play would start. Max Dearly told me plays were always late because the audience wasn't there. The *affiche,* the newspapers, and the box office would never agree. Once, after waiting till three-thirty at a Sunday matinée of a comedy by the genial Alfred Savoir, a spectator demanded the manager explain the delay. When he came before the curtain to say the leading actor had been caught in a traffic jam, some one asked her name. My neighbor shrugged when I wondered why audiences accepted such abuses: "It has always been like that, monsieur. *Que voulez-vous?*"

As we entered, *les dames du vestiaire* took our belongings, to be paid for per article. They received a small nightly sum, and the manager pocketed the charges; or they might follow the example of Harris Dickson's old negro mammy, who would disappear for days "to organize the heathen in China" and say, "I gets what I collects." Then we were greeted by the *ouvreuses*. Originally they opened the boxes; now they eagle-eyed the whole theatre. It was portioned off, and no spectator could escape. The proper one would find our seats; if we did it ourselves she would charge down the whole row to demand her tip. The program was sold by a man whose patron had bought the concession. It was all "the old hat-and-coat racket." One *ouvreuse* told me not to blame her: the play was a failure [*four*], and she was losing money since she had paid "for the privilege."

Yet these harpies were interesting. Many were retired actresses, clinging to the fringe of the theatre which had been their life. Others had been *habilleuses*—in France even the actors had female dressers. (What consternation this was to cause Jim Hackett and the English actors who came over to the Odéon to do *Macbeth!*) Yet how they could retail the gossip (*potins*) of their world! And is anything more fascinating than such irresponsible gabble, smelling of grease paint? What strange alchemy makes us "theatre folks" brothers and sisters under the skin? I could not have been more at home in a Belasco dressing room than I was with these women—or than I was later in a little town in France, idling an hour with a troupe of those "playing the fairs," talking to the ticket seller who explained, "We give them comedies and social dramas during the week; but on Saturday night we always have to do melodrama to please the working people"; nor that evening when Fola and I went with Lenormand in Rome to a first night of his *Le Simoun,* and sat in the Italian star's stuffy dressing room as he blandly explained, in three languages, "how the paper scenery he had to use in traveling about Italy seldom caught fire."

What was that kinship in being asked, during those endless intermissions—to make theatre going in Paris a social affair and to encourage the bar: Did I know who was really the father of Maurice Bernhardt? Did I know Yvette Guilbert had only one kidney? Did I know that Réjane's breath had become so bad no one wished to act opposite her, and so she always carried a heavily scented handkerchief? They knew all the answers or had them. Did I ever hear what Sarah Bernhardt, then seventy-six herself, had said when she learned that Réjane had died at sixty-three? "Now it is Jeanne Granier's turn"— Granier being eight years younger!

Was it here I first heard that famous reply of Rachel? When she was on tour a much smitten son of Louis-Philippe, from his box, sent back to her dressing room his visiting card, on which was tersely written: *"Quand? Où? Combien?"* And the greatest of her day replied on its back:

"Ce soir. Chez moi. Pour rien."

One *habilleuse* had seen Yvette Guilbert in the early nineties when she startled Paris at the Scala. Then slim and flat-chested, with long neck, pudgy nose, carrot hair, she even shied from the devices of make-up. But her angularities inspired caricaturists, among them Steinlen and Toulouse-Lautrec, who often sketched her.

"Ah, monsieur: then she sang her risqué songs with the voice of innocence and the face of an angel," I was told.

In later days, for those songs, she would don the familiar green satin gown—much ampler, of course—and the long black gloves, originally conceived to accentuate her slimness. *Les Chansons de gants noirs,* the group was called.

When I had first met Yvette, in New York, she asked me to write her a play. Only uncertainties as to her own future kept me from trying. Many writers, in fact, had urged her to return to the stage, where she began. George Moore was wanting her to do *Esther Waters;* but the novelist and Edward Knoblock, the dramatist, disagreed as to the treatment. When she announced each night she would "now sing some songs of my youth," the house would applaud. Then she would add significantly: *"Oh, là, là!"* In those three syllables she suggested the stretch of her professional years.

Yet even then I felt something tragic about this gifted woman. Her restless intelligence had, in fact, long since led her away from those songs which had made her fame, and of which the public never tired. During a prolonged illness she had collaborated with Gaston Paris, the leading authority, to resurrect hundreds of lost folk songs, some from as far back as the thirteenth century. With this grew a passion to instruct; her recitals soon expanded with erudite comments. This weakened Yvette's popular appeal, though many, of course, were aware of her great contribution. Today, in fact, the folk song has come into its own. She was among the first to popularize it. She once summed up her career: "Ten years of boulevard indecencies and twenty-six years of the lovely songs of France."

Of course, Fola and I now followed her current recitals in Paris. They turned back the pages of a France we were striving to know. One night, too, we saw Duse there, behind the scenes. They were intimate friends. From Yvette we first heard of the Italian's tragic years, struggling to come back from those personal depths that lay in her tragic love affair with D'Annunzio. Recitals were planned together: Duse to do poems; Yvette, songs which would blend. But nothing happened. Duse a few years later went to tour America and died there. Only yesterday Yvette also passed from the scene; but there still remain the songs from which she shook the dust of years. Younger and better voices will sing them—but no one as Yvette Guilbert, I am sure.

While in Paris Fola and I had an unforgettable measure of her art. She asked us to lunch in Montmartre with Jehan Rictus ("John Grin"), the "poet of the poor." With a few of her pupils we ate under the trees, back of the old Café aux billards en bois. A downpour drove us indoors, and Rictus, who had been a cabaret character, recited, in a lugubrious argot—obviously an echo of an earlier time, when in such little *boîtes* a strange poetry was born. Soon, with the rain, the talk slipped back to the singers of another day: La Grande Thérésa, Bruant and Paulus, all famous when Madame and Rictus were young. Their songs were resung for us; their styles imitated. Then the two recited their own hard beginnings, not far from where we were sitting:

"Do you remember, Rictus, what good comrades we all were then? There was such joy in creating. It was all for the thing itself. Has youth changed any?"

But the realistic Rictus snipped the nostalgic mood. "Youth was also unfair and naughty then, madame. Do you recall how vitriol was thrown and one of the 'new ones' disfigured?"

I urged Yvette herself to sing some of those famous songs: "Les 4'z Etudiants," "L'Hôtel du Numéro trois," "La Pocharde," among others. I see her now, her black-tipped fluffy parasol and her full white flowing gown, with a cigarette hanging in the corner of her mouth. There, lolling in a chair, with only her change of expression, for an hour, she peopled the room with those who sang their songs through her. No *diseuse* could so endow each *chanson* with the personality of the fictive singer; for her range was phenomenal, as she switched that day from youth to old age, amid varied social strata and centuries. Even in this silhouette of her genius she was unapproachable.

To the end Rictus remained true to his pen name, for he left the world "grinning." In 1938 he died of starvation in a garret. His body was discovered by an officer of the Legion of Honor, who had come to make him pay for the decoration which had long since been granted him, but for which he had never called. The cross was then pinned to his left breast.

The last time I saw Yvette, in 1928, she inscribed her photograph, I am proud to quote: "A vous Middleton un ami de la France et de moi." With a wistful smile, she said: "That is the first photograph I have ever let them touch up. But, you see, I am past sixty now." To talk with her of her work and her old associates was to know those dazzling decades over which she was one of the acknowledged queens, outliving all the others, to die in 1944.

Le Nouveau Cirque! Le Scala! Les Champs-Elysées! Les Ambassadeurs! Only a few still stood, as I sought them out; for I have often been homesick for what I have never seen. The others were faded. Yet Yvette Guilbert herself had brought their glory back to Fola and me with hers that rainy afternoon, in a sordid, stuffy little café—and Paris visible over the treetops of Montmartre.

I never took a photograph of Paris from our balcony. But we cherish a portrait of Fola by Waldo Peirce, with the egglike dome of the Institut de France in the background. On a book she held he had painted, "A la plus sage des folles." Though Waldo's highly individual art—now in nearly all the leading museums—was only feeling its way, the bewhiskered painter was famous as a type in the *quartier*. His New England ancestry, his wealthy parents (who would have been shocked to see how he made a belt out of several neckties), and his notorious voyage on a cattle boat with Jack Reed, from which, miles offshore, he jumped overboard to swim back to Boston because he didn't "like the smells"—were already known to us. He used to climb our stairs at odd hours. Once, in return for some small favor, he threw a canvas on the table. "Here's a bunch of spinach, Fola." It was the lovely flower piece which now hangs near his portrait of her in a yellow gown.

Waldo's shaggy beard inevitably calls up the full-fledged appendage sported by Jo Davidson, the sculptor. When we last saw him in Washington he was as full of vividly told anecdote about his host of friends and acquaintances all over the world as when he and his fine-lined wife, Yvonne, descended from Mirabeau, had lived near us in the Paris days. But aside from all personal contacts he brought us I am most indebted, as I look back, for an absorbing vice he started me on, to add zest to all my wanderings ahead. Jo bought me my first piece of *bois sculpté:* a carved, rural, eighteenth century Virgin. She eyes me wistfully as I write.

From her my budding interest in religious art soon flowered, as it were. I studied styles and iconography. The primitives also, which, years before, I could not endure, now spurred my curiosity. At first the approach was literary; but slowly I felt their naïve charm and full accepting faith. Soon I could spot an influence and a period by the way the Child was held in the Virgin's arms, or the Sacred Loincloth was draped. The crossing of Christ's legs upon the Cross, with three nails instead of the twelfth century's four, was its own calendar. My study has images lovingly gathered in many quests, which seem to look in wonder at their strange displacement; and, oddly enough, they often recall Jo—gambling with me at the Deauville Casino, near where he bought my first Virgin with his winnings—which I am sure was not the carver's intention.

Jo also gave us the provocative Gertrude Stein. His statue of her suggests the squat body, cropped head, rounded face, and all-embracing eyes; but only through hearing her speak could you feel her devastating scintillations and scornful intolerances. Fola and I both enjoyed going to her much publicized apartment, in the rue des Fleurus, with its celebrated Picassos, Cézannes, and Braques, in which she had pioneered. To me, it was all new; for "modern art" was then something I also had to be led to.

After a luncheon at the Davidsons' I scribbled some comments to Fola:

Gertrude Stein was there and we fought royally. Jo said I was a marvel to make her talk art . . . She has little sympathy for those who get emotion out of art. "That's such an easy thing to get," she says; she gets "a lot" just driving her Ford about Paris. . . .

I fought for my right to be ignorant and my wish to try to *understand* painting, etc. . . . I refused to be overwhelmed even when she said I was "an adolescent, like most Americans." She tried to make me interested in her writings because I "shouldn't be interested in any new paint movement without also being interested in new literary efforts." That, she felt, was "a pose." Jo says she hates milksops. I think my ignorance amused her. . . . As she expressed it concerning my aesthetics: "You've opened the door but there's nothing there."

I suppose there's some hope for me, as she feels many others "don't even turn the handle of the knob, and thus the door is forever closed." We talked pictures and her work, which I confess is a closed book to me as yet . . .

I never could reconcile her own experiments in a new literary form with her eager anxiety over the weekly arrival of the *Saturday Evening Post*. But one day Fola pleased her. As she was looking at some of Picasso's drawings in the corner, Gertrude began reading to

Yvonne and me several compositions she called "prose poems." Fola did not know the subjects, yet found herself listening. "That's odd," she said, "There's nothing in the context to indicate who they are; but they sound to me like Roosevelt and Wilson; or rather they bring them to mind." Gertrude was tickled. Fola had guessed right. I was amazed; but then, Fola always was more sensitive to words than I.

Through Yvonne Davidson streamed other worlds of French life—none so fascinating as the dressmakers' kingdom. At that time Yvonne had her own shop. Though I stumbled badly in the technic of style exploitation I understood perfectly the marvelous mannequins. What materials they wore, and what stories they inspired! Once we all went to Lanvin. Though the lady herself was then inaccessible, I later sat with her in the orchestra at a Guitry rehearsal. Between suggesting tucks and lifts in piquant Yvonne Printemps costumes, she let me into the mysteries of how stage gowns were cut and their lines artfully designed to bring out "special enticements" or to switch the eye from frontal looks or limitations. It is important to understand such matters.

James Joyce also had posed for Jo. The bust catches the ascetic thin-pointed face, tight lips, and sharp nose, though his dark, heavy-lensed glasses hid much of his quick questioning expression. He was tall and lean, ever with a cane, and I never saw him assertive or other than shy with strangers. The Irishman once climbed our stairs to show me a long, and, I thought, devastating letter which Bernard Shaw had written about his *Ulysses*.*

When I first met Joyce he was awaiting its appearance, after stacks of proofs, rewritten in the Balzac tradition. Holding his hand was clean-cut, businesslike Sylvia Beach—to whom Archibald MacLeish later wrote a poem—a young American who ran the Shakespeare and Company bookshop. It specialized in the advance guards of literature

* Shaw had written me: "As to quoting letters of mine I should like to see copies of them first, as there might be passages in them which for private reasons I'd rather have deleted." So when I wrote him for permission to use his letters in this book I also asked whether his letter I had seen about Joyce had been written to Joyce or to someone else. It was characteristically gracious that, fearing mail under then existing submarine activity, Shaw should cable me: "You may quote my letters I never corresponded with Joyce." I might here cite another instance of his inherent kindness. As this manuscript was going to the printers and personal illustrations were possible, I found I did not have his photograph. I clipped one just published in a newspaper for the occasion of his approaching ninetieth birthday. I pasted it on a card and airmailed it, requesting his autograph. Shaw signed it, as it happened, on his birthday itself and so parenthetically noted in his vigorous handwriting, which showed no signs of his great age.

whom I had often observed in their razorlike amiabilities. Hearing Joyce could not get an American publisher, she sent the script to a printer in Dijon. Though literary historians have recorded the despair of French compositors setting up such a script in English—Joyce's English, at that—its delayed birth was not entirely due to his itch to recompose. I contribute a clinical detail: stories of strange doings in the printing establishment itself floated to Paris, as successive young male assistants, after being broken in, seemed to quit, and work stopped during replacements. Euphemistically, one might even say the delay had elements of manly sin in it. However, in time, *Ulysses* appeared, with its blue and white cover, which Joyce selected because they were the colors of Greece.

I had met the Irish writer through my college mate, William A. Bradley, and his wife, Jenny Serruys. She had many literary friends: her brother-in-law was Pierre Mille, novelist and feuilletonist, over whose salon his wife, Yvonne Serruys, the sculptress, presided. Jenny and Will took us into their home and opened difficult doors for us. Later Jenny was to translate my one-act plays. Will, a fine poet and critic in his own right, had been building up his agency to become and to remain, in his widow's hands, as it is today after the war, the most important link between French and American literary markets. Jenny had befriended Joyce when he came penniless to Paris from Trieste, finding a place for him to sleep and work. Will gave him his army cloak. Joyce had a sort of fated feeling that the gods would provide. Whether he offered up prayers of thanks or not on receipt, I am not so sure.

It was Jenny who also took Fola and me to see Anatole France, at Villa Saïd, in Paris, and at the home of his literary executor, Dr. Couchard, at Versailles, as well as later in Tours near his Bechellerie. The sprightly quality of the great writer, then seventy-six, was well caught in the bust Jo Davidson had just done of him. Only a few months before, he had married his housekeeper, possibly with the same motives which had prompted Rodin to regularize a similar situation.

The foxlike expression, which still lingers in the well known Choumoff photograph he autographed for me, was subtly present in his long face and close faunlike ears, which the white beard did not hide. He first greeted us *en négligé* in the library of his Paris house, which looked out on the Bois. As he made his entrance I noted the effective multi-patterned bandanna, twisted carelessly about his head: but Fola said afterwards that it had probably taken him a long while to achieve just that careless effect. No one could have been more gracious. Though he did not know my work from Adam, he gave me *Petit Pierre,* the story of his own youth, and wrote "Confraternel hommage" after my name. Jenny may have told him that I had read almost all he had written.

France discussed politics with entertaining Gallic skepticism. It was here I first heard broached his belief that the natural destiny of his country lay in an economic *rapprochement* with Germany. How he phrased it, I don't recall, though some less important words have lingered. I was admiring a Greek marble torso in the best fifth century, ensconced in a window. As I walked around it I moved my thumb to feel the rhythm of its line.

"Vouz pouvez le toucher," he said: for seeing my admiration he joined me. And then he reached for the little knob and turned the torso around on its socle.

"Oh, Maître, elle tourne!" I exclaimed.

"Oui, monsieur: comme toutes les femmes."

And from Lady Bountiful Jenny came the entrancing Charles Seignobos, Professor at the University of Paris. Though I was privileged to know him, and he once wrote that I was *sympathique,* it was Fola he took to heart. I used to see him at the Sorbonne. Far off, he would be seated at the inclined desk which held his notes, over which he would be leaning, as the lamp shone down on them and lighted his face. He was a little mite of a man, with a stubby white beard. He seemed lost there at the desk he was to honor so many years.

Then nearing seventy, he would climb our five flights with agility and talk in the same rapid manner, looking quizzically through his corded eyeglasses as he queried Fola on woman suffrage or Wisconsin. But mostly he revealed his immense knowledge of the American scene, for the passing present was his specialty: his book on modern history still a classic. He was one of those, too, who understood her father's position on the war; the very first thing he said when he met her was: "Your father was right. It was a blessing for France but against America's interest to have entered it."

One night we went to the apartment in the rue des Écoles, near where I had been a *pensionnaire* on my first romantic Paris trip, in which he had long made his home with the gracious Madame Cécile Marillier, great-granddaughter of Madame Roland. It was to her that

Ida Tarbell had dedicated the life of the Revolutionary heroine since she owed her "a debt of gratitude for sympathy and help which I can never repay." She was very old when Fola and I first met her, "freed and mellowed by a tragic life," as Ida Tarbell, who also knew her story, later put it. She was small, too.

As she sat that night, by his side, before an old-fashioned piano— she playing with hands already tight with age, and he singing in a gentle voice the old Breton ballads he knew by heart—something unforgettable slowly took meaning in me. I felt the unconquerable spirit of all that was best in France which sang that night, out of the hearts of that old couple, side by side—sang, and will sing again, I know.

There was then no conscious storing of any of this in studied sequence, and the stage doors of Paris still remain to tell about. Yet, as I look back, nothing now seems isolated or unrelated: each individual and each experience brought some radiation, some enlargement of view; each beckoned to new interests or enhancements. All were to help me grasp something of the spirit of France, which I then hoped to envelop in the play on Balzac I was still mulling over—Balzac who once, a hundred years before, had lived just below our balcony.

Whatever each day brought, Fola and I would always be glad to come back to our studio. We would grope up our darkened stairs; open the heavy door with our big key; then go to that beloved balcony and look out. The roofs and the gay terra-cotta chimneypots, the dour domes and gilded steeples would be in the shadows, with only the city's glow to tell they were waiting for the morning light to brighten them to life. We never knew a city could be so quiet.

As we stood there together I would realize I was completely myself in the new background, unafraid as I had seldom been, and uninhibited, as I had never been. I was strong and well, with energy as boundless as my curiosity. I was keen and zestful. I could modestly afford each caprice that caught me. Somehow I saw, too, as those months were passing, that I had never felt like an alien there. I belonged. By some strange atavistic impulse, though I had no French blood, I was at home. I was happy: Fola was with me and there was Paris, sleeping each night like a tired giant.

Early each morning the church bells from Saint-Germain-des-Prés, a step away, or from Saint-Séverin, farther off and deeper pitched, would waken us. As we lay and listened the ancient street cries of the itinerant scissor grinder, or glazier, or herb seller would rise from the rue Jacob below, and mount, through the narrow canyon the old buildings made, to our welcoming window—the cries now forever stilled, perhaps, but which Charpentier has kept immortal in *Louise*.

The city Fola and I thus came to know in those two years is dead. But a loved one lives again when we think of her. And Paris will remain as I loved it for as long as I can remember.

CHAPTER XV

I GO TO LONDON TOWN AND
BERNARD SHAW EXPLAINS

BUT THESE enhancing adventures were interspersed with professional activities in both Paris and London. Gilbert Miller was to produce our *Polly with a Past* at the historic St. James's Theatre, which had just come under his management. A foggy February again found me in London to assist at rehearsals.

Gilbert came of an established theatrical line. I had often called on his mother, Bijou Heron. Daughter of Matilda Heron, the first Camille to be acclaimed in America, she was herself, as Professor Odell records, a "marvelous" stage child. She later joined Augustin Daly's company, and during his production of *Odette* she met the young English Henry Miller, who was beginning a striking career.

I valued my contact with Henry and respected his art. Nobody could be better company. The last time I saw him he was calling on Ethel and Al Thomas, whom Fola and I were visiting, and delighted us for hours with satirical comment and anecdotes. One I recall of why he bought Charles Rann Kennedy's *Servant in the House*. Walter Hampden, just back from England, asked Miller, whom he had never met, to hear the modern morality play. As the dinner was good, Henry dozed. He murmured after each act, "Um—very good," and, to Walter's astonishment, accepted the play. But the script was not the reason. While listening Henry saw the tall, handsome actor was just the personality he wanted for Alla Nazimova's leading man. It was only when he himself had read the play that he sensed its value. Its later production, for a song, made theatrical history, and it served many seasons in Walter's repertoire. I wish every time a manager had fallen asleep on me things had turned out so well.

Henry Miller never did a play of mine, worse luck. A. E. Thomas, Arthur Richman, and James Forbes, who were produced by him, thought him the finest of stage directors. "He gets inside a play," Al put it. A rehearsal was an exhilarating and often explosive experience. Cyclones might develop, to be followed by calm contritions.

Yet, as Al said, "he was generally right, though he never insisted on his suggestions." His wit was ever on tap. At rehearsal one star said:

"Mr. Miller, do you know what I would like to do?"

"Don't bother to tell me: you will anyway," he replied.

As the same lovely lady let fly a series of picturesque oaths, he called out: "Please be careful: you'll shock the stage hands."

When I first knew Gilbert Miller he lodged in a furnished room near the Players. He was slim, with roving eyes and an on-guard smile. He had been hard up, doing every hack job the theatre offered. When he suddenly blossomed into a London personage during the war, by importing established American hits, we all rubbed our eyes in amazement. He had seen his chance and taken it.

While the real invasion had always been upon our shores by perennial English favorites, stray American stars had from time to time hibernated in London. Tallulah Bankhead's hectic stay, however, is hardly to be described with such a word. (Wasn't it Mrs. Pat Campbell who explained why so many important people constantly hovered around Tallulah: "She's always skating on thin ice, and they want to be about when it cracks"?) Though American plays had scored in London the war had obviously increased their production. I even heard that some English authors had apprehensively stroked their chins.

Gilbert aided and abetted, since he had not agreed with the prevailing pessimism that the war would ruin the theatre. He saw that the flow of soldiers to London would boom it. Even when I went over in 1921, though long runs with old favorites still held sway, audiences had markedly changed. With the shift in wealth a newer audience, that relished a coarser fare, had taken over the expensive seats. The need also created a new crop of producers. The vacuum into which these had rushed had been increased by the passing of the actor-manager.

There was nothing in America then quite like this British institution. Our few actor-managers seldom continuously had their own theatres. But in England they had been the residuary legatees of a tradition, tapering off after the Lyceum and Sir Henry Irving. My fellow dramatists spoke to me of the change with diverse feelings, depending in part on their own financial concern. Sir George Alexander, Sir Herbert Beerbohm Tree, and Sir Charles Wyndham, brother-in-law of our Bronson Howard, had for decades brought a distinction and personal cachet to all they touched. But these had now died off before they had themselves realized their reign was over. Whatever their contribution, it was generally admitted that the London stage had been more or less subservient, as John Drinkwater once put it, "to their marked personalities."

A new substitute had sprung up: "the soulless syndicate." It was impersonal: a hodgepodge of individuals, who combined to produce for quick profits, with drama and acting subservient to dividends. It was a foretaste of the bootlegger-backed productions soon to sprawl over our Broadway stage. The bidding by these for popular actors and theatres, the outrageous rentals upped by speculation in leases and production costs forced these pseudo producers to seek short casts and one-set plays, with smallest investment risks.

In England, as elsewhere, such factors reacted on the writer, always sensitive to changing conditions. Certain types of plays now found it harder to reach the footlights and often rested stillborn in the author's dreams or portfolio. Those managers who might appreciate artistic effort could seldom compete financially with new producing Richmonds. The semi-failure could no longer be nursed to success; the old chances could no longer be taken. In fact, the law of economics again caught up with the wayward theatre, where the odds had once meant everybody might have a look-in. In this era of quick openings and quicker closings those who labored—the salaried actors, stage hands, and musicians—had felt they must protect themselves with even tighter organizations. Among those concerned the American author was to awaken last, as I shall tell; the British author has never yet effectively organized.

The bewilderment of veteran playwrights over the transformation did not arise from aging vision. The theatre in which they had lovingly labored was stranding them—they could not write for it nor appraise it; restless, they would not even glide gracefully into their memories. Truth was, the theatre was shedding its skin, and the new skin was strangely spotted—while the motion picture, on the side lines ready to lure the coming generation away, had a host of new troubles in store for the stage. Such was the pattern we writers everywhere now saw emerging.

Though St. John Ervine himself could not calmly describe this postwar English theatre, he told me about a hardened convict in jail who, being given a Bible by the Warden to read for the first time, tackled the book of Lamentations. At the end of the final chapter he scribbled: "Buck up, Jeremiah."

Of course, things are never so bad in the theatre as they seem. They couldn't be.

In these muddy waters Gilbert Miller had been fishing with skill. He had, what the new pundits and raiders lacked, real bait; and he loved the theatre as his parents had loved it. He had gone through every department the hard way—hard for himself and possibly others, since he had also acted. Further, he had flair and daring, as his first adventure reveals. I add some words from a letter he wrote me in 1942, to show how he had fortified his position when he first landed in London and laid the basis of his private fortune:

> I had no interest in leases at that time, George. I wasn't quite clear what they were; but I had to find a theatre (for *Daddy Long Legs*) and there simply wasn't one to be had in London. Finally, some one told me that the Charles Frohman lease (he, of course, had perished on the *Lusitania*) of the Duke of York's Theatre had six more weeks to run and that the Trustees would let it go for a song for this short period.
>
> In desperation I took those six weeks over, figuring that if the play was a failure six weeks would be more than I wanted. Whereas, if the play were a great success, a theatre might be forthcoming. As a matter of fact, the play was a great success, and two days after it opened, the owner of the theatre, Miss Violet Melnotte, sent for me and asked me if I would like to continue at the Duke of York's on a week-to-week basis as long as the business kept up.
>
> The play ran for sixteen months—during which time the dear old lady made desperate efforts to get me out, as the theatre rents kept soaring higher and higher and she could have got double the rent I was paying her for our agreement.
>
> It was during this time I had the foresight to grab the leases of the Garrick and the St. James's Theatres on the theory that if a bomb hit them my obligation would be actually cancelled and if it didn't, I would make a lot of money. I eventually sold the lease of the Garrick for a very large profit: the St. James's I still have [1942].

Gilbert, who speaks four languages fluently, became almost the only international manager of standing to survive the First World War. He flew about Europe, piloting his own airplane—to glide in on the bland, moon-faced Molnár at Budapest for morning brioche, or to have chocolate that same afternoon in Paris with tall, saturnine Henri Bernstein and his many Manets I so admired. Gilbert's financial stability gave him the pick of European plays. He emulated

Charles Frohman, whose interests he briefly took over; he was to transfer American and French successes to London, while English and foreign hits came here in first cabins. Though Sidney Howard, Arthur Richman, and Robert Sherwood were commissioned to adapt his foreign manuscripts—since 1926 the Dramatists' Guild Basic Agreement obligates a manager who has signed with it to have his plays adapted only by Guild members—Gilbert has, with few exceptions, given scant encouragement to the American playwright. However, he is still a young man; that is, younger than I am. I have never lost hope.

So I was happy, old friendship aside, to have him do our play which he now cast with individuals on the threshold of spectacular film and stage careers—one of whom was to achieve world fame. As David Belasco would rehearse no new script without the author, I had not missed one of his rehearsals. Thus I knew every bit of business or "reading." These I now gave to Gilbert's company. In a letter I wrote Guy, who was busy in America with *Sally*, I quoted Gilbert as saying "he didn't know what he would have done without me." Truth was, he couldn't have kept me away: it was fun to see how differently they did things in London—including that rigid split-second stop for tea—and to work with such a talented company. Edna Best, Claude Rains, and C. Aubrey Smith (now "Sir") were all to be picture personalities, and Edith Evans (now Dame), one of London's brightest stars, illumining with her inspired spark many an old English comedy at the Old Vic. We in America were not to forget her Nurse to Katharine Cornell's moving Juliet.

Flanked also by two featured favorites, Donald Calthrop and Arthur Hatherton, the smallest part in the comedy was handed to a tall, slim, no-stomachy young fellow, with a puckery smile, and eyes as alert and nervous as his hands. At rehearsals he was irrepressible—what the musicians might call a "flying staccato." That was, in fact, the way I first thought of Noel Coward. He was only seventeen when Gilbert had given him a part in a play which starred Charles Hawtrey. I give a sidelight on Noel then from Gilbert's letter:

I had had a very expensive "throw-away" (or folder, as we called them) made for *The Willow Tree*. It looked like a black lacquer screen and cost about ten cents apiece. Noel distinguished himself by papering his dressing room with these at an approximate cost of $700. However, I forgave him and gave him that bit in *Polly with a Past*.

Noel always complained about the theatre piano which he had to play.

You will recall we had a powder-blue set with black furniture. Noel came in one day; he had just seen a beautiful small black Steinway—for £200 —and thought it would be just the thing for the set. He was rather stunned when I told him to order it. The point was that the government took over 80% of my profits (as I had no "Pre-War Standing"), it was a good investment to buy a piano which I would still have after the play closed. As a matter of fact, I still have it!

It was at this time that Noel started writing plays and, as he states in his book, I produced the first play for him which was called *I'll Leave It to You*. This very bad title was my contribution to the literary side of the venture.

Noel hasn't changed so much during these twenty-odd years, as I had reason to notice one day a winter or so ago when I accidentally saw him rushing out of the Senate Gallery, in Washington. In fact, since London we have been bumping into each other in the strangest places, including Hollywood. Of course, the freshness of that early youth has gone; but the pertness, the clipped manner of speech, the butterfly-alighting-for-a-moment, the fluttering cordiality, and the quick scampering away still remain unchanged, after all the richly deserved applause that has since been his.

Once he even impulsively said that during those rehearsals I had been "kind to him." One couldn't have been cross even at the bubbling desire I soon saw he then had to rewrite our lines, especially since he pinged and improved them in his own special fashion. In fact, in his autobiography, he himself says of *Polly:*

"I was the feed. By the end of the run, however, I was embroidering and over acting to such an extent that they had to fight like steers to get their lines over at all."

It is pleasant to recall, among other London adventures, that I met Noel Coward on his start upward.

My experiences in London will further emphasize the hazards of play writing. I ran head on into an unexpected one while rehearsing *Polly*. It adds another sidelight on the English theatre. To me the Lord Chamberlain had always been a sort of Gilbert and Sullivan shadow. I was now to feel his personal pincers. It had to do with my one-act play *Collusion,* which Alla Nazimova had originally produced in New York, and which was in for further adventures there some years later.

It dramatized the cynical comment that in some states there are only two causes for divorce: adultery and perjury. A husband goes to a hotel with a prostitute whom he registers as his wife, and, through prearrangement, is found by his wife's detectives. What I felt gave it some originality was the character of "The Woman" and her indignant reaction against "being used" to protect the good name of a guilty wife, per the accepted "gentlemen's code" as to what "decent people" should do.

It had been received by José Levy, a young Englishman who was successfully producing a program of one-act plays at the Little Theatre, *à la Grand Guignol*. It was to be featured in his third bill, starring the equally enthusiastic Sybil Thorndike. She had recently scored, as Hecuba, in Euripides' *Trojan Women* and was soon to capture London, as Saint Joan, in the Shaw masterpiece. Now Dame Sybil Thorndike, she was then recognized as the most brilliant graduate of Miss Horniman's Gaiety Repertory Company in Manchester, one of the most fertilizing factors in the English prewar stage. I had seen her in a dress rehearsal and was thrilled at the prospect of a gorgeous performance.

But, during a rehearsal of *Polly,* Levy telephoned: The Lord Chamberlain had interfered. Levy gave me the original letter "as a souvenir," expressing the belief that this was the first time a visiting American playwright had been "so honored":

CEREMONIAL DEPARTMENT, ST. JAMES'S PALACE, S.W. 1
24th February 1921

SIR,

With reference to a play in one Act entitled "Collusion," which you have submitted for a Licence to be produced at the Little Theatre, Adelphi, I am desired by the Lord Chamberlain to inform you that he regrets that he is unable to grant a Licence for this play.

Yours faithfully,

[Signature illegible], *Comptroller*

José Levy esq.
Little Theatre, Adelphi W.C.

Levy immediately wrote for an appointment with the Lord Chamberlain, stating:

As the play has already been fully rehearsed, I would be prepared to give a private performance in order that His Lordship may judge for himself the way in which it would be produced here. It is hardly necessary for me to point out that Miss Thorndike, who has been cast

for the part of the Woman, is an artist whose reputation is beyond
reproach, and that Mr. [Lewis] Casson, who would play the Man and
also produce the play, is sufficient guarantee that the play will be handled
in as sincere a way as possible.

He was informed the interview would be "useless."

I was disappointed and baffled. This action had ruined *Collusion*
as a stage property everywhere in England. I appreciated that a guest
must observe conventions of conduct which would not concern one
on his home soil. I knew nothing of the crosscurrents of the English
theatre, which might, through some tactless action, in some way
prejudice *Polly*. Political experience warned me a definite action could
bring scattered results. So I sought advice.

I thus found how the English "licensing system" differed from
ours. What limited legal and local censorship we had generally
operated *after* and not before production. The Lord Chamberlain,
by refusing to license my play, had confiscated it as stage property.
He could enforce this by the licensing power he also had over theatres.
My script had been sent to his Examiner, who was hedged by numerous interdictions. Amid the nebulous so-called "immoral" realms the
Censor moved loftily in a discretionary area of self-communion.
Caprice alone determined his decisions on subjects in the twilight
zones of morality. What most shocked me was to learn that the
dramatist alone was reduced to such scrutiny. The novelist could
publish whatever he wrote, subject only to common law. While the
stage writer might publish he could not produce his play—its sole
reason for existence. Nor had he any legal appeal, as I was now to
find out myself.

Of course I turned to St. John Ervine, whom we had known in
New York—keen-eyed, of glowing speech, sturdily built, though crippled in the war. Author of successful plays and novels, he had also
managed the Abbey Theatre. The Theatre Guild had done his *John
Ferguson* and *Jane Clegg*. At this time he was dramatic critic on the
London *Observer*, which I religiously read in Paris as much for news
about Paris as for his comments on contemporary London productions. He was interested in the business of authorship—so much so
that later, when special critic on the New York *World*, he was the
first to analyze our Dramatists' Guild Agreement as it affected British
authors in America.*

* London *Observer*, Aug. 5, 1928, and Mar. 24, 1929.

I might have hesitated to intrude upon him except that in personal letters he had been generous towards my published plays. So when he said he would hear *Collusion,* left his own rehearsals of a play he had written with H. G. Wells, and tucked up on my bed as I went through it, I felt that I was in friendly hands.

I knew, of course, that *Collusion* was "immoral": but only in Bernard Shaw's sense of being "non-customary." I wondered, however, whether it might offend some canon of British taste, which a foreign playwright always risks. On this at least St. John reassured me. As to what steps I might take, he suggested I should talk it over with Shaw, who had had so many catch-as-catch-can conflicts with the Lord Chamberlain. But when I hesitated so to presume on my slight acquaintance with Shaw, St. John, one of his closest friends, said he would arrange it.

On a previous visit to London I had hoped to see Shaw, but he was unable, as this characteristic postal card explains:

20th Nov. 1920

Unluckily I have had some rehearsals sprung on me for a performance on Tuesday; and I have to go to Lancaster on Wednesday to deliver a political oration. This means that I shall not be in London until the 26th; so we must put it off until February. That may seem a distant date to you; but it will be upon *me* before I have time to gasp.

G. Bernard Shaw

A Shaw play in New York, as it happened, had also been my first contact with censorship. Out of it came an amusing episode, which, by an odd twist, I was now to tell the author himself. It dealt with *Mrs. Warren's Profession.* Mary Shaw and Rose Coghlan had both been playing the notorious lady in separate companies. I had seen Mary's first hectic performance, with all New York fighting to get into what it was thought would be its only presentation. I speak of a revival after the censor had finally permitted it.

Mary's career, which dated back to the old Boston Stock Company days, was then at its height, after her celebrated interpretation of Mrs. Alving in *Ghosts.* She had a trenchant mind, was a strong suffragist, and her name was on the roll of many reforms. Though she was a monologist one chuckled at her scalpel-scrapping stories of pretentious people or her own lively experiences. Savoring her wit, I was calling one day when Rose Coghlan barged in.

The latter was nearing the end of her stage life, which had seen

Vandamm

EVA LE GALLIENNE IN "MADAME CAPET"

SCENE REHEARSAL AT ST. JAMES'S THEATRE, LONDON, OF "POLLY WITH A PAST,"
PRODUCED BY GILBERT MILLER

(Seated) Edith Evans, Noel Coward, George Middleton, Edna Best, Donald Calthrop

her one of the queens of her time. Still flamboyant and picturesque, with her rich contralto voice and broad gestures, I was happy at this close impression of one I had admired, as a youngster, from my top gallery in *Peg Woffington* and, as Countess Zicka, in Sardou's *Diplomacy,* one of the most expertly constructed plays I know of. And how she talked that day! Mary held her own, of course. I would have put my oar in if I could have found water enough; only my past was still so shallow. Out of it all, one line of Coghlan's has stayed: a phrasing a playwright would envy. She was speaking of her husband: "He died," she said, "with his head in my lap and another woman's name on his lips." Maybe I have used it somewhere.

As we were talking a student from the Art Center called. Anthony Comstock the day before had raided the shop where "September Morn" was exhibited—a painting of a nude girl, with hands clasped before her, shivering in her lakeside bath. The student opened a package and planted it triumphantly on the table. It was a nude plaster caricature of Comstock shivering *à la* September Morn. The two women eyed it appraisingly. After all, it was something to be so expertly judged by two, not one, Mrs. Warrens!

When I now told Shaw of this plaster appraisal, he tossed back his whitening head in the heartiest laugh any mortal ever had. Then he revealed what I had never seen in print. He was unable to get *Mrs. Warren's Profession* passed by the stage censor for production in England. To protect it legally, however, he had one of those then necessary stage "performances," where the actors read the lines. But in this version Shaw had changed the lady's profession: instead of running a chain of immoral houses, Mrs. Warren taught boys to be pickpockets!

Ervine had remarked that Shaw was "essentially a kind man." As I then told the eminent author my tale no one could have been more considerate. He has been the same ever since, when occasion prompted me to seek his cooperation in matters of authorship or organization. One letter very severe in its condemnation of an action by our Guild, as I shall show, was signed, "Your all the same quite friendly G. Bernard Shaw."

He then lived in his flat overlooking Adelphi Terrace. It was near the hospitable Savage Club, directly across from where Sir James Barrie was to reside until his death. As I had heard Shaw was always punctual I arrived ahead of my morning appointment. I thus had a chance to take in the room, which instantly impressed me with its symmetry and oriental decorations. I also got a close look at a Rodin drawing on the wall. It reminded me that I had heard Shaw had posed for the great sculptor's *Penseur,* brooding in bronze before the Panthéon, in Paris, but a few streets from where Fola and I were living. *

When he came in, on the dot, straight, tall, and friendly, my timidities vanished. He took what I came to know was his favorite seat, and motioned me aimlessly to another. The talk circled easily about until one thought would swoop to another concerning his own experiences with the Lord Chamberlain's office. He sat deep in the low upholstered chair, tenting his fingers at times and always leaning back against the head rest, as he laughed. His hair was much whiter than when I had seen him a dozen years before. I could note in more detail the well known features to discover, for the first time, the extraordinary blue of his eyes. Once seen, they were never forgotten. They were the most innocent eyes I ever saw—till they twinkled. Perhaps Montaigne's eyes may have had the same wise look. As I write I recall Augustus John's celebrated painting, on which I later happened in Cambridge. The blue of those eyes is used as the color motive throughout that most striking of Shaw's portraits.

When I sketched the scheme of *Collusion,* he instantly told me I had erred in dealing with the problem seriously: "For adultery, you know, can always be treated frivolously on the English stage." The "fake" corespondent in comedy, he recalled, was an old device: several recent plays employing it had been licensed. Apparently I should not have suggested the prostitute might have "an economic place in our social system." And it brought to mind the famous paragraph in Lecky's *History of European Morals* about her being the "eternal priestess of humanity blasted for the sins of the people." I told Shaw that Levy had written me he intended "to start a campaign against censorship." Would it be bad taste for me to do what I should unhesitatingly have done at home—join in the fight? But Shaw laughed. "He won't start a fight," he said.

I had already noticed that Gilbert Miller hadn't seemed much concerned. The truth was, as Shaw then explained, the British manager himself almost without exception, favored retention of "censorship" *before* production. Charles Frohman had vigorously opposed it,

---

* In Hesketh Pearson's *G. B. S.* (New York, 1942) there is a remarkable letter the dramatist wrote to Epstein, recounting all his experiences with sculptors. There is no reference, however, to *Le Penseur,* in this connection, though plenty about Rodin.

not only on principle but because of his close personal relation with many British dramatists who hated it. Yet Shaw rightly predicted that Levy would feel it "inconvenient" to start a campaign. He would realize it "would do no good and get nowhere." Some years before, Shaw recalled, the entire subject had been aired in a spectacular fashion; * but, while some concessions had been won, the Lord Chamberlain's power, after the most bitter attacks, remained intact largely because Sir George Alexander and other managers had come to its defense. The answer was, as usual, "self-interest."

In America our censorship situation had been hit-or-miss because of the confusions in state laws. Filth was often identified with any honest drama which questioned conventional morality. This same *Collusion,* in fact, was to be stopped there by a type of censorship, exercised through pressure groups, without legal status, as we shall see; but our police censorship was local and not Federal. One blanket law did not smother a play everywhere. Court action might let air in and allow the play to survive. American authors and managers were also solidly united against *any* form of official censorship and such confiscatory power.

Yet, as Shaw pointed out, British managers supported censorship because they thought it "good business." Once a play was passed— no matter how cheap or vulgar—no one would interfere with it. The license became "a certificate of decency." This made the manager of plays in questionable taste or treating "vicious themes frivolously" virtually exempt from police persecution. Only thus could the play become an actual commercial commodity. The provincial "routes" for a London success were arranged far in advance. Local towns had strict police laws: without the license the tour might constantly be interrupted; with it there was no trouble. For this security the manager preferred the risks of censorship. What if some magnificent play were barred? Like *Monna Vanna.* There weren't so many, and time might ease them to the stage.

But my friends said the number of plays prohibited gave no clue to the number that remained unwritten through fear they might not be licensed. Such brakes lock the creative processes at the writer's desk. Every important author had protested having a censor looking over his shoulder. It is therefore impossible to measure the extent to which this institution had hobbled a serious drama. The plays of

* See the Report from the Joint Select Committee of the House of Lords and the House of Commons, 1909 (375 pp.).

Pinero, Jones, Galsworthy, Granville-Barker, and even Shaw were
not as untrammeled as the social dramas on the Continent, revealed
in Ibsen, Strindberg and others. But what outraged me was the indignity of such dramatists having no appeal. Unimportant as some
might quite properly consider my play, I felt at least entitled to a
hearing. Shaw smiled: he knew his Lord Chamberlain.

But our *Polly* had now successfully opened, March 2, 1921. I had
survived the first night, astonished at the trick of the pit in applauding not only the entrance of each actor but each celebrity who edged
into the stalls. I had put on my new full dress with all the fixings.
Gilbert had told me I "should be prepared to take a bow." At the end
I appeared expecting to be booed, for that was a popular pastime at
the moment. But somehow I got by. Gilbert gleefully eyed me from
the wings as though saying, "You lucky stiff!"

So, having gone through this, I felt courageous enough to tackle
even the Lord Chamberlain himself. I had permitted no publicity
to leak out about *Collusion*. I had been told that through "personal
appeal" I might "smooth out" the difficulties. Others had been granted
that privilege. Without affecting the integrity of my script I could,
at least, shove the bed off into an alcove and modify some of the
tart lines of dialogue.

But in my naïveté it was only later that I discovered one reason
why my play had been stopped. A Liberal Member of Parliament
had obtained his own divorce through the same shenanigans as my
hero! Later he publicly admitted the collusion to create propaganda
against the very stringent British divorce laws, which happened then
to be under attack. Incredible as it may seem, *Collusion* was actually thought to be a dramatization of that recent scandal. Knowing
nothing of this personal parliamentary contretemps, I wrote the
following letter, as a last resort, to the Lord Chamberlain on
March 4, 1921:

My Lord:

I learn from Mr. Levy, who has obtained the producing rights of my
play "Collusion," that you have refused to license it, and that you have
also felt it useless to grant him an interview concerning the matter.

May I ask that you give me an interview in order that I may find out
more specifically what your objections to this play are, as I confess I am
unable to understand the point of view of the letter you have written him.

I need not tell you how embarrassing this matter is to me, as an

American dramatist, especially if you deny me a personal interview, since I would only be too happy to do everything possible to meet any objections which you may have to the performance of this play. I quite appreciate that it is difficult to argue the ethics of this play in a letter, and I am prompted to request this interview in order to obtain more clearly your point of view.

I had expected to leave London, but I am waiting here now until I hear from you, and I therefore appeal to your sense of fairness at least to grant me this interview at your earliest convenience.

I am, My Lord,

Yours faithfully,

GEORGE MIDDLETON

I never had an answer.

As a postscript I may add that, several months after *Polly* opened and was enjoying good business, the national coal strike closed nine London theatres. The St. James's was included. Such are the hazards of play writing.

CHAPTER XVI

SIR ARTHUR PINERO:
"A MODEST GENTLEMAN"

I WAS ALSO discovering London's hospitality. The city itself was so overwhelming that I could never feel at home in its streets. Appointments took time, though the great museums welcomed my waiting hours. But nothing could be more charming than when doorbells might be rung. Perhaps I may tell of one intimate dinner given me by Mr. and Mrs. W. J. Locke, since it affords me an occasion to speak of Sir Arthur Pinero.

Besides the dramatist only W. B. Maxwell, the novelist, made up the little party. Unlike his mother, M. E. Braddon, with her popular melodramatic books, Maxwell dug into the mysteries of human nature. Though I was to see him on various visits, it was not until he came to New York to represent the British authors at an Authors' League conference that I felt I knew him a bit. He was a tall, well built man, with a high forehead and deep-set brooding eyes. He had wanted to be a painter and had even ventured on play writing. He was astonished when I told him I had read his little drama, *The Last Man In,* for my lecture material. He shyly remarked: "You are the only man in England who has."

Locke had more surface quality: his humor continuously bubbled; he had ready opinions on everything. One felt immediately at home. I had frequently met him in America and once was tempted to dramatize one of his early books. In fact, I had admired nearly all his novels, especially those which, while showing the Anatole France influence, * reflected the debonair spirit of the land he loved so passionately. He urged me that night to spend my time in France. "Don't bother about Switzerland and Italy," he airily added, as he promised me a list of inns near his favorite Mediterranean. He was a ready raconteur and an exquisite host to boot. I wrote to Fola:

* At his request, I later arranged through Dr. Couchard for him to see Anatole France. But Locke, who would not sit in the same room with Bernard Shaw during the war of 1914, was very uncomfortable, as he himself confessed. For France was then in his best pro-Bolshevik mood.

It was a wonderful dinner—gastronomically and otherwise. . . . He gave me a bottle of special whiskey to take home in hand, to say nothing of all sorts of marvelous drinks I carried away otherwise.

I include this alcoholic content because his cellar in London was as famous as his open-house "bar" in Cannes. Al Thomas recently told me of a lunch at Locke's villa. After the cocktails—which his adopted daughter had been taught to mix—and a parade of wines with each course, Al but vaguely visualized the butler by his side, about to pour some brandy. Self-protectively he waved a refusal. But the vague figure lingered, and he heard a significant whisper: "1840, sir." Al quickly countered: "My mistake." The snifter received its golden-hued treasure. The situation was saved. Al's brother-in-law, Frank Dodd, who was Locke's publisher, says this happened to him; but both agree on the date of the brandy.

My letter to Fola casts a new light, I believe, on the emergence of Mrs. Pat Campbell:

Pinero was asked about *The Second Mrs. Tanqueray* [out of which, incidentally, I heard he made over $150,000—which was a very large sum for the period]. He denied that he had waited years till he found someone to act it—as the story has always gone.

It appears that when he wrote it he took it to Alexander, who accepted it for the St. James's Theatre but got cold feet—for it was rather radical in those days. Pinero offered to let him do it for nothing at a matinée: for, as he said, "I wanted the picture hung."

There is still in existence an agreement whereby the play was to be done without royalties for the first performance and with royalties for subsequent Wednesdays. But [R. C.] Carton—whose play, *Liberty Hall,* was being done in the evening bill—quite naturally objected on account of the effect it would have on the success of his play. So the matter was called off. But that play finally began to peter out, so A. decided to put on *Tanqueray* late in the spring, not expecting much of a run.

Then the question came up as to who would play it. They could find nobody—some refusing it on moral grounds. They heard of Mrs. Pat, who was playing in a melodrama at the Adelphi; but Gatti would not release her.

Anyone could have had the part and it was finally offered, Fola, to your friend, Elizabeth Robins. She had been successful in the Ibsen plays, and while she hadn't Mrs. Pat's strange personality she accepted it. They felt confident she would be splendid in it.

Pinero had made an appointment at 3:30 to read the play to the company. But when he went to get Alexander, at a friend's house, the latter rushed out and said: "We can have Mrs. Pat"—the matter having been arranged through the courtesy of Sims, the author of the play in which the lady was playing.

But Pinero felt it was not fair to Miss Robins and finally he said: "I will take a walk in St. James's around the Chinese bridge. At four I will be there and read the play to whomever you have there."

When he got back it was Mrs. Pat; for Miss R. said: "This is the chance of my life; but Mrs. Pat is my friend, and I will not stand in her way."

Some day that story ought to be told, for it is so exceptional.

Brander Matthews had given me a letter to Sir Arthur a decade before. I was to see him on all my subsequent visits. Shortly before his death, in 1934, he sent me his photograph, inscribed to "my good friend." Perhaps he may have felt the warmth he always kindled in me. Though he had areas about himself upon which one never intruded, there were no limits to his own outgoing interest in his friends. He was singularly well informed about their fortunes and would earnestly inquire of those we had in common. Indeed, no man I have known, except Justice Brandeis, ever so possessed this quality of concern about people or in making you, in particular, feel he was really interested in what you were doing.

The first time I went up his doorsteps, I realized that no English dramatist had meant so much to me. His contribution, in fact, to us youngsters, had been important. Even today, when it is fashionable to deride the "well made play," its contribution to certain types of stories has again been vindicated in one of its most brilliant exponents, Lillian Hellman; for her *Little Foxes,* with modern trimmings, is in the tradition. No better way to perfect one's own technical skill could have been found, as William Archer had emphasized, than to analyze the plays of such an expert as Pinero in exposition and scene structure.

Each of his plays thus had become a textbook for us who were trying to master stage mechanics. All my copies, beside those of Dumas *fils* and Augier, were annotated. I had often loaned them to beginners. At each line in dialogue, which had special importance, I would note *why,* in relation to the whole. For dialogue has functions beneath its seeming spontaneity. It must conceal the hinges which scene transitions need to keep them from being linked together like sausages. It is the covering over which the action must gracefully glide, easily to carry on the intrigue. Its verbal variety expresses character; its very phrases may contain technical devices and aids in the strategy—or trickery, if you will—of the writer's hidden intentions, his surprises, his *coups de théâtre*. For beneath apparently unimportant lines, which cluster consciously about a situation, or beneath casual bits of stage "business" (also forms of dialogue since they speak to an audience) may lie "plants," which, like coming situations, or laughs, cast their suspensive shadows before.

One could comb his plays for other dexterities which so pleased those anxious to learn "how it was done." In getting people on and off the stage, in giving life to characters while they were off and until they came back, or in the logical unfolding of a plot, no one, in those days, was a better English model than Pinero, though Henry Arthur Jones knew many a trick and Shaw began by having forgotten them. Take but one example: *The Thunderbolt*. There an entire family group is individualized, with every factional relationship clearly defined, by a witchery that will ever be a dramatist's admiration and despair.

Sir Arthur pioneered in squashing asides and soliloquies, with the help of electricity which lit the actors' faces. Before he tackled more serious themes he had learned much about his business as an actor, being five years with Henry Irving. But Pinero did not jump full-fledged into his mastery; he had first groped amid conventionally sentimental themes and the more exacting technics of farce—now almost relegated to the movies. Farce writing, previously, put impossible people in impossible situations. In his series of Court farces —*Dandy Dick, The Hobby Horse,* etc.—Pinero soon found it was funnier to place real people in impossible situations. This became a new farce formula. On these he laid the basis of the fortune that enabled him to experiment in what might prove to be less profitable social subjects.

He was also the first dramatist, I believe, who had a prompt copy privately printed * before rehearsals. By this means each actor could have the entire script, instead of our ridiculous "sides," giving only the actor's answers to "cues" (the ends of the other fellow's lines). Every bit of stage business was worked out and rigidly followed.

* Thirty-seven original manuscripts of the fifty-two plays Pinero wrote are now owned by Harold Moulton, the American actor and collector. He told me that, when Mrs. Pat Campbell dined with him shortly before her death, he showed her the original script of *The Second Mrs. Tanqueray*. She wrote across it: "Beatrice Stella Campbell I envy you this wonderful possession."

While composing, Sir Arthur spoke his dialogue and thus made his words easy to utter and to wing. He also knew the visual requirements of his art, which makes gesture and pantomime the aid to acting—as in the "mirror scene" in *Tanqueray,* where Paula looks into the glass and sees the drama of her aging years ahead. No one ever devised a more telling bit of stage business.

He staged his own plays, like Fitch and Thomas. Actors have told me of his courtesy at rehearsals. "I try to understand the individual temperament of each member of the cast," he said. Once he called from the top gallery: "I'm so glad you are enjoying the play. But why do you want to keep it all to yourselves?" Mrs. Pat also told me that at the final rehearsals of *Tanqueray* no one was allowed in the auditorium as he sat alone "with a lantern, the prompt book and a pencil."

While Pinero could admire the looser technic of a Wedekind, he seemed to be influenced most by Ibsen—though he denied it— an innovator with this type of social drama. Yet he was not a revolutionary moralist, nor was he attracted to the economic problems that agitated Granville-Barker and Shaw. In our talks I felt an instinctive conservatism, which probably never let him fly entirely free on the stage. His plays, however, did pose, for almost the first time, certain questions of sex. He thus spoke out for its recognition as a topic and his right to select whatever themes he found dramatic. His own plays were never the heavily seasoned dramas that then filled the menus of Europe; but he made his offerings palatable even for those who had to swallow hard at the nourishment the English theatre then needed. "I never thought of the censor while writing the play, and when it is finished I could never sleep thinking of him." Sir Arthur was not a polemist, as Shaw and Jones: he was the first of his craft, though, to be knighted for achievement in his profession without any collateral qualifications. It was the generous Shaw who did most to bring that honor to him.

There must have been hard moments when Sir Arthur's later plays failed or were not even produced. Once he said:

"I am too old, Middleton, to send my plays around. I had a letter from a manager the other day who misspelled two words. I can't spell myself: but I don't want that sort of man to judge my plays."

Yet I never heard him ungenerous to the younger generation "tapping at the door." Some men, like Bernard Shaw, live long enough to be aware of their own immortality in their chosen field; others, like George Meredith, only to see their contemporary fame slowly tarnished by creeping neglect. Yet Sir Arthur was enough of a philosopher to know that, however a coming generation may appraise any man's contribution to his art, all streams and what they carry make the land on which new structures, or even temples, may be built. Pinero made the play, rather than the actor, the important factor in the theatre of his day. He has thus a secure place in the history of the English stage.*

So perhaps there was contentment in the kindly smile which twinkled about his black eyes, beneath those enormous brows the caricaturists loved, when I told him at our first luncheon what he had meant for a freer theatre and what an example he was to us, who were youngsters then.

One didn't drop in on Sir Arthur. He hated telephones: but a letter brought a speedy response. Lunching was an aesthetic experience. His table was exquisite, with its silver pieces precisely placed amid ferns upon lace coverings. The food, of course, was perfection. But I loved the odd-shaped library above that one reached by the narrow, curving stairs. Upon the walls and low bookshelves were photographs, framed with programs, of stars who had acted in his plays: Mrs. Pat, who received fifteen pounds a week for Paula and rehearsed "on approval"; the suave Gerald du Maurier, whose role in *Trelawny of the Wells* (one of the most autobiographic of Pinero's plays) first brought him recognition; Sir Johnston Forbes-Robertson; Sir George Alexander; Sir John Hare, who turned down *Tanqueray* because it was "immoral"; and Marie Lohr, Fay Davis, together with brilliant Dame Irene Vanbrugh, whom the dramatist directed through many roles to the magnificence of her Sophie, in *The Gay Lord Quex.*

Though Sir Arthur told me he never wrote for a particular star, his position had early enabled him to choose the most desirable artists, who in turn were assured of effective roles. His American list of stars was equally impressive. I caught a glimpse of Ethel Barrymore, the unforgettable wind-tossed Zoe in *Mid-Channel,* clean-cut John Drew in *His House in Order,* Virginia Harned in *Iris,* and

---

* I have drawn a paragraph or two, with modifications, from my article on Sir Arthur, written after his death at the age of seventy-nine. (*New York Times,* Dec. 24, 1934.)

the young, eager Katharine Cornell, who brought such beauty to
The Enchanted Cottage.

And there was Duse! At Locke's we had been speaking of her
and Bernhardt; for Pinero had seen both in their prime. In 1895,
the two stars were playing in London. He would go every night,
he said; and in a letter to Fola I quoted him: "When I saw Duse
in *Camille,* I did not want to leave my stall, for I was in the presence
of a woman who was suffering greatly." Of Bernhardt, whom he
saw a few days later in the same role, he said: "I admired her art
and thought her conception of the final scene, when at death's door
she became almost the maid again, was very remarkable." He
summed up his feeling: "I admired Sarah, but I loved Duse."

It was during this visit of Bernhardt's, I believe, that she mastered her audience when a stage accident nearly wrecked the play.
It was Dumas's much acted *La Femme de Claude.* In the final scene,
as her perfidy is unmasked, her husband's father shoots her. But at
this theatrical moment the audience had breathlessly awaited, when
the trapped Sarah snarled like swift-ripping cloth, and shrieked as
only she could in such frenzied moments, the gun did not go off.
Three times the trigger missed fire. Sarah saw she could not fall.
Her famous death scene was ruined. But her electric personality
held the audience. No one moved. No one laughed. Then she drifted
to the footlights, with a wonderful open-armed gesture and a wan
smile as though asking pardon, and murmured: "Too bad." The
audience cheered.

The brooding photograph of the Italian actress was framed with
a program of *The Second Mrs. Tanqueray.* I had forgotten that she
had played it.

"Oh, yes: she had insisted upon appearing only in D'Annunzio's
plays. Her season had been a dire failure. Her manager asked
permission to do my play, and what would be the royalty. I gave
him permission, of course, but I said that for Madame Duse there
would be no royalty. I only asked that she send me a photograph.
She put a little rouge on and played Paula. The season turned out
well for her."

As he gazed at the photograph, silent, I asked: "And that is the
photograph she sent?"

"No." He shook his head. "I bought that photograph." Perhaps
the manager never told her.

Similar recollections inspired me to ask whether he had ever written his memoirs. He shrugged it off. I recall little he wrote which ever betrayed his more personal life. Perhaps, too, Pinero's essential dignity is best expressed in some lines from a character who speaks in *The Big Drum*. This brilliant and unsuccessful comedy, produced during the war in London but never in New York, is a bitter comment on phases of the author's trade. It might be his own creed of good manners he was stating:

I have no dislike for publicity, for fame. I covet it, if I can win it honestly and decently. And I humble myself before the men and women of my craft—and they are many—who succeed in winning it in that fashion, or who are content to remain obscure. But for the rest—the hustlers of the pen, the seekers after mere blatant applause, the pickers-up of cheap popularity—I have a profound contempt for them and for their methods. . . . No amount of ability, of genius, if you will, absolves the follower of any art from the obligation of conducting himself as a modest gentleman.

It was Sir Arthur who first took me to dine at the Garrick Club, a few days after *Polly with a Past* opened:

It will give me a very great pleasure if you will dine with me—just you and I—at the Garrick Club next Thursday night at a quarter to eight.

I congratulate you most heartily upon what appears to be a solid success at the St. James's.

Yours very truly

ARTHUR PINERO

And he added to the carefully typed script, in his own clear hand —never in his letters is there a correction:

As I have to attend a committee meeting at the Garrick Club on Thursday, and shall remain on there afterwards, I shall be in morning clothes. Come as you please. Morning dress, evening dress or in spangles—I shall be delighted to see you.

P.

Of course the club, named after the great actor, brought the Players to me. Founded in the eighteen-thirties as a place where "actors and men of education might meet on equal terms," its very object reveals the social attitude towards the stage a century ago. The present stately clubhouse was occupied in the sixties. Like the Players, it is a priceless repository of stage mementoes its distinguished members have given. When I later lunched there, I was always taken to the "strangers' dining room," though guests for dinner were permitted in the main room above. While comfortable, the house lacked the informality of London's other theatrical clubs, the Green Room and the Savage, which exchanged with the Players.

Almost the last time I was to see Sir Arthur he invited me again to the Garrick, with genial Sir George Frampton, whose statue of Edith Cavell had just been unveiled: "Patriotism is not enough." Over the port for which the club is famous, I listened in a mellow mood as the talk meandered from their early London days, through the doings of the Rossetti group, with its odd fellowship, to other famous club members. With a twinkle in his eyes, which were the most observing I ever saw, Sir Arthur then told of "a young clerk who had studied law to please his father, but who used to snatch a bite of lunch so that he could stand outside on the street corner and watch the great men of the theatre enter or leave the club. The clerk wondered whether he would ever be permitted to enter the club —even as a guest." The clerk's name was Arthur Pinero.

Within the span of his life—to his seventieth birthday as a famous dramatist, in 1925, when in that same club literary England feted him—Pinero was to see England's later theatre glow with a new meaning, glow and fade again. Naturally, I never could have dreamed on that night I dined with him, that it would be my official privilege some years later to cable greetings on his seventieth birthday to the "modest gentleman": *

Kindly convey to Sir Arthur on this auspicious occasion the heartiest congratulations of the Dramatists' Guild representing all American playwrights. We are happy to join our British associates and many other distinguished personalities present in this universal tribute to one whose art has always been an inspiration and whose unfailing courtesy and helpfulness have set so high an ideal of personal relationships in the world of the theatre.

GEORGE MIDDLETON, *President*

As we walked that misty night from the Garrick Club to his "little house on Harley Street," past the St. James's, scene of his greatest

* The text of his speech, on this occasion at the Garrick Club, is published in *Sir Arthur Pinero*, by Wilbur Dwight Dunkel, University of Chicago Press, 1941. It was based on the anecdote I quote above, and is probably the most personal communication the dramatist ever publicly made.

This study, incidentally, is recommended to all students of the English drama for its scholarly approach and discriminating judgments.

triumphs, and other theatres his plays had so often filled, somehow I had the impulse to slip my hand through his arm. He gave it a friendly reassuring hug, as though he understood of what I was thinking, while we walked on in silence.

When I left him at his door I felt I was saying goodbye to another epoch.

CHAPTER XVII

THROUGH THE STAGE DOORS
OF PARIS

In 1926, Edouard Bourdet came to New York to see Gilbert Miller's production of his Parisian success, *La Prisonnière,* which had been skillfully translated under the title *The Captive* by Arthur Hornblow, now a successful producer in Hollywood. It played to capacity at the Empire Theatre; but its homosexual theme, in spite of the delicate treatment, brought attacks upon its morality, and the police closed it. Regretting that its "real meaning" had been unappreciated, Bourdet wrote me he was consoled by thinking that all Americans hadn't judged it the way the police had, and that many had disapproved their action. He was astonished that it should be stopped after being played four and a half months. He did not know the erosive tenacity of our pressure groups.

I had met Bourdet in Paris in 1922, when Belasco commissioned me to adapt his popular *L'Heure du berger,* in which Marthe Régnier had starred. After trying to lure Maude Adams out of her retirement, Belasco did my adaptation, *The Other Rose,* at the Morosco Theatre, New York, with Fay Bainter.* She remains one of the best troupers with whom I have ever been associated, a most ingratiating actress, now also firmly established in pictures, who knows her business to her fingertips. Bourdet and I naturally had had much correspondence about it. So when he came to my home town in 1926, while *The Captive* was still running, I asked what I could do for him. He made one special request: to meet some American playwrights.

Fola corralled the strays who were in town: Sidney Howard, Owen Davis, George Kelly, A. E. Thomas, Arthur Richman, Don Marquis, and Percy MacKaye, I recall. Eugene O'Neill, whom Bourdet especially wished to know, was away. We talked shop all eve-

---

* Also in the cast were the gifted Henry Hull; Carlotta Monterey, who shortly afterwards became Mrs. Eugene O'Neill; Ernest Stallard; and Effie Shannon, who dates from old Lyceum days and remains one of my personal admirations as woman and actress. The play had 84 performances but did not tour.

ning.* I mention this because of something Bourdet said about our group, when next I lunched with him in Paris:

"I did so enjoy meeting your playwright friends at your home," he remarked, over our apéritifs. "It was my happiest evening in America. You all seemed to know and like one another so well. I wish I could do the same for you here in Paris. But I can't." He added cynically, "You see, I know so few French dramatists."

Bourdet's frank admission throws light on that lack of comradeship among French dramatists I had quickly discovered for myself in 1921 and 1922. Having, through *Polly* and *Collusion,* learned some problems facing English authors, I wanted to watch how the French theatre ticked. With the themes of its many serious plays I had little sympathy; any maturing dramatist, for example, would probably tackle the middle-aged-writer-losing-his-mistress plot. I soon realized that only a small segment of French life was portrayed in the dolled-up triangles or its intense preoccupations in the trivial Parisian scene. Indeed, the social theatre since Dumas *fils,* Augier, and Becque, except for Courteline, Brieux, and possibly Curel, seldom approximated in scope or variety the interpretation of solid French life and character which French novelists continuously achieved. Nevertheless I enjoyed the amiable deceptions of the boulevard stage, though its shallowness soon made me yearn for the vitality of our own developing drama.

I was, therefore, less interested in the appraisal of individual authors than in aspects the visiting academic critic might not care to explore: the *practical conditions* in which the French author himself functioned: how he plied his trade, *our* trade. This was, in general, my approach in the articles I was now sending the American papers.† Nothing in books could help me: nor could mere theatre going. I had to go behind the scenes, to see grease paint close. So

* It was later that Bourdet was appointed administrator of the Comédie-Française and initiated striking reforms, calling in Dullin, Copeau, and Jouvet to revitalize its classic productions. But he had achieved further outstanding successes with *Vient de Paraître,* a vicious satire on literary prizes, and *Les Temps difficiles,* a study of postwar conditions. His carefully organized plays, meticulously built up by minute brush strokes, dipped in an accurate observation, were to make him a highly respected dramatist. He died in 1945.

† Any one interested in contemporary comments will find my newspaper articles on various occasions as follows: *N. Y. Times,* April 18, 1920; July 4, 1921; Feb. 12, July 4, Sept. 3, Nov. 22, 1922; Feb. 12, Feb. 18, Nov. 18, 1923; Jan. 20, July 13, 1924; June 7, 1925; Jan. 16, 1927; Dec. 2, 1934; Oct. 23, 1938. *N. Y. Herald,* July 9, Sept. 24, 1922. *N. Y. Tribune,* Oct. 8, 1922; Oct. 23, 1938. *N. Y. Sun,* Sept. 28, 1928. *Paris Comœdia,* Jan. 28, May 27, 1921.

I talked hip to haunch, and even cheek to jowl, with actors, authors, and producers. Groups were arranged for me to question. They were amused, as I was, with my intensities—while my notebook filled.

Lenormand, whose *Les Ratés* was to be done by our Theatre Guild under the title *The Failures* (I urged it for Jack Barrymore), Denys Amiel, whose *La Souriante Madame Beudet* also went Guild-wise, René Fauchois, on whose play Sidney Howard founded *The Late Christopher Bean,* Alexandre Arnoux, whose *Huon de Bordeaux* had been done by Dullin, and Victor Pellerin, another *jeune* just pro-duced (whose father, incidentally, owned the great collection of Cézannes and had in his gardens a number of statues which looked like Renoir and were, to my astonishment), were among the writers I buttonholed as to special problems facing "the young." Aside from the mass of technical information about salaries, house receipts, and trade customs, light on the *terra incognita* of touring companies was supplied by glittery-eyed, long-bearded Tristan Bernard, author of that witty classic, *L'Anglais tel qu'on le parle,* and famous guardian of prizefighting lore. Incidentally, the fact that I had once read James J. Corbett a play established me as quite a fellow, I am sure.

I wrote a friend about something else which had puzzled me —why so many of the playwrights were also critics:

I couldn't dope it out why they should want to take such punishment until I discovered something about rehearsals. The French don't have our tryouts; every play opens "cold" in Paris itself. No "dog-towns" for them. But they do have a lot of oddly named official rehearsals, supposed to be for dressmakers, scenic artists, decorators, and what not, where they hastily do their repairing.

The performance, however, everyone wants to see is the *répétition générale.* This final dress rehearsal is more important than the opening. In the old days, *tout Paris* was there—and the playwrights naturally thought they were important enough to be included.

One cynical author frankly told me he became a critic so he could always be sure of getting tickets!

Though both French and English dramatists had been uniformly kind to me I soon realized they felt differently towards one another. On the whole, in personal relationships, the English appeared to be more mutually cooperative; indeed, in Paris I found much personal jealousy. They may have thought they hid it. It recalls what Stephen Phillips once said to Mrs. Brown Potter when she was rehearsing

Calypso, in his *Ulysses*. After some comment on her interpretation she flared up before the company:

"Mr. Phillips, ever since I've been doing this part you've not attempted to conceal your contempt for me."

He smiled suavely: "Why, Mrs. Potter, I thought I had."

Sacha Guitry admitted, "My contemporaries don't like me." He —like Bourdet—had met few of them personally. There was at this time, in fact, a definite split between the younger and the more established French playwrights. The reason lay in one fact which also explained many of the obvious limitations in the French theatre.

France centralized early under its king; Paris became his throne as well as that of all the arts. To triumph there, was to succeed in France; in fact, as Yvette Guilbert once remarked to Fola, in speaking of her own early days: "Success in Paris was *mondial.*" So Paris alone was the center of the French theatre. Within France itself there had never been the competitive inspiration which, before the war, had stimulated the German theatre to such splendid achievements in the rounded art of the theatre. Germany centralized late, and then only politically; Munich, Dresden, Hamburg continued to vie with one another for stage supremacy; and Berlin was never the center of the German theatre.

All French playwrights sought the few Parisian stages. It was a fight for self-expression and existence. Outside the capital there were no French producing centers. The "road," in fact, only received what Paris exuded. The best possible publicity for a traveling troupe was to have a play by an author who was a member of the French Academy! Most theatres outside Paris were municipally owned. They were thus compelled to start on time. If they started before the advertised hour any spectator could demand that the play begin over again! But, aside from the important actors of the Comédie-Française, many stars never even toured; Guitry admitted to me he "didn't like the inconveniences."

The French had nothing to compare with the Abbey Theatre, or Miss Horniman's Gaiety Theatre in Manchester—which produced two hundred plays in fifteen years, half of them new. From it alone emerged two splendid directors: Basil Dean and Iden Payne, director for years of the Shakespearean Festival Playhouse. Yet even the authors' royalties from such theatres in England did not equal their returns from the great number of British amateur groups, producing their older plays. No important amateur groups, like our Amateur Comedy Club, stood out in France. So, for the young, it was Paris or nothing: "Pikes Peak or bust." No wonder the French stage seethed with bitterness.

But Paris did have one famous theatre, with a long tradition, which London lacked. I argued for what I felt was even the tarnished greatness of the Comédie-Française. True, aging ladies still simulated virginity, and foreign plays seldom reached its footlights. But its Molière anniversary cycle, in which I saw all his comedies, could not be excelled by any theatre in the world. Nor did any possess finer artists than Maurice Féraudy and Piérat, then in their prime. (For hours I once sat opposite her in a Spanish train going to Saragossa, and to this day I never have understood my timidity in not telling her of my admiration.) Yet I seldom heard a good word about this national theatre from my young dramatist friends. They could not break through its regulations or its personal politics. Hence they felt that it was another "dramatic museum." They even called it, as some called Sarah Bernhardt, "an historic monument."

But there was a custom in Paris which delighted us both. Neither New York nor London could boast it: mainly because the reasons that caused it did not exist with us. I wrote to my friend:

Fola and I have been gorging on the great number of revivals here: the best plays of the decade to gobble! In New York we bury our hits once they've played their tune. Yet the system here I find in reverse, is tough on the young door-tappers.

Rich authors, like Bataille—who recently had five plays running at once—are so mighty they won't hand over a new script unless the manager agrees to revive one or more of the fellow's old plays! Particular ladies often figure in part of the bargain, and nobody knows what financial arrangements are made by authors to keep their names before the public.

Ever hear of the *ristourne?* With us it is called a rebate. Though strictly forbidden by the French Society it's more honored in the breach, etc. Few people knew or asked *where* the producer got his money, or who made up the producing syndicates. The author, after the royalty due him has been cleared through the Society, might very easily pass some—or all of it—back to the reluctant producer. How could the latter refuse without offending?

Most of the boulevard stages are thus occupied, and only a few down-the-side-alley theatres are available. Another device completes the strangulation of the young. The established writers have "turns"—that is, an order in which plays of respective authors shall "pass" or go on at leading theatres. Having a nice clique, they surrender or accommodate dates to one another—sometimes for a consideration—only within the charmed circle.

In spite of all this I decided to do a little proselyting and get some American plays on—including my own, of course. I was now writing for *Comœdia*—the daily *Variety* of Paris—to encourage a more open mind. It happened that season that New York had seen some twenty-odd French plays, while only two American successes had hit Paris. I pointed out that, in almost every American city, clubs or study circles read the best of French drama, while few American plays had even been translated in a country where nearly every kiosk sold published plays.

One American name, however, was beginning to mean something: Eugene O'Neill. As yet, he was unproduced on the Continent. I had still not met him: but, as I have said, I had early felt his power and international stature. So I took him up first with Copeau for production at the Vieux Colombier and later, more successfully, with Gémier at the Odéon. Copeau didn't like my plays for his theatre— I had slipped my short ones in, more or less casually—but wanted to read more of O'Neill. So I wrote to Provincetown. The answer came along, in due time:

April 12 1921

Dear Middleton:
  Your letter reached me today. I am having a copy of the book of short plays sent to Copeau and to Levy at once. It is sure glad tidings to know Copeau is considering doing *Beyond the Horizon*. It would be a good dream come true if he should decide to put on something of mine. I hope he will like the one-acters. I will also send him a copy of my new book which is due to come out any day now. . . .
  I can not thank you enough for what you have done in my behalf in bringing my work to the attention of a man like Copeau. It is sure kind of you, and I hope I shall have the pleasure of meeting you and thanking you in person when you return home again.
  All my best wishes.

Sincerely
Eugene O'Neill

I learned more about the workings of the French theatre when my one-act play *Circles* (first produced at the Lyceum Theatre, in New York) was put on in Paris. Constant Lounsbery, a well known

American who knew her Paris, brought a French translation *(Cercle)* to the attention of Irénée Mauget, the director of the Nouveau Théâtre, who had first produced Tagore's plays in France. The law of averages let him take a chance with me. Constant also had a short play on the same *affiche.* This little boulevard theatre was secreted above the Musée Grévin—the famous Parisian waxworks. To enter the theatre, however, one had to pass through the museum with its figures of Marie Antoinette on her last ride and Charlotte Corday killing Marat in his tin tub.

What I thought might be an amateur lark became an occasion, because I was able to get three fine professional actors, including the superb Marie Kalff for the complex leading role. Her husband, H. R. Lenormand, * I had come to know well.

The day of the first-scene rehearsal, Marie Kalff and Fola both thought the theatre's regular "drawing-room set" distressingly ugly and inadequate. Fola took the problem in hand, and secured the cooperation of the amused stage hands in repainting it. She also spent a desperate day making curtains and borrowing furniture from the antique shops in our old quarter. On the opening night the set was a fairly harmonious frame for Kalff's outstanding performance, and the audience could think of the drama without visual distractions.

A one-act play produced in a small theatre in New York might have gone unnoticed by first-line critics with few dramatists in the audience. But in Paris these out-of-the-way productions often aroused special interest. Then, too, most of the critics were playwrights, as I have said, and that night a distinguished group filled the theatre. The irony of the plot seemed to appeal to French logic. The daughter leaves her husband and child to return to her parents. Also unhappily married, they had, on the contrary, stayed together for her sake when she was a child. They now find that she married to escape her own unhappy home. She reproaches them for what they did for and to her, only to be coldly asked by her father whether her child may not in time reproach her for her course. Hopeless . . .

When the curtain fell there was an ovation. As Nozière, the

* Gene O'Neill told me recently that Lenormand has translated his *Mourning Becomes Electra* for Paris production. He was the most interesting of the younger dramatists. When I first met him, his plays had already been produced by Gémier, Pitoëff, and Reinhardt. He steered from conventional themes to the effect of climate on character or the then novel dramatic possibilities of psychoanalysis. I wrote an estimate of him in the *New York Times*, Nov. 18, 1923.

dramatist, who reviewed *Cercle* for *L'Avenir,* said of the play: "It was short, but it was long applauded." Alfred Savoir, whose *Bluebeard's Eighth Wife* tickled America, wrote: "By its treatment, its concentration and all that it unveils and suggests it is not far from being a chef-d'œuvre. It obtained a very great success." I recalled "Strindberg" to one and "Ibsen" to another—which would have riled both. I was "most promising" to a third. Jane Catulle-Mendès, Edmond Sée (for *L'Œuvre*), and Charles Méré, on whom part of Sardou's mantle had fallen—all dramatists—made me believe in critics.

In addition to *Cercle,* my *The Reason* was also done at the Théâtre Albert Premier. E. H. Sothern and Julia Marlowe had been present to sponsor what was hoped to be an Anglo-French season. I might here add that it was soon noised about that Belasco had commissioned me to adapt two popular comedies. However, it was through the production of *Cercle* that my acquaintance among my fellow craftsmen was extended. The competitive jealousies which often separated them from one another did not create barriers towards me, because I was an American. It is not cynical to add that some of them thought I was also a critic.

So my progressive education into the workings of the French theatre through "learning by doing" continued. Next, it indirectly brought me into contact with the French Authors' Society, then the strongest in the world. Shortly after the *Cercle* production Firmin Gémier "received" our *Light of the World* at the Odéon. I had a literal *(mot à mot)* translation which gave him the general plan, though later he insisted on a retranslation. With Guy Bolton's consent I had this made by Alexandre and Amaly Arnoux who were our close friends.

Amaly spoke a perfect English and had an intimate knowledge of French "protocol," as it were; for she had been social secretary at the American Embassy under Herrick. Her letters were exquisite examples of French epistolary art. Alexandre had a joyous interest in every phase of life. While holding a bread-and-butter job he had written a dozen variegated novels that had already brought him acclaim. Early interested with Charles Dullin in the French cinema, Alexandre was almost its first scenario writer. With these backgrounds Alexandre and Amaly's translation of our play enhanced it.

In the press cables to America, the news angle, of course, was that ours was to be "the first play of American authorship ever accepted by a French State theatre." Wythe Williams, close friend of Clemenceau and correspondent for the *Public Ledger,* had introduced me to Gémier. It was with them that I talked over a list of plays which the Drama League had sent for the French actor's contemplated "Franco-American *manifestation.*"

Thus I had the privilege of urging upon Gémier the plays of Eugene O'Neill. He had a translation of *The Hairy Ape* at hand, and accepted it, as he later wrote me, "because it was the first of O'Neill's plays which I had read." On my return to America he wrote to ask me whether I would see the author:

Recently I read *The Emperor Jones.* This is the play with which Mr. O'Neill should make his début in Paris because the meaning of that beautiful play is clear and more understandable to us French than the idea and symbolism of *The Hairy Ape.*

This is how, as it turned out, O'Neill was actually the first American dramatist to be performed at a French State theatre. And it was as it should have been. Other prospects were also in the wind, as Gene wrote me:

I certainly appreciate all you have done to help me to a hearing in France. Things seem to be stirring quite a bit lately in that direction—but I'll tell you all about it when I see you—also need all the advice you can give. Again, all gratitude.

Firmin Gémier was an outstanding stage personality. Some ranked him, as an actor, with Lucien Guitry and Féraudy, though he never so excited me; but as director of the famous Odéon, with broad international sympathies, he had a unique place. I had come to know him a little under amusing circumstances. For on the very boards where I was now hoping our play would soon appear, with Gémier himself in the leading role, I had earlier blinked out beyond its footlights when I made a brief "personal appearance" in that venerable house. Of course I was merely an "extra"; but my name was on the program in a role Shakespeare had never mentioned. I was the First Lord during the banquet scene, when James K. Hackett stormed Paris with his *Macbeth,* the first American actor to be so honored in a French State theatre—thanks, I am told, to the political influence of Loie Fuller of the swirling skirts and colored lights, whom our daddies gaped at. The souvenir program I have before me is a formidable affair. Under the patronage of the French President and both English-speaking ambassadors, it meanders on to

Henri Bergson, James Hazen Hyde, and Otto Kahn—which, to combine American and French slang, is some *salade*.

When Jim Hackett had paid off his overwhelming debts, dollar for dollar, out of an unexpected inheritance, some years after he had produced my *House of a Thousand Candles,* he determined to do better things. One much better was *Macbeth.* Not setting New York on fire, Jim went to the more inflammable London. While I was rehearsing *Polly* he was ending his run, at the Aldwych, with Mrs. Pat Campbell as the sleepwalker. Jim had made a sensational success. I was surprised, and asked Pinero, who also was greatly impressed, to explain it. As I wrote to Fola, he said that it was "partly because of its breadth and sweep of style, which is so lacking nowadays."

Jim planned to take the production to Paris and wondered whether I would help out. It was for a benefit. It had been arranged with Gémier to hold "a Shakespearean Festival." They planned to do two plays on successive nights: *Macbeth* and *The Merchant of Venice.* Gémier's mean and revengeful Shylock was his greatest part. *Othello* was to be done together, with Gémier as Iago. But Jim found that Gémier not only could not speak or understand a word of English, for even the ordinary exchange of rehearsals—which hadn't bothered Booth and Salvini when they did this stunt—but also was hard of study and of hearing. So, at the last minute, it was decided that the second bill should consist of individual scenes. Jim played Othello, and his wife, Beatrice Beckley, played Desdemona. Oh, yes, the Iago was delivered by airplane from London.

I had completely forgotten my promise to appear until the morning I returned from Italy, when I found in the Paris edition of the *New York Herald* the head: "MIDDLETON JOINS CAST OF MACBETH—American Playwright Combined with Hackett Forces for Performance Monday." The story said I had volunteered. If it "should be fully cast he could at least be relied on to carry a spear with grace and abandon." As it turned out, I compromised on a goblet.

But what made me feel that for once I had, unintentionally, matched a master of publicity was to see in the next column, in *no* larger type: "MORRIS GEST SEEKING BALLETS."

When I rang up, Jim told me to report for rehearsal at ten. There I found some old friends: John Drinkwater, who was playing Banquo, and his talented wife; Mary Young, wife of John Craig; ebullient Mary Boland, who arrived too late to get on the program—

drat it; and gorgeous Sybil Thorndike herself, who had been loaned by Levy (with proper program credit) to be Lady Macbeth. My college Shakespearean appearance, in 1902, came back—with Irving and Terry. Oddly enough, Sybil was wearing Ellen Terry's robe from the Irving production.

Opening on June 6, 1921, Jim had a triumph. Julia Marlowe and E. H. Sothern were present (though I could never get them to comment), together with literary and official Paris. In an intermission, after one of the murders, the music struck up, and President Millerand came in with the Crown Prince of Japan (who has recently called on General MacArthur). The English and American Ambassadors were already there. Each national anthem was played and recognized, for we were all Allies then. After the death of the Scottish King himself the applause was thunderous. Jim was cheered and cheered.

As he "took the call," with the old familiar breath-exhausted trick, my mind suddenly shot back to the first time I had seen him, from the wings, when he played Don Caesar de Bazan. Then his curtain line was climaxed by a sweeping feathered-hat-flourish and rushing hand-up-in-the-air exit. He stopped quickly by his dresser in the wings, who handed him a comb, and held a mirror for him. Jim carefully arranged his hair, as the applause continued. The curtain rose. Jim went out for the bow and resumed his hard breathing. He had the same difficulty with breath and hair at the Odéon twenty years later.

I drove home with him the next day, after the *Othello* rehearsal, and translated his notices. The French critics had never seen such a Macbeth, with so magnificent a physique, so kingly a mien, and so rich a baritone. He smiled. I was happy, too, for he always had been a square-shooter.

"Isn't it odd, George!" he said with a twinkle. "They always called me a ham actor in the States. I seldom got a good notice. And now I come to London and Paris, and they call me a great actor. I don't feel I am any different."

As he went upstairs Jim found the future Emperor Hirohito had sent him and his wife a Japanese tree, five feet tall. It wasn't so bad, all of it, for a New York City College boy!

But what especially impressed me as a foreign playwright was that I *had* to become a member of the Société des Auteurs et Compositeurs Dramatiques before Gémier could produce *The Light of the World* at the Odéon!

American dramatists make their play contracts directly or through personal agents with individual managers: in France the theatre managers made them with the Society, which drew up all the rules, had its own agents, and collected all royalties. These had to be paid "whatever should be the composition of the spectacle or its nature and even if the spectacle is composed of works called in the public domain or of works composed by persons foreign to the society." This means that, even for performances of Molière and Shakespeare, royalties go to the Society's sick and pension funds. The dead authors are thus called upon to help the living. (Once I boldly suggested in the *New York Times*, February 18, 1923, that small royalties should similarly be imposed to assist authors, actors, or even managers in distress: but it wasn't popular.) Of course, if the French manager couldn't resist my script he could produce it; but he would still have to pay royalty to the Society. In addition, he would have to pay me. To any manager the thought would be appalling. Yet all I had to do as a member was to sign my *bulletin de réception* for my play, and everything else was set: royalties (depending on the status of the theatre); time for production (two years with indemnity for failure, at so much per act); no script changes; sole control over cast (principals and even understudies) and full knowledge of their salary arrangements, to say nothing of the number and location of the free seats at every performance—with extra ones at the final rehearsal, which in old days went to the claque. Among the many odd and amusing provisions I also found that a dramatist could freely enter the theatre where he had had his own play acted, to see the plays of his confrères. This was only good for one year if he had a one-act play done, but for life if six acts or over had been performed. *

* In the *Bulletin*, Feb., 1929, I analyzed this Society. I was happy to have its contents officially endorsed by the eminent Academician, Paul Claudel (then French Ambassador to the United States), whose *L'Annonce Faite à Marie* (*The Tidings Brought to Mary*) was produced by the Theatre Guild: "I have read with great interest the article so precise and so true which you have written for the Authors' League Bulletin on the Société des Auteurs et Compositeurs Dramatiques. It affords me great pleasure to congratulate you for what, I consider, as the first attempt to make a thorough study of this important French association in English. The chapter devoted to 'the agent and the French author in America' required no comment but congratulations for its accuracy and I would like to have it carefully read by French authors and dramatists." My brochure was subsequently translated into French; but I heard nothing more about it.

I began asking myself again why some modification of this couldn't be worked out in our kid-gloved Guild. Scraping away all the barnacled abuses which age had fastened on the French Society, I was fascinated by one essential fact: the managers and the dramatists could deal only through a tight organization and by means of a negotiated, enforceable contract! This principle gave me the basis for a suggested adaptation in our Dramatists' Guild fight three years later. So while *The Light of the World* was never produced—for a variety of reasons, including Gémier's death—the contract he gave me, with the Society's blessing, was to return unexpected dividends.

But the Society controlled its members only where French was the official language. The French dramatist, unlike the American, always retained *all* his motion picture and foreign rights, and was free to make any contract for them; and, because Belasco, as I have said, had commissioned me to adapt two plays then running in Paris, I now undertook another interesting part of a journeyman playwright's job: adaptation.

Belasco had cabled me to see Sacha Guitry's *Une Petite Main qui se place,* then running. He wanted my impressions. He had bought it under a blanket agreement to do three of Guitry's plays—two of which, *Deburau* and *Le Grand Duc,* he had already produced.

I bought a seat in my favorite front row and had the time of my life. I can be a good audience: my laugh is loud and hearty. So I cabled Belasco favorably, yet cautioned him its success would rest in the casting and in capture of the French style. To my surprise he cabled me to see Guitry, and make the adaptation if it were agreeable to him. Of course nothing could have pleased me more. Whatever else might come of it, this gave me a chance to explore another plane of the French theatre, through its most popular playwright and actor. Further, I could hover over the upper crusts with one who for years had been the darling of Paris. But I had never met Guitry. How could I persuade him to let me do the adaptation, as he spoke no English?

After the next performance I sent my card in, with Belasco's name on it. As I entered his dressing room *(loge)* he moved rapidly to greet me with his open ingratiating smile, sparkling eyes, and caressing words, but stopped, astonished. All he could gasp was *"C'est vous!"*

I admitted it was I, with a look asking, What about it?—for his behavior astonished me equally. Instead of explaining, he rushed to the dressing room for Yvonne Printemps, his wife (then). *"C'est lui!"* he exclaimed, pointing dramatically, as she came hastily to the door in her kimono, still wiping off her make-up with voluble *"Oui-ouis."* Hearing the general excitement, a distinguished gentleman moved into focus from an anteroom. The bald dome and familiar mask told me at once it was the great Lucien Guitry himself.

Then Sacha introduced me to his wife and father, explaining in his rapid, crystal-clear French:

"Yvonne and I saw you sitting out front, monsieur, at the matinée yesterday. I also told Papa. We knew, from those heavy-rimmed glasses, you were an American. You see, all our stage Americans always wear them so that the audience will be sure to know they are Americans! We saw how much you enjoyed the play. Everybody in the cast spoke of it. You may have noticed we were watching you. I didn't see how an American could get the lines or laugh at all the right places. I told Papa about it. I almost sent out to ask you to come around to my *loge*. Now it is you! Belasco cabled me he wants you to do the play. Of course, you can, you must. Come lunch with us tomorrow."

And that was how I met "the three Guitrys"!

CHAPTER XVIII

SACHA GUITRY: THE ART
AND ACHES OF ADAPTATION

PREVIOUS TO the war Sacha Guitry's talking pictures, in the various theatres over the United States dedicated to foreign films, had begun to make his name better known here. Acted and written by himself, *The Cheat* and *The Pearls of the Crown* had been hailed: but they afforded only skimpy examples of his scalpel-like skill as writer and actor. At first, he looked down on the films. His *Pasteur* was inferior to Paul Muni's later version, for he would make no concession to the medium and almost literally transferred the stage play, which his father had made famous and Henry Miller had briefly acted in New York; but later pictures soon revealed an innovator. When war broke he was already experimenting with new technics as he had done, at seventeen, with his first stage comedy.

However, when I first met him in 1922, he had seldom acted even outside Paris except for annual trips to London. Once at a luncheon of cold salmon and champagne, when I was prattling of the little towns in France, Yvonne Printemps eyed me with astonishment.

YVONNE: Why, Sacha, monsieur knows France better than we do.

MIDDLETON (with a deprecating gesture): Being unknown, I can get around easier.

YVONNE (nibbling daintily, for reasons of weight): Oh, monsieur, it *is* difficult for us! (With a sigh) We could never be alone.

MIDDLETON (in his best French): It's damn tough all right to be famous.

(They both nod and think they believe it. MIDDLETON takes more champagne.)

But Sacha Guitry was a Parisian. He hated to budge; he rarely took a walk. As he has been infrequently translated or performed here, American critics and drama groups know little about his dozens of plays. Historically, his work may remain only a personal expression; a sharp observer of character, he has created no universal sym-

bols, which make the enduring genius of
Molière. Yet to me, through his many gifts,
he had been one of the exciting personalities in the French theatre; a real *homme
du théâtre.* The hours I spent with him,
adapting his comedy, during my subsequent trips to Paris, and on the visit he
and Yvonne Printemps made to America
in 1927, add up on the credit side of a
writer's job. I was also to learn some of
the art and aches of adaptation.

There was a photograph on Guitry's
table which once caught my eye. It was of
Sarah Bernhardt as a young woman, when her Semitic ancestry was
more strongly marked. He told me she had lunched with him the
day before. On it she had written (he let me copy the words):

"A mon cher Sacha: Tu n'étais pas né quand cette photographie a
été faite; mais déjà mon cœur se faisait tien." *

Shortly after she had given the photograph to him she was rehearsing with his father her last role, written for her by Sacha, when
she broke down and was taken home. They telephoned him. He
found her lying on the lounge. "She put her arm up and drew my
head to hers and whispered: 'Pardon!' "

The episode recalls that Lucien Guitry was acting with her in London when he married Mademoiselle Pont-Jest, and Sarah was their
witness. Sacha was born in St. Petersburg, where his father was
engaged at the Imperial Theatre. He knew the continual uprootings
of an itinerant actor's family and was dismissed from some fifteen
schools. Each time he went to a different school he was placed in the
same grade. He told me that at sixteen he was "still with the eight-
year-olds."

During his young manhood Sacha knew all the famous personalities of his father's salon. They differed so that he could not decide
which profession to enter. His father discouraged him from the
theatre "since the name of Guitry was already so celebrated it wouldn't
make the path easy. But," Sacha added (he had asked me to write an
article about him for America †), "I suppose I started writing plays

---

* "To my dear Sacha: You were not born when this photograph was taken; but
already my heart was yours."

† See the *New York Times,* Jan. 16, 1927.

to prove Father was wrong." He did ten for his father after their quarrel and thirteen-year separation. In most of the others Sacha himself acted; unlike many French dramatists he thus entered the theatre through the stage door. He became, in fact, the only important actor-author in Paris: most of his confrères were also novelists or feuilletonists. His alone has been a complete full life in the theatre.

He had married Charlotte Lysès—a fine actress, too; then he spied Yvonne Printemps in a music hall. They were married. And to round out the circle Sarah Bernhardt was *their* witness, as she had been at his father's marriage, thirty-seven years before! It is only the Sacha Guitry of this happy artistic collaboration with Printemps of which I here write. I never saw him after their separation.

His house was a museum. Books galore. On the floor we once sat journeying through his literary treasures: not only first editions of Molière (who greatly influenced him) and the very rare La Fontaine, but a complete collection of first editions, dedicated copies, of the writers of the late eighteenth and the early nineteenth century. This period, indeed, has always so fascinated him that his plays have oscillated between the chic modern comedies and comedies of fast-fading days. He admitted once that his plays were never intended as "literal historic documents," but rather as expressions "of some mood of the Gallic spirit," as efforts to arouse a certain emotion in the audience "by the evocation of a famous personage." *Mozart* (lovely Yvonne), *Béranger* (with its subtle study of Talleyrand), *Deburau* (S. G. always loved clowns), and *La Fontaine* (probably his favorite) are but a few such plays.

Tucked in with the manuscript of a Baudelaire comedy (the only one he ever wrote), the Liszt copy which Gérard de Nerval dedicated, and a verse of Verlaine he deciphered for me, were the more personal books dedicated, of course, to him in phrases which made him proud to show them: by Anatole France, Octave Mirbeau, Georges Courteline, Jules Renard, and Tristan Bernard, who, incidentally, also gave him the short two-foot cane which the misshapen aristocratic Toulouse-Lautrec had leaned on as he sketched. Among others I read one

from Bernard Shaw, on a copy of *Saint Joan:* "To Sacha Guitry who, like myself, does not write in chains and who, indeed, should have written this play."

He would talk of them all, as became a cultivated man of letters. But he seemed equally proud of the collection of modern paintings that I used to linger over at his own home and then at the house his father willed him.

"Why don't dramatic critics realize in making their judgments that there are as many kinds of plays as there are paintings? Oil and water colors cannot be judged by the same standards. Sometimes, too, the greatest art may be expressed in a few strokes *à la Forain*. There may be equally as much art in a revue as in a tragedy."

When I first entered his study I was startled by a gaping female torso, by Rodin, so realistic were the long leg muscles reaching into pelvic mysteries and *genitalia*. On its base was engraved, in French:

"Rodin gave this to Mirbeau. Mirbeau gave it to me. They are both dead. I give it to you.   LUCIEN"

And Sacha told a story of the controversial Balzac statue which I repeat because it led me later to incorporate Rodin as a character into my Balzac play, in order to "place" my hero:

"Those who remember the tortured face and figure he made of the great novelist have often wondered at its inspiration.

"Rodin first made a nude, quivering with the travail of creation: the head flung back, the body exhausted, and the hands grasping each other in front.

"Some of Rodin's friends saw what the sculptor sought to express: how tied together was the literary and biological effort to produce. But others laughed at the strange posture. So Rodin covered Balzac's nakedness with a bathrobe!"

I'm not sure this is the literal truth since the monk's robe, which Balzac often worked in, has sculptural values in directing the smooth planes to the head: "the head that held a world." But, after Sacha told me, I went to the statue again. The expression took on a new meaning: I ventured to have Rodin call it "the orgasmic moment of creation." *

* This statue was completed in 1898, after five years of sketches and maquettes—the most literal of which is in the Metropolitan Museum of Art. Owing to the storm of protests it raised, unequaled in fury since Victor Hugo's *Hernani* shocked the French artistic conservatives, it was not cast in bronze until 1939, when it was placed in the heart of the Paris Balzac loved. I am indebted to my *Balzac Bulletin* No. 15, issued by the Balzac Society of America, for the following: "The famous statue of Balzac by

I had sensed the influence of Claude Monet and other Impressionists upon Sacha's own play technique. He was seldom occupied with a story as such; it was "the mood and color which attracted him." Yvonne Printemps told me: "He never will write a play till he has it all in mind. Then he shuts himself up and does about an act a day. He walks back and forth, talks to himself, and writes it down. It gushes out." He wastes little time in neat scene hinges or over-all structure. The first version he lays aside, to revise it completely in a few weeks. He must write absolutely alone. "Not even a dog may look at him," she added with one of her sly glints. How my Skippy would have resented that!

"There is only one thing an artist must do," he said to me, "—follow his own impulse, create as he sees it. The rest will come." I may add another aphorism, which his friend Alphonse Allais once put to him: "Never lie in your art." And Sacha explained: "I always try to keep his words before me—which is probably why I don't write so-called situation plays: they never seem true to me." Yet he dramatized *Jacqueline* for his father. When asked about its powerful situations he waved it aside: "Oh, I did it to prove I could write an old-fashioned play."

(So Sacha fibbed a bit: but how can one ever be completely honest about oneself? Writing this autobiography, I often blush at my omissions.)

Sacha's emphasis, however, has been on little things rather than pistol shots. Once in illustrating their inherent drama he recalled a phrase in a Capus drama which he felt was most moving: "The former wife is in a restaurant, and as she rises to leave she sees her former husband there with another woman. All that Jeanne Granier had to do was to say 'Bon jour' and pass out. The way she said that brought cheers from the audience. There could, of course, be no greater drama than further repercussions of such a short sentence."

Perhaps this explains why his plays are full of short sentences—pages of them, often: packages of baby firecrackers, bursting one on top of another, amid puns, double-entendres and quick flashes of obser-

Rodin, which had been hidden in the vaults of the Observatoire to escape the Nazi demands for metals, is once again in its place at the corner of the Boulevards Montparnasse and Raspail." Organized by William Hobart Royce, one of the most erudite and indefatigable of Balzacians, this society now has 430 members all over the world. It holds a yearly dinner, which I attend when I can, and publishes this intermittent *Bulletin*, full of pertinent data about the novelist and the books or articles he still inspires.

vation. Always the treatment rather than the story. "Yes, it is like the time Claude Monet took his first studies of simple landscapes to the dealers. They all wanted him to paint figures in them—so that they could 'tell some sort of story.' The managers wanted me to put in more situations."

As recollections of his old friend came to mind Sacha was silent. "The last time I saw Monet at Giverny," he told me, "he was seated hunched and despondent with his arm over the back of the chair. They used to tie the brush to his hand so that he could more easily hold it. I sat beside him and asked how he felt. He was past eighty then, you know. He turned his eyes to me, eyes scarred by operations for cataracts. I noticed he held in his hand a tube of paint. Monet smiled sadly. 'Ah, Sacha, I can no longer see the yellow!' " *

I know of no more tragic phrase which ever fell from an artist's lips. Somehow that day there was not much more for us to talk about.

I saw *Une Petite Main qui se place* ten times. It was not easy to adapt: turning a play into another language rarely is. Dramatists who have tackled such jobs know each script is its own problem. If the adapter cannot read the language of the original he is up against it. He must first rely on a literal translation. His headache begins there, for it is generally hard reading. Where the plot is a series of situations, with a "stunt" part such as Sardou loved, adaptation is not complicated. But comedies or plays with some literary quality, as well as those which are rooted in special local customs, double the complications.

The Berlin meeting of the International Confederation of Dramatists in 1928 devoted an entire session to this subject. My own experience made me beg the foreign authors there to insist on a decent English translation.

Of course, translators everywhere have been underpaid—especially when agents sent scripts overseas on speculation. A play requiring only straight translation may be well enough done; but, ideally, only a dramatist can translate a dramatist. Stage dialogue, as I have said, is shaped to be spoken. The translator should have the same feel for the language of the theatre as the original author; if not, the translation misrepresents the original.

* Sacha Guitry repeats this story in his impish autobiography, *If Memory Serves,* translated sensitively and with amusing notes by Lewis Galantière (Doubleday, Doran and Co., 1936).

It took a poet-dramatist, in Brian Hooker, to translate Rostand's *Cyrano de Bergerac*. "It was impossible to translate, and Hooker did it," was Brander Matthews' estimate.

One Spanish drama, which I was commissioned later to adapt for Katharine Cornell, had had two "rough" translations, adjusted respectively to French and German postwar susceptibilities. As I read no Spanish, how could they tell me surely the author's conception?

I also pointed out to the Confederation that a script as published is often not even an accurate transcript of the play as performed—and the text furnished to the adapter should be the form finally acted; generally a garbled or unrevised text is supplied. I recalled the *Illustration* version of Brieux's *L'Avocat*. It was stark dialogue marked with only necessary exits and the like. When I adapted it for E. H. Sothern and Belasco we sent to Paris for the prompt copy: a stiff notebook, beautifully inked to illustrate the action. The stage business had not been incorporated into the text—probably a French precaution to keep it secret from all but the oversea purchaser. Incidentally, the French author always hustled his script into print, possibly fearing it might not come out before the play came off.

With the Guitry script I had my troubles. When I first sat "out front" to register the laughs and effects, I lost my place the moment Guitry stepped on the stage, with that authoritative way he had. Tall, getting weighty, handsomely tailored and suggesting he had just left his valet in the wings, he was instantly arresting. His large, frank features needed little make-up; and he was never shy at turning his profile, which was slowly approaching his father's sculptural outline. His crop of wavy brown hair, however, was as personal as the lofty bald pate of "Papa." Several times in his *cabinet de travail* I had caught him noting his face, in the mirror, with a comparing glance at the portrait of his father hanging there.

Yet when I referred to the script I couldn't find what he was saying. So I did, what we all have done when tempted, gave up and enjoyed. But I grew curious. It was not until I took out the *souffleur* (prompter), for drinks and other gifts, that I was able to set the text as spoken. "Monsieur Guitry improvises," he confessed. "He changes at every performance. This is the very latest though. It is the old *commedia dell' arte* method, monsieur," he added, with elaborate historic apology. But the only scenes which remained as written were those in which Sacha didn't appear.

The personal style in which any such play is written or acted may also cause an adapter pain. And Guitry both wrote and acted! As he composed his part he stage-managed himself. I watched how the two gifts cooperated or complemented each other, how closely he timed his byplay and "tricks" to point the lines, using only enough dialogue or leaving it out for a shrug if necessary. Pantomime was the willing bride to speech. Indeed, this particular comedy was full of those "old-fashioned" asides and even monologues, which we had been taught to abhor. But his was in the old tradition. He believed that whatever was effective on the stage was right. Eugene O'Neill about this time was also rediscovering the virtues of such self-communion.

"The theatre is not life," Sacha said to me. "Take a stenographic report of a conversation, and see how impossible it is as stage material. In a monologue, as a dramatist, I recognize the audience. I do not play to give the impression the audience does not exist. The self-questioning I make in the monologues of my own motives and what I intend to do in the play as an actor is so presented as to give the impression of questioning the audience. My monologue is thus confined to what one is thinking." *

Some of my friends were never so keen as I for Sacha's acting: they kept the greater father too much in mind. But the younger man's urbanity and style made him, with the exception of Victor Boucher— of the sudden little bleats and slow credulities—one of the finest light comedians. Yet Sacha's distinctive personality also explains why his plays seldom succeeded when revived by another.

But I must hasten to add that he was then abetted by a gorgeous comédienne—Yvonne Printemps, "the little Guitry," who could sing like a lark. Her piquant face, turn-up nose, large open eyes, and husky laugh made her a risky attraction for any normal male. Sacha had studied her capacities, and she herself had mastered her father-in-law's underplaying. Nothing was easier than for her to pack every subtle implication into an "Oui," a "Non," or a "Fallait-pas?" I sensed how impeccable was her ear when Sacha once asked me to check up on an English poem she recited in *L'Illusionniste*. It was perfect; yet she didn't understand a word. Always she would hit the same exact tone, when once it was pitched for a desired effect.

---

* Yet when my adaptation was later submitted to Richard Bennett, for the Guitry part, he scribbled:

DEAR GEORGE:

I wonder who wrote this play—how many years ago? Why not fool the critics by titling it *The Asides?* I adore it but—Guitry must have delved. Why pay 10 per cent?

DICK

To watch her and Sacha bat verbal bubbles back and forth, as they winked naughtily in mid-air before they broke under our laughter, was delicate stroking that had no parallel. Only the Lunts equal it today. What is skating on thin ice, in French, risks being indecent exposure, in English; the delicate innuendo of one, vulgarity in the other. A responsive audience, in Paris, clothes such comedy scenes for a stranger with a deceptive charm which loses its felicities in our more precise vocabulary. We Americans understand and handle the thrust better than the finesse. In such scenes, alas, poor adapter!

From this extended experience with Guitry, I learned not only that the personalities in an original performance must be taken into account, but that the adapter ought to *see* the original performance. The fact is, only a performance of a play can ever reveal its full values.

This suggests how ticklish a problem it is to cast a foreign play that was originally devised around marked individuals. Personality, in addition to acting ability, is essential. This was realized when we tried to produce the Guitry comedy in New York. Among the men who wished to do it, Cyril Maude, the English star, would have been ideal; but no outstanding actress was available. Belasco asked me to read it to Eva Le Gallienne and see if she would consider it.

Although I had long known Eva, our professional association was not to begin until 1938, when I adapted *Madame Capet* for her. Fola and I had admired her devotion to the theatre: always more interested in making a contribution to its art than in her selfish advancement as an actress. Her Civic Repertory Theatre admittedly has a notable place in stage history. Its record of intelligent production of the classics, as well as in the development of young talent, is unequaled by any American theatre of recent decades.* Its closing, by the force of circumstances, was a great loss. It seemed to be the swan song of the repertory idea: but Eva's own intense interest in it persisted. So much so that plans have been announced, in cooperation with Margaret Webster and Cheryl Crawford, of the late Group Theatre, for a 1946–47 season. The American Repertory Theatre (A.R.T.) will include plays by Shakespeare, Shaw, Barrie, Chekhov, Ibsen and one by an American author. Walter Hampden will be in the company.

---

* More than three dozen plays—including works of Shakespeare, Ibsen, Chekhov, and Molière—were in the active repertoire. Among the actors who there had their first opportunity were Burgess Meredith, Edward Bromberg, Richard Waring, and John Garfield. Alla Nazimova, on her return from Hollywood, also became a member of the company; later Ethel Barrymore joined Eva in a production of Rostand's *L'Aiglon*.

Only those who know of the terrible accident, which might have blighted Eva's career as an actress, can appreciate the gallant courage which enabled her to triumph over her ordeal. There are few with whom Fola and I so enjoy spending an evening as with Eva, in the modest farmhouse discreetly off a Connecticut highway, where she has her innumerable little dogs, her countless books in five languages, and maintains her alert interest in all that passes. She inherited from her mother a God-given sense of humor which lights everything her mood may dwell upon. It was once while we were gossiping over our many stage experiences that she urged me: "Put yours down, George. No American playwright has your story."

But at that younger time, when Belasco suggested she come to our home to hear the Guitry comedy, I saw she was disturbed. Before I started to read, she put her hand on my arm.

"Can I be frank, George?" I got ready for almost anything. "I don't know this comedy; but I don't want to act for Belasco. I don't want to offend him; but I just know, after talking with him, that he and I couldn't get along."

This was the second time a star's refusal had kept a play of mine from a Belasco production. It was a hard position. I knew if Eva refused that he would not try further to cast it. But I saw she had made up her mind. That, too, was like her. *Que voulez-vous?*

"I tell you what, Eva: let me at least read a scene or two. Then you tell me you don't like the character, or it doesn't suit you. Then we'll talk of cabbages and kings."

It was one of my strangest reading chores, and Belasco was furious the next day.

"Didn't think it suited her, eh? I know she could have done it beautifully."

Of course. That was what had bothered me.

In the end Belasco agreed with me that the comedy would have little chance unless properly cast. Indeed, it never has been acted in either America or London, though frequently revived in Paris. The only tactful way I could reconcile Sacha Guitry was to write: "Where is there a Guitry and an Yvonne Printemps in America?" Naturally he understood that and agreed.

I was left with an adaptation on my hands. But it was worth more, in the amusement and association it had brought me, than the cash which might have come to the family till.

CHAPTER XIX

DUSE, BERNHARDT, AND
LUCIEN GUITRY

DURING this time Sarah Bernhardt and Eleonora Duse were frequent visitors to Sacha's home. He was planning a play for each without the other's knowledge. He would tell me of strange exits, hastily arranged, so that they should not meet. He said Duse was "afraid of Sarah." It was a confusing story of temperaments, jealousies, and misunderstandings that had begun when Sarah offered Duse her theatre in Paris. The guest opened in the part of Camille, which Sarah regarded as essentially her own role. After the first night, Duse called on her and, kneeling at her feet, asked her pardon for "having dethroned her." At least so history ran—touched up, no doubt, as it had come to Sacha through many retellings. All I know is that the two actresses weren't having chocolate with him at the same time.

One story he told me suggests the life which pivoted about his home and *loge*. He and Yvonne were acting in London. As the curtain fell the enthusiastic house called for a speech. Sacha begged the audience to stop applauding them, and applaud "two of the greatest artists in the world who are in the audience: Chaliapin and Duse." Amid the cheers he saw the actress and the singer rise and look about. But neither was bowing to the audience: each was trying to see what the other looked like! Afterwards both went behind, where they met Lucien Guitry. When the manager saw the five celebrities on stage together he threw up his hands. "What a cast! But it would cost something!"

Too bad only Sarah was lacking. But I shall boldly borrow her, Duse, and Lucien Guitry for the faint silhouettes which follow: the moment or two I was honored with a sight of them. All three, as it happened, moved from the earthly scene within two years.

I first saw Duse offstage in the *loge* where I first met Lucien Guitry. It was furnished like a room at home except for make-up lights around the inevitable long mirror. Half-hour intermissions with the Guitrys were not unusual. Sacha always received during his.

Movement everywhere, comings and goings, backslapping and hand-shaking, whispers, refusals, evasions, and conversational confetti. It seemed like an old-time monarch's *petit lever*. One of the first radios added operatic airs to the background.

Into this confusion Duse quietly passed. In a few moments she came out, bewildered. I had a glimpse of her harrowed face as she hurried past—to stop abruptly and cry out: "Mon chapeau! J'ai oublié mon chapeau!"

A year later I met her in New York by arrangement through her manager, whom I had known in Paris. I recalled this incident.

"Oh, yes! Sacha had asked me to go back to his *loge, en camarade*. It was so full of noise. How can he stand having people there when he is creating a role? I had to leave—pleading a headache. I was so confused. That is why I left my hat."

While admitting Sacha's "brilliancy" she believed he was the essence of what was "worst and best in the Paris stage." Naturally, by association and temperament, she was more attuned to his father. "Il est de lo grande ligne," she said emphatically. I saw the father late, but in one or two of his best parts. I tried to analyze his method. I also had some talk.

To many Americans who yearly visited Paris, Lucien Guitry was already an institution, easily its most striking actor. I have an early photograph of him as Coupeau in Zola's *L'Assommoir*. Already his body was massive and firmly set, although later he became heavier; somehow it seemed to be the proper medium for his individual technic. His hands, like those of Duse, were unforgettable, though he used them less often—for a Frenchman, his gestures were few.

His face was the actor's perfect mask; his jaw was heavy; his mouth, large, constantly opening and closing a trifle, with just a suspicion of nervousness; his nose, long and prominent. His head and body seemed to be almost of a piece. This made his eyes important; their very movement, in fact, became startling, placed as they were in a mass which itself seldom moved. Sometimes, too, they seemed all that was alive, as quick shifts of emotion or thought would flash like sparks sharply struck off.

Comedy and tragedy, he managed equally well; and in both economy was the rule of his art. Like George Arliss, he was a master of understatement, and he wisely capitalized on the very limitations of his marked physique. When he was on the stage it held no vacant moment, yet he never made a useless motion. Each gesture thus had its own studied importance, without nervous waste. I have watched him light and smoke a cigarette so that the mere flick of his finger conveyed his unphrased thought. Further, his movement was seldom rapid, save when the occasion demanded. Then, though still controlled, the possibilities were terrific. The audience always sensed something beyond words held in reserve. I never saw such power under restraint; and, in his huge form, more force was thus suggested than any actor ever could actually express. Pinero told me he always had felt that if Guitry ever let go "all would be swept away." He could be a great oak shaken in the most strenuous Gallic storm: yet he never was blown over. In spite of everything even the leaves somehow had held on.

Though he appeared to be the most natural of actors, through this understatement, his method was constantly conscious of its effects. He would rest his hand flat on a table; then his fingers would tap, once or twice, or curl under—and the audience would be riveted, awaiting his next move or word. Another characteristic trick was his habit of pausing before each reply. It was the orator's way of getting attention; but with Guitry it significantly charged what was coming. Few actors have ever used this as skillfully as he, though his daughter-in-law successfully transmuted it into something quite her own. I was talking of this once with Gene O'Neill when he told me that George Cohan had so studied Guitry's "delay before speaking" that "by the end of the run *Ah! Wilderness* was twenty minutes longer than when we opened."

It was Yvonne Printemps herself, however, who surprised me by acutely observing that Lucien Guitry had been responsible for many bad actors.

"They try to imitate his method, monsieur; but they cannot, for they do not have his great personality. They merely catch the ex-ternals: they have no reserve power with which they can arouse the imagination."

There were lessons to be learned by every student of acting from this rigid economy, as well as from Guitry's capacity to assume an un-derlying mood and sustain it during an entire act. How he loved cynical contempt, for example. In another player what might become monot-ony supremely suited his own endowments. Yet a company of actors, all with Guitry's method, would never make the impression he made alone. His difference was his great asset. The awe, too, which I felt in some degree each time I was with him, followed him on the stage.

In his best moments he seemed like a chained force, awful in implication. Lucien Guitry was then a Rodin statue come to life.

I talked to Sacha of his father after his death. Concerning one of his plays about an actor, the son once observed:

"I was interested in showing what I believe is true with most of us on the stage: that we often carry over our roles in real life. My father, for example, if he were playing an aristocrat, always unconsciously at breakfast the next morning would order his coffee in the same courtly manner." *

The last role his father played, when he was taken ill, was that of an actor playing a role for the last time:

"He never asked me to change a line. Once I saw a sentence had too many words in it, making it difficult to speak. But he said I had written it, and it was for him, as an actor, to play what I had written."

As Sacha was talking he finished the pencil sketch he had been making of his father. He handed it to me; he had written under it, "Hélas." Alas, indeed! Sarah was right: Lucien Guitry had been "the first actor of the French stage."

Perhaps I may publish here one spontaneous tribute which Edward Knoblock was moved to write by my article in the *New York Times* when Guitry died. Theirs had been a close relation springing out of his having acted in the playwright's *Kismet* in Paris. It gives, better than my small contact could, some indication of the warm emotions the man himself inspired:

HOTEL ALGONQUIN
Oct. 9 '26

MY DEAR MIDDLETON:

You sent me the analysis of Guitry almost two weeks ago. I was in the throes of writing a play. I've had to do a three act play plus prologue and epilogue in twelve days—so I know you'll forgive my silence. In fact I didn't look at your article till just now—I've finished my work ten minutes ago—and reading your words on top of all this effort they came to me with a singularly unusual force. I can see the man I loved so clearly—and

---

* Press agents have always loved this assumed "coloration" the actor carries over into private life. There are many tales about Richard Mansfield's Mr. Hyde. Charles Laughton's wife attests to her husband's similar identification in his offstage hours.

the great artist—both. And frankly—my eyes are full of tears as I write you.

He was a great man—a rock in this sea of uncertainty and pretence that the theatre mostly is. And such as Lucien Guitry makes one realize after all why we care for the art at all—is that there *can* be beauty and truth and something divinely human in it all—if we will but put aside all the sham and look beyond the tinsel—into the heart of things.

Am I a bit sentimental? Possibly. He might have smiled at these very words I write you—but a kindly smile—the big generous delightfully cynical man he was.

So I know you will forgive this letter. I don't let myself go often. But then how often does a Guitry happen in our lives?

Sin. yours,

EDWARD KNOBLOCK *

I happened to be talking to Lucien Guitry in Paris a few days after I learned of Eleonora Duse's death. I told him what she had said about him. He smiled and mentioned he had been trying to find "the many letters she had written" him when he was acting in St. Petersburg.

"I often urged her to return to the stage. I told her she should go back and offered her my theatre. Staying in retirement for an actor means nothing." And then he added a sentence one does not forget: "Our roles are only garments hung in a closet until we put them on."

Yet Duse, too, might have replied in Balzac's query: "Why wear robes when one can no longer play the role?" It was what the Italian had felt, as Yvette Guilbert had related, before that last tour in America. So I had been prepared when I called upon her in New York. Disliking interviews, which she believed had often misrepresented her, she graciously arranged to see me when she heard I merely wished to talk of plays. Of course I was fussed: I knew it would all have to be in French.

While I was waiting outside her door there flitted the memory of her palace Fola and I had seen from a gondola in Venice, where she and D'Annunzio had lived. There was a remark, too, a friend had once heard the poet make in a hotel in Rome. On the sofa looking anxiously up the long staircase was Duse, seated. As D'Annunzio came down, he saw her.

"Oh, you are still waiting for me?" he said brutally.

---

* Upon his death, in 1945, he willed to Harvard University his extensive collection of British handbills and programs.

"I am always waiting for you," she replied quietly.

There were other fragments Isadora Duncan had told us from the time when she and Duse lived near each other in solitude, each trying to forget the personal tragedy which had touched her: Duse's parting with D'Annunzio, and the accidental death of Isadora's children in Paris. But, as I heard the apartment door open, the past slid back.

She came in quickly and went straight to her manager without looking at me. After he had greeted her and murmured my name, her eyes turned, her lips moved as she extended her hand. I saluted in Continental fashion. Though she was absolutely natural I noted the trained actor's unconscious art of registering one point at a time: the entrance, the meeting of one and then, clear-cut, the other. There was no blurred embracing of the three.

White strands wove through her iron-gray hair. Her face was sallow, yet, except the brow, not so wrinkled as I had expected. Her neck was a bit gaunt; her high cheekbones, perhaps more prominent than in that lovely Lenbach drawing we had seen in Munich. Otherwise she seemed as she had that thrilling night when she returned at the Metropolitan Opera House in *The Lady from the Sea* and the capacity audience had risen on her entrance! Her eyes remain my most vivid impression now—mysterious yet kind. I had anticipated something more wan: an epic woman bowed by a world of sorrows.

She spoke with great rapidity, without any letdown in her verbal vitality. Somehow it astonished me, since her manager had told me, as her train left Paris, she had huddled in her compartment asking timidly, "Do you think there is a place in America even for me?"

Her French was fluent though with a pronounced accent. She generously divined my meaning when my own phrase halted; for I was recording my impressions while trying to think in another tongue. After some words about the Guitrys, she asked if I had a play which would suit her. Though she would only act several times a week, her management had to keep her company on full time, and carry scenery for her repertoire.

As I knew touring thus presented special problems I had therefore come to suggest the possibility of an evening of one-act plays. This would not require a large company yet would permit her public to see her in a variety of roles. She liked the idea, which she apparently had never thought of before. She saw its value since people came to see her and not the plays. I quote from notes I made immediately on leaving.

"It is practically impossible for me to find new roles," she said. "The Italian dramatists now only write for young-women stars. The problem of the young alone seems interesting to the public. I understand it is the same here in America. Yet there are so many problems that come late in life. I feel I shall find something here that I can use. I cannot explain it. As I came nearer to America I felt my own vitality increasing. And I do feel so much vitality here. I have so many young people coming to the theatre to see me. But I must change my repertoire. I realize my present plays are not suitable. I cannot play Camille and Sardou. I am too old. Times have changed, and I, too, must have new things. Perhaps I could more easily find a repertoire of one-act plays."

When I suggested the possibility of such an international program her eyes lighted.

"I might do two on an *affiche,* with some music between. That would be enough. In fact, I had thought of doing Synge's *Riders to the Sea* for my return; but it was too short a play in which to make my reappearance after an absence of twenty years. . . . I understand you have written many one-act plays. Have you any that would suit me?"

I had brought one along, *The Man Masterful,* which I had had translated into French so that she might read it. I apologized for the condition of the pages; I had carried it over Europe in the hope I might have an occasion of presenting it to her.

"Oh, I am used to that. If a manuscript is all done up beautifully I am a little suspicious of it. I like to see a manuscript that has been worked over."

I told her I had written it six years before with her in mind.

"Why didn't you send it to me? I should so like to have been remembered. . . . Yet six years is a long while when one is young. . . . Perhaps if I don't think it suits me you will write me something else? It is so hard to find plays which suit me—now."

There was a momentary glance as though she were looking far away. "Tell me," she asked, "how do your young artists endure playing every day? Your young Eva Le Gallienne tells me that she must give nine and ten performances a week, and that often a play will run for a year or more continuously. . . . How can one keep the springs of creation fresh? And yet they seem so willing to learn. . . . They do not come to see me act because I am handsome and young. . . . Perhaps I have something to give them."

When I rose to go she leaned on the arm of the couch fingering my manuscript. Her eyes accidentally fell on a phrase which was a sort of text I'd put upon the title page. "I like that," she said, " 'Les arbres morts restent longtemps debout.' " *

She smiled enigmatically. I kissed her hand and left her standing there.

Some months later, wedged in the compartment of a French train coming from Le Mans, where I had gone to see the cathedral, I read in a local paper two lines telling me of her death—in Pittsburgh.

After France was invaded, in 1870, and Paris occupied, the first clarion voice poetically to prophesy that she would rise again was George Meredith. Thinking of her during the recent occupation, I took down his ode *France, December, 1870*. It thrilled again with the same hope for the France to be. It repeats, too, as though written yesterday, the causes which brought her where she was:

> She sees what seed long sown, ripened of late,
> Bears this fierce crop: and she discerns her fate
> From origin to agony, and on
> As far as the wave washes long and wan
> Off one disastrous impulse: for of waves
> Our life is, and our deeds are pregnant graves
> Blown rolling to the sunset from the dawn.

As I turned its worn pages I came upon a pressed red carnation!

I tried in vain to remember what fugitive emotion had made me keep it; or which girl's eyes, out of younger days, might have smiled as she gave it to me. Slowly she did come back to me, vivid, as I had seen her but once up close: Sarah Bernhardt, who made her first American appearance on October 27, 1880, the day I made mine.

My one meeting was at the Players: a reception, one of the very few our club ever gave a woman. She plucked the carnations from a vase on a tea table by which she stood. She gave me mine. I can see the smile yet. I'll wager I am the only one who still has his flower. I have always been sentimental about the great ladies of the stage. Sentiment is all I could ever give them in return for what they have given me. Ada Rehan moves into my thoughts often, and even now, as I write. . . . But *place à Sarah*, for her little scene.

It is hardly anything—a flower, and a woman in a crowd; but I

* Dead trees stand long.

have kept the impression. She was more than an individual, of course —such personalities suggest so much beyond their mere being; she was a world of emanations, the countless memories others like myself have kept alive which she gave birth to! She was a tradition that those of us still living helped to make. She was to be the last of a royal line and, in her turn, had made the theatre of her time great. Also, she was unquestionably the most famous woman then alive. Yet, only a few years later, I was to stand at her grave with two whose fame already had far exceeded hers, and . . .

She came to the Club June 20, 1911, with a couple of secretaries and Lou Tellegen, her last romance. She was still able to walk in spite of her bad leg. She stood by the stairs to greet us with the spontaneous grace which had, no doubt, become a mechanical habit. She wore a toque, on the side of which a bunch of grapes seemed mysteriously to dangle. Her hair edged about this—it was not gray, of course. The gown was of yellow lace, with golden buckles around her waist. The collar reached chin-high so that her neck was hidden; the sleeves ended in long points which left only the fingers visible. It was all designed to mask her age; for even then she was past sixty.

Her face was a marvel of make-up: the eyes shadowed, the cheeks without a wrinkle! The only time her age showed was when she smiled; for nothing could conceal the way the skin sank back around the mouth. She carried her habitual long scarf, wound around her back and over both arms.

Francis Wilson, Vice President, greeted her in French. He didn't know French; but, to our astonishment, he had acquired this perfect sample. That was like Frank.

She responded, full of emotion. How happy she was to be there! Her arms lifted up ecstatically and held high and pausing, for a moment, as I had so often seen her on the stage—while the long scarf hung from them, lining her in its frame. Her face at times was innocent, almost virginal: yet, in profile, it was a sphinx cynically guarding every secret of life she had herself devoured. It was a double woman I saw. As she talked, the scarf wound constantly with the serpent life she gave it.

We went out where tea was served. She stood by the table and poured. She hesitated to put sugar in one cup, as there were no prongs. A member gallantly begged her to use her fingers. She smiled and did. It was then she reached for the red carnations and gave them to us— to me: just so that I could write this now, perhaps.

A telegram from John Drew, our President, who was on the road, was passed to her. I was standing behind her when she eyed it, clasped it to her heart, overcome with sentiment. But I noticed that she held the wire upside down. With the resource of one who had forgotten a cue she handed it over and motioned that it be read out loud. Some one translated it. She got it that way. How moved she was!

A tactless, well intentioned member brought forward a photograph she had given the club many years before. The sun had faded it even more than time had touched her own youth. She looked at it and murmured softly in French, so that only those of us near could hear: "I will give you another, but not so pretty."

She kept her word. There hangs now in the clubhouse a striking photograph of her as Pierrot. Under it she wrote:

"C'était pour les aveugles, fermez les yeux et admirez."

Years afterwards I was to take Douglas Fairbanks and Mary Pickford out to Sarah Bernhardt's grave. She lies in Père-Lachaise, the cemetery overlooking Paris. I had known Doug back in pre-screen days. They were now at the height of their fame. As we rode through the streets of Paris people everywhere called out "Dou-glass', Mary—Dou-glass', Mary." They were as unable to guard their privacy as Sarah had been in her great days. We left the entrance and wandered among the memorials to those who had made history and art: and theatre folks, too: Rachel, Talma, Lemaître. Soon we came to Sarah's grave—then inconspicuous, with a raised covering, so simple and so unlike every moment of the decades she lived. Instinctively, Doug and I took off our hats. We three stood silent.

I saw her again as I first remembered her. I was a young admirer in my top gallery and she was even then in the autumn of her art. And that last time, at the theatre which still bears her name, as Athalie. They carried her on to act but a brief scene or two: one, with a little child, effective in the emotion awakened by the notes of her golden voice still with some sheen.

I glanced at Mary and Doug. The screen had made them known in every tiny town of the world; known to many more millions than the most traveled of actresses, in all her tours. I remembered, too, that, bankrupt, aged, with but one leg and an indomitable spirit, this old relic, if you will, had also turned to the screen for the last francs she was to earn, when she was so feeble that the camera had to be set up in her home.

What was that strange motion picture camera doing *to* and *for* the theatre Sarah had kept a living art? Would it, in its far perfections, guard for the generations ahead the records of such as she? She who before could only vaguely survive in word or recollection? Would it harbor great stage actors of the future? the Bernhardts and the Duses, who, as it happened, on early flickering films, themselves left but silent hesitating gestures of their genius? Or would such as they be put aside for actors who took good pictures or merely had some pretty tricks?

What of the theatre itself, I wondered, as I looked from her grave to the famous couple by my side. Were they and Sarah the symbols of two opposing arts, or might each in turn be merged to the benefit and beauty of both? What did the strange machine portend for the theatre I had loved since boyhood? What was it to mean to us dramatists? For already we writers had begun to seek the answers to the questions I shall tell of, in their turn.

Doug and Mary had stood silent. Maybe they were thinking of the fleeting quality of fame when such could come to her. Sarah had it as none. Now she was buried in a narrow grave more than large enough to hold her genius, which once had overflown a world.

Our eyes met and then looked again at what we saw, as we walked to the other side. There, on an upright support to the covering slab, a bronze plaque was riveted. It was put there to commemorate the fact that the Orpheum Circuit had first invited Sarah to play in vaudeville. It had, perhaps, been thought to be an American decoration.

Douglas Fairbanks and Mary Pickford at Sarah Bernhardt's grave! A bronze plaque, from a vaudeville circuit, its only decoration then! What a time to moralize! But they must hurry back. Photographers! Interviewers! Appointments! Cables to be sent!

We hastened through the gate. As we rode back to the Crillon through the streets of Paris, where Sarah had been queen, the crowds cheered:

"Dou-glass'! Mary! Dou-glass'! Mary!"

CHAPTER XX

INTERMISSION: FOR CHANGE OF SCENE, NAZIMOVA, AND TWO FORCED CLOSINGS

When I went to Europe in 1920 I had been a disillusioned liberal. The war had mangled my proportions. Aside from the interests I was to find in new friends and professional activities, only man's destructive habit kept intruding itself as I went over battlefields, watched the crippled soldiers in London anticking before theatre queues for pennies, or traced the wrathful writing of Big Bertha on the walls of Paris.

Yet one happening, in an autumn twilight, soon restored my sense of values: to endure through all the world bewilderments since. It was to open a retreat which no one could ever again take from me. As it was thus one of the memorable moments in my inner life, it asks a page in this personal record.

I had been gazing at Notre Dame Cathedral—"the dear old thing," as Henry James had dubbed her—recalling how the Revolution had profaned the holy figures which for five centuries had graced the great portals. A number of those now standing guard in their stone rigidities, I knew, were modern; the noble originals, so lovingly carved by faith, were but the scarred and scorched relics that I had seen the day before in the Musée Cluny near by.

With this still in mind I had wandered along the left bank of the Seine into the cloistered walk of old Saint-Julian-le-Pauvre. Again I gazed at the Cathedral, across the swift-flowing river. The pink rays of reflected light rested upon the stone crockets which edged the early Gothic mass. They caught the light, as it grew faint and strong, and faint again, under the subtle movement of the passing clouds and the fast-sinking sun.

I stood spellbound. The cathedral slowly moved with life. It breathed. For the first time I fully experienced the emotion of beauty. It *was* beauty to me. I could not put it into phrases: for once the writer did not try. Yet when my mind caught up with my emotion it suddenly came over me that man had made that cathedral. The hand which had broken its statues had also built the House of God

259

itself! Beauty, too, was still striving for its place in the sun—and always would be. It was asserting its right to be seen, enjoyed and to *be,* even to an ignorant pilgrim like myself. Then I realized what I had never, in the bitterness of preceding years, accepted: beauty, as well as hate and ugliness, was a property of human expression, as warmth and cold were of the air itself.

Beauty! Why not give it a chance with myself? Why not go find it and the new values it held out? But would *I* know it if I found it? What was its test? Only how I felt, perhaps? Very well. Maybe, by constant association, it could in time be coaxed to reveal its secrets to me, freely and unafraid. "Seek, and ye shall find," took on a new meaning as I pieced out the message which opened a new world, in the pink light upon those wise old stones. And somehow in the silence my spirit was lifted and equilibriums restored.

But time was short. I might never be able to go again. A voice inside kept at me: See the best over here which man has made—it can be unmade by man also. *Go.* There are Italy, and Germany, and Austria, and Spain, and England, and the Low Countries, with every cranny of France outside your doorstep. Go and explore. Your treasure will be only where your heart is.

So, a truant from my theatre world, I had gone forth from time to time, mostly with Fola till the pace tired—more often breathlessly alone, to write her of it all each night. Reading in advance about each town, I had known exactly which church or picture or relic I might wish to see. I had thus kept to an inner schedule of desire, with hours always open for the unexpected. Henry Adams expressed my own feeling in one of his letters: "As for me, I am always content when in motion and ask no better than to wander on."

For years I could recall everything I had seen in every town, and all the items would march to my wish in regimented order. They string together now in careless sequences, disdaining year or place, sometimes even mingling with recent recalls in our own rich museums here at home. In burning log or, foolishly, in heavy traffic stray recollections unexpectedly leap to mind of white-frilled egg-shaped Greco heads, hung in a row upon a Prado wall to tell, better than books, what the Inquisition was like; or that single Delft landscape by Vermeer in the Mauritshuis; or that slim thirteenth century virgin, bent gracefully to the shape of the wild elephant's tusk, smiling at me again across the years, as I write, from her little chapel beyond the "bridge at Avignon."

In addition—for my Balzac play—there were the towns which his intimate life had touched: Tours, the room where he was born;* Vendôme, for school days; every nook in Paris, full of love, work, and phantasmagoria; Fougères, scene of his first acknowledged novel; Provins . . . What fun! Never had I been so happy as while scenting on all these double quests. Everything in me was sharpened to a point: to go; to see; and then to keep on going.

With these, too, were happy living encounters: guides, guards, priests, specialists. . . . If one were passing through a museum's corridor and caught upon the door a name last seen upon a book one had devoured, what was more natural than to tap and ask for the man himself?

"Whom shall I say, sir?" one secretary asked me at the British Museum.

"He would not know me. But tell him I merely wish to thank him."

The famous scholar came out, much puzzled. Before he could speak I said: "Mr. Dalton, I want to tell you what pleasure your history of Byzantine art has given me. It is a wonderful book. Thanks." I shook his hand and turned away.

"Wait a moment, sir," he said, as he hurried after me. He gulped for a moment or two, embarrassed, and then smiled as I stopped. "If you are interested in our Byzantine collection, won't you let me show it to you?" And the greatest English authority himself took me about, opened cases, and let me touch the jewels which an Empress on the Bosporus had worn!

There was, too, the sad-eyed aristocrat in Rome, of subtle smile and nuance, whose lineage, perhaps, reached back to the very Forum he was telling us of to earn our stray lire. There could be tales of the erudite sacristan at Mantes, friend of Emile Mâle and Charles Diehl, who achieved the heights of sacrifice, for a Frenchman, by forgoing his *déjeuner* to explain to me for an hour the tricks of his cathedral's architecture. And then, in the Seville Cathedral, another Madonna brought me a happy encounter. . . . She was known to art students, resting already for four centuries in her high stone niche. I had found her after much search—gazed, felt her charm, and walked on. I noticed an elderly oak of a man, ruddy, with a shaggy fringe of hair and baggy pepper-marked tweeds, glancing about the celebrated grilled *coro,* with his grandson, who wore an English school tie and an

* The house was recently destroyed by bombing and fire during an air raid.

eager look. I had observed the very negligee pair the evening before at the hotel, immaculate in their smoking jackets.

"Are you looking for the Madonna?" I impulsively ventured. "It's the famous one—one of the earliest, I've been told, where the Christ child is sleeping in his mother's arms . . ."

"Never heard of it," he answered, with a smile. "But, by all means, show it to us."

An hour later we three sat, in the Arabic Alcazar—just talking. Of course, I didn't conceal that I was a writer. But I could draw nothing personal from his studied English reticence except to register his casually authoritative culture. As we separated, I to go for my train to Granada, he shook my hand and volunteered to arrange for me to meet Kipling, who was there.

"I wish you would look me up when you come to London. My name is Augustine Birrell. You see, I am a writer, too."

The famous statesman and distinguished critic and essayist smiled modestly as he saw my astonishment combined with recognition. Happily there flashed out of nowhere his name on another book I'd read.

"Oh, Mr. Birrell, I'm so glad. For this gives a chance to tell you how much I once enjoyed your *William Hazlitt*."

It was now my turn to smile at his astonishment.

But no need to intrude a further itinerary of dead excitements. To remember is personal and intimate; often it serves best as an intermission between harsher realities. So these memories have been my retreats in the years since: those things I saw and people I met beyond the fast receding shores and now recalled, as Fola and I were sailing home.

Our slow, reluctant boat docked at Hoboken on September 26, 1922. My brother met us. We had exactly five dollars in our purse. But we had prospects and the busiest of days ahead.

Save for a six weeks' dash in 1924—paid for, and more, by a re-write job,* to which I didn't sign my name at the time—I was to let

---

* *The Bride*, originally written by Stuart Olivier, whom I never met. I didn't want to do this, as it looked so hopeless, but was offered $2,500 advance and half of all royalties. I naturally was persuaded, with the understanding I could sail in three weeks and need not attend rehearsals.

I managed to get an angle on play and suggested complete recasting. We engaged Peggy Wood, an old and valued friend, Ferdinand Gottschalk, who had been in our *Adam and Eva*, and Isabel Irving, a splendid comedienne from Daly days who, in this play, made almost her last stage appearance. They alone gave the script importance.

Europe get along without me until 1927. In the three years immediately ahead I plunged, for a change, into my job: writing plays. Five were to come on and, almost as quickly, off: for, to put it delicately, all except one were "flops." My promised beds of roses only yielded me a poison ivy rash.

The fact would be stated, as "the rub of the green," and forgotten were it not that two of them—*The Unknown Lady* (our old friend *Collusion*) and *The Road Together*—did not pass quietly into the obituary columns. They both died violent deaths, one after the other, and, in so doing, became front-page news stories. Ironically, this publicity soon started the tradition that they were among my most popular successes. But the cold fact remained: *The Unknown Lady* lasted initially but two performances in New York; *The Road Together,* with an equally distinguished star, survived but one—to establish a record.

Alla Nazimova brought *Collusion* to life again. It was seven years since she had given it a single benefit performance, arranged by Daniel Frohman at the Century Theatre in New York two years after the Lord Chamberlain in London had said nay. Alla had a chance to reappear in vaudeville: I, of course, was willing. There is no delight in the play-writing game like seeing dead ducks wing again. I was also glad to be a small part of her career, for hers was as romantic as any in our theatre.

Fleeing that earlier abortive revolution in Russia, she came here by way of London with a ragged troupe headed by Paul Orleneff, then the most brilliant of Russian actors, who pooled their poverty to give performances of modern European classics in an obscure East Side theatre. When she and Orleneff went to their flat after the performance, they would have to throw their shoes from the doorway to scare off the rats!

Suddenly they became the rage of New York. Later uptown to Broadway; her quick resolve to go it alone and stay in America; then, only six months after her first English lesson, that startling opening performance of *Hedda Gabler,* which I watched with amazement. No

While the comedy ran a number of weeks—being less interesting to New York than the Democratic presidential convention, but really more entertaining—it turned out to be a good stock piece and was sold to the pictures, I think for the world-admired Pearl White.

I mention these trivial facts to show, that the return from plays is as illogical as the relative returns from certain professions: movie executives and college professors, for example. I probably made $8,000 for the three weeks' job.

Slavic actress since Modjeska, in fact, was so frequently to impress our critics with sheer acting skill, expressed through an exotic but exciting personality. For Alla, in spite of the handicaps of accent—which Modjeska herself never lost—was predestined for the theatre. It had held a power over her from her early youth, for she told me that, when a schoolgirl in her teens, she had fainted at the beauty of the first play she ever saw: Stanislavski's amateur production of Hauptmann's *The Sunken Bell.*

Fame at twenty-seven! Henry Miller. Skyrockets and her own electric lights over a theatre named after her! For ten years, with Mrs. Fiske, the most provocative interpreter of Ibsen. Charles Frohman. Exotic, unworthy, but popular *Bella Donna* stuff. Then the thrilling *War Brides.* Silent pictures, world-wide publicity, and thousands per week. Overambition and picture production with her own money. Broke. And after more dips into Ibsen and Chekhov, with Eva Le Gallienne at the hospitable Civic Repertory Theatre, in and out, with Gene O'Neill's *Mourning Becomes Electra* and an unforgettable Mrs. Alving in *Ghosts.* Then in talking films, looking as young and vibrant as in the days she did my little play.

Though I had met her before she spoke English, Fola and I saw her often during her early expanding years of triumph. She had rare humor. One afternoon Alla and I were at a reception. The salon was crowded with the socially prominent, and Alla felt it was "very respectable"; for she said something to me which inspired my little play, *Among the Lions.* It told of a celebrated actress with a lively past, made everything of by the very people who were the "guardians of morality" but, for the luxury of basking in an artist's fame, blinded themselves to her infractions of the moral law she knew they would impose on one of "their own class." My fictive star felt impelled "to tell all," and did. But Alla had only smiled significantly and tossed me the thought.

All such strange contrasts in which she found herself amused her; none more than, in the Russian language days, her being, with Orleneff, a dinner guest of the Marshall Fields in Chicago. It was shortly after McKinley had been shot. The police were searching for Emma Goldman, who had once talked with Czolgosz, the assassin. No one knew the actors had brought to the dinner, as interpreter, "Miss Smith," who was Emma Goldman herself. Emma later told me that her hardest job that night had been to put into polite English the vituperations the poverty-stricken Orleneff was blurting out in

Russian to his wealthy hosts, with the sweetest of smiles, as they beamed back in approval.

At one period a change came over Alla which grieved everybody but her press agent. She became more aloof, artificial, and bizarre in manner and dress. Her conversation struck the same note. One evening at a large formal dinner she happened to notice that I refused both cigarettes and drinks. She waited till no one was speaking and then volleyed:

"Oh, George! You do not smoke and you do not drink. What do you do? Do you go with women?"

When I recalled her challenging question, during a rehearsal of *Collusion,* she smiled:

"Ah, yes! You see, in those days, I was trying to live up to what they told me Americans think a Russian actress should be like."

But she was on to herself and what all that studied posturing had been doing to the inner Alla. For after acting, not so happily in a variety of artificial roles, she finally came upon the deeply moving *War Brides,* by Marion Craig Wentworth. It afforded her a part into which she could pour her heart, and was among her greatest successes. A day or so after it opened she wrote Fola an impulsive note which revealed the Alla which lay hidden in the opening chapters of the autobiography she read us years ago, and which, in spite of our persuasions, she did not finish until just before her death:

Not that I have anything to say—just because I *must* let you know how superhumanly happy I am. I breathe again. I have a right to look myself into my own eyes and not blush. I am doing honest work, work that gives me a *reason* to be on the stage, work that makes me better . . . I feel that you know all about me and are happy with me now.

When my divorce play, *Collusion,* was first revived in San Francisco, I was in Los Angeles rehearsing *The Road Together*—whose spectacular finish was still months ahead. In view of what finally also happened to *Collusion* I must add Alla's wire on the opening:

MATINEE ELEVEN CALLS NIGHT NINE THEY LIKE IT AM HAPPY

ALLA

In a follow-up letter she added:

I find no prejudice against the theme except in one paper. The people are neither shocked nor "anything." They love it, are very attentive and laugh and cry with me. . . . . I find that your ironical title "a domestic comedy" is not understood and is misleading them.

I saw it in Los Angeles and was happy over its obvious audience appeal and its showy acting opportunity, which Alla took in her stride. She was magnificent in the only slangy American role she had ever ventured. I was tickled when she sent me a copy of Judge Ben Lindsey's letter which she had received in Denver. Ben told me some time before his death, when I last was with him in Washington, that his vigorous defense of my play had contributed to his defeat for re-election! As the title was not arresting I had changed it to *The Unknown Lady*—the moniker it was destined to wear on its tombstone.

DENVER, October 10th, 1923

Madame Alla Nazimova,
Orpheum Theatre, City.

MY DEAR MADAME NAZIMOVA: At the Orpheum Theatre last night my wife and I had the very great pleasure of witnessing your magnificent production of Mr. Middleton's one act play *The Unknown Lady*. A brilliant performance was assured by the very fact of the production being under your skilled direction and the leading role being in the keeping of your artistry and genius. No one was disappointed in this expectation.

May we also add our commendation of the play itself. An experience of twenty-five years in the Domestic Relations and Children's Court has given us an unusual opportunity for knowing society as it is and the causes of its misery and unhappiness. It was therefore a most hopeful experience to us to find in *The Unknown Lady* one of those vital themes constantly suggested by the work we are in. The subject matter and its wholesome treatment is not only proper for the theatre, but especially for the Orpheum Theatre. What the people of this country need is the truth about their own hypocrisies and the monstrous injustices of stupid laws still permitted to remain on our statute books; laws, that because they are established and maintained in ignorance and defiance of the real truth about society are doing hideous wrong and contributing to more vice and immorality than they could ever hope to prevent.

The rather sordid phase of life the play shows up in its true light is not only nothing against it, but, in the delicate way it is acted, calls for special commendation. It is without any of the vulgar suggestiveness of certain phases of domestic relations used in so many of the farce comedies and sketches for mere commercialism and cheap amusement and that too without any question from the critics. In *The Unknown Lady* that phase of life is properly used without offense or harm to anyone, in the interest of a high purpose and the cause of justice. It is hard to have patience with

the captious critics who, in such a circumstance (probably from the ignorance they suffer about injustice, people and society) insist upon seeing
immorality in something that so sincerely and successfully attacks immorality.

We cannot attack a festering canker in our body politic any more than
we can attack burglary or murder without showing what it is. The crying
need of this age is fearless people who have learned that the surest way to
conquer evil is to show where evil lurks. This is just as important whether
it be in a bad law or in a bad habit.

As a champion in this struggle to which you have brought the light,
force and courage of your genius through a great piece of work like *The
Unknown Lady,* may we, in behalf of outraged justice and suffering
humanity, offer you our sincere congratulations.

Sincerely yours,

BEN B. LINDSEY

What followed can be briefly stated. *The Unknown Lady* was
greeted with the same enthusiasm everywhere. It was such a "smash
hit" on the Orpheum "time" that Albee sought it for the Eastern
Keith circuit to begin at the New York Palace, then the prize
"booking" in vaudeville. The play was announced as "dramatic Dynamite." The press agents blared the fact that the Nazimova role was
"sensational." The opening matinee house was packed. The play had
a wild reception. In a note I sent to my Washington family at the
time I reported there had been between "twelve and sixteen curtain
calls." It was also given one night performance. Then it was closed!

Pressure was brought on Albee by an individual who asserted that
he spoke on behalf of a religious organization. My play was admittedly
killed on a one-man protest. I had no appeal. Naturally I was not
consulted. I knew nothing of it till the papers rang me up for a statement. That it was not a police matter is evidenced by the fact that
Arch Selwyn, managing the Grand Guignol Players, immediately
engaged Nazimova to do the play as their guest at the Frolic Theatre.
They had been starving to death; but, surrounded by French *cuisine,*
the highly spiced fare the papers had made of my play did not blend—
for my play could not live up to its suggested immorality. At any rate
Alla didn't do it again in vaudeville. She wrote me that the management would book her in "anything but that."

There was, however, a sequel I never knew till I read it in Douglas
Gilbert's fascinating *American Vaudeville.** I quote what happened

---

* *American Vaudeville: Its Life and Times* (New York, 1940), pp. 363–365.

after the contracts booking her into the Keith circuit had been sent
to Alla:

Now the Keith contracts contained what was known as an "elimination"
clause. This clause was the keystone of the Keith-Albee vaudeville policy.
It gave the managers authority to censor any word, line, lines, business, or
costume that violated the Keith-Albee idea of "cleanliness."

Nazimova crossed out the clause and wrote in her own to the effect
that not one line or bit of business was to be tampered with and that the
act was to be presented exactly as she played it. With these changes she
signed the contracts and forwarded them to New York where they were
filed—unexamined. That any performer, from Bernhardt and Bayes to a
honky-tonk hoofer, would dare to scissor this clause, let alone change it,
was inconceivable in the Keith-Albee offices.

So when the righteously indignant Albee . . . descended on Nazimova
she produced her copy of the contract and bade him look at his. He did,
and paid her $11,000. The sum included not only her salary for the
truncated week at the Palace, but for the entire booking time.

So is virtue sometimes rewarded: by trying, quite properly, to
protect my script, Alla's feelings were financially salved. I received a
front-page funeral, including flowers and plenty of sympathy.*

And another cortège was also rounding the corner. It was *The Road
Together*. The title was to prove prophetic.

Henry Holt had originally published this play in 1916. The idea
hovered amid the conflicting claims of sex and habit in marriage.
Undoubtedly it was a hang-over from the romantic interlude in
bachelor days. I rewrote it in Paris, of all places, after some actual
experience in marriage not gained solely by looking over its fence at
forbidden preserves. The theme remained, but the emphasis was naturally changed. Though the book reviews had been generous, I couldn't
sell it for production till my return from abroad. Then it was agreed
with Al Woods that I should let Tom Wilkes's stock company in Los
Angeles try the play out, with the ideal star I had wanted, who was
to "give a season" there. I went out to stage it and persuaded
H. Reeves-Smith, who had been with *Polly,* to join the stock cast.

The play succeeded; in fact, it ran five stock weeks. The star gave

* *The Unknown Lady* was published in the *Theatre Magazine,* Jan., 1924. I did
not include it in any of my collections, as I planned to enlarge it into a long play
and did. Though only the idea and one situation remained, the entire character of
the story was changed. The play was sold three times but never produced. Maybe
if it had been, after the first advance payment, I shouldn't have made any more out of it.

me her photograph, on which she wrote: "Many thanks and congratulation, George, for having one of the finest plays ever written." According to the *Theatre Magazine* the star appeared "in what she herself had spoken of as the best part she had had in years." With such reports, and every picture company eyeing it, Woods and three partners—George Cohan, Sam Harris, and Wilkes—decided to bring it to New York. The final preliminary tour looked promising; Buffalo and Stamford perked up; the press was good as the play edged nearer to the Broadway test. On the strength of the star's draw, a splendid company including both H. Reeves-Smith and A. E. Anson, and road reports, the ticket agencies had made a four weeks' "buy" before it even opened.

My star was second to none in the type of part I had provided. Though she lacked soul, she could assume its trappings. Beautiful, too, and eye-arresting, she impressed by the commanding way she moved about. Mistress of stage strategy, gained from hard years in stock, she could handle resourcefully almost any demand of emotion or comedy. With vitality and a perfectly controlled voice she had become so popular that her presence in a play guaranteed it a public. Whatever the critics might do to me, I felt, from the brilliant performances I had seen her give, that the play would at least have a respectable run, a road tour, with ultimate stock and picture money.

Perhaps the report of that first-night performance, however, can best be epitomized by the way Otis Skinner once greeted Leslie Howard, after his performance of *Hamlet,* which Otis disliked. He went behind, opened his arms wide, and rhapsodically exclaimed, as he strode across the stage towards Howard: "Oh, Leslie! What a night!! What a night!!!" The critics of my play sensed something was wrong, and some blamed it on me. It will suffice, for descriptive purposes, to quote only one notice, from the *New York Herald*. It is unsigned, but since it is stamped with the limpid accents of the late Alexander Woollcott, it may have an added value as one of his unknown items:

Instead of being a play *The Road Together* last night turned into something suggesting a tug of war. Playwright George Middleton and the cast assembled by A. H. Woods didn't seem to pull together. One might call this an uneven, faltering and turgid piece, if one was not restrained by the fact that there seemed to be something fundamentally wrong with that part of the universe enclosed in the Frazee Theatre.

But the lenient and indulgent old hand is stayed by the fact that the

times appeared out of joint. . . . In the first place the star of the occasion
. . . was apparently laboring under some mental strain, which made her
lines somewhat unruly. Her pronouns seemed a bit obstreperous. Several
times the "me" or the "you" or the "him" became sadly mixed. It would be
impertinent to inquire what this particular stress of spirit was, but it
seemed to draw a veil over her native talent for acting. At times she would
valiantly endeavour to put her shoulders in her acting—and what beautiful
shoulders they were! But at other times the incubus seemed to hold her,
and her voice sank low. She whispered—and she did it so confidentially
that some of the spectators moved up a seat or so. And she muffed a fairly
easy word like "thermometer." . . .

In the circumstances, it was proof of the vitality in Middleton's underlying idea that one could still find interest in a play dealing with a married
woman who gave up a pilfering lover to help her husband win the District Attorney's office, only to find that he cherished his own secret love
affair and was at bottom as dishonest a man as the man she turned away.

. . . It seemed hardly possible that an author who collaborated on the
sparkling *Adam and Eva* could write a play so obfuscated. Part of it
might have been written by Strindberg. It is to be regretted that matters
might not have been so composed that . . . [the star] could show her
undeniable talent, instead of being in such an overwrought state that she
put on her voluminous cloak in a topsy turvy manner.

Instead of giving a final judgment, one might suggest that what the
play needs is a second first night. Every one concerned might heed the
advice of the bemused drawing professor who saw a dilapidated cab horse,
learned from the cabby that it was actually a horse, and then said absent-
mindedly: "Well, better rub it out and do it over again."

In view of what had happened I made up my mind to close the
play at once, if I could. I knew of three stars that season who, from
time to time, were giving performances decidedly below par. Yet with
me it had occurred on a first night when the outcome of the play itself
was also at stake. I consulted experienced playwrights who had sat
through the entire evening. They volunteered to testify, should a court
issue be made of my closing the play, and agreed that this was the
only dignified action for me to take.

However unworthy a play may prove to be, the actor, after accepting of his own accord the part entrusted to him, is enlisted for the
duration in a cause which permits no disloyalties. There can be no
treacheries behind the lines or with them. I have seen actors racked
with pain or grief heroically carry on, and I have been grateful where
on such occasions my own ventures were concerned. But no allowance

can be made where an obviously inadequate performance lacks that excuse. *The Road Together* itself took on persuasive importance when the star fulfilled her obligation to it and to the audience that then loved her.

Once Mary Shaw played *Ghosts* in Madison, Wisconsin, when Fola La Follette was a girl. As it was Christmas Eve, few were in the audience. Yet Mary gave a thrilling performance. Years after, in our home, Fola recalled that night to her, and her splendid acting "to the empty house."

"But, Fola," she said, "there was *one* there who cared, wasn't there? I always play for that one." So it should be.

How much I rationalized my feelings at the time, I don't know. I was perhaps too hurt and sick. Closing the play was the hardest decision I ever had to make in my professional career. But there was a larger issue involved. It lay beyond being chivalrous to a lady. Gus Thomas told me later that he wished he "had had the guts to do what you did" when he had suffered the same experience. But mine was no case of intestinal courage: my emotion was further up. I was indignant that the play of *any* author could be subjected to such treatment.

In those days there was no effective Dramatists' Guild contract; but mine required the management to perform the play a certain number of times before it could come into its share of stock and picture rights. The day after the opening, I went to Martin Herman, Al Woods's brother, and offered him an interest in those rights provided he would close the play at once. After consulting with his partners he agreed. The following stark notice was sent out after being read over the telephone to a lawyer:

A. H. Woods closed *The Road Together* at the Frazee Theatre last night at the request of George Middleton, the author, who was dissatisfied with the performance given on the opening night.

I declined to make any further statement, merely adding that what happened was "a secret of Polichinelle." As some reporters didn't know who that fellow was I amended it by saying, "What happened was obvious." The papers, of course, took the author's unusual action to their front pages, and the *New York Times* reported:

The occasion marked the first time that a play having an established star has closed after a single performance in New York and it was agreed last night that only unusual conduct on the part of the principal performer could have brought about the sudden closing. . . .

The closing of the show was not altogether unexpected by the first-night audience which noticed something was decidedly amiss.

One further notice from the *New York Herald* may be added:

. . . This abrupt termination was all the more unexpected since favorable reports of the piece had come from Los Angeles and other towns on the preliminary tour.

But there was never to be anything "doing" with that script again. Though I had offers to revive the play, on the strength of the publicity alone, and another star was proposed for it, I would not. I knew it couldn't possibly live up to the hullabaloo its closing had created. No. This was another dead duck. Let it be buried where it fell. I put the battered prompt copy away. I have never opened it since. Until I reread Alec's review I had even forgotten the plot.

The day after the closing I sailed for Bermuda. I had to buy tickets when I went aboard, and the boat was so crowded that I had to sleep in the hospital. Well, after these two experiences, I felt that was the proper place for one playwright.

While rummaging in old files I came upon a bright and glistening clipping from the glossy pages of the *Theatre Magazine* for April, 1924, that touched at length on these two ventures and my others of those days. I reread it and for a moment or two felt quite sorry for myself. I reprint the season's mortuary record for budding playwrights to ponder on, in the exultations of hope or even the enthusiasm of their first successes:

Consider George Middleton. If ever a playwright encountered a tidal wave of bad ill-luck, certainly this is one. When the present season started, Middleton's outlook was, perhaps, the rosiest of his contemporaries. . . . It might [have been] safe to prophesy that the playwright could expect to have two big royalty-paying propositions, and even the most conservative estimators in the show business would [have been] willing to gamble on the success of certainly one of these enterprises. But the wager would have been lost. One after another Middleton's seeming good fortune was marred by a series of *débâcles,* only one of which might reasonably be laid to any fault of his own. . . . If any playwright has ever known such wholesale disaster in the brief space of half a season, it certainly hasn't been within the memory of your present correspondent.

It is one record my fellow playwrights have never been anxious to beat. I hope they don't.

ALLA NAZIMOVA

DAVID BELASCO

CHAPTER XXI

DAVID BELASCO: THE LAST OF HIS LINE.
E. H. SOTHERN AND INA CLAIRE

OF COURSE all the preceding had not shown in the cards when Fola and I landed in Hoboken and drove to 158 Waverly Place which had been waiting two years for travelers who had left it expecting to be away two months!

The place looked dingy. A movie sale came along, so that Fola could make it over. All my wooden saints and virgins, a plaster original of Jo Davidson's *Ida Rubinstein,* an English fourteenth century *Christ,* and loads of French books moved into the places they were to hold for nearly twenty years. We had brought back with us some of the Europe we loved. Always we were to be reminded by our frail statuettes of those rich years in a new world some called old.

It was months before the rounds of friends were made and threads picked up. Fola was soon centering on progressive education. Of course, rehearsals claimed me with the other ventures now coming to a head. Happiest of these theatre experiences were the hours I spent with David Belasco, now that old days with him were to be supplemented by two further productions.

To his fingertips and the ends of his small, slim, shoes, Belasco was a man of the theatre. His clerical garb with its closed collar and black rabat effect set off his marked oriental features. Were it not for his rich-lipped mouth and inscrutable dark eyes a casual observer might have suspected something ascetic in the parchmentlike face that I never saw flushed. His reverence for the stage often took strange turns: he eyed suspiciously the new production heresies of groups which challenged, or made him question himself—heresies which, in earlier days, he had himself defiantly embraced. Yet he loved the theatre; it was the first law of his life, his heaven and hell. And it is what I came to know of that theatre man, through a decade or more as his years began to curve downward, that I write. In all, I worked with him on six scripts, advised on others, and shared three childbirths.

273

It was a complete experience in a glamorous theatre which has gone. The conditions which made him possible can never come again.

I first saw David Belasco, in his black-haired days, at the notorious trial of his suit against N. K. Fairbank, the Chicago capitalist, for fees promised him as Mrs. Leslie Carter's dramatic coach. I was sixteen, satisfying my hunger for court trials and press-absorbing personalities. Here I heard legends of his cruel methods with actors that I was to find so false; here I first learned how theatrical "angels" backed plays—the history of which, by the way, is an unfilled blank.

I was twenty-five when, seeking every possible work contact, I next saw Belasco and Mrs. Carter together; he was high on my list. As it happened, the little play I then begged him to let me read did lead to our long association. (It was intended for Blanche Bates, who by then had become a star in *Madame Butterfly* and *The Darling of the Gods*. I had seen her eastern début with Ada Rehan and had hoped I might in time do a play for one so colorful and compelling.) He asked me to the tiny room off the stage of the first Belasco theatre—later to be known as the Republic and bloom with busts and burlesque queens. It was there that, after *Zaza* and *Du Barry,* the flaming-haired Mrs. Carter was mechanically performing a commonplace concoction called *Adrea.*

I remember my shock that night at the imperative, irreverent way she called to him as the curtain fell, while the applause filtered backstage:

"Come along, Dave! You know you are waiting to take the call with me."

He hurried with her on stage. Then, with studied deference, she left him. From the cluttered wings I watched him make the gesture that a star herself generally makes, of gracious reluctance, when by prearrangement the rest of the cast simply insists on leaving her alone. Indicating it was impossible to recall Mrs. Carter (then hurrying to her dressing room anyway), Belasco turned, defeated, to the audience. He stood, almost shrinking, without a smile, his left hand guarding his heart, as the other plucked at that iron-gray lock which, through two decades, I was to see slowly whiten under that same digital caress. Then he murmured his hesitating thanks in sibilants, the mimics always stressed.

In Hollywood, long after their nationally publicized quarrel and Mrs. Carter's marriage to W. L. Payne had ended their collaboration (no longer financially successful anyway) the elderly lady, with lips deeply receding as she smiled but with hair still heavily coiled and flaming, eagerly asked me about "Mr. Dave." When I later repeated to the old gentleman, then past seventy, that Mrs. Carter had "sent her love," he grunted a bit reminiscently. What stage waters and excitements had gone over the dam between my final glimpses of them both and my first!

What a part of a theatrical tradition Belasco was, for nearly forty years! "Super" with Edwin Booth and Adelaide Neilson, "bit" actor doubling up, stage manager, prompter, hack playwright at a few hundred per job, barnstormer, co-author with a half-dozen well known names—including Steele MacKaye and Henry C. De Mille—early producer of Bronson Howard, theatre operator, associate of A. M. Palmer and Charles Frohman. When I first met him he was fighting the Syndicate, the best known personality in the managerial world— to be the last of his line!

Critics can more accurately appraise his place in that stream of drama history. But I may serve some purpose in a more intimate record of how he worked, and what a production with him meant to a dramatist. I had no illusions about his limitations: he had no broad culture and was unaware of social and economic readjustments in the world about him. He produced no important play, I recall, which reflected the new moralities touching on man and society. Preoccupied always with sex, he would dare a bit, as in *The Easiest Way;* but the revolutionary *Doll's House* or any plays which suggested the claims of a mild feminism were beyond him. With few exceptions, the American plays he did were amiably unimportant, though among the best of their kind. Yet, within his capacities, no one surpassed him as a producer. Everything he touched became sheer theatre. To thrill or amuse an audience so that it escaped from realities into a make-believe but recognizable world, is one of the theatre's functions. There Belasco seldom failed.

My entire relationship with him was happy. There were disappointments, of course: the Frances Starr play that died of anemia; the Guitry play I have told about; and the Cornell play, *The Desert,* for her and Basil Rathbone, that shriveled up from inner combustion and cast trouble, with Godfrey Tearle, Brian Aherne, and others involved. But, no matter how long the waits or furbishings in dry dock, a venture received every right of way, once it was launched. There was no skimping on cast or scenery, no corner-cutting with an eye to a non-expansive budget, no quick closing or notice given, even before the New York opening (such as Eva Le Gallienne suffered when she stepped on the stage for the final rehearsal in my adaptation of her *Madame Capet!*).

Belasco was not a solitary worker. He seldom retreated alone into that book-lined, memento-stuffed studio on top of his theatre, loaded with curios of all epochs: Gothic cloth, Dalmatian Christs, French cherubs, drawers full of jester's baubles, and one locked cabinet, guarding the many necklaces a daughter he loved had in life herself loved. He needed somebody to talk to, plan with, or listen, as he moved about in pajamas and a flowing purple dressing gown, acting out new scenes, scribbling notes on his sewing table he used for a desk, or pinning them upon the black cloth screens always within reach.

His large office force was ever ready for action: no mere skeleton set-up which only came to life with intermittent production. Belasco was then an institution. Every department was manned throughout the year. He instinctively resented all labor unions and Equity. They imposed restrictions, refused to live on benevolence, and altered the claw-and-fang habits of his early years. When the Dramatists' Guild came along—with its time limits on the holding of plays and prohibition of script changes without the author's consent—he saw another effort to curb his free enterprise, though I was able to persuade him to join, as we shall see.

No one gave him greater loyalty than Ben Roeder, his business manager, who became my good friend and ally. Starting as his office boy, Ben survived a lifetime of storms and dead calms to settle his employer's complicated estate and keep a guarding eye on its ever unraveling threads.* Belasco also had a play reader; Miss Ginty, a personal secretary, now herself a playwright; a scenic artist on tap; a music specialist; a costumer; a social secretary for appointments and buffer jobs; a permanent press man who expanded; and the necessary stenographers. Howard Bookbinder wove the mystic figures of his extensive bookkeeping. In the box office were "Bob" and "Jo," who had been with Belasco for years. Behind stage "Matty," his property man, Louis Hartman, his electrician, who grew old in his service, and others whom he kept on salary even when the theatre was closed. All this did not make for great plays, of course—they have often sprung from

---

* On his own recent death Ben left to the Players, of which he had been a member for half a century, many of Belasco's valuable "props," associated with Edwin Booth and the leading actors of earlier decades.

bandboxes; but it is detailed here to show the aid which instantly rushed to an author's script when Belasco took hold. He was, as I say, an institution; and he must be so considered in the appraisal.

With all these, as well as a staff of authors who came and went— some writing under a weekly salary, in the early days *—"D. B." was essentially a collaborator: on the whole an easy one, who welcomed suggestions if properly timed and tactfully put. When crossed he would rage; but "blow-ups" were often assumed or directed to some specific purpose. He moved by indirection, though the whip could crack. I had my misunderstandings; yet I felt he respected what talent I had or perhaps, even more, my willingness to work. I was never to miss a rehearsal nor an appointment. My drive, at least, equaled his. There I could meet his enthusiasm. When on a scent he also never knew how to relax. I grew fond of him with time. I was touched when, shortly before his death in 1931, he told a friend he hoped "George will come back from Hollywood so we can work together again."

Today managers can no longer inflict either directors or actors upon an author. So important did it seem to keep this control as well as the integrity of our scripts, that the Dramatists' Guild was to make one of its hardest fights when the issue was joined in 1926. The relation of author to director is an especially delicate one; for here temperaments meet head on. It may require the most tactful handling. While today an author has the right to be at all rehearsals it is not compulsory. An author who takes a play to certain managers has the option of adapting himself to their well known peculiarities; he can measure the compensatory values.

Guthrie McClintic, for example, will go over every scene with the author, scrupulously follow the script as mutually agreed to—except after further consultation; but he simply cannot rehearse "if the dramatist is hanging around." He feels an author should thereafter be neither seen nor heard, unless script emergencies arise. Belasco, on the other hand, back in the days when the Guild had no power to define these rights, would not rehearse unless I were glued to the prompt table. This was a constant lesson to me: but he wanted at hand some one to make the numerous verbal changes to fit the new business he was constantly devising, which any author well knew in advance he would seek. There was no deception. Such a voluntary

* For a further discussion of payments to dramatists see Chapter XXIV.

relationship between an author and David Belasco was understood and accepted.

I was thus to see him intimately at work on every phase of a production. Without wishing to discourage any dramatist, who may be under the delusion that sanity necessarily rules in a play's coming to life, I will open a peekhole, where I can, on various parts of the Belasco process. There is little like it today: there was nothing like it then. But it was Belasco. No theatre man I ever knew had his mania for perfection. That must also be remembered in any appraisal.

Though I early did an adaptation of a German play, *Georgina*, which he planned for Frances Starr, and saw much of him during his fight with the Syndicate, it was not till *Polly with a Past* got under way, in 1915, that I began to know him. Some idea of the preliminary work on that I have already indicated. Not only was it tried out in stock, condensed from four acts into three, and then held up a year till we could get Ina Claire, but even after the spring tryout, including seven weeks' rehearsal in all, polishing still went on. One of many such letters shows the enthusiasm to which Belasco was always geared:

I have engaged another Clay and I think he much improves the cast. I am doing all sorts of things with our scenes [sets]. I am also sending a woman to Paris to get the latest models from Callot for Miss Claire's third act costume and Callot's dresses, you know, cost over five hundred a piece.

I want you and Mr. Bolton to do as much for your comedy as I am trying to do, and there are certainly some final touches to be made if we hope to carry off the comedy honors of the season . . . so as soon as Mr. Bolton gets back, come to me with both your coats off.

The Governor's very laudable habit was to rehearse in the sets, as soon as possible, so that the actors would become used to the "feel of the scene." That union rules made this an added expense mattered little to him. At an early rehearsal of *Polly* our first interior was thus set up. He gave one scornful look and hit the metaphorical ceiling. His sibilants hissed: "What is *that?* Why is that fetus in this flat?" And between more *why*'s and *what*'s he called out: "Matty, Matty— where is the ax?" The property man reached behind him and passed it over with perfect timing. (He told me he could always tell about when it would be called for.) Meantime the Governor had thrown off his black coat and, grabbing the fireman's ax, started swinging. As he let fly everybody got out of the way—especially the authors. Two or three long gashes completely ruined the canvas. He threw the ax down, triumphantly turning to the undisturbed scenic artist: "Now I guess I'll never see that fetus again!"

He breathed hard a few moments. The carcass was removed. A lot of us, of course, helped him on with his coat. The chair was replaced for him. He was handed his Japanese fan. The inevitable green bottle of smelling salts appeared. But, as he motioned the rehearsal to begin, he moved over to the still astonished authors and whispered: "Must keep these boys on their toes: I've got to pay for it anyway." Then he handed me a quarter. He was very superstitious. The gift took off whatever curse might be floating about. It probably went back to Chinese ways in his Frisco days.

At another time I was sitting in back, as a scene model was brought into his studio. It looked all right to me; but he wasn't satisfied. He blew up. In fact, he had seen some sets by Robert Edmond Jones the night before. And though *Polly* had been tried out he still desired to change the opening set for New York. I took down part of what he said, it was so revelatory. I found the copy in my notes the other day: here is a page of it, with a few fumigations:

"I have been near the top all my life, and I'm not going to fall back now. I'm not going to be made to look old-fashioned. They'll be glad when Campbell takes me. I know these young fellows are serious.

"When I came to New York I saw the sort of melodramatic acting that was going on and I helped put them all out of business then. Now they want to do the same with me. But I shan't let them.

"You know when a fellow's getting on he wants to push things a bit. I'm broke now; but I'm not going to let them beat me. . . . These young fellows are serious and are going to do things. We're going to have real competition from now on. I go see these young fellows. I see *real* rooms and *real* sets.

"But I'm going to sue every manager in New York about the way they've stolen my lights. All I want to show is that I was one of the first to use these things which the young critics praise because they say they've come from abroad. I'm getting all my things together and going to make lithos of them, if it takes my last cent; just so they'll know what I've done as a pioneer. . . . I've wasted a lot of time all my life paying attention to details, and as a result my plays have been heavy. . . .

"Think of the way they have talked about Pinero, these young snots. One of the greatest dramatists of England, with no recognition of what he did for the theatre.

"Sometimes I think I'll retire, sell my studio, and yet keep just enough going so the girls will think I still have something to give them."

I have quoted this because beneath the jumbled, undisciplined phrases, with their pettiness and cynicism, another rare quality is revealed. He did fear the younger generation. He heard it knocking on his door. It kept him awake. But he did not shut it out, as Solness tried to do in *The Master Builder*. He sought to find out what it had to say. He recognized its capacities and enthusiasms. He wanted to profit if he could. He was determined, by the example of his own productions if possible, not to let the younger men better him. That he often failed, under the test of newer standards time had remorselessly moved into the scheme, never kept him from striving.

But, as with the gestures of aging men, which through overeffort unwittingly betray the toll of time, so with him. He hated the thought of death. He would seldom admit its slow approach. He had things to do. He died at seventy-six still planning! David Belasco had the courage of his inner urge: magnificent courage. He was never disloyal to that. It is that which I most admired in him. The detractors have forgotten it—if they ever knew.

The Governor hated to rehearse until the members of the company had their parts "out of hand." So he made me take the company and break it in. This was as hard on the actors as it was on me. After two weeks he would sit out front, as we "ran the play through." He said nothing till it was over. Then he came on stage, hemmed or yessed and rearranged all the furniture. This automatically changed every position I had painfully worked out. I sat beside his efficient assistant, Burke Symon, who managed each morning to have all the changes neatly typed for the next day's work. Sometimes these got very complicated. With *The Other Rose,* in desperation, we used to go to Fay Bainter herself. She remembered every verbal variation. I never saw anyone quite like her.

I soon made a discovery: Belasco thought in immediacies. He was not interested in arrival, only in the going. When he altered lines I would call attention to the effect that would have on "something coming." He would smile: "We'll cross that bridge when we come to it." I soon learned to bide my time. The next day, before rehearsal, I would put my suggestion as though recalling something he had himself previously proposed. If he liked it or saw the error of what he had already done, he would pat me on the back to thank me for reminding him. I didn't fool him by my tactics; but it was a more comfortable method to get my way or let him retreat from his. Indirection can only be met by indirection.

Sometimes I got burned. Once I spontaneously objected to a change. He glowered: "I did that trick before you were born." He spoke so sharply that I nearly got temperamental myself, only Burke kicked my foot off the gas. Yet out of it I learned a lesson which has remained with me ever since. It came through an actor in the company—and a fine one, too: Herbert Yost. He saw me walking up and down behind the set, trying to cool off.

"I hope you won't mind my butting in," he said. "I heard what happened, and it was hard to take, I know. But may I make one suggestion?" He smiled and put his hand on my arm. "Never forget the end in view."

He was right. I wanted the production by Belasco, the experience, and the cash. Herb certainly said it at the right time. Never afterwards did "D. B." get under my skin. Maybe, when he saw he couldn't, he didn't try. "Never forget the end in view." It is a good motto in almost any enterprise where others are concerned.

Apropos of text changes Belasco appears as the author of many dramas. Often, too, his collaboration was hinted or implied by his producing a play, as George Kaufman's collaboration is today. But while his was often the guiding structural spirit in so-called situation plays, other types, where values lay in constant eye-tricking and ear-tickling, often were dialogued by others. One bizarre but typical episode I recall to illustrate how he might develop a scene; for it was on the stage rather than in the studio he was best stimulated. In fact, I soon came to believe he never really knew a script's potentials until the actors began to unfold it before him. He was always visually excited.

In a costume play he wanted a lady to call a man a coward. Belasco felt the straight phrase lacked period subtlety. He called Matty. (We used to bet that if Matty were asked to produce an elephant he would go into the property room and lead one out.) This time the Governor shouted:

"Matty, Matty! Get me a fan—a large fan, with feathers; yes, white feathers."

Presto—it arrived. Then Belasco gave it to the actress. "Here. . . . You have been fanning yourself . . . before . . . so . . . so . . . it won't seem like a device. . . . See? Fan slowly . . . See, this way. . . . Now . . . when he speaks— What is the line? Oh, yes! When he hesitates to go to fight for his country . . . You smile . . . Lady on top—claws underneath . . . See? Now—fan yourself. . . . That's it. . . . Look at

him . . . Look at the fan . . . Yes . . . Now you get an idea . . .
See? Feather? See? It's a white feather . . . See? Now you pluck one
out. . . . No emotion . . . Brain . . . Yes . . . Wait. . . . Now throw
it into the air. . . . No, blow it up—over your head . . . Yes. Natural
—as though amused . . . See? Now fan it. . . . Not too much. . . .
Fan it—and watch it as it settles slowly to the ground . . . You both
watch it. Now . . . you speak." He turned abruptly to the playwright:
"Now get me a line there for her to say." And for a hundred nights
the actress murmured what she thought of a man "who showed the
white feather."

Belasco's long experience gave weight to his instructive acting
direction. But much of the surface fluidity of his productions came
because he recognized it was the actor who finally carried the play's
interpretation. Primarily, he got results because he engaged the best
actors. He had sense enough to leave them alone. Belasco never dia-
grammed out stage movements, as some authors and directors do—
Shaw and Pinero had every move worked out. He gave the scenes little
advance study. He let each one develop as it came along, with the
chairs, tables, and sofas so located that movements up and down
stage would break naturally. Sentences, too, were bent or expanded to
put the actor at ease. Indeed, that was his first law. "Are you happy,
Fay?" he would ask. "How about you, Henry Hull?" If he noticed
certain sentences didn't come readily, he would have me change the
arrangement of the words.

"Oh, what a terrible thing to make a nice girl like Polly Shannon
say! George Middleton [exploding the -ton], I'm trying to protect that
little girl with the audience. I'm not thinking of your lines. . . . I
know a girl's heart. I once went to the morgue, and they let me hold
a girl's heart in my hand! . . . There's something human here that
I miss."

No volunteered suggestion from an actor would go unconsidered.
It was one of the keenest things about his direction, which included a
constant concern over tempo; for, as the play began to jell, he would
sit with fan in hand and make them run the lines. The words would
have to march or leap with the varied beats of his fan.

Aside from obvious stage mechanics, he aimed to get the author's
thought across—if the play had any: for plays which could be batted
about verbally weren't strong on psychology. No important play could
be. *Polly with a Past* and *The Other Rose,* like a dozen comedies he
successfully produced, were entertainments. The authors were content

to let the old master do his tricks. But what he added to such plays in warmth, color, and charm!

Once, during a rehearsal of a different type of play, *Accused,* I wrote out a few of his typical stage directions:

"Don't think: agree with him."

"You're talking to his brain: don't look at him."

"You bring the feeling of uncertainty with you into the room."

"Punctuate. Pause and yet no pause. Only a comma's worth. His hesitation makes you supplicate."

"You mustn't anticipate that. It's a new movement, and a new passage of interest."

"Almost get into the chair without the audience seeing it. They must be thinking of him, not watching you."

"Now you're building up the air of mystery."

"Now we're nearing it. This scene is final. Then comes change. A new interest suddenly builds up. That other scene was the end of the world. The iron curtain has fallen."

"This line is just as big as though we had the kick of an elephant."

"That's what I call a dangerous moment. Get over it quickly. Don't give the audience time to think."

"Each sentence here is a bullet. [*Stamping foot*] *Bang! Bang!! Bang!!!*"

But he had no tolerance with incompetence. When he saw faults or a bad stage habit, even with a star, he would often resort to his favorite indirection—oriental in its cunning and as cruel. I once saw him force an unimportant actor to a dozen repetitions of his scene, to convey a thesis on acting to the leading man—whose faults were indirectly commented on. Belasco thus got over what he wanted to the leading man without offending him.

I have already said that Eva Le Gallienne considers Ina Claire to be one of our best actresses. I heartily agree. The gifts her maturity now brings to any scene are rooted in an unerring instinct for stage effect, mellowed by an alluring personality. Polly Shannon, I believe, was her first legitimate part. She had an uncanny gift of mimicry, and was excelled only by Cissie Loftus, to whom I quite periodically lost my autumnal heart each time I saw her. Ina's acute ear thus made it possible for her to assume our French siren with perfect intonation.

After a lesson or two, her French was perfect. She could catch the tonal sincerities of almost any mood our text called for. But she then lacked stage strategy: the physical movement in a scene which focuses or expands as the values in a situation may require.

I am not sure how much Ina profited by a lesson in acting Fola and I saw D. B. give her; but it was a treat to us. Here was a great actor, for a moment or two slipping in and out of ebbing emotions, as he moved in and about the stage his improvised action required: acting that made us forget him as an old man, puffing hard in the inherent absurdities of what he was doing, amid the tide rip of his assumed excitement.

He told Ina to make a sweeping exit through the door. She turned to him:

"But, Mr. Belasco, I can't go out that door: there's a chair in the way."

He became icily polite as he said: "Miss Claire, when you've had more experience, you'll learn that on the stage *nothing* should ever be in your way."

Then, to illustrate, he dashed up the runway from orchestra to stage. He began to patch-quilt dialogue from his many plays—his eyes flashing and his white hair rumpled. He fell on a chair as though dying, with legs aimlessly distended and arms limp. Then he slipped easily to the floor—he had thoughtfully cushioned the place—moved over, turned, came to apparent consciousness, realized his imagined grief, beat his hands in agony amid sobs, rose slowly, half tottered to a large round table blocking the way. He edged up to this with his back against it, murmuring "Bernhardt," to show how his favorite actress would get about it. All the time talking gibberish, he slowly backed around it till he faced the door. Then with hand on high he sailed out amid more sobs. But without a second's pause he rushed back to the center of the stage, where Ina was supposed to start from. With more disjointed words, as he ill recalled our lines, he moved to the chair, majestically swept it aside, and strode out with a bravura cascade of words—as he wanted her to do.

We were watching spellbound, so dynamic was that electrically charged man, the master of his medium. We all—including Ina—burst into applause.

When he joined Fola and me in the orchestra he chuckled: "I guess that will give her something to think of." Yet he felt maybe he had offended Ina in front of the company, and his conscience (sometimes confused with his business sense) began to hurt him. Before the scene was over he had an expensive blue kimono brought down from his studio. He knew what a find he had in her, and he was afraid she might walk out on him. I'm sure she never really knew why she got the kimono. But trust Ina. She also knew what a part she had in *Polly*.

At our final dress rehearsal D. B. threw out a hand-carved telephone booth he had ordered. Lenore Ulric and Frances Starr—seated on different sides of the auditorium—didn't like the scene played around it; and they were right. We had rehearsed the action with a substitute screen. As so often happens, the effect of the booth could not be foreseen. Myrtle was to go into it and come out all hot, and we expected the sight of a perspiring heroine to disillusion the young lover. Instead, Belasco felt it visually "disgusting," and his two stars out front, in different parts of the house, agreed. So he called me on stage.

"George, you've got to get a better ending to this act. I don't intend to have this play ruined by such a disgusting scene. If you don't, we don't open tomorrow."

I nearly passed out. It was a situation Guy and I had planted with great care. But Guy was away frying other fish. Then and there D. B. ordered the booth sent to the storehouse ("Three hundred dollars worth of nice carving," Roeder remarked). He broke all his engagements that night. We worked four hours. I suggested that more anger and less perspiration might do the trick. So we locked poor Myrtle in a room. *Bang! Bang!! Bang!!!* on the door. He then had Polly sing again a little song she had done in Act I—always aware of the exploitation value of Ina's sweet voice. The curtain came down on sentiment and charm. Out of that midnight session evolved our second-act ending—where it was needed most. The Governor, too, could dip into the past in an emergency. I always suspected he might have done that ending also before I was born. At any rate in play writing a little memory is not a dangerous thing.

So rehearsals with Belasco were never dull. During the actual tryout he did not immediately go out front. He sat backstage where he could judge effects orally, and his secretary took down the notes he dictated. He was the only director I ever saw do this. After the fourth performance of *Polly,* however, we stood together in the back of the house.

Suddenly there was a ghastly stage wait. Cyril Scott had just said

to George Christie: "Ah, here's Myrtle coming in." He looked off for
Anne Meredith, who was playing the role. But no Myrtle. Scott, ever
resourceful, gallantly improvised, "Ah, I'd better help her out of her
car." He rushed off to find her, leaving Christie to fill in the empty
stage with eloquent *hem*'s and *hum*'s.

After what seemed like hours, Cyril rushed back, smiling but out
of breath. "I couldn't persuade Myrtle to come in," he panted, and
rushed over to poor H. Reeves-Smith, who was awaiting his cue, aware
of the fact everybody would think he was responsible for the wait.
Cyril pulled him on, and the play went on, too.

When the usual "notes" were given to the assembled company after
the performance, Belasco spoke of everything, except that stage wait.
I felt sorry for Anne. It was slow torture. Finally he ventured: "Anne,
you were a little late today."

Anne (who later became Lady Sackville and has spent many hours
every year showing itinerant American actors over the famous four-
teenth-century castle and family estates at Knole) burst into tears,
expecting to be fired.

"Oh, Governor, I went to my dressing room and completely forgot
that scene."

"I rushed all the way down to her door and banged on it," volunteered Cyril Scott, "and yelled for her to come on stage."

"But I couldn't," Anne blurted. "You see I didn't have a stitch on."

Belasco's eyes gleamed during a long suspensive pause. We all felt
so sorry for her. Lightning hovered. Thunder backed up. But he only
smiled sweetly, like Coquelin in *L'Abbé Constantin*. "That's all right,
Anne." Then, with a sudden satanic glitter, he turned to me.

"You see, George, that scene was no good anyway. I've been trying
for weeks to get you to take it out; but you were too stubborn. It's
out now."

All of this shows how some plays are rewritten and improved—
in spite of the author.

But it would be unjust to suggest that D. B. changed all scripts.
My adaptation of Brieux's thoughtful study of a lawyer's conscience,
Accused (*L'Avocat*), is one I know of. Too bad that circumstances
prevented the cuts needed for the American tempo; but here another
factor entered. It leads me to speak of one of the most delightful and
cultivated actors with whom I was ever associated.

With people he did not know well, E. H. Sothern had many

reserves based on a native shyness. His aloofness, which so many felt, was a defense. His inherent human sympathy peeks continuously out of his well written autobiography, his occasional verse, and an outstanding speech he made on a Founder's Night at the Players.

Of course I had known E. H. Sothern (I was now to call him "E. H.") many years at the Players, in the usual come and go of theatrical life. But it was in Paris, snooping about its odd corners with him and Julia Marlowe, or at their hospitable apartment in the rue de l'Université, that our friendship ripened. I soon felt at ease and sampled his rare humor, though it was not until Belasco engaged him to star (at 20 per cent of the gross) in my adaptation that I was to appreciate him at his full stature.

With a lifetime of stage experience—and I suppose I had seen him in everything from the old Lyceum light-comedy days through all his Shakespearean roles—he remained simple and humble toward his art. Never once in our relation did he presume on his eminent position, which I so respected. I can testify also to his kindliness, which still breathes through charming letters that I treasure.

A few lines from one or two letters * will convey the consideration he was to show while discussing my version:

It is good of you to let me make these suggestions and I am grateful.

I have no wish to push my own views for one can see how deeply you have considered it all and my suggestions are only on the way of helping to paint the lily so to speak.

Once more thanks for your tolerance and my prayers for a successful issue.

And the final words of the last letter I was to have from him: "All good and kind thoughts for you always."

Because of all this I shall always remember this association as one without a flaw, and I proudly guard the letter I received after his death:

* In one letter he wrote: "I want you to see some things I want to give to the Players club—pictures and curios about my father—some of his Dundreary clothes and the whiskers, eyeglasses, etc.—in case they would be acceptable. I don't want them to accept the things and then have them 'in corners thrown.' If there is room on the wall for my father's picture I have a lovely one of him. And also props belonging to Forrest, Booth, Edmund Kean, Charles Kean and so forth. Tell the librarian about it and see if he is receptive." I had long urged him to give these souvenirs to the club, and I am happy that they now safely rest there amid so many priceless treasures of the theatre's past.

BEAU RIVAGE PALACE, OUCHY, LAUSANNE
December 17, 1933

DEAR GEORGE MIDDLETON:

You had Edward's admiration and regard always, as you have had mine. Know how much I cared to have your sustaining message. Whenever we are in the same place let me see you—please.

Sincerely yours
JULIA MARLOWE SOTHERN

Although E. H. was in his middle sixties when *Accused* went on, his white hair belied the ruddy almost unlined face. With little make-up save the blackening of his hair, he easily passed for the man of forty in the play. Every movement kept the same early electric elasticity. Only on profile did the body show a middle-age sag, as he humorously indicated by an arrow to his tummy, in one of the casual sketches with which he loved to thumb-nail his notes. He had compared my version with the French original, and the modest verbal changes he had suggested, I, of course, agreed to. But when he walked into the green room for the first rehearsal he was already letter-perfect. It was to excite my wonder and prove my despair. For E. H. could not unlearn!

When Sothern and Belasco shook hands before the company I couldn't help recalling stage history: it was young David Belasco who, as stage manager, assisted young "Eddie" Sothern in his first starring venture at the old Lyceum Theatre—in 1885! I was playing then as a tot about those very streets, living but three blocks away. I used to see him come from the stage door as time went on. Almost forty years later they were working together again. He had now given the actor a wonderful cast. The performance, in fact, was to be flawless.

But I was embarrassed beyond words to have to take the company with two gorgeous directors as well as E. H. himself to be told what to do: Lester Lonergan and Henry Herbert. So we all agreed to help one another till the entire company had the parts out of hand. I had gone to Montreal to see a French troupe give the play, and so knew certain effects I could incorporate.

Following my custom with other plays, and knowing D. B.'s ways, I had made few cuts but rather had verbally expanded certain scenes in order that he might have his "room to work about in." Imagine my horror then at rehearsal to see—as did Belasco when he took over— that, with Sothern never leaving the stage from curtain rise to fall, we could make no cuts without wrecking him. On that basis D. B. rightly staged the piece within the limits imposed. Twenty minutes out of the play would have sharpened its intensities and probably made it more than a season's success.

Actors differ, of course; but E. H. was very nervous on stage. He admitted his first contact with an audience each night was always "disconcerting." The least thing upset him. Every position and bit of business had to be carefully timed and always the same. Chairs must never be moved, and all "props" must be checked—with "duplicates" hidden in odd places against accident or mislaying. If anything went amiss he would go up in his lines. This was not fussiness: it lay deep in the habit of a lifetime, which made each performance a highly concentrated, well ordered mental effort. He was not an improviser, like Noel Coward or Sacha Guitry, nor did he move in stage fluency, like Margaret Anglin and Fay Bainter. I never noted any variation in his performances: they were always literal and as minutely timed as they were intelligently composed. But over all lay the scholar's thought.

Aside from all the subtleties, which D. B. none the less got into stage movement and readings, there was one moment of direction I shall not forget. There he let his genius express itself. It affected no lines and solely concerned the opening of the second act. When the curtain rose and the dialogue started he stopped E. H. He turned to me and said, "George, you don't dramatize each situation enough." I had followed the stark economy of the French script. The audience knew that the lawyer had worked all night preparing his defense of a murder charge brought against the woman he loved. His conflict was over allowing his reputation for probity to be used to win his weak case—since he suspected her guilt. I had had the curtain rise, telling Sothern merely to walk up and down and express his mental agitation.

But Belasco rushed to the stage. He clapped his hands for Matty. It went something like this:

"Matty, Matty. [*Matty appears.*] This man is a lawyer—lawyer . . . Yes. [*Gazing about.*] That bookcase—the glass is covered . . . It has no books in it . . . Fill it with books . . . Open one of its doors. [*He does it himself.*] Take out several. [*He does it himself.*] He has been worried, hasn't he? . . . He has been wondering how he could save the woman he loves, hasn't he? . . . He's desperate . . . He loves her. His conscience is torn . . . Books . . . Get me larger ones . . . [*As he walks up and down large law books suddenly appear.*] That's it. . . . Now. . . . Open one here. . . . [*He does it himself.*] On table . . . Paper . . . Get me paper slips. [*He tears a French newspaper on table into long slips and puts them into several books to mark place.*] Throw one on floor by couch . . . It has nothing in it to help him. . . . All night he has worked—all night. It is morning now. Those curtains . . . Pull them to. [*He does it himself.*] The sun is up . . . He hasn't noticed it. See? Have a fan offstage to blow those curtains a bit . . . Have a shaft of sunlight come in—on wall. . . . The lamp— keep it on. . . . See? [*He turns desk light on.*] Papers on floor . . . Notes . . . Wait. . . . Pin some about. [*He does the way he pins his own play notes in studio.*] He mustn't forget that thought—it may save her. Cushions on floor . . . Throw some down. [*He does so himself.*] Throw that big one on sofa—ruffle it . . . See? [*He thumps cushions himself.*] He has thrown himself down on it to try to get some sleep . . . His head was there . . . See? [*He buries his fist in cushion to make impression of his head.*] There. . . . There. [*He stands surveying the room.*] There. That's how the room should look when the curtain goes up. That shows at once what the man has been through! Now any one can see, right away . . . [*To me.*] You don't dramatize enough, George. When will you ever learn?" [*George wonders, too.*]

The last time I saw David Belasco was in the rehearsal room beneath the stage of his theatre. About were hung the photographic records of all the plays he had produced. They filled the walls. I had come back after three years in Hollywood. I walked through the old familiar door, as I had so often done before. He looked up and smiled. He was seated there at the table where I had so often worked with him. About him were seated the same stage assistant, the same secretary, the same art director and electrician—fiddling with the same detail over a new play.

Only the author and the script were different.

CHAPTER XXII

FAMILY INTERLUDE:
A PRESIDENTIAL CAMPAIGN

WHEN I came back to New York from Europe in the summer of 1924, our comedy *The Bride,* with Peggy Wood as star, was at the Thirty-ninth Street Theatre, and the Democratic Convention was still running, with John Davis in the lead, at the Madison Square Garden. Out in Cleveland my father-in-law was being nominated for President by a gathering of Progressives.

For thirteen years, my Washington family had made me feel part of its varied activities. Mater had asked me to write for *La Follette's Magazine,* and my first article was on the Dramatic Museum which Brander Matthews had inspired at Columbia—unique in the historical stage data so carefully assembled. I became Literary Editor and for years had a weekly column entitled "Snap Shots" in which I gossiped about books and plays, with uncensored forays into politics and opinions. Though Mary, Fola's sister, was only ten when I had my first family dinner as an acknowledged future member, she at once became my ally. (Her son, Robert Sucher, was the only one of six grandchildren Pater lived to see.) Mary was interested in politics, of course, but found her personal expression in painting. Lincoln Steffens had recognized her gifts even as a child; and examples of her work later brought appreciation from artists and critics who saw it at various exhibitions. Bob, Jr., and Phil, the lads who had put on their first show for me in 1909 with monocles and top hat, had grown up to self-sustaining manhood with their public activities just ahead. Phil had married Isabel Bacon and was practicing law in Madison. Bob had become his father's confidential secretary, and a few years later married Rachel Young.

Through Pater himself, as I've told, I had learned how bitter could be the intolerance bred of war. He had also let me peep behind the scenes on other dramatic occasions, including the Teapot Dome scandal—the far-reaching investigation of which, he had initiated. In this 1924 Presidential campaign Pater likewise discussed with me some

intimate decisions of political strategy or analyzed the problems inherent in any third-party movement: the mere conflicting technical
and legal difficulties, for example, of getting the name of any independent candidate on the ballot in each state, as well as the delicate
tactics necessary in selecting local and state candidates, from dog-
catcher and sheriff up. He opened for me the doors of a political
laboratory and explained many formulas inherent in our democratic
process, devised more or less by the politicians to preserve the two-
party system. His study door remained always open to me, and as I
passed he would often call out: "Come in, Mid, and let's have a powwow." How I should welcome that call today!

But what I remember most warmly is that, whatever he may have
felt about my political immaturities, it never lessened his appreciation
of my loyalty and affection. Even amid important demands he never
made me feel that my reactions were unimportant. It was the quality
of the man. He really cared about what the other fellow felt.

The story of that 1924 campaign, in which I now became absorbed,
is Fola's to tell in her father's biography. It will include a family story
quite unique in political records. Phil, then twenty-seven, and Bob, Jr.,
twenty-nine, I now watched step out upon the national scene. Bob
was his father's personal campaign manager: he traveled in the special car and sat by his side at each meeting, guarding his energies.
He had his fingers on the pulse of every campaign headquarters.
Phil was to precede his father at many of the capacity meetings,
thus early winning his spurs upon the platform. Mater, too, went
on the stump, making an early speech in Town Hall, New York: the
first time, I believe, a Presidential candidate's wife ever so spoke in
her husband's behalf. When illness forced Mater to stop, Fola took
over her speaking schedule. Having heard them all I admit, confidentially, that Fola was second to no other La Follette in eloquence.
I record these family facts, aside from a speech or two I also made,
to indicate how exciting were these months while I was also carrying
on my trade.

For me it was naturally an outstanding experience to have a Presidential campaign in the family. I soon realized—a bit cynically, perhaps—that proportion is retained in politics, as in life, only by remembering the boos amid the cheers. The lights I saw blazing in La Follette's honor had been bonfires under his effigy seven years before.
No man, in fact, during forty years of public life had encountered
such twists of circumstance—beyond the power of a dramatist or a

movie writer to make plausible. Here was my chance to make a throbbing study of audience reaction, if only how at different times one public man could arouse such varying degrees of hate and affection.

I went with him to a half-dozen meetings, as a spectator of the hullabaloo which surged about. It fascinated me to observe the push of devoted admirers, the backslapping of those who might wish to be earning their right to "a place on the platform," or the minor candidates who wanted occasion to say "only a few words" to the huge audience they could not themselves draw. All these were fringed by cynical reporters who knew that campaign news lives on personalities, surmises, editorial abuse, partisan praise, and other "baloney," and that, while the vital issue for the average candidate may be to get into public office or stay there, a nod must be given to the many who are unselfishly prompted by a desire to serve in the public interest. No stage play could embrace all the changing daily dramas I felt were framed in that American election. What was claimed and hoped, for example, shot my thoughts ahead to what would or might be. Such a moment, I recall, was best pointed when La Follette met with Sam Gompers, as the A. F. of L. for the first time officially pledged its support to a Presidential candidate. As I listened to these two veteran fighters I thought what might occur if labor's four million votes could be delivered. What if other groups similarly pledged to support our man—estimated at nearly a dozen million—came through?

But already I was seasoned enough to know what was more likely to happen through the confusions wrought by skillful propaganda, with a predominantly hostile press and our lack of a large campaign fund and a down-to-the-roots organization. Honest or understandable doubts would soon stalk among the salaried groups with the fear of "losing the job," the difficulties in many states of splitting the ticket, and other political imponderables entering the mass mind under "local conditions." So, however deeply my sympathies were engaged, my training as a dramatist made me sensitive to the piling up of each day's suspense while the campaign advanced towards the November curtain. But nothing could curb my zest in those passing excitements. I was grateful for my seat in the wings.

La Follette opened his campaign in the Madison Square Garden which I had seen built, and on whose wind-swept tower I had seen Diana mount. I walked beside him that night from the entrance to the platform. Twelve thousand pairs of eyes fixed on the man beneath the snow-powdered pompadour, now near seventy, smiling, happy at the cheers. In that very amphitheatre when I was sixteen, I had watched a young Bryan come out of the West; and I remember how odd it seemed nearly thirty years later, even amid such campaign delirium, that I should be walking towards that platform with another Presidential candidate equally loved and hated. What twisting circumstances through the intervening years had led my feet to keep step that night with his!

One open-air meeting had its special personal thrill; for I was in his car when, escorted by a motor cycle squad with screeching horns, it whisked him at full speed through halted traffic, to the awaiting thousands at the Yankee Stadium. My eye kept picking out the scenes of fading episodes in those New York streets I had loved for their rich panorama of life. How often I as a lad had gaped at just such cavalcades of mounted police at the gallop, hedging the open carriages of hat-raising candidates. In such conspicuous moments as I was to live through with Senator La Follette I could not forget their sharp contrast with the concealments that same lad had once sought. There was always to be a conscious rim of irony around such exaltations.

How the old war horse tossed his head and, with all his eloquence, faced as tumultuous a reception there and everywhere, even hostile newspaper men told me, as any candidate had ever received! My experience of the intense evangelical zeal he threw into that campaign was an unforgettable one. This was his last appearence on a public platform.

There is a catharsis life itself brings, through some men at some moments in their lives, that is as moving and as purging of littleness in the beholder as the ancient Greek dramas of the gods and heroes. One is the better for having felt deeply through them. I knew, during that campaign, such moments.

Eight months later he died, planning further fights ahead. His family was with him, as he would have wished. Afterwards I stole down into the darkened room, alone, where he lay. Only the sun edged the drawn curtains. No one ever knew I stood long by his side. I felt all the intimations of such an hour. Even in a professional writer some thoughts are too deep for words. But one thought he had expressed to me I may recall now as I did then.

It was almost the last time I talked to him. It was late at night. We were alone. He was speaking of his life; he seemed, as he looked back, almost prouder of what his children had become and might be than of any of his own accomplishments.

"I'm not leaving them much money," he said. Then his lips tightened as they often did under stress of feeling, and his eyes flashed, "But, Mid, I think I'm leaving them a pretty good name."

Even his bitterest critics would not deny him that.

We all went to Wisconsin on the special train with him. Crowds were at the passing stations. "They brought Bob home on his shield," a reporter wrote in the *Chicago Tribune,* which had always bitterly opposed him. He lay in state in the Capitol at Madison. I watched the lines of folks who believed in him and loved him—fifty thousand of them in the one day—pass the flag-draped coffin. They seemed to think of what he had meant to each one. Parents brought their children from over the state—"so they could remember his face," as one said. Never before had I been so a part of massed grief. Again the spirit of the lad in his teens who had passed by the bier of Henry George stood by me. How life ties up!

He was buried quietly, under an oak tree. There, every year on the June anniversary of his death, a memorial meeting has been held. I was to read a poem about him that I had written and to speak, as I did on another occasion in John Haynes Holmes's church in New York. But while I could speak of some things I have told here, I never could phrase what his outgoing warmth had meant in my life, or what a world, through him, Fola had brought me.

The statesman belongs to history: what the man meant to me is mine. I have been content throughout to leave appraisal to others: the emotion he inspired in me properly enters into this story.

Mater would not become a candidate for his unexpired term. Admittedly she could have been the first woman ever to be elected to the United States Senate. She preferred to carry on his work in *La Follette's Magazine* (later renamed *The Progressive*). She was to begin his biography. On her sudden death, some years later, it became Fola's to complete. Bob, Jr., ran for his father's seat and was elected. He was just thirty, then the youngest man ever to become a Senator. As it turned out he was to serve longer than his father. The copper plate which had been tacked on his father's desk was embedded on his. I recently noticed it had begun to wear smooth, with the books and papers which have rubbed over it in the forty years a La Follette has sat in the United States Senate. Through Bob and

Phil, who moved into the Governorship of Wisconsin for three colorful terms, I have kept a continuing personal interest in the events and
actors on the national scene.

It remained as much theatre to me as in the early days when I first
moved into its more personal orbit. And nothing in Bob's long congressional career was more tinged with dramatic irony than that his
defeat—by a few thousand votes in the primary on August 13, 1946—
should have come only a few days after the passage of his Congressional Reorganization Act. Following many months of study and
extensive committee hearings, under his chairmanship, Bob had ma-
neuvered it to the floor and strategically steered it through an amazed
but consenting Senate, to the unanimous applause of a nation's press.
In order to secure its passage and to contribute what he could to other
vital legislation then pending, at the season's end, he had deliberately
chosen to remain in Washington rather than return home to campaign
for renomination. "My record is my platform," he said. There it was—
and is.

But Bob, a realist, knew the rip tides and cross currents sweeping
over postwar American politics. Weeks before the election he had
accurately appraised to Fola and me the campaign of falsification and
misrepresentation which the extreme right and left groups, though
opposed to each other, would employ successfully against him if the
independent electorate, on whose votes in large part he had always
relied, should be apathetic and stay away from the polls—as hundreds
of thousands of them did. In a public statement, when the result was
known, he gallantly said:

"Naturally I am disappointed that I did not receive the nomination; but I have no regrets or bitterness in my heart. I want the
people of Wisconsin to know that I deeply appreciate the opportunity
they have given me to serve them during the last twenty-one years in
the United States Senate.

"I have served to the best of my ability during these years and I
have always realized that an elective office is not a vested right but
rather a temporary honor and privilege accorded to the citizens of a
democracy. I sincerely thank all who gave me their support in this
and in past elections."

A letter I wrote to Bob immediately after he was first elected in
1925 has the autobiographical value of a contemporary hope and belief
in the future I was so amply to see realized. So I quote it as I close
these family annals:

DEAR BOB:

I need not tell you how deeply I feel what has happened to you. It comes all the more to my heart because you so richly deserve the recognition of all you gave into the great life that has gone on. I loved your father very deeply; he caught my imagination and filled it from the day I first heard of him—long before I even met Fola. All those who touched his life closely felt his great spirit, and no one is better qualified to have it breathe into a continued living force than you.

We all know how that memory will spur you on; we all know, too, how he would want you to carry on into the new things that time and place will bring. What *was* must continue to inspire you; nothing can excel the high integrity and courage of that inspiration; but your father made much of his success by growth and study; so you must keep looking ahead and making your own path into the future now so brilliant and beckoning.

I also love you deeply, Bob; I have the greatest faith and belief in all you can and will do. I just want to tell you what you must know in your inner heart: that your responsibility to a great memory must not alone be enough; you must grow with an open mind to each new circumstance. The politics of it all will be easy for you—no one knows them better. And you have lived through courageous days and been tested. You are ready for the great undertaking.

Good luck to the splendid harvest that will be at hand. How happy Fola and I are . . . for nothing could have pleased your father more. . . . How well he built. . . . It is ever with me.

MID

CHAPTER XXIII

TROUBLE IN OUR MARKET PLACE

WHEN I turned, in 1925, from the national stage, so personal to me, the theatre seemed small. Yet in its market place was my work-world, amid whose ill regulated traffic I pedaled and sold my wares as managers' caprice then decreed. It is natural that academic critics appraising a play have seldom considered the effect of this motley market place upon the author and his output. Who hung up the rules by which the script was cast or staged? Did power alone have the final say as to the integrity of his text? Did the circumstances under which it was produced bring out its essential qualities, help or hurt it? Did the author get his full penny's worth out of his occasional successes so that he could eat through subsequent failures? Was he, in other words, short-changed out of any of his legitimate rights? What were his rights, anyway? And what were the manager's? This phase of the theatre, as an institution, has seldom been taken into account by stage commentators, though the surrounding atmosphere always affects any perspective.

Dramatists had spasmodically sought a more vigorous control over production canditions; but we did not become effectively aroused until the fall of 1925. How we protected ourselves against new and startling invasions of our rights is one of the most picturesque unwritten tales in the theatre. Some program notes about a few of the contrasting personalities will supply a necessary back-drop to the battle.

Vivid then, and still alive, were two sturdy survivals of an earlier ruthless, clashing, and now nearly forgotten theatre. A. H. Woods was only a producer; William A. Brady, like Belasco, had been actor as well. Both Woods and Brady were born gamblers; both knew what it was to be penniless and rich; both had come up from the soil, and some of it stuck. Both had marked personalities.

Brady was long the eloquent spokesman for the theatre's business interests. Politics and prize fighting, having a common ring strategy, were his meat. His racy anecdotes of both were told with broad Irish humor which never braked his easy emotionalism: for often I have

heard him on the verge of platform tears. But this was the stuff of
acting; it was as a barnstormer that Bill first learned about audience
reactions, by taking the beatings with the bouquets; here, too, he
first directed. It was said, "Give Bill Brady a mob to stage and
he is in heaven."

No such picturesque type of theatre man survives today. Brady
knew backstage and front office; he pushed through both the hard
way. Compare the endowment of some present-day amateurs with
what such a rich if crude background brought to a production. Brady's
own contacts made him favor elemental, sentimental, and melodramatic stories. Knowing this, we playwrights generally funneled
to him that sort of script, in spite of the more ambitious forays he
made for his wife, Grace George.

He had two famous successes: *Way Down East* and Jules Eckert
Goodman's *The Man Who Came Back*. Both made millions. Brady
circused the former. The vista of that earlier theatre opens up when
one recalls how it was then possible for "an old showman" to exploit
a play. Produced in 1896, this rural snowstorm drama toured for
twenty-two years! Often it had six companies. The total box-office
returns were over $14,000,000—more even than those of any motion
picture until *Gone with the Wind*. I might add that the author, Lottie
Blair Parker, sold it outright for $5,000.

Though we authors considered Bill as a hard businessman I early
found he was full of sentiment. His greatest ambition was to make
Grace George a famous star. Recently in Washington, Fola and I
were walking with her to the hotel after seeing her in *Spring Again*.
I told her of a curtain speech I had heard Bill make, at the turn of
the century, on the opening of a play in which he had first starred
her, voicing his passionate faith in that young woman's future. And
now—forty years later—walking briskly between us to keep her nightly
long-distance date with her husband, the little lady had indeed become
a mistress of high comedy, playing in her late autumn with a facility
and subtle implication given to few of her younger sisters.

Al Woods was the most mysterious character on Broadway. I
would watch him edging rapidly down Forty-second Street to his
own theatre: hat turned down and collar up; hands deep in his coat
pockets. The wayward hair, his one good eye, his cynical smile flitting
in and out of an ever assumed humor, plus his picturesque profanity,
always fascinated me. He reminded me of the obvious character in
Treasure Island. Tradition said that he slept in a lighted room, and

that in early days he diabolically changed his underwear in a taxi, with the shades down, leaving the discarded garment to startle the next fare.

He was devoid of "book learning," but he got along. He made his own business rules and followed his own particular ethics. He once offered me a thousand dollars I didn't need and then went shy with me for weeks after I sent him some flowers in appreciation. But his ambition, he had told Owen Davis, was "to have a million dollars in actual cash." When he did he took Owen, whose popular-priced melodramas had helped make it, to his safe-deposit box to show the stack of bills. How Al later found the box empty is another story. Somehow that seems symbolic of the wide swing of his career and of another theatre epoch which could only have brought forth an Al Woods.

To read him a play, as I have said, was an adventure. His feet would sprout from the desk, his cigar puffing emotionally to the scene's tempo. His criticisms were elemental: he acted on a hunch. But nobody ever has thought out a better rule to guarantee a play's success. Al was one of the largest purchasers of scripts; in fact, I heard him boast of the number he bought without producing. One of my scripts helped to make up the two hundred or more he actually did produce—a developing pride soon entering into their selection. How romantic had been the possibilities in our theatre, that the man who early gave to the world *The Queen of the White Slaves* and *Secret Service Sam* could climax his career by bringing to America Sacha Guitry and Yvonne Printemps in the exquisite *Mozart!* There was nothing of a Belasco about him. He contributed little at rehearsal; he engaged the best directors and cast. Al was a merchant prince with a rumpled fedora. He paid and let nature take its course.

Nothing could better express our theatre's democratic hospitality than a Broadway anecdote based on some strange twist which had brought together Al Woods and Winthrop Ames, as possible partners in a play. The author came to summarize its plot to both.

"You see this —— —— is a dirty —— —— ——! See? He is nuts over a Moll, who thinks if she can rope the —— —— she can get the other —— —— to deliver the goods. See? So she pipes up to the —— ——: "You dirty, —— ——!""

Winthrop Ames, a refined soul and a Harvard Unitarian, interrupted:

"I beg pardon. But is it necessary to use such language?"

"Sure," replied the playwright. "I want Al Woods to understand it."

It was the art rather than the gamble of the theatre which brought
Mr. Ames behind the proscenium. (I never called him Winthrop.)
His thin, pointed, sallow face, with its keen eyes, bespoke a kind man
who, through some atavism, passionately loved the stage. With plenty
of money he of course became the magnet for special scripts. He could
write a charming rejection—I have quite a collection—and tempered
it with an "I might be wrong." Which he was with two of mine. He
had card indexes of all the performers he had seen and an uncanny
memory for a plot. He was a perfectionist, with exquisite taste. All
my friends who worked with him spoke of his unfailing courtesy.
I recall Archer's enthusiasm over *The Green Goddess*.

Whatever the business methods of certain other prominent producers whom I need not name, having the Theatre Guild or a man
like Henry Miller, Ames, young Brock Pemberton, William Harris,
Jr., Arthur Hopkins, or George C. Tyler see one's play through to
birth made its normal pains a joy. Of two of these I would say a
further word here.

Owen Davis summed up Arthur Hopkins not long ago: "A man
of dignity, George, who insists plays be real." His productions of the
Anderson-Stallings *What Price Glory* and O'Neill's 1922 Pulitzer
Prize play, *Anna Christie*, as well as most of Clare Kummer's joyous,
irresponsible so-like-her scripts, proclaimed a worthy merchant in our
market place. But above all must be remembered his no-contract
partnership with John Barrymore and *Redemption, The Jest, Richard
III,* and *Hamlet,* which came out of their only partially realized
dream of a repertory of stage classics: a high-water mark in our American theatre. In Gene Fowler's moving biography of Jack, *Good Night,
Sweet Prince,* are to be found phrasings of that dream which best
reveal Arthur's own hopes for it. Since that decade Arthur has known
all the seesaws of theatrical fortune, and now, in 1946, he has again
had an outstanding artistic and financial success: *The Magnificent
Yankee,* a play about Justice Holmes by one of my favorite playwrights, Emmet Lavery.* Yet throughout I've always found Arthur
the same: taciturn, with a wise smile and, for me at least, an eager
ear for Washington gossip. It is my loss that so far we have never had
a business association.

* Lavery's play *The First Legion* has recently been voted into the permanent repertory of the Comédie-Française, a unique distinction.

But the contrast of past and present could never have been more vivid than when I saw George C. Tyler, before his final illness. His office door, in the New Amsterdam Theatre Building, was open. Save for the rumble of Forty-second Street the empty room was quiet. But the reading glasses were on his desk. So I waited alone. At the side slept a tall, dusty cabinet from which protruded old scripts dating, I'm sure, from the early nineteen hundreds. On the walls were fading photographs of many he had managed, largely until 1918 under the firm name of Liebler and Co.; among them the gifted, never-able-to-make-up-her-mind Pauline Lord, for whom George had bought one of my plays. Instantly, from French days in 1927 there came back my trip to Contrexéville to read him the script, only to have him at once set me to work typing a letter to Mussolini, who had wished him to undertake an international dramatic festival!

The photographs spoke the stretch of George's activity. He was the first to bring to America the Irish Players, Mrs. Pat Campbell, Cyril Maude, Mme. Simone, Réjane, and Duse. He, too, had found Eleanor Robson for *Merely Mary Ann.* There was Helen Hayes, whose childhood letters, he told me, he had given to Princeton, where they now snuggle with hundreds from Booth Tarkington, Zangwill, Hall Caine, and his other pet dramatists. He made stars of Viola Allen in *The Christian,* George Arliss in *Disraeli,* Mrs. Le Moyne, Arnold Daly, and Lynn Fontanne. In his companies Alfred Lunt, Jeanne Eagels, William Faversham, William Hodge, Doris Keane, and Laurette Taylor first obtained outstanding recognition. There were older faces, too, staring at me: Mrs. Fiske, John Drew, James T. Powers, Henrietta Crosman, Margaret Anglin, and May Irwin, of his famous "all-star revivals," which gave a new refulgence not only to the great classics of comedy but also to veterans of a passing epoch. And there was Ada Rehan's co-starring tour with Otis Skinner. "I loved to bring back the old-timers," he once told me. They were there again for me that day; I had seen them all many times.

By some inexplicable association, I felt my emotion slowly mounting, and a warm glow filled me; it seemed akin to the reverence I had so often felt in Europe, as I stood silent and alone in its great cathedrals. But this glow was for the art of the theatre and for a high priest who had loved, served, and enflowered its altars, where from childhood I myself had humbly worshiped.

As I stood gazing out his window I could see across the street the theatres herded together which had housed his ventures. Seven of them in 1925—all movie houses in 1943, with "double features," flaming posters, and strange names no stage ever knew. When I went down to the street, after that last time I was ever to see George, I passed a flea circus almost next door! Even in 1925, truth was, such attractions had already begun to inch uptown, into our market place.

The varied backgrounds, racial stocks, and cultural roots of these and other producers were shared by us playwrights. Managers weren't all bright: but some writers had also run into the money through a curious flair where, on occasions, pure intelligence alone might have been a handicap. For instinct in play writing, as in love, may pay better than brains. Only in my own decades were dramatists to sport a college degree: Clyde Fitch, Edward Sheldon, Owen Davis, Robert Sherwood, Sidney Howard, Philip Barry, Arthur Goodrich, Percy MacKaye, to call a few at random. Some, too, with or without academic blessing, had earlier come into the theatre via the newspaper world like Channing Pollock, Maxwell Anderson, Lawrence Stallings, Jules Eckert Goodman, George S. Kaufman, Marc Connelly, Don Marquis, and A. E. Thomas. Others, like Eugene O'Neill and George Kelly, grew up in the theatre itself.

Authors and managers, with the actors and directors, made up our world. Let it be said at once that one could find in each group the same average individual probity, art, and intelligence. Scripts are poor things indeed without the actor's art and the director's skill. A play that is to come to life needs us all, plus an audience. The layman must grasp this mutual interdependence in order to understand what now follows.

In 1925, Arthur Richman, author of *Ambush* and *The Awful Truth,* was president of the Dramatists' Guild. Never ruffled, but with tenacity, humor, good judgment, and a sense of fair play, he was to prove an ideal leader. Early he had complained about the Guild's inability "to hold managers to our existing non-enforceable agreement." He and I thus first came together with a common sense of the Guild's futility. He called a Council meeting, at the request of Channing Pollock and John Rumsey, the agent, "who had important matters affecting all dramatists to disclose." There is no record of the half-dozen others who were there at Cosmo Hamilton's apartment.

What we learned set off a train of events which was to fill my next three years to the exclusion of nearly all else, to lead me twice to Europe for the Guild, and to widen my knowledge of the problems that faced writing men everywhere. But best of all it was to bring me new and closer friendships with many of my fellow playwrights here and abroad.

Yet even this was not the first effort which had been made to bring dramatists together. In 1878, Steele MacKaye, one of the remarkable theatre men of his day and father of our own Percy, wrote, "The time has come for the organization and founding of a society of American dramatists somewhat on the plan of the well-known society in Paris." He later joined with Clay M. Greene in the short-lived American Dramatic Authors' Society to secure protection of their works. But the first effective group was founded in 1891 by Bronson Howard, who became its president. This Society of American Dramatists and Composers was in reality the granddaddy of the present Dramatists' Guild of the Authors' League. Though it started as a social group with thirty-three members, "in a spirit of fellowship and for whatever artistic or business ends discussion and experience might support," Howard's fight, in 1896, revolutionized the status of dramatic ownership. With a small committee he had invaded Congress to try to amend the copyright act; later he succeeded in revising many state laws. Play piracy thus became a punishable crime. No single dramatist ever made a greater contribution to his fellows.

In April, 1913, the 350 members who had answered the first roll call of the Authors' League of America included about a dozen playwrights.* As my book of one-act plays, Embers, made me eligible, I had joined in the preceding February; later I became a life member. Only three dramatists were on the Council of thirty, and none on the Executive Committee. Quite rightly the League could then center on but a few problems: copyright protection, both international and domestic, and the legal rights and remedies pertaining to all business relations with publishers and editors. Not until October did the Council include the dramatic field, at the urging of Owen Johnson; and it was over a year before the first "dramatic subcommittee" was appointed: Bayard Veiller, Harvey J. O'Higgins, Edwin Milton Royle, Edgar Selwyn, and myself, now the only survivor. Our initial task was to work "toward the standardization of the dramatic contract" between managers and dramatists.

Back of Bronson Howard's copyright fight had also been a plan for a "model contract." But he soon gave up the effort, as theatrical

* The facts are drawn from the official records, as published in the Bulletin, passim.

E. H. SOTHERN IN "ACCUSED"

Produced by Belasco

SENATOR LA FOLLETTE, WITH HIS SONS, BOB, JR., AND PHIL, AND
GEORGE MIDDLETON, IN THE 1924 PRESIDENTIAL CAMPAIGN

MARY LA FOLLETTE

conditions were then too chaotic to be boxed into a formula. In 1915, however, we ventured our model: the first, such as it was.* Admitting it was subject to changes "to meet special conditions," we boldly published its thirteen clauses, some of which today have become part of the accepted code. It was sprinkled with spunk, though we naïvely added that "as long as its terms and stipulations are followed with tolerable fidelity [!] it will be found a trustworthy instrument." We also suggested six "warnings to dramatists." But, feeble as this now seems, here was the *first* effort to stake out the ill defined rights of our small membership. The playwrights outside our group gave it the cold shoulder; the managers, a boot.

Another attempt came two years later. A committee headed by Cosmo Hamilton, in which Edward Childs Carpenter and Channing Pollock began their yeoman service to dramatists, drew up a new "standard contract." While some individuals were cooperative, those who dominated the powerful Managers' Protective Association (M.P.A.) resented our "gall." I believe it was at this time, during an informal meeting with a half-dozen managers, that Owen Davis said, "Why, there's *one* manager here now who owes me over a thousand dollars in back royalties." The next day, to his astonishment he received checks amounting to more than five thousand dollars from four of those who had been present. They all apologized for the "oversight"!

Augustus Thomas soon brought a message from Lee Shubert, M.P.A. vice president, that the Shuberts would "close their theatres sooner than sign the proposed contract." Lee also squashed our effort for a settlement by insisting that managers would treat with authors individually and in no other way, and that the part of good business was for a manager to get the best and most he could. We were indignant; we threatened "a white list"—we would give first choice on our scripts to those who signed. But we didn't say we would not submit to those who did not sign. We boldly hinted we *might* take "concerted action." So we published the contract for "educational effect." † Then we went on sputtering, while business went on as usual.

When the Actors' Equity struck, in 1919, for recognition and a Basic Agreement with the managers, our plays got caught in the crush. Being helpless bystanders between two tightly organized fac-

* Text in *Bulletin*, Nov., 1915.
† *Bulletin*, Aug., 1917.

tions, we herded together for protection. Channing Pollock's original suggestion that we dramatists in the Authors' League be allowed to form "an autonomous committee" was belatedly granted by the Executive Committee. Thirty-two new "working dramatists" joined and a "Dramatists' Committee" of one hundred twelve was created. Out of this the Dramatists' Guild was born. Channing was midwife and then its first chairman.

To make the Guild an integral part of the League, however, our Constitution had to be revised. I was happy to be asked to represent the dramatists. The League became "a sort of holding company or a federation of Guilds." Owen Davis, who had the confidence of all groups, logically became our first Guild president. The years have given ample testimony of his dedication to the theatre he still loves at seventy-plus with an absorbing passion.*

Once again we went after that Standard Contract, and succeeded mainly, as the records disclose, through the efforts of James Forbes, Roi Cooper Megrue, and our persistent chairman, Channing Pollock. It was rumored that Owen whispered in the proper managerial ears that the Guild, like Equity, "might join the A. F. of L."—a thistly idea that the League itself had fingered and quickly dropped four years before. This new threat, which was only a bluff, sent such shivers down certain spines that creeping paralysis alone would then have prevented the new standard contract between the League and the M.P.A.

In spite of some modern improvements, however, the agreement had two fatal defects: *its use was not mandatory, and its terms were not enforcible.* Neither individual managers nor authors were required to become members of their respective organizations, and nobody could be penalized for not using it—nothing except hisses could prevent its protective clauses from being red-inked. Some firms, in fact, soon made the contract a gory mess. Truth was, the Guild patted itself on the back to keep from admitting this. It still floated in the lofty realm of moral suasion, while managers and actors had already

---

* Edward Childs Carpenter (who succeeded Owen) was vice president, with Jerome Kern, representing our composers, the first secretary. The Council was: Porter Emerson Browne, Eugene Buck, Edward Childs Carpenter, Owen Davis, Anne Crawford Flexner, James Forbes, Avery Hopwood, Montague Glass, Cosmo Hamilton, Otto Harbach, Louis Hirsch, Aaron Hoffman, Anthony Paul Kelly, Jerome Kern, Edward Locke, George Middleton, Channing Pollock, Edwin Milton Royle, Mark Swan, A. E. Thomas, Augustus Thomas, Rita Weiman, and Rida Johnson Young. Later Bronson Howard's society affiliated with the Guild, and the two groups, with the same officials, were known for a time as "The American Dramatists."

realistically dug in for self-leverage on the more solid ground of organized power.

When the Actors' Equity Association, which had been recognized, proposed its "Equity shop" our Guild lined up futilely with the managers to fight it. Equity intended that none of its members should act in any company which was not composed exclusively of Equity members. Our Guild hysterically joined the cry that this meant a "closed shop." We bitterly condemned the "czaristic actors." We even adopted a "statement of principles," which now makes comic reading:

The principle of the Dramatists' Guild of the Authors' League of America Inc. is that no matter how great its power may become, the Guild will never desire the closed shop; the Guild will never induce a Manager to produce plays only by members of the Guild; the Guild will never endeavour to force any other Dramatist into the Guild, but will only ask him if he care to join; the Guild will never refuse membership to any serious minded playwright who cares to join the organization.

So much heat was set up that no protest of mine would have availed had I been in America. But it was with amazement and chagrin that, weeks later, I read this polite and unrealistic manifesto in the *Bulletin*. At that very time, in fact, I was confirming in Paris my earlier knowledge of what a tight Authors' Society in France *had* done to protect the rights of its members. They already had an enforcible Agreement, which our Guild so far had not had the boldness to demand nor the strength to achieve.

On my return, therefore, when I was placed on a committee to try to prevent another strike to enforce the Equity shop, I stated in the New York *World* (March 27, 1923):

If the firing begins we [dramatists] can only sit on the side-lines and be the perforated goats. What we think of the merits of this whole controversy has therefore little force, since it lacks a punch back of it—at present. Without power opinions are mere phrases; power only respects power. Our action can only be individual and so, ineffectual, since, frankly, we are as yet by no means unanimous.

Until an economic situation arises which forces us authors into a close organization we are only a lot of languid lilies with good intentions; until we have as strong an organization, watching only our interests, as have the actors and managers, we can merely smile sadly when we are about to be sat on.

Such, in hasty outline, was the bumpy background, for the "economic situation" which arrived with bells on two years later. John Rumsey of the American Play Company rang them in our startled ears that night I've spoken of, at Cosmo Hamilton's. He brought convincing data that certain managers, with the Fox motion picture company, were already using a form contract which would seriously lessen the authors' share in the film rights of their plays. Our dear old 1920 contract was not only violated: it was dead. It had suddenly become a museum piece.

Yet it cannot be tucked away in a glass case, with the other contracts, without a word of tribute to those who made them possible. Each had progressively pegged out rights from which there would be no retreat. Each League member who gave even a mite to that end, since its organization, has an implied credit mark throughout this record.

That night, as Arthur Richman and I walked home from our little meeting, we took stock. We must move on beyond our old contract since it was not geared for the hills ahead. We had realized that a myriad of little abuses had slowly weakened it. What a few managers were now cooking up, with a powerful film firm, as I shall explain, had dramatically exposed the weakness of our whole set-up. Further the M.P.A., with which we had drawn the now much abused "standard contract," had itself been split into opposing factions since the Equity fight. So our fancied securities were not even partial retreats. Now was our chance!

Raiders were abroad. Yet we had no arms. We weren't even a cohesive pack. Truth was, in the past four years, many members had dropped out or become indifferent, feeling, quite rightly, that the Guild had little of value for them. Scores of leading playwrights had never even joined our organization, as neither self-interest nor a desire to cooperate had forced or persuaded them. We had no money. But we had a grievance. If we could dramatize it we knew we could make the pocket nerve of every dramatist jump.

That night one fact was also clear: nothing could be accomplished unless *all* the leading dramatists would band together. Yet, because of the unfortunate attitude the Guild had taken towards the Equity shop, we faced an admitted hostility within our own house towards anything which savored of a union. Thus there was really but one problem: to convince our fellow writers that now they *must* get together in as tight an organization as the French dramatists or even, ironically enough, as the very Equity they had opposed. It presented nice difficulties; but, once they were overcome, the rest would be easy. A play was the cornerstone of the theatre. On its primary need of a script we might build our own bombproof shelters.

So we got busy in the market place with our surveying kits, plumb lines, fresh mortar, and, I may admit, whatever bricks were handy.

CHAPTER XXIV

WE COLLECT AUTOGRAPHS AND
GIRD OUR LOINS

SIX YEARS after the then impending battle was over, Shaw wrote me about the Dramatists' Guild.

In 1927, I had signed him as a member, in London; and he has always observed his obligations though castigating us for the concessions he thought we should not have made at the time we were organizing. Yet the cause of his complaints, in a degree, had initiated the very fight on which we were embarking. To grasp how threatening to us was the entrance of motion picture companies into play production, under the specific Fox proposal, the reader may not mind having a doffing how-d'-do with the accepted author-manager relationship; and Shaw's caustic letter, perhaps, will best open the way to a simple understanding of it:

4 Whitehall Court, S.W. 1
30th Dec. 1933

DEAR MR. MIDDLETON:

Your Guild seems to me the worst calamity that has ever overwhelmed our unfortunate profession. Instead of resolutely keeping our various rights separate and independent, and giving no countenance to the assumption that a manager with a performing right is entitled to a rake-off on the film rights and all the other rights he has ever heard of, the wretched League actually draws up a Basic Agreement in which this assumption is recognized, accepted, and regulated.

Why is it that an American cannot believe in the possibility of any business transaction being possible until he has induced half a dozen totally unconnected and irrelevant persons to accept a rake-off on it?

It will be impossible for British authors—imbecile as most of them are in business matters notwithstanding—to go on working with your League if it persists in selling all the passes to the enemy for nothing in this fashion. Your Basic Agreement isn't good enough for a three-year-old British baby.

Your all the same quite friendly
G. BERNARD SHAW

Even in 1941, he again wrote me that the Guild

has conceded to the managers an interest in all new rights which it should have defended in their integrity in the last ditch. It is [in] effect a manager's agency.

No American author, however, has ever retained in their entirety the "rights" of which Shaw speaks; he has exacted a contract which we never could have demanded in 1926 for all playwrights, big and little. Our first Basic Agreement put a floor but no ceiling on production conditions. If the manager consented, an author could obtain even Shaw's terms—which generally retained every right except that of regular stage performance; in joining the Guild, however, each member had to agree to accept no lower terms than those it had negotiated with the managers. While we knew a minimum basic agreement would tend to become maximum, we felt we must first get an enforcible contract and then improve it—as, in fact, we since have done. Any ship must often tack to arrive in port. Besides, there were strong reasons why Shaw's so-called "passes to the enemy" had come about in the United States.

To take but one example, the present system of royalty percentages on "performing rights" was no ordained gift to playwrights: it worked out episodically in a chaotic theatrical set-up, where the rules jelled slowly.* A century ago *Metamora,* which served Forrest for four decades, brought its author only the initial $500 he won as prize money. The man who dramatized *Uncle Tom's Cabin* received a watch for his job; even Harriet Beecher Stowe, on account of the lack of protection in the copyright law, only got a free box to see the show. Up to David Belasco's day many writers were "staff playwrights," "resident" or "house" authors, hired to "fix up" vagrant scripts or older plays. By agreement they had to turn over everything they wrote to the manager. Bartley Campbell, a popular author of our granddaddies' melodramas, at one time received a weekly salary of $25, and $10 for

---

* Margaret Webster's scholarly *Shakespeare Without Tears* speaks of a playwright's fees. There were no continuing royalties. Authors got from £4 to £6 for an entire play, which would be around $100 today. A few shillings were paid for revising old plays or for added scenes (this work is somewhat akin to the "added dialogue" for which thousands of dollars are now paid in Hollywood). Plays were done in repertoire, and changed rapidly; forty performances, in the three or four years a play usually lived, was a record run. Shakespeare made his money mainly through being a shareholder in the theatre. He collaborated on many scripts to turn them into successes, and not to confuse the scholars.

each performance of his script. A flat sum was long the rule. Those interested in one author's financial returns, during this transition period, can find a detailed record in *Epoch*,* Percy MacKaye's absorbing biography of his father, Steele MacKaye. Though under a yearly salary with the owners of the Madison Square Theatre, which required him to do everything imaginable, he received no royalty from *Hazel Kirk*, one of the most successful plays of all time. MacKaye's name was left off the programs as author, while the management made several million dollars from its more than five thousand performances.

Richard Mansfield, in 1889, paid Clyde Fitch $30 a week in salary to write *Beau Brummell*, and $7.50 for each performance, until the total reached $1500; then the play passed to the actor to serve him, as it turned out, the rest of his life. Aside from numerous cases in which playwrights had sold their scripts outright—for sums varying from $500 to $10,000—special types of royalty arrangements were also practiced. Owen Davis explained his arrangement to me: on his long series of "popular-priced melodramas," which circled for years around the well established Stair & Havlin "wheel," Owen got 8 per cent of the "company's share." As this was 60 per cent of the weekly receipts, which averaged over $4,000, Owen banked from $125 to $250 on each play. Since he sometimes had a dozen plays running, the young Harvard graduate and future Pulitzer Prize winner (1923, with *Icebound*) didn't do so badly.† Yet even then royalties paid to French dramatists were far beyond those any American author could command. I recently saw the contract Kathryn Kidder made in 1893 with Sardou for the American rights of his *Madame Sans-Gêne*, which Réjane had done in Paris. He got $2,500 advance royalty against 8 per cent up to $5,000 and 20 per cent on all over!

* Originally commissioned by Boni & Liveright, the publishers, to consist of 80,000 words, for which the author received $500 in advance royalty, it took four years of research, in which his wife, Marion MacKaye, shared. The final manuscript, as submitted, had nearly a million words. After being cut to meet the two-volume requirements, it was published just as the 1928 depression hit the book trade. It turned out to be indeed a labor of love; for Percy told me that he had never received any royalty beyond the initial advance.

† Owen wrote his hundreds of plays in long hand, and the typist who started doing them as a young woman has done them throughout his career. He didn't save the original scripts, because his apartment became too small, as he put it. "You know, George, there were only three tried and true formulas for those audiences: the Western, which was the good sheriff against the outlaws; the Prodigal Son and the Magdalene. But," he hastily added, "you had to make her suffer a lot for her sins before those out front could be asked to forgive her."

These few random examples will suffice to show the lack of standard royalty rules; and it might also be added that, even where they were stipulated, there was practically no way to check on them. This lack of uniformity applied to all the other contractual terms and conditions between authors and managers, equally unenforceable.

When I began writing, in 1902, a sliding scale of royalties, based on the total box-office receipts, was the accepted system. Clyde Fitch by then could thus command more royalties in one week than all *Beau Brummell* brought him. But few new authors could be sure of getting a whiff of even the 5 per cent flat, which decency thought proper. Meantime, as I've said, factional fights among producers had increased the need of theatres, companies, and plays. The manager who first produced the script took to handling and leasing all subsidiary rights, which likewise had increased in an expanding theatre. I can find no protest against this by any author. I myself recall that it seemed natural to divide all the "extra take" with the manager, 50-50.

When silent pictures caught everybody unawares and cash was actually offered for these new "film rights," the old 50–50 division, then the accepted trade custom as to other rights, was automatically extended. No one of us thought we were giving the managers a "rake-off," as Shaw puts it: we thought we were splitting up unexpected manna from heaven. I remember my own pocket emotion when I accepted $200 for a play long since entombed. Few, in fact, had any idea at first how valuable film rights would become. George C. Tyler told me the first play to be filmed, in 1905 (in a thousand feet), was *Raffles,* which cost the picture producer nothing. Even the year before, George added, the much talked-of duel on the staircase in his production of *A Gentleman of France* had been filmed to "advertise the title": a fact which film historians have overlooked.

In addition, our courts soon held that any film made from a play competed with it, because it might damage the performing rights, and the manager who had contracted for these, without any film interest being mentioned, had automatically a right to protection. Unless the title were cleared of all possible claims *before* the picture was shot, film companies, in turn, would not risk an expensive infringement suit. The manager, if not appeased, could thus block the film sale. To avoid all such threatened hold-ups, plus a confused legal situation, compromise was the easy way out for everybody. Such were the established trade custom and other complications regarding film rights which the Guild faced in 1925. What was worse, many dramatists simply didn't agree with Shaw: they believed the managers were honestly *entitled* to half of all "subsidiary rights." So, as the Guild came to grips with the picture problem, its ranks were split.

Yet, once the terms of the Fox contract came to light, we knew every author would fight, since a secret clause, in the way of a weekly salary to the manager, assured him *more* than even the then established 50 per cent of the film price. To get his play produced, the author would have to take it or leave it. As Fox had already tied up six managers, he boasted that he would practically "control all of the stage output of those producers." We knew the answer: If all producers went along, *only plays with film possibilities would receive such backing.* Ergo, starvation for the others. There it lay stark. No, no, we didn't like it!

But art—and, I blush to whisper, our pocketbooks—pointed to but one way to protect our property: the manager must be deprived of his existing control over the conditions of a film sale. Thus, though Shaw and other British dramatists later complained at what the Guild had conceded to the managers in 1925, our initial problem, weak as we then were, had been to form *an organization strong enough to preserve our 50 per cent division and give us some voice in the sale.* So we took our coats off.

Our immediate need was a lawyer—one who knew the ropes; but we decided to avoid a Broadway tie-up. Fortunately, Arthur Garfield Hays and his partner, Dudley Field Malone, agreed to take a chance on a contingent fee.

Arthur had been my college mate at Columbia, and I admired his social sympathies. He was and still is an earnest defender of civil liberties and minority causes.* A shrewd lawyer, always good-natured, he served us with a devotion and skill no fee could have covered. I know we also amused him as we coached him in theatrical sleight-of-hand.

Dudley also was a personal friend. He and I had campaigned together for woman suffrage. He had been close to my father-in-law in his 1924 Presidential campaign. Never was there a talker with such persuasive charm. Though he had not his partner's patience with detail, on one occasion he proved his worth to us. Early we asked Dudley to make a much needed "pep" talk. He knew little of our grievances, and before the meeting he came to me.

* In his autobiography, *City Lawyer* (New York, 1942), Arthur has given a picture of this adventure.

"What the devil must I say, George?"

"We must be united! Only through union is there strength! The individual is lost today when up against organizations! The young must be protected—"

"I get you," he interrupted.

He talked for nearly an hour. No one could have been more eloquent, as economic formulas and anecdotes armed with humor flashed. The audience was swept along, and answered with cheers. Every Jack and Jill left the meeting feeling like part of a crusade. It didn't bother us a bit.

The secret confab at Actors' Equity Headquarters on December 7, 1925, brought our first direct move. Though we feared to scare off our own head-shaking conservative members, and so had to move step by step, we knew a strong hint of our having Equity as a possible ally would impress the managers. We thus back-pedaled the unfortunate attitude the dramatists had earlier taken towards it. John Emerson, a playwright himself, and his tiny dynamic wife, Anita Loos (who made blondes famous), had now returned to the Guild. As former president of Equity and a resourceful organizer, John now agreed with our audacious strategy.

Behind closed doors, with Channing Pollock as chairman, we had a prepared resolution endorsed. In part, it said:

Whereas the authors, composers and dramatists have certain grievances which they are unable to correct individually . . .

Now therefore, we, the undersigned, in meeting assembled, do associate ourselves together to consider what steps, if any, can be taken for our mutual protection and to promote our common welfare.

Arthur Richman named a committee * "to consider the abuses and report to the signers for their ratification what measures should be deemed advisable to cure them." More than thirty authors agreed to be bound by the report if it "shall have been accepted by a majority of the signatories hereto." † Further, every one thereafter signing agreed

---

* Cosmo Hamilton, George Kelly, Roi Cooper Megrue, A. E. Thomas, Rita Weiman, Arthur Richman (chairman), and George Middleton (secretary).

† The original document, on file at the Guild office, has the following signers: Don Marquis, Arthur Richman, Lynn Starling, George Kelly, Gladys Unger, Sidney Howard, Lewis Beach, Rita Weiman, Alice Leal Pollock, Isabel Leighton, Kate Jordan, A. E. Thomas, Thompson Buchanan, Jane Murfin, Vincent Lawrence, Roi Cooper Megrue, Gilbert Emery, Arthur Goodrich, Clemence Randolph, Owen Davis, Edward Childs Carpenter, George S. Kaufman, Bayard Veiller, James Forbes, Percival Wilde, J. Hartley

to forfeit to the others $1,000, "as liquidated damages, in the event of any personal breach." We tactfully did not ask who of us had that much money; but it made the members realize they must be subject to discipline. This first agreement was signed by all—except one. As it turned out, this was the only time that, on a final vote, we were ever to lack a unanimous accord!

We started at once to list abuses and to get more dramatists signed up. Thirty was not enough. As we had no paid organizers Arthur and I took over this particular job of autograph collecting. A wag said we would go down the side streets, tap on the doors, and ask: "Does a dramatist live here?" One manager, who thought the Fox agreement was unfair to authors, showed it to me. Under pledge of secrecy, he let me copy the committing clauses and remove all identifying names. I merely had to show this to each author and watch his pocket nerve jump. Some reached for the fountain pen at once. That was fun. Others made us work. That was fun, too, since we always got our man. A few took being hooked quite hard. The old individualistic wiggle, of course.

But organizing writers was no new difficulty. The solitary nature of their work made them individualists and not good pack runners. Since many were also economic conservatives, smelling salts were needed to offset the mere thought of trade unionism. Others had opposed the Equity shop because they themselves were interested financially with the producers in their own plays. When we, in turn, came to sign up our fellow dramatists the same divided loyalties were involved, for they still had the manager's slant. But an author, at heart, is always an author first. Ultimately, every one came in and has stayed.

We followed set tactics. We signed up one leading writer close to each manager: that is, one who made him money. If trouble came, we wanted "persuasive elements" in each important office. Since Arthur and I were not after anything for ourselves, the fellows had to listen. Every morning we would ring up each other: like schoolboys, we counted our scalps and the stragglers we had waylaid. They were the symbols of the power we saw the group was gathering.

I recall going to Noel Coward, who was acting here in his first hit, *The Vortex.* I had not seen him since London days. Without a moment's hesitation he joined. Noel felt that "British authors having

Manners, James Gleason, Gene Buck, Cosmo Hamilton, George Middleton, Channing Pollock, John Emerson.

their plays done here should at least meet what the American dramatists asked." Other British dramatists also signed: John Galsworthy,
Somerset Maugham, Michael Arlen, and Ian Hay Beith—many
through their agents' persuasion. This was another bit of strategy:
to make the agents our allies, which they hadn't always been in the
past. We rightly suspected some authors might have more confidence
in them than in us walking delegates.

I was touched when I went to sign up Eugene O'Neill. He,
Robert Edmond Jones, and Kenneth Macgowan (now so successful
in Hollywood) were producing Gene's plays at the Greenwich Village
Theatre. I had not yet met Gene, though of course in some small
way I had had to-dos about getting his plays on in Paris. He had not
forgotten, and when I asked him to join us he said:

"Well, Middleton, I'm not much good at such things. I'm busy
and—"

"Can't we have your signature? We want your name on our
committee. You need not do another thing."

"Have you got a piece of paper?" he asked.

I gave him a scrap. He wrote his name on it and handed it to me.

"There. Use it any way you want." And he was good enough to
recall some words of mine at the start of his career.

Though Gene never got around to our meetings, few ever knew
how he cooperated. Later, for example, he refused to let his plays be
leased to a certain management which owed royalties to another Guild
member. And in 1936, when our third Agreement was up and we
feared a management which had produced his plays might refuse to
sign it, I motored down to his Georgia home and laid the matter
before him.

"I won't do anything, George, till you tell me it's all right," he said.

So on January 7, 1926, when Arthur Richman opened the meeting
to ratify our report at the Hotel Roosevelt, we had one hundred
twenty-one pledged instead of thirty! All within a month! I linger on
this unique meeting, for none ever brought such significant results to
any group of authors.

Practically every American playwright faced our committee, which
flanked the president. By us sat Owen Davis, vice president of the
League and chairman of our board, primed to give his benign blessing. Our counsel was ready. Near by sat hard-working Luise Sillcox,
our executive secretary (she fortunately still is), who had seen the

Guild through puberty and was proud of, if a little frightened at, our obvious virility.

It thrilled me to look at those conspicuous in the theatre, with plays running, and at those who had tasted past glories. But best of all were the first-play youngsters knocking at the door. If we succeeded, how many still in college would be carrying on after us. It was a far cry from our little group who had met together "to do something," only six weeks or so before.

After Arthur Hays had surveyed the facts, Arthur Richman unexpectedly read the following letter. No one missed its point. Even those who had fought Equity hardest swallowed their canaries.

January 6, 1926

Arthur Richman Esq.
President American Dramatists.
DEAR MR. RICHMAN:

The Actors' Equity Association is delighted to learn that all American Dramatists have at last decided to unite in a homogeneous body. We feel and always have felt that without organization no group can effectively function. It goes without saying you will have our support.

There are to-day many problems in the theatre where the interest of actor and dramatist is identical. We are sure that harmonious action between the two Associations will solve those problems which may at any time call for our united action.

With all best wishes,

Very truly yours,

FRANK GILMORE
Executive Secretary

It is time for one of those convenient "little-did-I-think" moments. I had first known Frank years before at 'Sconset, and I remember how hot he was from our tennis match and the argument we had between sets over labor unions. If ever a conservative became converted by abuses he met in his profession, it was Frank; and he developed into a skillful leader when the going was hardest for his fellow actors. I smiled now to think that he should be writing such a letter to such a dramatists' meeting—as far from my thoughts on that tennis court as Equity had been from his.

Every signer was told that no one would be bound by our report unless the majority supported it. We had worked out our strategy: those who had done the talking at the other meetings were now to stay in the background. That was hard on Channing and myself.

Motions were prepared and timed for introduction. Best of all, George Kelly was chosen to read the report. Its reception would be the test.

Tall, slim, with dark eyes, a fine lined profile, and clean-living face, which, in spite of its tolerant, hovering smile, would light with the high idealism we had come to find in him, George's commanding position with the Pulitzer prize for *Craig's Wife,* and other outstanding successes like *The Show-Off* and *The Torch Bearers,* added to the respect with which he was now heard. Himself a master of stage direction, he sensed the need of a quiet simplicity. He thus endowed with a lofty dignity the words on which we had worked with such care. Afterwards one member said: "George, I'd have been for that report no matter what was in it, after George Kelly got through reading it. Why, you'd have thought it came down from Mount Sinai direct."

Kelly began, in slow measured tones: " 'We are convinced, that quite as important as correcting at the moment the abuses so well stated by counsel, is the necessity of forming a strong and powerful association which will be able, from its very nature, to remain alert to avoid future abuses.' "

The first applause broke in, as the color of the sentence suggested what was coming.

" 'One of the chief motives of this move for organization is the feeling among American dramatists that hitherto they have had no effective channel of expression regarding conditions which surround the practice of their profession. All of the other branches of theatrical art have long been organized—the actors last of all. But the dramatists, without whom there could be no spoken stage, have had no collective voice whatever. They desire to have such a voice in order that they may express their collective hopes, plans and ambitions bearing upon the traditions and the ideals of the theatre.' "

I could see that the solemn note had sobered the few cynics who had "gone along," with little hope that we could accomplish much.

" 'The dramatist must be vigilant enough and powerful enough to avoid the development of unfair practices and strong enough to compel respect for the continued observance of fair dealing.

" 'The genesis of this present association is due to the fact that, for once, the authors are all thoroughly aroused and are group-conscious. They must remain so!' " The applause now punctuated almost every sentence. " 'An organization must be formed along lines which will attract *all* dramatists to its membership and make them realize that only within the Association can their rights be adequately conserved. . . .

"'Therefore . . . we approve the fundamental principle that negotiations be conducted with managers by ourselves as a group, with the end in view of consummating a basic agreement between this association and managers or groups of managers *to the effect that no dramatist shall submit any play to, or rewrite any play or make any translation or any adaptation or any dramatization or any part of a musical comedy for, any manager who shall not enter into and observe such basic agreement, or who, without the approval of the Association, shall deal with any dramatists outside the Association.'*"

Our policy was out. Some had feared we would advise joining the A. F. of L. at once. They had come to oppose it. But we felt the wisest strategy was to hold it in reserve should the more conservative course fail. Relief thus added to the enthusiasm our decision aroused.

It was some time before George could continue. As I gazed at him, quietly facing that cheering crowd, my thought darted back to the first time I had met him.

"Kelly, the dramatists are organizing. Will you come up to Arthur Richman's this afternoon?" I had asked over the telephone.

"But, Mr. Middleton, I never take part in these matters. I never have had any difficulties with managers in my business relations and—" It was very restrained and dignified.

"I know it. That goes for a lot of us fellows, too. But I don't think you realize what's happening . . . and what this may mean to every young fellow who writes. Won't you at least come and hear our tale of woe? You won't be committed or embarrassed in any way."

On the dot he walked into Arthur's apartment. He never said a word throughout. I was careful not to have him drawn into any discussion. Tinker-Bell, Arthur's black cat, kept a chaperoning eye upon him, from the top of the bookshelves. Our counsel explained to the new recruits why we felt all dramatists must stand together. I could not tell how Kelly felt. I saw him waiting for me after the meeting.

"Well?" I anxiously asked.

"Mr. Middleton, I am indignant beyond words. I never knew *any* manager could do some of these things to *any* author. You may count on me in any way I can help."

So now he stood before more than a hundred men and women, moving them by his own deep conviction. It hit me hard. Such moments were compensations for whatever little leg-running and work one might have given. And George was also answering the one question which disturbed the more conservative-minded. Was all this leading to the closed shop?

" 'It is, of course, necessary,' " he continued, " 'that the requirements for membership in the association shall be such that it will be open to *all* dramatists, and that we deal with *all* managers who shall accept and observe the terms of the Basic Agreement.' "

Every young dramatist could join, and enjoy equal protection with every member no matter how important. The only obligation was that he, as they, observe the rules of the game. Our strength thus would rest only upon ourselves.

Our nine resolutions were unanimously approved. Not a peep opposed A. E. Thomas's motion that a contract committee be named to prepare a "Minimum Basic Agreement," to include the "Dramatists' Shop." We agreed that unless *two-thirds*—not a majority as before—approved the Agreement, it would not be binding. Every member, however, promised not to lease any play until it was ready for submission. This took all scripts out of the market. It was a new type of strike. It showed we meant business.

We could now move on to the next job with our little army in step. It was the most important action the dramatists had ever taken for their own protection in the history of the American stage. We had signed our Declaration of Independence.

Somehow I wish now we had thought of waving a silent salute to Bronson Howard, across the years.

CHAPTER XXV

THE DRAMATISTS' GUILD COMES
INTO ITS OWN

"The kids are getting nervous."

Such was Al Woods's comment in the *New York Times*. As he had himself signed the Fox contract the Freudian might understand the manager's troubled reaction. Martin Herman, his brother and businessman, put it more whimsically:

"You don't think playwrights will stick together, do you, George? You ought to see the bastards who come around here wanting something, with their asses out."

The *Times* news report, however, phrased the real managerial reaction:

The dramatists have added the further warning that if some managers refuse to deal with them, they have opportunities for production. Just what was meant by that George Middleton, who did a large part of the organization work, said he was not prepared to disclose at this time.

It was learned yesterday, however, that the managers have been so alarmed at the determined aspect of the playwrights' defiance and their strong strategic position, that they already are forming some sort of organization to attempt to cope with them.

The threat was valid. We had had outside offers "to back our plays"; but, as we had to hold our cards close to our chests, we didn't explain that the offer was *limited* to a half-dozen established authors. This offer was promptly turned down, "unless it were opened to all Guild members" with desirable scripts. This fight was not intended to better only the top-flighters.

The truth was, if a half-dozen established authors had thought only of themselves they could have obtained any collective agreement they might have demanded, and the Guild would have folded up. It was those very men, really with nothing to gain except a clarification of expanding rights, who now insisted that the occasion should bring full protection to the young author. This was not revealed at the time, but I can vouch for it; I know what was being offered to split paying lode from untested rock.

Meantime our contract committee * met daily for three weeks, at Rachel Crothers's apartment. As chairman, I wrote to each signer and agent for suggestions as well as copies of any bizarre contracts. Though most managers had played the game within the well established preserves, strange fish turned up. Never were we so convinced that the pools needed flushing as when we discovered what bait some of our youngsters had snapped at for a production. Our prize catch was an inter-office memorandum accidentally left pinned to an author's contract when it was returned to him. He was putting money into his own play, and the manager had directed his lawyer, "Draw this so I can get out of it." We kept it iced for emergencies.

I urged the committee to weigh each proposed remedy with a how-would-a-crook-beat-it? test. What potential rascals some of us might have been! I admired their business acumen and the way their own experiences had shown them the side doors and shady alleys.

Channing Pollock, for instance, not only had backed his own plays, but had press-agented for the Shuberts. John Emerson, aside from his Equity service stripes, had once been on the Charles Frohman office force. Roi Cooper Megrue for years had been a play agent with Elisabeth Marbury (no slouch herself), and so had inside knowledge of

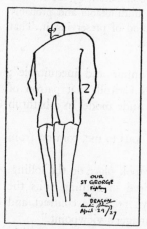

OUR
ST GEORGE
fighting
The
DRAGON
and the
April 29/27

every producer's contractual career. J. Hartley Manners (husband of Laurette Taylor and father of *Peg o' My Heart*) knew the workings of the English theatre, in which he had grown up. George S. Kaufman, already starting his meteoric rise, had covered the theatrical water front for the *New York Times,* to learn its tides, eddies, and backwash. All the pizzicato and semiquavers of musical comedy agreements were taken care of, at a glance, when Otto Harbach, author of *Rose Marie,* took hold; while Gene Buck, then president of ASCAP, author of many

* Eugene O'Neill, John Emerson, Eugene Buck, Otto Harbach, George Kelly, Roi Cooper Megrue, Channing Pollock, J. Hartley Manners, Le Roy Clemens, George S. Kaufman, Rachel Crothers, and George Middleton (chairman). Others were consulted. Richman, as president, was member of the committee ex-officio.

Ziegfeld *Follies,* was an expert on "small rights," destined to be one of our hardest fights. The rest had tussled with business problems in other incarnations—some of mine being probably French.

Owen Davis was not on the committee, but I took every clause to him. He was an ideal yardstick. While he resented any intrusion on a writer's inherent rights, his many personal relations with managers made him understand their claims. He smiled himself over the dual pull. But his long career and personal integrity carried great weight with both groups. When the time came to submit our Basic Agreement for ratification, February 2, Owen was so pleased with what he considered our common-sense approach that he himself moved its adoption, at my request. This had been barely two months after our first confab at Equity Headquarters.

A few managers signed at once. Henry Miller, without even reading it, said to Arthur Richman:

"I know you fellows. Anything you boys want is all right with me."

We sat on our haunches, licked our chops, waited developments, and read the front-page stories. The *Times* in a long editorial analysis said:

In the present contest the intelligent public is vitally interested. . . . It is highly significant the leading American dramatists have joined their American brethren in the fight against further domination by the movies. That the spoken drama should cease to exist is unthinkable and probably impossible; but there is wide choice in the method of preserving it. That of the Dramatists' Guild is both timely and wise.

The managerial reception was chilly: "unfair and inequitable"; "unworkable"; "we will never sign it." Earl Carroll, that patron of pulchritude, took time off, before dunking a nude model in a bathtub of champagne, to remark:

"Concerted effort like this sounds incongruous to me, coming from a profession predisposed towards brains."

The most picturesque of several meetings took place on the lolling, affluent sands of Miami Beach, where "attired in bathing suits the managers sat in a circle while Edgar Selwyn read the contract and checked the clauses objectionable from a manager's viewpoint."

But the agitation had unsettled Broadway business. The withdrawal of our plays promised empty larders. No quick jobs of adaptation, dramatization, or revision were taken on by authors. The theatre owners, who loved their regular rents, recalling the lean days of Equity troubles, heard another season rolling around without the backlog of scripts to fill the stages. Even an anxious Equity now wondered whether its actors might have fewer jobs. So pressure began for a quick settlement. While some of us listened wistfully to the mating call of managers for spring scripts to "try out," not one violated our pledge of continence. Right here I may add that, in the twenty years since, only a half-dozen known violations of the Basic Agreement have merited suspension! Violators who came back into the Guild paid a thousand-dollar fine.

So our members' voluntary compliance with Guild rules began early. They knew that they had the best contract ever; that royalties from all sources would now be paid when due, and sent directly by both managers and agents: that arbitration would be compulsory, saving thousands in lawyers' fees; that cast and control of script would belong to the author; that plays could no longer be kept out of circulation; that foreign and picture rights would be regulated in fairness to all, and that "corporate entities" could no longer swing in and out of bankruptcy with the greatest of ease, to recostume with a new team name in full air. But, above all, the authors knew that *if any manager violated this agreement all other Guild members were bound not to give him a script; that the managers who had signed the agreement were bound to refuse production to any Guild member violating it.*

While we had made compromises we knew we were accomplishing a miracle in obtaining so much as this for the young authors. The dramatists would possess a new dignity. They knew, too, that the Basic Agreement and a rejuvenated Guild had been welded together solely through their own cooperation. It was their contract. All of this, however, would be possible only if our Dramatists' Shop was recognized. On this the agreement's enforcibility depended. So the members were content to wait and support our planned strategy.

The rest can be quickly told. Brady asked for a joint conference. Richman refused until we were assured the managers' committee would have "the power to bind the entire group." When we met the forty managers, who found our membership out in force to lend moral support, it was quite a thrill. We now had two hundred forty members signed to stand together—"some of them dramatists," one manager cynically remarked.

Arthur immediately nominated Brady for chairman. Bill offered to pledge in writing that he was the managers' authorized spokesman. But again we went lofty and refused. Bill also promised that any contract the two committees could agree on would be the basis of our future business relations.

Two committees were named * and met daily for several weeks. Two subjects nearly broke us up because we wouldn't back down: "small rights" (which the Shuberts did not want ASCAP to control) and the right to change scripts in certain cases, which Lee Shubert in person came and pleaded for. Owen Davis, on this, rose up in all his Harvard wrath against "ever turning over to anybody the right to change one syllable without the author's consent." A majority of managers upheld the Guild. Our fight was won.

Five months of intense activity had come to an end. On April 27, 1926, the Basic Agreement was signed by all managers who had been party to Brady's pledge—except one! As Arthur Train, later president of the League, summed it up: "The compact and highly vitalized Dramatists' Guild has succeeded in doing that which was never dreamed of, to wit, compelled the collective discussion of equities between authors and producers and the collective acceptance by the latter of a minimum basic agreement guaranteeing from Broadway only slightly less than the Barons exacted from King John at Runnymede."

We had set up a large organization: wide discretion and responsibilities were given to the Council. Percival Wilde and James Forbes helped us feel our way through increased carrying costs, due to expanding services. How those growing pains eased up, as we grew up, is for a later story which would cover the presidencies of Edward Childs Carpenter, who was to succeed me, Sidney Howard, Robert Sherwood, Elmer Rice and, at this writing, Richard Rodgers, the first composer to fill the office.

Glancing ahead for a moment, however, one could never have appraised the radiations of so fundamental a reform, the abuses prevented or the benefits automatically bestowed. Ours was to prove no

* For the authors: J. Hartley Manners, Roi Cooper Megrue, Owen Davis, James Forbes, Otto Harbach, Gene Buck, John Emerson, Channing Pollock, George Middleton, Marc Connelly, and Arthur Richman, Chairman. For the managers: Lee Shubert, Sam Harris, Arthur Hammerstein, John Golden, Arthur Hopkins, Joseph Bickerton, Edgar Selwyn, Brock Pemberton, Warren Munsell, Laurence Weber, and William A. Brady, Chairman. The meetings were held at ASCAP's offices. Full stenographic records are available. They are picturesque but technical.

perfect instrument: trial and error were to reveal inadequacies to meet constantly changing production conditions or holes where abuses had not been plugged. Justice to all parties was to be considered with adjustments made in four future revisions of the Basic Agreement. Until I joined a government war agency I kept sufficiently in touch, as a council member, with Guild activities to know that the leaders were making every effort, through a negotiated line, not only to harmonize any differences between authors and managers, but to protect their mutual interests before the ever increasing power of mechanized industry with its normal hunger for copyrighted material.

What specific financial benefit the Guild was to bring its members may be persuasive proof of its effectiveness. Though in the first dozen years over 5,000 play contracts were examined and approved, as to terms and required royalty advances, the success of our film control program was to be spectacular. I am indebted to the Guild's film negotiator and counselor, Sidney R. Fleisher, for the figures through 1945. The sales of film rights in our plays, since reorganization, were to bring $24,480,066! This did not include additional percentage items, which raised the total over $25,000,000. Up to 1936, the authors and managers shared equally in such proceeds; but after that, through Guild effort, the authors were to obtain 60 per cent. Thus in the ten succeeding years, the authors were to profit $1,500,000 more than under the initial Agreement which Shaw complained about.*

But beyond the unestimated royalties collected, the economies to authors through arbitration and avoidance of lawsuits together with all the other protections given the young oncoming playwrights, there is the outstanding fact that over a hundred different members were to serve on our Guild council, without compensation. This might well be capped by a few lines from a letter Arthur Richman wrote me, quoting what Rachel Crothers said to him, after a council meeting, in 1938:

"I can't tell you how much I admire you men who helped organize the Guild. Now that it is the splendid thing it is, I find you—more than twelve years later—working for it as unselfishly as you did then. I don't believe there's a group of people anywhere who have worked with greater loyalty and unselfishness than all of you."

---

* In the *Bulletin*, Jan., 1939, I detailed the abuses which the various Basic Agreements corrected, as well as a record of the entire Guild set-up, services and the like. This was completely revised, in brochure form, in 1943; and a further revision, covering the 1946 Agreement, will bring the record of widening activities up to date. Since much of this is trade jargon it is sufficient merely to call it to the attention of any stage historian, interested in what has been accomplished through organization.

But this present chronicle, limited necessarily to the Guild's early days, must speak of the cooperation of the Authors' League itself, with a salute to the late William Hamilton Osborne, its lawyer. Though no committee member asked for even personal expenses, we had spent $20,000 for printing, postage, and secretarial work. As we had no cash to swing it, a few League members borrowed $12,000 on their personal endorsement. Among them were George Barr Mc-Cutcheon (then president), Owen Davis, Ellis Parker Butler, Orson Lowell, Tony Sarg, Fannie Hurst, Jesse Lynch Williams, and Rex Beach. The mention of their names brings back the close friendship I had with some still living and others, like Jesse, who have gone on.

So often, in fact, as I put down this personal story, I realize how rich I have been in knowing those whose faces hover in my memory. Of two I must pause to say a word: my college mate, Roi Cooper Megrue, who died just after we had completed our reorganization, and Arthur Richman, who lived into the writing of this record. Roi's sense of satire, with his chuckling amusement at anyone's polite pretensions, made working with him a joy. He never missed a meeting though he knew he was fatally stricken. He left personal souvenirs to all his associates and willed the Guild $5,000 in $500 yearly prizes for the member writing the best comedy. Arthur, of all, became closest to me. When I came to Washington in 1939 he kept me in touch with all Guild activities, in which he took an active part until his sudden death, on September 10, 1944. At his funeral, there was no religious ceremony; but I was asked to conduct the services. I told of what he had done for the Guild as perhaps only I really knew it. The distinguished men and women from every branch of the theatre who came to pay him the final tribute evidenced his enduring record of service. I know too that, of all that had happened in his successful career, he cared more for what he had been able to do for his fellow writers in both Guild and League, of which he had also been president.*

But back in 1926, even after the ratification of the Agreement, there were still some who stayed outside. I wrote to those I could. We all respected then the uncanny doctoring and stage managerial skill which Winchell Smith possessed. Author of *The Fortune Hunter*

---

* I wrote of Roi's activities in the *Bulletin,* Mar., 1927. In the *Bulletin,* Sept., 1944, and later in pamphlet form, are the words I spoke at Arthur's funeral. At his death he was on the Board of Directors of the American Theatre Wing and of its Club for Merchant Seamen; and he had appointed me, as a bus boy, to be the Guild representative at the Washington Stage Door Canteen.

(shade of that beautiful young actor, John Barrymore!) and collaborator in too many plays to mention, and partner with John Golden, "Billy" earned far over a million dollars. Though he and I never worked together, we did have a pleasant association at the Players. It was from there I wrote. Here is part of his long reply:

MILL STREAMS
FARMINGTON, CONN.
May 22, 1926

DEAR GEORGE:

Thank you for writing me about the new author's contract. Frankly my feeling has been strongly against it. . . . It gives me a much better and freer feeling to go my own way and arrange for the production of a play of mine exactly as I please without any regard to any authors' society.

I've written all this because you have taken the trouble to write me most pleasantly on the subject and I wanted you to know the way I honestly feel about it.

On the other hand all you fellows have felt strongly in favour of this scheme, have talked about it and worked at it and *done* it.

I know it makes very little real difference with any one except myself whether I come in or stay out; but I wouldn't feel happy if I thought I was making things even slightly harder for a society who sincerely think they are helping the younger playwrights.

So, though my personal feelings are opposed to it, I'll sign on the dotted line and sincerely hope that the majority are right and that I am wrong.

Yours sincerely,
WINCHELL SMITH *

When the fight was thickest, Belasco had suddenly asked:

"George, do I understand that, unless I sign, you won't do any more work with me?"

"I can't, Governor. We've all made a pledge. Nobody yet has even thought of breaking it."

He said nothing. We never discussed it again. The summer passed. One day, his manager, Ben Roeder, said:

"George, why don't you make it easy for him? Write him a letter, asking him to join, and see what happens."

I did, to have the following come back:

DEAR GEORGE MIDDLETON:

Nothing has ever moved me more than your letter. It is fine and frank and more than friendly. I am with you all, of course, and will gladly

---

* In his will he left a selected income to the Authors' League Fund, which has averaged $3,000 a year, especially earmarked for dramatists!

become one of you. In a way I was one of the founders of The American Dramatists. I remember Bronson Howard talked with me about the organization many times before it was formed. We would sit at his home —this long before many of you were born—and talk over the details and advantages of such an association.

I produce plays to be sure, but I never think of myself as only a producer. I am in the ranks with the play writers too, and my heart is with them and for them, and their cause is my cause, so we are all together and God bless us all.

And above all, dear George, I want you to know how much I appreciate your wonderful letter. So send me the contract. My pen is in the inkwell all ready for signing.

Faithfully

NEW YORK, October 21, 1926   DAVID BELASCO

Nothing better reveals the author-manager complexities which had been developing during his long span than our Agreement, with its twenty-four lusty sections, and the two timid extracts concerning the above I came across in the *Clipper,* of April, 1890, which foreshadowed it:

The subject of play piracy was discussed, and it was decided that all action against pirates should be taken by the society itself, on behalf of members of the society. There was also some discussion of a minimum price which members should be allowed to receive for their work.

The object of the Society is to secure protection for dramatic authors, and it was decided that no member should do business with a manager who has fallen three weeks in arrears in his royalties to another member of the society. It was also decided that all royalties should be collected by the secretary, in order to make sure that the authors kept the managers up to their contract.

One other opposition lingered: the Shuberts for a year refused to sign. So no Guild member could or would write for them or submit scripts. But I was fearful this powerful firm might seriously hamper us by taking out long options on plays of foreign dramatists, especially the British, where no question of adaptation would be involved. Though we had appointed Ian Hay Beith our representative among the latter, I believed missionary work was necessary to persuade their important authors to join us. A *Times* story had appeared that Austin Strong, author of *Seventh Heaven,* Channing Pollock, Marc Connelly, and myself were slated to go to Europe "to arrange closer bonds with European authors."

Hardly a week after this was prematurely announced, however, the Shuberts—who had participated in our conference, to be bound, as we thought, by Brady's say-so—"started a war on the dramatists." An injunction was asked against the Guild: Arthur Richman, still president, was served. The Guild was charged with "secondary boy-cott," by William Klein, the Shubert lawyer. He stated, "The proceedings are an effort to restrain the Guild from interfering in any way with the manager who desires to have his plays written by an author." Arthur Hays, unruffled as usual, promptly announced that the Guild welcomed the action, as it was time the matter came out in the open.

This was the first occasion any group of American authors had ever been hauled into court on the issue of trying to protect themselves.*

After the preliminary hearing the Judge asked counsel to file briefs. We were naturally in a dither. Though we might lose, we knew no law could make us work for any manager; but temptation is less persuasive when removed. So again we got busy. The Guild Council instructed Richman to name a committee to "reconsider the possibility of our joining the A. F. of L." A union charter might clear away any doubt as to our legal status. We gave this proper publicity, though I don't believe the committee was ever named. Then a strange thing happened. The Shuberts withdrew the suit. Lee sent for Richman and signed. Nobody knew the reasons: they didn't matter. Arthur told me that Lee had said, "It has cost me about $400,000 to fight the Guild."

The last influential manager thus signed: every important playwright, too, had come along. The door was opened wide to young "associates"—mostly those not yet produced on Broadway. But they came from over the country, bringing to the Guild their interest in the theatre and their dream of being a writing part of it. At the end of the first year, as we counted our chicks with the "regulars," we had nearly 1,000!

That lawsuit was a trying time for those who had the prenatal and postnatal care of our Basic Baby. But I already had my passport. I intended to see whether, as a further precaution, I might tie up all the British authors. From my friends in England I felt sure of both advice and cooperation. I kept my plans to myself. As Owen Davis had become League president, I succeeded him as chairman of the board. It gave me a bit of a handle with which to act.

* See *Bulletin*, May, 1927.

So Fola and I once more stepped up a gangplank: again on the *Roosevelt*, with Captain George Fried. At his table we found two unusual people: Sir John Adams, whose shrewd humor and enclycopedic knowledge we greatly enjoyed, and Lady Adams, his match on any ground. The grace and wit of two such brilliant Scots recalled our other crossing with William Archer, seven years before. We have always been lucky seafarers.

To Fola it was a special delight to chat with the white-bearded Sir John, one of the great teachers of teachers, who had earlier done much to overcome English prejudice against Education *per se* as a subject for university study. After twenty years as Professor of Education at the University of London he had retired and was lecturing everywhere, to be dubbed "the first citizen in the international world of Education." He questioned Fola closely about Caroline Pratt's highly reputed City and Country School, one of the pioneer progressive educational experiments, whose staff Fola had joined. Her work there enriched both our lives, for it brought into our home an ever expanding circle of new friends and deepened our relationship with others we had long known. Among these were Caroline Pratt, Leila Stott, John Dewey and his daughter Evelyn, Horace and Rachel Kallen, Charles and Mary Beard, Alexander and Helen Meiklejohn, and Helene Scheu-Riesz of Vienna, who had written many books for children and translated *Alice in Wonderland*.

I was glad to have Fola with me. She had been so understanding with a temperamental husband during the many months of strain, while carrying her own heavy teaching schedule. I would need her advice, too, in my personal adventure ahead, for she had never lost her own interest in the welfare of theatre folks. My portfolio was full of literature, Basic Agreements and blank applications for membership. I had written to Shaw, Barrie, Pinero, and the others. I asked the British Society to arrange a public meeting of its members.

It was good to glide from Plymouth through the smooth English countryside on the way to London, and to find harborage in quaint little Carter's Hotel. Everything was crowded, of course, at the season's end: yet we got two rooms, by my willingness to sleep in one—which held our tub.

But I was a mighty nervous speaker at my first meeting in a Bloomsbury Street hotel, a week later. I had, however, brought it on myself.

CHAPTER XXVI

FORTY BRITISH DRAMATISTS
JOIN US

The Society of Authors, which Sir Walter Besant inspired, had in turn inspired our Authors' League. It started in 1884 with an imposing membership, and Tennyson was its first president. George Meredith came next. On my 1927 visit to London, Thomas Hardy was filling out the last year of his life in that high office.*

I had talked over its beginnings with Sir John Adams. While boldly declaring the primary need of a legal definition of "literary property" and an even greater need of unscrambling the conflicts in local and international copyright, the Society's Committee of Management had apparently moved with caution. In spite of the example long set by the French Gens de Letters, which, through Beaumarchais, Balzac, and others, had done vigorous fist-shaking at all unfair practices, the British authors wooed each reform in a gentlemanly fashion. This was the instinctive technic of those engaged in so polite an occupation as "the literary life." We also had to face it in America. With time, however, the growth and pressure of the British Society got results. It gave its members precise information about literary trade habits and pertinent laws in all parts of the world. As the United States was the largest outside market, our own confusions became its chief focus and concern. It also gave legal aid wherever the special case might concern all writers.

This our League, being a corporation, could not do—as I often had to explain to British dramatists who had trouble in the States. English law permitted their Society to practice law for them: American law forbade any corporation to do so. Further, when I first appeared before the Society it had nothing but a "subcommittee" to handle the affairs of playwrights. This, too, had been our pattern, from which our Dramatists' Guild had emerged. Perhaps our example impressed the British authors; for in 1931 the League of British

---

* Sir James Barrie succeeded him. John Masefield, the Poet Laureate, is now president. Its membership is over 3,000.

Dramatists was to be formed, with Sir James Barrie at its head.* This was to bear approximately the same relation to the Incorporated Society of Authors, Playwrights and Composers (the Society's later legal name) as our Guild did to the Authors' League. But neither of the British groups has had anything resembling our "Dramatists' Shop." They have no enforceable contract, no power to discipline either managers or their own members. The more conservative or wealthy members have blocked every such effort: the old self-protective individualism has stood more or less heroically on the burning deck.

From the start there had been an amiable affiliation between our two groups. In fact, Channing Pollock had even gone to London in 1921 to propose a joint membership. He then came to Paris and saw me as to a three-way tie-up with the powerful French society. But while the latter already could and did automatically protect American and British interests in Paris, neither of us could do anything at home for the French. This common weakness likewise made futile our suggested union against managerial abuses in both countries. But the balance had changed in 1927: the Guild had a strong "shop" and a Basic Agreement. While, of course, no one suspected that we had any remote idea of using "a big stick" to force the British to join us to protect our own front yard, the realistic Bernard Shaw was aware of its possibilities, as a question he asked me will show. Knowing something of the above cross-currents which might flounder me I resolved to take out all the insurance I could. Any of the important dramatists I could sign up through direct personal appeal, *before* my public meeting, I knew would carry more weight there than words. So I first sought Bernard Shaw.

I had found only two letters when I landed—from Pinero and Shaw. Perhaps others to whom I had written recalled a reply of W. S. Gilbert.

An actor in London wired both him and Barrie, "Tonight, as Beerbohm Tree is ill, I shall play Macbeth." The matter came up when the two dramatists lunched together. Barrie had thought it quite kind of the actor to let him know that Tree was not playing. Gilbert grunted, "I had one, too."

"Did you go?" asked Barrie.

"No, I wired him."

"How nice of you! I meant to. What did you say?"

* St. John Ervine has been its president since Barrie's death.

"I said, 'Thanks for the warning.'"

The efficient Blanche Patch wrote me to call on Shaw the day after my arrival. He had changed little; his hair was a bit whiter, perhaps, but he was vital as ever. I had sent all British authors my various reports; but the Basic Agreement was too long and imposing. He alone asked to have it. He is the only one, I believe, who has ever troubled to read it—plenty of Americans haven't, even yet. He said he would not join the Guild until he had. Other British authors would sign only after they knew who had already signed. Their attitude was somewhat like that of the reactionary American Senator Lorimer, as he explained his votes: "You see, in the roll call my name comes after La Follette and Lodge. If La Follette is for a bill, I'm against it. If Lodge is for it, so am I." Authors, too, in business affairs often have and need a bellwether. So Shaw was important to me.

He gave me two hours. I guard the memory of one of the acutest of minds, playing over every business cranny of our profession. My notes, hastily scribbled in the darkened doorway when I left, show how far we ranged. In the placing of plays he felt that "the agents always tend to trim to make a sale." He had little interest in permitting them to be done "for nothing at charities or where no admission is charged." He insisted that the author get his pence: "The necessity of paying something, however little, is the only way to instill a sense of literary property."

When Shaw first needed a play contract, he told me, he asked Henry Arthur Jones's advice and then "worked over" the conventional contract even so successful a playwright had used. From that day he made his own contracts such as no other author ever approached. Shaw had a unique method of charging fees for amateur and professional use of his plays. On a performance which an American dramatist would consider amateur and therefore subject to a flat fee, Shaw would ask the same sliding scale of royalties as on a type of performance we would define as professional: 5 to 15 per cent on the gross (as he once put it) "applying alike to a first-class metropolitan production and to a performance on a village green. Checques for $1,500 and a stamp value of 36 cents arrive on the same morning and are acknowledged with equal courtesy." Shaw defined as amateurs those who gave performances to amuse themselves and had no intention of engaging in the theatrical business. These he charged a stiff 5 guineas fee. He thought it would be unfair, however, to inflict so heavy a fee on any group striving to establish a permanent organization or make a profession of acting and producing.*

Shaw never sold any part of his plays outright. Even managerial participation in the film rights never occurred. A film fortune thus remains in his plays still unscreened. Nor had he followed a good old American custom of selling outright the "Continental" or "Scandinavian" rights. Most American plays had brought a flat sum. But Shaw had cannily found out the prevailing royalty rate among the leading native dramatists, and he got that. The managers shrieked in German but paid in pounds—half of which, as I recall, Shaw split with his translator. In fact, he remarked, he thus had helped raise royalties all along the line and kept managers from picking up British plays for a song. He narrated with zest certain of his deals with managers, some of which have become traditions. I recall one, perhaps unrecorded, with Marc Klaw, who had come to arrange for the production of *Caesar and Cleopatra* in New York with Forbes-Robertson and Gertrude Elliott. Klaw felt Shaw's terms were high.

"It's art, Mr. Shaw; but the play will lose us money."

"I accept without a blush," Shaw replied.

In telling of the experience he added, "You know, Middleton, it's art when you are writing a play, but business when you are selling it."

Of course, I analyzed for Shaw the Guild program and our desire to have him join. I found him instantly sympathetic, since he had himself made futile efforts to tighten up the British Society.† The arrival of the forthright Mrs. Shaw warned me that my time was up, and I left an application blank, promised to send a copy of our Basic Agreement, and mentioned casually the assessments for Guild expenses we asked on performances. With a twinkle he queried, "Would you take instead a life membership for a man of seventy?"

Trying to see people in London consumed time. Pinero had written: "A hearty welcome though our skies frown on you—I hope your advent will improve our weather." But the date he made for Fola and me to lunch with him was for some days later. In spite of fog Fola had her own plans, people and nursery schools to see—especially Margaret McMillan's, about which she wrote in *La Follette's.* While she was also investigating various educational aspects of British

---

* The *Bulletin,* Sept., 1928, prints an exchange of letters between Shaw and Percival Wilde, concerning this distinction.

† A full account of this venture will be found in Hesketh Pearson's *G. B. S.,* previously cited.

International

G. Bernard Shaw
Ayot Saint Lawrence
26ᵗʰ July 1946.
(my 90ᵗʰ birthday)

to George Middleton.

SIR JAMES BARRIE

broadcasting, I went after such authors as I could reach by telephone. I pause with a few playwrights I did see, to show what friendly cooperation I had.

Arnold Bennett, the co-author of *Milestones,* asked me at once to his spacious flat in Cadogan Square. He was unassuming, easy to talk to, like a methodical but casually efficient businessman. He had a slight impediment in his speech, and his large eyes were lustrous, somewhat like Professor Woodberry's; his mustache had a military firmness. Above the tasteful furniture I recall a striking Modigliani that startled me: its elongations didn't seem to fit its host. But then I remembered Bennett's extremely intimate knowledge of France, its literature and art, though his French wife could have accounted for the stunning picture.

After talking shop I asked to see his manuscripts. I knew he was proud of his calligraphy. He turned to the bound volumes in the cases. While he ran his thumb over them I could see how clean of correction they were. He told me the script of *The Old Wives' Tale,* his masterpiece, didn't have "a blurred or blotted line." After painstaking research, he knew exactly what he wanted to say once his pen started on its long journey through the pages.

In his published *Journal* he mentions that I called to see him "about English authors joining the American Guild for their own protection in regard to American production of their plays. I signed myself up at once." He had apparently read the material I had sent— and I was to receive letters of approval for later reports—because he also wrote a piece about our meeting in his daily column in the London *Evening Standard.* As I left he offered to help in any way he could; and he did in the article.*

The next day I saw both John Drinkwater and A. A. Milne. The latter lived in Mallord Street off Church. The author of *Mr. Pim*

* In commenting on the Shuberts' withdrawal of their suit, concerning which I had given him the requested information, Arnold Bennett, also wrote in the *Evening Standard* (June 9, 1927):

"The Shuberts did not fight the case out. They came to terms and signed the standard agreement, which is a very fair one. My contention is that the Guild's victory is an event which is honourable to artists and which will have a favourable influence upon the artistic development of the drama in America. My contention is further that anybody who thinks otherwise is a woolly thinker.

"American dramatists now stand on the same firm ground as French dramatists. In Britain dramatists have not so far had the gumption to combine in sufficient strength to enforce all-round justice from the theatrical managers. The Authors Society tried for years to arrange a satisfactory standard contract with the theatrical managers. The society failed on account of our notorious British individualism. Art suffers."

Passes By and *The Dover Road* (which marked Guthrie McClintic's début as a producer) lived up to my idea of him with his frail figure, alert eyes, and pushed-far-back light hair, which seemed to go with one who touched with fancy all he wrote. Milne had just begun that long series which was to make his son, Christopher Robin, famous. But it was his experience as a struggling writer in Grub Street, before his *Punch* days, which made him realize the service we might render to his plays in America. Of course it probably meant something to him, as it did to John Drinkwater, that Galsworthy, Coward, and Maugham had already joined us in the States.

The tall, handsome author of *Abraham Lincoln,* to whose house in Chelsea I hurried next, already knew of our fight, having just returned, I believe, from that favorite English indoor sport in America: lecturing. Of course he joined up. Granville-Barker and others I had known were out of town, and so I had to fall back on the efficient, good-natured, meticulous Mr. Thring, who had been secretary of the Society of Authors since its callow days in 1891. He arranged a luncheon for me before my meeting.

While the fight was on in America, Sir Arthur Pinero had written me of his sympathetic interest, adding:

I rejoice to see that all you fine American playwrights are firmly opposing the oppressive attitude of some of your managers. I am wondering what line the agents in New York, who represent the English dramatists, are taking in the matter.

When he honored me by coming to the luncheon I was sure he would sign. So did the others at the table—my two old friends, St. John Ervine and W. J. Locke, and Clemence Dane of the Committee of Management, who had come up from her home in deep Devonshire. I was impressed with her brooding, handsome face. I knew the lyric joy of her *Will Shakespeare* and the psychological power of her *Bill of Divorcement*—two plays in which Katharine Cornell mounted to stardom. We talked of Kit between shop and parsnips; for she was then under contract with Belasco to do my adaptation of *The Desert,* and I was, in odd moments, trying to persuade Brian Aherne or Godfrey Tearle to play opposite her. It would have been Aherne's American début. Another author present, who had already signed and was to be chairman of my meeting, was also chairman of the Committee. I was happy when Major John Hay

Beith (Ian Hay) said: "I'm inclined to think that we have got a very good bargain." With such names I felt fortified.

But I had not yet heard from Shaw. Though I had wanted to announce his official adherence, I heard Pinero's name would carry more weight with certain groups, since he "was considered less radical." Nevertheless I walked around to the Palace Hotel, in Bloomsbury Street, with trepidation. I was happy to know Fola had promised to tuck herself in a distant corner. But she would not come up to the speakers' table. I didn't urge her. She might be safer in the back.

As soon as Beith introduced me I felt at home. After all, they were authors, too: the Guild was bringing them something, not asking anything. A number of their own leading playwrights, whose names I gave at once, had already joined. I wasted little time retailing past wrongs. The fact that we Americans had felt the need of, and had put over, the Dramatists' shop was its own answer. But I asked cooperation because it would bring us added strength, and because only those British authors who joined could share the benefits we had won. As I was repeating the old Basic Agreement theme song I had hummed at Yale and other colleges, Bernard Shaw walked in and moved briskly to a front seat. My thoughts spattered as the eyes of the crowd turned towards him.

I managed to conclude with a ten-minute résumé, though I knew Shaw had my whole story in hand, and speeded to the question period. The questions certainly came. I was struck by the revelation some made of the business ethics of one American management. As it happened, Locke had told me a story which I fitted right into my meeting. It appears that this firm had been sued in London and had unexpectedly won its case. Its representative cabled the New York office, "Justice has triumphed." Within a few hours the cable reply was, "Appeal at once."

Beith then asked Shaw if he had "any comments to make." I had never heard Shaw speak in public: but when he began a special charm cloaked his words, as his eyes sparkled. (It all came back in a startling fashion five years ago, when, at eighty-five, his face and voice flashed out of the screen, preluding his own film, *Major Barbara*. Stowed away in a suburban theatre in Virginia, Fola and I thus heard again the voice of the man who had risen at my little meeting in London to speak to his fellow authors.)

He mentioned his own attempts to tighten the British organization and his general sympathy with our purpose. He was "particularly impressed" with what I had said about our compulsory arbitration: its "comparative cheapness" appealed to him. John Balderston, soon to author the lovely *Berkeley Square,* but then covering the meeting for the New York *World,* cabled:

A strenuous attempt to get George Bernard Shaw to sign the Minimum Basic Agreement of the United States Dramatists Guild failed today after a sparring match between Shaw and George Middleton of New York. But when it was over Shaw said he probably would sign up. . . . he said he had been unable to obtain a copy of the agreement. Middleton retorted he had left a copy with Shaw's maid, but Shaw said he never got it.

Some idea of how Shaw would mix his thistles with the bouquets was a sentence quoted in the dispatch: "My experience with contracts drawn up by authors is that they mean the precise opposite of what the authors mean them to mean."

John told me later, when we were doing Hollywood chores together, that he had never felt so sorry for any one as when Shaw's next question was suddenly shot at me:

"Am I to understand, Mr. Middleton, if I don't sign up with your Guild that my plays can't be done in America?"

I knew if I hesitated I was lost. So I replied instantly:

"Yes, Mr. Shaw: that is the general idea."

I suppose the picture of a band of American authors, like little King Canutes, trying to stop the most eminent of living dramatists hit everybody's funny bone; for, to my relief, there was a burst of laughter, in which none was heartier than Shaw's himself. Perhaps I was also suddenly flooded with the sympathy which must have gone out to the Christian martyrs in the arena when the javelin just missed. At any rate I felt a wave of friendliness sweep through the audience which gave me a much needed moment to ease into an explanation:

"You see, Mr. Shaw, we went on the assumption that every fair-minded, distinguished author would want to stand by his follow writers in, at least, *one* aspect of our endeavor: to protect the young writer from exploitation. Of course, if any British author does not wish to join in that end, and operate in American waters under the same conditions which all American authors impose upon themselves, we should be very happy to make exceptions."

The following account, anticipating a bit, was also cabled to the *New York Times:*

BRITISH PLAYWRIGHTS SUPPORT GUILD HERE
Sixteen Agree to Limit Production in America to Producer-Members

LONDON, June 17 (AP)—Led by the dean of playwrights, George Bernard Shaw, a number of British dramatists at a meeting today addressed by George Middleton, American playwright, agreed to produce plays in the United States only with producer-members of the Dramatists' Guild of the Authors' League of America.

Others who followed Shaw's example were Sir Arthur Pinero, W. J. Locke, Clemence Dane, John Drinkwater, A. A. Milne, St. John Ervine and Arnold Bennett. British dramatists who already have signed the agreement include John Galsworthy, Somerset Maugham, Noel Coward, Michael Arlen and Ian Hay.

The last named, who acted as Chairman of the meeting, declared he did not think the British dramatists ever would be able to organize against the British managers, as the American playwrights had done in their country.

Mr. Middleton is leaving for France next week to carry the movement to that country. He announced that Channing Pollock was now in Spain, after visiting Germany, for the same purpose. The American playwrights seek to induce all Continental dramatists to market their plays in America only through producing members of the Guild.

But the British custard could be still better browned. There were names I needed for prestige or cooperation. So I went a-hunting. John Masefield asked me to lunch at his simple flower-bowered home, Hill Crest, at Boar's Hill, Oxford, not far from where Gilbert Murray lived. I left London early so that I could steal another glimpse of the Michael Angelo drawings at the Ashmolean, and have a silent hour along the Magdalen Walk, where twenty years before I had wandered alone with what I romantically thought was a broken world.

It was not so much the poet—the Laureate to be—I sought to sign, as the dramatist who wrote *The Tragedy of Nan*. I had met Masefield in America, but had not realized how his deep interest in the theatre had found a practical outlet. Now, as we lunched—he waited on me himself, carrying the dishes through and receiving the food from a mysterious opening into the kitchen beyond—I found he had a wee theatre on his own grounds.

"I felt I had to do something to bring poetic drama back to the people; so I started this theatre here. At first we did our plays in the recreation hall in the village of Boar's Hill, a half-mile away. It seemed odd that, living within only six miles of a great university town, the people knew so little about the real poetic drama."

We later walked through the garden to the theatre which Masefield and some friends had built. It was not large, but it had a stage and a balcony with appropriate dressing rooms. The lighting was simple; the audience room could hold a hundred or so. Here a half-dozen plays a year were done. Masefield himself directed and sometimes acted. He admitted he had once played King Lear on three days' notice. The costumes were made by his daughter; his wife tended to business matters.

The plays were always poetic dramas. Masefield had made the translation into verse, including the great French classics. He had recently done a version of *Tristan* which played, in addition, three weeks in London, with the cast of sixty from the neighborhood. Scant work could be done in the summer, he said, as so many worked in the fields. During the winter, however, they rehearsed three evenings a week, "which added to the communal interest." The admission fees were less than a dollar for the best seats. The company of ten traveled to near-by villages. They tried to give two performances free, so that every one might come. There was no thought of financial profit though they aimed to earn expenses.

"It is surprising," Masefield said, "how instinctively they scan and find the rhythm. Even when they may not know the meaning of the word or ever heard it pronounced before, the flow of the line gives them the proper cadence and swing."

Life on that hillside seemed so far away from the industrial age that beckoned us in the screeching of a distant train. Here, too, was a living effort to attain beauty which the poet himself had so often himself caught in his verse. I was so interested that I almost forgot my mission; but his fountain pen was ready when I asked him to join our Guild. As I started for my bus, he gave me a rose from his garden.

"Give my regards to your brother. Scudder Middleton is an authentic poet," he said, waving a farewell.

It was a lovely interlude. I thought of it as the spires of Oxford Cathedral came again into sight, over the hill; thought of him and his country players—"who have no name," he had told me.

Fola and I had been the guests in London and the States of the author of *Waste* and *The Voysey Inheritance,* and I should have enjoyed seeing him again. However, his feeling towards the Guild is best expressed in two tiny notes, written at different times, which I add "for the record," as the politicians put it.

NETHERTON HALL, COLYTON, DEVON
June 23, 1927

MY DEAR GEORGE MIDDLETON:

Yes, please do let me become a member of the Guild. I am, as I said, fully alive to its importance and the excellent time-saving and dispute-saving work that it has done. I enclose my paper and a cheque for £5 more or less.

My kindest regards, please, to Mrs. Middleton and to you.

Very sincerely yours,
HARLEY GRANVILLE-BARKER

TUCSON, ARIZONA
2.2.29

MY DEAR GEORGE MIDDLETON:

Many thanks: my wife has her "trade union" ticket now and all is well.

You really have done a great job with and for the A. I congratulate you. I wish we had your powers of cohesion in England. . . .

HARLEY GRANVILLE-BARKER

I did get to see Henry Arthur Jones, who was then seventy-six. I was shocked as I approached his invalid chair, with its enclosing red rubber rings, in his suburban garden. He had written little for six years, except that, as usual, the congenital old Tory moralist would still burst out in polemic print. It had colored all his plays and let him pose human problems, only to have some avenging code ruthlessly judge and punish his puppets. To the end he was to be a propagandist and pamphleteer. He had kept an eye on a social world he was not born to. Yet his biggest successes were in such comedies as *The Liars,* not in the serious drama nearest his heart, as *Michael and His Lost Angel.*

But forty years of expert play writing looked out at me as I sat registering his sharp-pointed beard, eyes that would squint quickly, and the two deep ridges from his nostrils to the mouth corners. The face was ruddy, for age had lined its own peculiar year marks. Over eighty scripts had flowed from his pen, including *Mrs. Dane's Defence* and his first money-maker, *The Silver King.*

This melodrama held that famous line: "O God! Put back Thy universe and give me yesterday." A friend of mine was once present at a revival by the Stage Society of a long forgotten melodrama. Suddenly all eyes turned to the stage box in which Jones sat. For a character had just shouted: "O God! Put back Thy universe and give me yesterday." If true, I'm glad he lifted and thus rescued the grand line from oblivion. How else would I have had that thrill, when I heard it first as a youngster?

While I sat beside this shrunken old man, I recalled our various meetings back to my college days at Brander Matthews' home. He had fought for a National Theatre asserting the right of a dramatist to be considered as a literary figure. Jones had early impressed me with the need of play publication. Indeed, I still have copies which he gave me from time to time. He had a little trick of traveling with extra ones to distribute. Even this last time he had his daughter hand me *The Divine Gift.* One of his best plays, I think; yet one he never could get produced. And with the same pen with which he autographed it he gladly signed the Guild application blank.

No one in England, not even Shaw, had more eagerly advocated a union of dramatists. He murmured something to the effect that he wouldn't be "much more use." But I told him we were honored. I was pleased to think, when he passed on, two years later, that his name had been on our roll in those days of our youth.

I could not help being amused at the contrast when I signed Frederick Lonsdale, who had inherited much of Jones's milieu and none of his moralities. For the author of *The Last Mrs. Cheyney* was in bed when I called, in lavender pajamas, the picture of languid ease. He didn't mind signing a bit, as it turned out, was witty during our quick talk, and probably went back to sleep after I left. I think I went from there to Sir James Barrie; for, in response to a second letter, I received the following with its characteristic final line:

ADELPHI TERRACE HOUSE, Strand, W.C. 2

DEAR MR. MIDDLETON:

Thank you for your letter and I shall be glad to see you if you can kindly call here on Thursday about 5.30. I am so sorry to hear about that other letter and fear it is in an unopened pile that someone ought to tackle. Please forgive!

Yours sincerely

J. M. BARRIE *

Barrie lived opposite Shaw. They could wave to each other when so disposed. A little lift timidly rode me to his flat. The only impression I retain is a sense of its being brown. In the late afternoon half-light he made the same impression. He was even shorter than I had

* On a photograph he gave me for the club he wrote: "Decision of The Players, 'He looks like a Detective in the films.'"

expected, with something owl-like about his face, accentuated by its roundness and heavy pouchy eyes, fairly large ears, and high forehead. I felt ill at ease since he walked about, all the time I talked of the Guild. It was not discourteous, for I felt it was habitual. When I offered him a few short documents to read he waved them aside.

"Has Galsworthy signed?"

"He was one of the first."

"Then it's all right with me."

I passed him our application blank. He went quickly up a few steps to a table and signed, without further ado. I noticed he used his right hand to write his name but his left for the replies. When I commented on this he told me that he had contracted writer's cramp. It explained the difference between the text of the letter to me and its signature.

I don't remember much that he said. I had been so anxious to get over to him what the Guild stood for, in my limited time, that I didn't do much recording. When I spoke of dues and taxes he did some more waving and referred me to his agent. As we were waiting for the lift to steal up to his floor, he did mention his admiration for Eugene O'Neill and the striking performance Pauline Lord had given in *Anna Christie*. That is all I remember of my half-hour with the author of *The Admirable Crichton, Peter Pan,* and *The Little Minister*. He had written also practically nothing for seven years. I tried to murmur some appreciation for all the pleasure his pen had given me. But the elevator had started slowly down.

I had Sir James Barrie's signature, yet Shaw's had not arrived. In fact, I counted up to find we had now forty British members. I knew Shaw for years had tried to organize British authors; he had urged young playwrights to assert themselves against what he called "the dramatic ring," the close corporation of the elder British writers in the Dramatists' Club, to which women were not admitted and the young not encouraged. I also knew that, because of his war views, Shaw had been expelled from it! I resolved to take the bull by the horns—if that describes it—and rang Shaw up. Miss Patch answered. The conversation went something like this:

"Miss Patch, I'm in quite a dilemma. Perhaps you can advise me. Mr. Shaw promised to let me know whether he would sign the Agreement. I must leave tomorrow for Paris, as I have some engagements with the French authors. Since I talked with Mr. Shaw I have been successful with every one I saw, including Barrie who signed yesterday. The Associated Press has promised to send a story over if and when Mr. Shaw signs, and I haven't heard—"

Just then the well-known voice broke in. "I have read your Basic Agreement, Mr. Middleton. Much of it wouldn't hold water in British law."

When I recovered I managed to stay on my feet: "That doesn't interest me a bit, Mr. Shaw."

"Why not?"

"Because the British author is perfectly free to make any contract he wishes for the initial production of his play in Great Britain. This contract is only concerned with its production in America. This will protect the British dramatist there. It will hold water in American law."

"Well, I've signed it. I'll send it up by messenger. Where are you stopping?"

"I'm at Carter's Hotel. I can't tell you how much I appreciate—"

"I hope you have a pleasant trip. Just let me add that the American dramatists won't thank you for what you have done for them. The British authors didn't thank me."

Before I could say anything he rang off, with a chuckle. Shortly after, his application blank arrived. I have it before me. He had inked out the printed formula, "I am the author of the following plays." Instead he had written in his characteristic perpendicular hand:

"I am the author of several notorious plays, and need not enumerate them. They have all been produced."

CHAPTER XXVII

ISADORA DUNCAN SAYS FAREWELL

So ONCE AGAIN Fola and I climbed the five flights of No. 20 rue Jacob. Much water had flowed under our Seine bridges in the five years since we had stood together upon our little balcony "which Balzac himself probably saw when he looked from his own window a century ago." Death and birth had moved in and out of our lives: failure and success. But there had been no blank spaces for either of us: our years had been exciting and full.

Now there were to be visits with old theatre friends and new ones: André Rivoire, foxlike in appearance, with a penetrating Toulouse-Lautrec sketch of him peering over his shoulder as we talked; Romain Coolus, who succeeded Rivoire as president of the French Society— robust, spilly-talker, Gallic to fingertips and a cultivated professor to boot, when not writing risqué comedies like *Les Amants de Suzy*. However, I saw that nothing like a tie-up could be attempted during the *vacances*. And I was suddenly tired. Paris was a jealous lady. I had long carried on an affair with her. She put on her best lure. Friends of our other worlds tapped again on our doors. I am afraid I played hooky from my self-imposed and self-financed organizing quest. Paris! Paris, as we knew her then . . .

There was dancing with the Alexandre and Amaly Arnoux in the streets on Bastille Day. How the French could enjoy their fêtes! What abandon! What camaraderie! Real democrats. Real individuals. Then a visit to Jo Davidson's studio in Auteuil to see the plaster model of the La Follette statue, which, taking on its marble vitalities, was about to become, admittedly, one of the finest in the National Capitol. How lifelike the two qualities of the man alternated, as looked at from side view or in front: the fighter about to rise from his Senate chair to object; the man who deeply loved and believed in the people! The externals, too, were fixed, for the family had sent the shoes and clothing he had worn his last year. But the head had been modeled from life: in 1923 Pater had sat for Jo in that very studio after the visit to Russia with Lincoln Steffens, the Basil Manlys and Bob, Jr.

Then a dash to Jo's other home in Bescheron. As we were getting off the train he let out a whoop: "Just what I have been looking for, George: you must pose for me tomorrow. I'm doing a statue of ——, and you have his left leg." The slight bow which had been the bane of my self-conscious adolescence was thus to achieve an anonymous immortality! Left leg and all, the next day we went to the near-by château at Saché. Here, in a little souvenir-filled room under the roof, Balzac wrote *The Lily of the Valley*, tribute to a fading love, while nearly getting himself married to a *bon parti* in Tours close by. Then another sortie to Prémery, in Niève, to Auguste Lambiotte, industrialist with the largest formaldehyde factory in France, who had a broad, embracing culture in which Rose, his wife, shared. We four had been friends since Belgian days, motoring about from triptychs to quiet cathedrals. In fact, I heard Rose's father, Senator De Meulemeester, ask their witty chauffeur why he didn't have more children. "Monsieur travels too much," their chauffeur shot back.

They come to mind here because Balzac slipped into my pen again. Auguste knew I wished to write a play about him. (It was, in fact, now only nine years away.) One morning two letters, which had started on their way over eighty years ago, landed with my breakfast tray, in 20 rue Jacob, not far from where they had been written. One was from Balzac, the other from Madame Hanska, who became his wife. Originals, too! Auguste had picked them up at the Claretie sale, and he generously made them mine. They are here, in my files, fresh as when they were hastily penned.

Some of the French artists of my earlier pages had quit the earthly scene. Late leaves fall fast. One of the great still remained. So Fola and I were to see Isadora Duncan dance again.

Will and Jenny Bradley had invited us to share the stage box Isadora had sent. He was her agent and mentor for her celebrated autobiography. She never really finished it, though it told of her best days. It had been years since I had seen her. But, as I sat in the theatre, my thoughts went back to her and "the Duncan girls" who had come to America with her. The Children's Society refused to let them appear. Her secretary appealed to Fola. Could Fola do anything? Fola did. She saw Mayor Mitchel, who had been at Columbia in my time. He arranged for her to interview "the obstructor" at the Society. Fola found his chief concern was how short the dancing shift would be, and how high the children exposed their naked legs in the dance.

She apparently satisfied morality's latitude and modesty's longitude. The children were allowed to dance. "Why don't you come see me?" Isadora telephoned Fola one day. So we went. She then had a studio on Twenty-third Street. It was hung with blue cloth to serve also as a rehearsal room. A trivial episode happened.

I was sitting beside her on a couch. She had draped herself against the high pillows. Visions of Greek statuary came to me, Elgin marbles. Suddenly she took my hand. Not being alone with her I didn't mind. The vitality I thus gave her, however, surged right out of her to an approaching male vision. It brought Isadora with a bound to her feet. My hand, of course, got dropped in transit.

"*Who* is this beautiful creature coming towards me?" She exclaimed so that all the room could hear.

Everybody was silenced. She reached her arms out in pictorial abandon. The man was dressed in brown: a baggy four-plus. The coat and long stockings toned in, with touches of complementary green. His short, well groomed beard also hesitated from brown to auburn. As he hastened towards her the elemental curiosity of the elemental female again rushed ecstatically to Isadora's lips.

"But who *is* this man?"

And out of a skyey *castrato* voice fell his demolishing answer: "I am —— ——!"

I was thinking of this experience as the dancer herself now glided before us on the darkened stage of the Théâtre Mogador.

Of course, it was not the same. Gone were the slim lines which had waved their own special rhythms with each undulation of hand and scarf, or spoke in poetry as her body moved majestically through the imaginary Elysiums of Gluck. Gone was the arrow swiftness of *La Marche Militaire* or that final, frenetic flash which I had once seen lift an audience to its feet as she tore aside her red shawl to let her breasts leap forth to meet the tumult of *La Marseillaise*. But now I watched unmoved, save for a sinking heart. I could see intimations of her genius: but to me, at least, the spark had been spent in life itself. Perhaps after the intermission . . .

When the house lights came up I noticed in the next box Cécile Sorel, the veteran *sociétaire* of the Comédie-Française, one of the most famous Parisians of her day. Did any woman know more secrets of the *coulisse?* How her long life had twined with those of France's public men! She was an institution. Clothes, influence, and an indomitable will had made her personality famous: never her art, which had brilliance without any warmth. Except in the artificial roles of the classic repertoire she had never interested me. But I confess I might have enjoyed one of her famous receptions as she sat propped up in Madame du Barry's authenticated bed, which time had moved, by strange chances, into Sorel's apartment on the Quai Voltaire, around my corner.

I had a word with her. She spoke, as on the stage, with sharp, clipped enunciation. She held her head high, her nose pointed upwards as though disdaining the words she uttered; the pose was perhaps to keep the long neck line from sagging with the fifty-odd years already unavailingly besieging her. How different, I thought, the mold of race had made Isadora, whose story, too, had done some twining on her own among the great: Gordon Craig and others. Yet Sorel was at her peak only as a person; Isadora, only as an artist.

I was thinking of that contrast after the intermission, when, to a Tchaikovsky adagio, Isadora moved slowly to the footlights. She looked down and knelt beside what she made us feel was a sleeping child. Then she carefully put her arms beneath it, gazing in its face as she tenderly drew it to her breast in an encompassing embrace. It was all of motherhood: the epic of it. Of course I saw, as did everybody else, her own two children who had been so cruelly drowned. I sensed the personal because, through her art, it was transmuted into something universal.

I have seen this phenomenon from time to time in a life of theatre and concert going. It is one of the most extraordinary qualities of great interpretative artists, expressing themselves before an audience. It is then that they sometimes seem to have the power to call upon the gods who listen; and for them to pull aside mystic veils, through which we witness and suddenly become part of something far beyond our mortal selves. It is where great art and mysticism meet. It is a gift not given to mere facility nor technical perfection. It lies beyond all training and instruction. Even those who possess it cannot always command its presence. But when it flashes out to a receptive spirit, as did one simple gesture of Isadora's on that far-away afternoon, in a French theatre, it becomes an unforgettable treasure in our deep memory.

They gave her an ovation. After a dozen recalls she moved to the front of the stage and stood there, silent. Then, as the house suddenly hushed, with a single magic outward flowing motion of arms and hands she expressed what no words could have conveyed.

It was a hail and a farewell to all her greatness; for it was the last time Isadora danced!

I tell of this because there was also a sequel. With a play going into rehearsal * I had to leave Paris shortly afterwards. Fola was to stay for the Progressive Education Conference at Locarno where nearly a thousand people from forty different countries were to meet: a group which had sprung from a few who "had believed the new education offered the most fundamental approach to constructive internationalism," as she described it in La Follette's Magazine. And for her ahead, too, were days at L'Arcouest, in Brittany, with Professor Seignobos and Jenny Bradley, as well as days with Phil La Follette doing France together. So I sailed on the Paris alone.

I knew Mercedes de Acosta, the playwright, was on board. Her drama on Jeanne d'Arc had recently been produced in Paris by Eva Le Gallienne, with Norman Bel Geddes assisting. Eva's story of that amusing experience has survived in her autobiography, At 33. Mercedes came to me on deck to say, "An old friend wants to see you." So I again found Isadora. She and her new Russian lover had gone to the station in Paris to see Mercedes off. They stayed on the train to Le Havre. She would have gone right on to New York except that she had no money and no passport. She wanted to speak to me of her autobiography, about to go to press. She was afraid that the tale of her many lovers might cause it to be withdrawn. Will Bradley had told her of the Authors' League fight against censorship, led by Elmer Rice. She asked my advice. I said I would do what I could. The warning whistle blew. I walked with her to the gangplank.

"Isn't one American going to give another American a goodbye kiss?" she asked, almost wistfully.

Of course I did. Wasn't her lover right there, smiling? So I gave her as good an American sample as I could muster—if that is the proper word—and planted it full on the lips. None of those pecky two-sided French embraces. Her eyes widened in a studied response and flattering admiration. How well and how easily she did it!

"How you kiss!" she said.

I wigwagged a naughty finger. "Old stuff, Isadora." She burst

* The play was Blood Money, founded on a story by H. H. Van Loan. It was produced at the Hudson Theatre, in New York, by Mrs. Henry B. Harris. It had an exciting first act but never could catch its breath after. It is now mainly interesting as the piece, I believe, in which Thomas Mitchell caught the eye of Hollywood scouts. If so, the play did the public a good turn while giving me several bad ones.

out laughing. So did the lover. It was all so Continental and jolly. The whistle blew again.

She stepped carefully down the gangplank. She paused. Then she slowly turned. Another pause, and her long scarf blew frantically in the wind trying to escape from her neck. Some figure on a Grecian vase I had seen somewhere came to life. I heard her call: *"Au revoir."*

She held the pose another moment with practiced effect. Her hand turned downward. Her arm tranquilly unfolded to her side. She waited. She turned away. I watched her out of sight.

Barely six weeks later I picked up the paper to read that Isadora Duncan had been killed in an automobile. Her scarf, blowing in the wind, had caught in the wheel, pulled her head suddenly down, and broken her neck.

I have often wondered whether it was the same scarf.

CHAPTER XXVIII

ON TO BERLIN

In October 1927, when I became president of the Dramatists' Guild, with Hartley Manners as vice president, it was already in tiptop shape. Squeaks and the squawks had been oiled out. I knew, however, that no organization could survive on the mere momentum of an accomplished reform. Once the pressure of abuses is lifted, exaltations in the ranks are hard to sustain. I felt the first problem of leadership was to keep selling the Guild to its members by having it continue to do things for them. The Council heartily supported this. Its meetings, at which we averaged a dozen members every few weeks, dealt with everything from "special concessions," plagiarisms, arbitrations, prize-play contests, and violations accidental or otherwise of the Basic Agreement, to the regulation of agents and the collaboration contract I've spoken of. Our office staff combed each individual contract, soon over 620; and only 21 were sent back for repairs. There were also handouts galore about copyright, new laws, or court decisions of professional interest.

But there was another job for which I kept thinking my previous experience might qualify me. I hoped to help complete our deeper plan: a Guild tie-up with the playwrights in every country for mutual protection and cooperation. The occasion, like Venus, arose unexpectedly. The International Confederation of Dramatists and Composers, which included all European societies, invited the Guild to Berlin. Since the Authors' League needed some one to make an official statement there regarding the Berne Convention, the Guild asked me to go and was able this time to pay my expenses. I had naturally done little writing. My *Blood Money* had failed, and Belasco had laid aside *The Desert*. Kit Cornell stood ready to live up to her contract; but we both saw she was not happy with either the play or the part. Hollywood had called Basil Rathbone and he had turned down the important male role. So another chance to replenish the pocket-book had crashed. However, this trip seemed the next thing to do,

and I found it one of the most exciting adventures in my professional
life.

Before I sailed, Luise Sillcox dug up all my official titles and
had cards printed. I recently found one hiding, abashed, among my
records of that trip:

GEORGE MIDDLETON

PRESIDENT OF THE AMERICAN DRAMATISTS
PRESIDENT OF THE DRAMATISTS' GUILD
PRESIDENT OF THE SOCIETY OF THE AMERICAN DRAMATISTS AND COMPOSERS
MEMBER OF THE COUNCIL OF THE AUTHORS' LEAGUE OF AMERICA, INC.
MEMBER OF THE BOARD OF DIRECTORS OF THE AUTHORS' LEAGUE FUND

2 EAST 23D STREET
NEW YORK N. Y.

I sailed on the old *Rochambeau* to get up my French. I spoke it
three days with one passenger before I found he spoke English and
four other languages perfectly. "I never know which one I am talking," E. Fernandez Arbós said. Pupil of Vieuxtemps and Joachim,
he had been concert master in the Boston Symphony and later conducted it; friend of Casals and the incomparable dancer Argentina,
for whom he wrote a ballet (she, also, was to give me a nod at his
bidding in Hollywood), he soon took me into his confidence. Reputed
one of Europe's best raconteurs, he brought a world of personalities
out of his sixty professional years. "Some of the anecdotes are naughty,
so perhaps I'd better tell them in French," he would say. As he had
seen our *Polly with a Past* and *Adam and Eva* in Madrid, I of course
asked about the Spanish Authors' Society, and obtained some handy
facts for use at Berlin. Beside his young, vivacious French wife,
he appeared frail. Yet with thick-lensed glasses, a full, gray-threaded
beard and a rakish beret, Spain's greatest conductor could not fail
to draw attention. Always in repose, he made me feel his great
vitality only later, when he imperiously held the baton. Every mu-

sician I ever spoke to of Arbós—Bodanzky, Iturbi, the intense cellist, Cassados—held the Maestro's musicianship in high esteem.

He invited me to join his Madrid Symphony and tour Spain: he was booked to play in many villages off the beaten track, or in bull rings where no concert halls existed. Like Gunga Din I might be water boy, distribute the scores, or be the claque. Had it not been for the Berlin convention I should have gone. I felt envious of Olin Downes when he told me later of making the tour. Arbós explained to me how he had recruited this orchestra—the first, I believe, to tour Spain and give the masses an opportunity to hear beautifully played symphonic music.

"In Spain there is no money for endowments and no aid for music from the government," he said. "I found many splendid musicians doing routine work in the government. I went to the department heads, cut through the red tape, and almost kidnaped the men so that they could travel with me for the spring season."

How I wish I had known Arbós in 1922, when I wandered alone through Burgos, Avila, and Seville—about which William Archer wrote me, "In my opinion the great Spanish cathedrals are the most impressive in Europe"—or brooded over the grim exterior of the Escorial, or lingered on the road below the Alhambra as the sunset colored its tawny walls!

Years later, after the revolution had swept his orchestra away, I had a long, tragic letter from Arbós. His relations with Fola and me had deepened until he could sign his letter, "Your affectionate friend." He outlined the autobiography he was writing and wished me to send it to a publisher. I did what I could. He was then blind and, I believe, was not able to complete it before his death.

Arriving in Berlin at the end of an April snowstorm, I went to the cosmopolitan Hotel Adlon, so changed from 1922, when galloping inflation had started. I had come from Paris with the French delegation: Rivoire, Coolus, Messager the popular composer, Besnard, and my old friend Denys Amiel, who was *Secrétaire général*.

Denys was a Meridional: he saw everything *en grand*. An early friend of Bataille, he had begun his play writing shortly before the war. I was to watch his plays, from *La Souriante Madame Beudet*, written with André Obey, mount to the stage of the Comédie-Française itself. I should have been lost in Berlin without Denys. I had met him when he was editing a French paper in New York.

We had seen much of each other during Paris years, and he had translated my *The Reason*.

On our earlier wanderings we had visited the house in Gambais where Landru, "the modern Bluebeard," had burned up some dozen overripe females. It was uncanny to stroll about that walled back garden, behind a perfect fictional house of mystery, to poke absently in the dug-up turf the law had left in its hunt for human bones. The stove also remained in place, inside the house, now for rent, with no takers. Above it, I recall an itinerant's chalk inscription, "Attention aux revenants" (Look out for ghosts). It is unkind to associate the kindly Denys with Landru; but both were so efficient.

From the opening session on April 6, 1928, to the last, a week later, Denys directed the convention like a ring master. We met twice a day in the Prussian House of Parliament, destined to see history ahead. Into it Fola and I had peeked during one of the early crises of the Republic, in 1922. Two hundred delegates took part, with nineteen accents from as many countries. Once two Russian authors tried to break into the hearings. A statement was read, but they were carefully shunted off the official floor. The Bolsheviki were not paying any royalties to foreign authors, and there was some talk of contagion; but I had known managers who hadn't paid any royalties, and had no such fear. They seemed fine chaps. I only knew they were writers, too.

I discovered I had been dubbed an "honorary vice president," because I was president of the Guild. This privileged me to be photographed on the dais, sitting right beneath Mussolini's relative, Senator Morello, who presided, and also permitted another photograph, outside President von Hindenburg's office, where only the vice presidents were allowed to pass the sentries and be received by him.

In his office the enormous old man, then eighty and obviously growing *gaga,* was quite impressive. As we were shown in each of us was assigned to one of the seven chairs, placed in a perfect semi-circle radiating from a large chair at the center. When the President entered we all rose. We were presented individually. He gave us each a pump of the hand and a sharp nod of his massive head. Then he went to his chair. As he sat, so sat we. His pancake haircut, marvelously curled mustache, and distributed weight symbolized an authority which even then was slipping away to a sign painter in the offing. But what impressed me was the bull neck, much thicker than Lucien

Guitry's, which made his head seem like part of his body. He spoke
to us in guttural German that I did not understand. He was formally
courteous. I ventured the hope "for a close cooperation among German and American dramatists." He grunted, "Ja." Never in my
wildest dreams, during the Guild war, had I expected to get a grunt
from the author of the Hindenburg Line!

Almost the first hour of the convention's first day I accidentally
got into the debate. A motion was put to which I would not commit
the Guild. I broke in and glided along beautifully until I suddenly
discovered I was speaking French. Then I went blank and apologized. But they called out, *"Allez, allez,"* and so I shrugged. After
all, if they could stand it I could. George Gershwin, whom I had
met over a cold Adlon breakfast, had come along. I had not planned
this treat for him, but George, who did not speak French, was highly
amused at mine. A friendly twinkle from him, now and then, helped
me to keep at it. Maybe it inspired a syncopation. I managed all
right throughout the week by secret talks with the official interpreter,
a wonder named Schmidt. He translated my one English speech.
(He later stood by Hitler at Munich and interpreted everything to
Chamberlain, except his master's intentions.)

When, weeks afterward in Paris, I checked over the stenographic report of what I had said I was astonished at the beauty
of my French—due to Denys Amiel's very efficient secretary, who
had made good all my verbs and genders. I made that one little
speech in English at the farewell session just so that they would know
I could speak it, and was violently applauded. Relief undoubtedly
played a part, for I then discovered that nearly the entire convention
understood English!

I have no thought of distilling the two hundred fifty pages of that
printed report.* But I learned what I was after: the trade habits
and copyright protection of each country, how royalties were collected and all the admitted author-aches with actors and directors.
I was able to suggest some practical reforms: registration with each

---

*In the June, 1928, *Authors' League Bulletin,* I offered a detailed study of the
make-up of the convention and explained the various groups present. Here also is
information on the European performing-rights societies which corresponded to ASCAP.
They were made up of "editor-agents," music publishers, and the like. It was because
the dramatists had united with these other groups, interested in protecting the "small
rights" of composers, that the British authors did not send representatives to Berlin. I
also discussed this in the *Author* (Jan., 1929) from the Guild's viewpoint. All this
matter is too technical for insertion here. But it may have value for some fellow who
wants to earn a doctorate by digging into the ways and means of authors' societies.

society of agents and of adaptation contracts, with the local names of the adaptations as well as their production dates and number of performances. Señor Eduardo Marquina, the Spanish playwright, good-naturedly challenged my statement that many American authors never received royalties from performances of their plays in Spain and South American touring companies, asking me to name a single author who had suffered. I did, and there was a laugh; but months later I got some $500 back royalties due to Guy and me on *Polly with a Past,* with the society's apologies for "the slip."

The genial Ludwig Fulda presided over these sessions. Besides writing many plays that were adapted in America (such as Lunt and Fontanne's production of *The Pirate*), he made a translation of *Cyrano de Bergerac* that became a German classic. A cultivated literary man, modest and kind with his associates, Fulda had done most to advance the protection of the German dramatist. Adaptation and translation, as Fulda said, were admittedly most important in our mutual relations—aside, of course, from being sure that we dramatists got our royalties. I pointed out that their best protection lay in cooperating through the Guild. I explained our own special trade customs and even tackled our Basic Agreement, which was hard enough to explain in English. But, since riches lay in the American market, every European dramatist hung on my words.

When I concluded, the French privately offered to join us; the Italians also, though already their government had demanded a place in their society under the encompassing Fascist formula. Somebody told me the German papers carried full accounts. But I wrote to Fola:

As I can't understand what they say about me I don't buy them. . . . Tonight is a banquet and all is over. It is a very complicated situation and I need another trip to accomplish what's necessary. However, I've been successful and I think they like me and my funny French. At any rate they say they never heard any American speak it better—which shows what judges they are. I can't tell you all that has happened of a gracious sort. Coming to Europe in an official position has its advantages. . . .

I know I have done something for the future—if only I can make the fellows see it. This is a big job and Lord only knows where it is all going to lead to. I sometimes wonder and then again I am content.

No convention could have been better run. Our hosts offered the best in the artistic world of that Germany. I had renewed impressions of leading actors, like Krauss or Moissi, and prominent producers. George Gershwin and I went to see the famous Yiddish Art Theatre do *The Dybbuk* (up to then, the German stage had ever been hospitable to such wandering groups). We went to a special performance of *Salome,* followed by a reception to which Richard Strauss himself came from his Bavarian home. He smiled graciously: I noted his intense eyes, sandy mustache, and high forehead. Then I passed on. And yet . . .

Fola and I had once heard him in Salzburg, conducting a dress rehearsal of *Cosi Fan Tutte.* Directly above him, stowed in the Burgomaster's box, we could watch him lure Mozart's beauty from the pages. I noticed, when he took his curtain bows with the Viennese opera stars, he seldom smiled: he seemed colder and more formal than when I had heard him in my bachelor days at Paris, twenty years before, from a box at the Opera House and let his music carry my eyes over the spaces, searching for one I knew was there, to find her with another, drat it!

To me much of remembered pain and pleasure loses its initial intensity. I can recall and phrase old emotions; but they remain like something I have read; the real and the fictive, in fact, often become synonymous. As I then faced the celebrated composer, beyond our polite exchange of words lay that strange sense of what his music had once intensified. Odd thus to meet one who had communicated through some far-away emotional association: in Paris *Ein Heldenleben* had held that unforgettable violin theme to the Hero's beloved, which then was personalized; his *Tod und Verklärung* had brought back another top-gallery exaltation in Carnegie Hall. Yet both emotions had long gone into my dead self to seminate the new, which now had hardly a bowing acquaintance with it. In shaking my hand, Richard Strauss little knew how, through his music, he had once aroused and coddled deep feelings. Here and there, too, even the humblest artist may unknowingly have likewise brought a communication to a stranger whose hand he was never to shake.*

In off hours I forswore sight-seeing trips for the great Berlin museums. I said hello again to Queen Nefertete, that most beguiling of painted limestone heads, with the sloping hat, discovered by Her-

* Strauss's American royalties on *Der Rosenkavalier, Salome,* and *Electra* have passed through my hands at the Office of the Alien Property Custodian.

man Ranke in a sculptor's shop, sleeping for centuries so soundly
beneath the sands that her color kept fresh. Years later, Dr. Ranke
autographed a photograph of the lady when I followed his lectures
on Egyptian art at the University of Wisconsin. There were more
Berlin interviews with Max Reinhardt and his staff, to answer all
business questions: tutelage, too, from Fulda, Lothar, and leading
commercial playwrights, as to their workings with the editor-agents
(*Verlags*).* But here I was most indebted to Fritz Wreede, already
mentioned in connection with *Light of the World,* when Reinhardt,
Strauss, and Hofmannsthal thought of doing it. Fritz also opened
every door and gave me an inside view of the powerful Felix Bloch,
Erben, Verlag, of which he was head. I was most grateful, however,
for the hour he arranged with Hermann Sudermann.

The author of *Magda* (*Heimat*) lived in Grunewald. The walled
villa was guarded by the largest police dog I ever hesitated to pass.
But he smelled Fritz, and that apparently was also good enough for
me. The house was comfortable, without pretense. The little library,
in which we were to have tea, was tasty, with a lived-in feeling. The
dramatist-novelist was waiting. He had a high forehead, with wisps
of hair on top, closely cropped at the sides by the hirsute poverty of
seventy years or by design. His eyes were large and steady. The mustache did not conceal his firm mouth and determined jaw. Yet he
spoke German gently with a peppering of French. Fritz was a skilled
interpreter; he had lived in England and could match me with American slang.

Of course, as always when I met such men whose plays had been
a part of my young enthusiasms, I recalled how affected I had been
when I first saw *Magda* (written in 1893), savoring the author's
theatrical finesse filtered through the thesis dramas of Dumas and
Augier. I fell for any dramatist, of course, who wrote of the individual's revolt against bourgeois respectability—so often Sudermann's
theme. *Magda* was the most widely performed play of its time.
Largely because the *bravura* role so stood out from its drab small-
town background, it became the vehicle of every star. Though later
plays achieved some international appeal Sudermann's tight technical

* In the Sept., 1928, *Bulletin,* I wrote a detailed analysis of this entire business
structure, with special reference to the *Verlag.* I was naturally gratified with some words
Arnold Bennett wrote me about these various reports: "It is all very interesting, and,
what is more important, it is extremely useful. I congratulate everybody concerned. And
while I am on the subject, let me say, I was immensely impressed by your report on
conditions in Germany. This must have involved an enormous amount of work."

methods ceased to be the mode; life itself was also altering the values of his social attitudes.

He had sent a telegram to the Confederation, regretting that he could not attend as he was engaged on work he could not interrupt; but in a private letter to Denys Amiel he indicated that he had left the theatre because of the hostile attitude of the press towards his later plays.

I had at once sensed, beneath his courtesy and tolerance, that the man was sad and disappointed. A reserve and poise kept this from words. Fritz later told me Sudermann had been deeply hurt when Germany failed to pay him the tribute it paid to Gerhart Hauptmann at his sixtieth birthday. Of course Hauptmann was a much more significant figure and was a Nobel prize winner. I never met the handsome author of *The Weavers, Hannele,* and *The Sunken Bell,* though I saw him once. He moved impressively down the well carpeted stairs of a Munich hotel, with the dignity of a Greek god bestowing his presence on our midst. He seemed to be carrying his aura under his arm; but he didn't put it on for me.

I felt sad when I said goodbye to Sudermann. I thought of him often. I do now. Hard must be such late days in a dramatist's life when, not content to rest on his laurels or accept the gray protective coloring of age, he feels his powers and will to write strong as ever, yet knows they are not wanted. There is the anecdote about Scribe being turned away by the director of the very theatre where once his fame was made: "Scribe? Never heard of him." When I first began my rounds in New York I saw one such dramatist shivering along with his manuscripts under his arm, after having seen him coldly greeted in the offices of the men he too, in his time, had helped to initial success. It is the law of life that it must often frazzle out, I know. Perhaps it is sentimental of me to speak of it. After all, Sudermann had had his cake and still could afford to munch the memory of it in comfort.

But, like actors who fade away from the footlights' applause, dramatists live on more than the bread which comes from their plays. There is something irretrievably lost when public favor fades. A playwright outmodes or his fighting spirit often weakens, under the unproduced scripts, so much more quickly than the novelist, who needs nothing but the printing press to keep him alive before his individual audience. I felt this when I last bade Sir Arthur Pinero goodbye. Old Henry Arthur Jones, too. I was now to feel it in Vienna when

I saw Schnitzler; and in Paris, a few weeks later when I visited Brieux.

In some ways, I am sure, no one of them minded the verbal tribute I brought them or that I looked them up. They had, I knew, little to give those of us in the Guild who were now trying to build better for the protection of the plays to come. But I was glad it was my privilege to tell what each had meant to me and my generation. Perhaps only those whose own shadows have begun to lengthen a bit can sense how deep the shades ahead may be.

Hermann Sudermann died a few months later. In some ways the memory of his sad but kindly smile stays clearest of those full, exciting Berlin days.

CHAPTER XXIX

THE END OF THE ADVENTURE:
MOLNAR, SCHNITZLER, BRIEUX

BEFORE keeping my May appointments with the French Society in Paris I now had time to visit some European authors whom I had missed in Berlin. Ferenc Molnár had whimsically written on April 16, 1928, in his purple ink and immaculate lettering, that because of his trip to America and the rehearsals of his new play he had not slept since the 30th of November, 1927. But he hoped we could pass some time together in Vienna. The most successful of Continental authors promised pay ore on what I was after. Wreede had arranged appointments with other authors. Heltai, president of the Hungarian group, had done the same, in Budapest. So I sallied forth.

Some idea of the interest these days held is reflected in the hasty and intimate notes I scribbled to Fola between times. In June she herself was booked to go with Evelyn Dewey, to Russia by way of Sweden, as a member of the American Education Delegation, headed by Professors John Dewey and J. McKeen Cattell. So beneath all the passing excitement I was anxious to return before she sailed.

AMBASSADOR HOTEL, PRAGUE
April 27, '28

. . . I sent a card from Dresden. The gallery is wonderful: one of the greatest. Do you recall it? And such Titians and Veronese! I delayed going to the Dürer Exposition and so missed it by five minutes. The ride towards the border was marvelous—after leaving Dresden—all along the Elbe, with the trees in bloom and the cliffs just back enough. I read between times Yvette Guilbert's *Chanson de ma Vie*. It is splendid: particularly interested in her account of Duse, some of which we knew.

I was met at station. They are giving me a lunch and then show me the town—which boasts a great Dürer. I have lunch, too, with Capek, who wrote *R.U.R.* I have already got a lot of dope * on the place, from my end.

* In the Jan., 1929, *Bulletin,* I analyzed the authors' societies and the general theatrical set-up—especially as they affected the plays of American authors—in Hungary, Czechoslovakia, Poland, Rumania, and Finland. I gathered this information in odd hours, from the amiable representatives of these countries at the convention.

It is not big; but it has one or two fine writers. . . . This situation in Europe is very complicated, and I feel I did the wise, if less spectacular, thing in not tying [authors] up as I did in England.*

I spent an hour with Reinhardt before I left and he was very gracious. There is so much cuisine amid all groups! . . . We must ultimately force them all in as [Guild] members and they all want it† . . . I've learned heaps and made enduring connections . . . I wish you were to be with me the rest of the trip. I meet Molnár, etc., and expect to dig out some more facts to write up. I hope to get my report to Guild done on boat or before I leave. I see so much to be done . . . speaking French saved me . . . Want to look up some Balzac material . . .

HOTEL DUNAPALOTA, BUDAPEST
April 28

. . . It is entrancing. I didn't let anybody know I was here as I came ahead of schedule. So spent the morning in the museum. Here is what I found [enclosure: photograph of Vermeer's *Woman with a Glove*]. I knew she was here but I didn't think she was so lovely; so calm and serene and distinguished. You'd love her, too. I only wish you were here with me. . . . They are coming for me now . . .

"They," who were coming for me, were Zsolt Harsányi—translator of O'Neill's plays and author of a novel about Galileo, *The Star-Gazer*—and Emil Lengyel, author of *The Typhoon,* with whom one day I played golf. Yet I now had my first perfect alibi for not keeping my head down and my eye on the ball: the distant Danube, and a fascinating musical comedy queen playing with us! The two dramatists, incidentally, had such attractive wives that I saw why most Hungarian comedies were about marital mix-ups. I wrote:

I'm trying to keep this a business trip, being a conscientious fellow . . . I have ten appointments in Vienna. . . . Honest to God, dear,—I know you smile—but I'll be glad to have some time all alone. I've talked for weeks about contracts, and I wonder whether it is all worth while. But I've put the Guild on the map over here, and that's something. . . .

Everybody has been wonderful with entertainment, etc., and Budapest is adorable. But I need sleep. I leave for Vienna tomorrow after having had the meeting last night I really came for. About twenty-five were

---

* I was also hindered by the fact that our Basic Agreement did not give us complete control of conditions under which the foreign rights to our plays should be sold in Europe. This was altered in 1936.

† In the 1941 Agreement, membership of British and foreign dramatists in the Guild became obligatory, with certain exceptions.

there, and I think they were pleased. I have at least established Guild connections that will lead to something. . . .

Spent an hour with an agent and got some valuable documents which they avoided giving me in Berlin. . . . Tomorrow I turn back, and from then on shall be going towards you. . . . I've been rather important over here, I suppose, judging by the attention I've received. But I know where I am at in the U.S.A.!

Harsányi said an American author might then earn $5,000 on a play in Hungary. Producers and publishers had always been hospitable to foreign plays; in fact, they had done everything to keep Hungary out of the Berne Convention, so that they would not have to pay royalties. As a consequence the home authors had their plays stolen outside Hungary. Molnár told me his own *The Devil* thus had two competing Satans in Manhattan, one being George Arliss. When there was a greater demand for the works of the Hungarian authors they themselves forced copyright protection at home for the foreign works produced there. Restricted geographically as Hungary was by the Versailles Treaty, with towns formerly important placed beyond its borders, Budapest still remained a germinating force in the international theatre.

I cannot pass from that city of wonderful bridges without re-.calling the party given me by Ince, the publisher of the Budapest theatrical paper. He had invited lovely women and stray dramatists. A regular stage scene. I came away at dawn, with a large bottle of native wine he had given me. I decided to walk to my hotel—to phrase it euphemistically. My train was to leave for Vienna in a few hours, and there was no need nor time for sleep. Alone, I strolled along the Danube. The Danube at dawn! The old houses of Parliament yawning into life beneath a lifting veil of mist, with the warmth of the growing day! And the old city of Buda sitting vaguely on the hill opposite, brooding on history it had seen sweep through that valley, wet with the blood of conquerors, drenched with music of its tziganes. What stuff for drama it had all been! What librettos!

It was good to be alive, taking in such beauty. I remembered how insignificant I had felt as a lad looking from a mountain top till I suddenly realized there was greatness in a human being's mere capacity to take in such space and color. So, I hated to leave the Danube for contracts and such. I wanted to go on to Belgrade, Constantinople, the Armenian churches beyond, and . . . Yet trains to Vienna would not wait. I called the hotel maid on my late arrival, and we hastily packed documents, Basic Agreements, and black ties; but it was impossible to take the wine with all my impedimenta. So I presented the bottle with a courtly bow to the wide-eyed, blushing, expecting-anything maid. She must share it with her favorite lad, I suggested. Her eyes sparkled. For a moment I felt like a part of some libretto myself. Here was just the place for a duet. But I didn't. What strange people, these Americans!

I did not see Vienna in its great days. I knew those only through plays or history. In 1922, when Fola and I were there together, I had been so depressed at the stalking tragedy on people's faces that I stayed in its great museums (it was a dentist, acting as guide, who had led me among the great Velázquezs, best of all those outside the Prado). Now as I rode past familiar landmarks along the Ring-Strasse the irrepressible spirit of Vienna spoke again. The Opera House had its usual queue. There I was to place a scene in my Balzac play depicting his great fame when Metternich ruled. The Burg Theatre loomed mightily; but I missed its performance of our *Adam and Eva* by several weeks. Yet there I saw a revival of *L'Aiglon,* which brought back that other Vienna in vivid contrast to the city outside.

When I arrived at the Hotel Bristol my room had not been reserved. The clerk was very sorry. My *commissaire* had not arrived. As I was protesting, the smiling, moon-faced monocled Ferenc Molnár moved into my orbit: he had come to call on me. When the clerk saw our greeting, there were quick apologies. A room mysteriously popped out of a hat, and all the porters pounced on my baggage. Any friend of the dramatist in Vienna . . .

HOTEL BRISTOL, VIENNA
May 2

. . . I had lunch and supper with Molnár. . . . Have got some fine documents and learned a lot. . . . Tomorrow Kálmán, Lehár, Schnitzler, and three others [including Siegfried Trebitsch, favorite translator of Shaw, and Sil-Vara, whose *Caprice* the Theatre Guild was to do with Lunt and Fontanne]. Took two hours off—by starting early—and saw again St. Stephen's, the blue Vermeer, portrait of himself, and the best at the Lichtenstein. What a Van Dyck!

May 3

I have a full day. Lehár, etc. . . . Molnár is a dear. We talked over an hour last night about the theatre and he gave me lots of inside stuff. Everybody here seems willing to talk. . . . Most of them have grievances against one American firm. "Can you help us collect money they owed us?" I was asked. I've already specific pledges for our protection. It's going to take two weeks to get my material in shape, and want to do it in Paris and on boat so it is as clear as I can make it. . . . But, oh! the cuisine here as everywhere! The *other* fellow is always dishonest.

I had met Molnár in New York. He then spoke no English. Once, June Walker who had acted in his *Golden Slipper,* rushed up to him. In effusive English she told what it had meant to play in his *"wonderful* piece!" He smiled but said to me in French that he "didn't understand a word." As an appropriate climax she kissed him plumb on the lips. "That is something I understand in any language," he murmured.

He took me now, of course, to Sacher's restaurant, which Bob Sherwood was about to use in his nostalgic *Reunion in Vienna.* Though Molnár did not wear military garb and was a bit roundish in front, he could have stepped out of his own comedy, *The Guardsman,* or any other, of the great Schönbrunn days. He seemed to be the eternal skeptic, or rather the amused spectator of life, savoring it as it passed his lips. There were no illusions left; only the old world's ennui, with a tolerant interest in the new world's effort to find something different in life. As though there were! He made me think of Meredith's line in *Diana of the Crossways:* "It is the test of the civilized to see and hear and add no yapping to the spectacle." I felt so at home with him, somehow. He was a character I had conceived but never written.

"I'm sorry I wasn't in Budapest when you were there," he said; "but it was too early for me to go home yet. You see, I only go there when it gets warm, for all my summer clothes are there. I come back to Vienna when it gets cold. I have to: I leave all my winter clothes here."

I should have liked to hear the stories of lovely ladies and intrigues he could have told me. Instead I had a job, and I questioned him about unromantic matters: the *Verlags* and the repertoire theatres in each city which dominated the German theatre. I had noted the fear among the powerful editor-publishers of the spread of the American "traveling troupe system." Molnár's reaction might be helpful for Guild members who had hits, when it came to making German and Austrian contracts.*

* I dwelt on it *ad nauseam* in a brochure I previously mentioned. For comment on it see *New York Times* editorial, "Theatre Business in Germany," Aug. 6, 1928.

"With my *Spiel im Schloss* (*The Play's the Thing*) I had fifty presentations on Easter Day alone," he told me. "Under our present repertoire system one could have three hundred and sixty-five performances a year, since a year happens to have about that number of days. There are some two hundred first-class theatres and others. In repertoire Hamburg, Leipzig, and Munich can easily give the author a hundred performances a year. The *villes de bain,* like Karlsbad and Baden-Baden, can in all account for another hundred. I made my verlag report to me every three months. It got 10 per cent commission; but some verlags took from young writers as high as 50 per cent. Verlags, you know, often act as brokers and frequently are speculators in the play.

"In an average repertoire a play might easily be done forty times at one theatre; whereas a play arriving *en tournée* in the same town would not do more than four weeks. It is booked for a specific time and must play that date; should it be a success it could hardly stay longer, as the theatre has its own troupe waiting. The resident company would not revive it after it had been done by a traveling troupe. *Eh, voilà.* It's all a matter of mathematics." *

What a contrast Molnár was with the pert, chubby, agitated Franz Lehár, who made a very Merry Widow famous, the suave Emmerich Kálmán, composer of *The Countess Maritza,* and Arthur Schnitzler.† Our meeting had been arranged by my efficient but mysterious *commissaire.* Of the list of agents and adapters I wished to meet, none escaped his net. He went along when I interviewed Kálmán and Lehár together. I knew their cooperation as Guild members might be of value to our musical comedy group in the event of another fight. I called on Dr. Schnitzler alone. I had never seen Rodin; yet, somehow Dr. Schnitzler recalled him. He was stocky, quick-moving, with a full fine head and warm embracing eyes. There was no indication of his Semitic origin. He spoke three languages, intermingling

---

* Molnár is living at a New York hotel, in one room of which he has filled the walls with a dozen colored reproductions of Gauguin, since "they make such a harmonious background to look at." Seventeen of his plays have been done in America. Fortunately, he had let all his royalties accumulate here, and so found them waiting when the war forced him to leave Hungary. "I always liked dollars," he added, with a contented smile. Since his *Liliom* inspired Richard Rodgers and Oscar Hammerstein's highly successful *Carousel,* he now has that exquisite pleasure of an old play bringing fresh fodder. Dick recently told me an amusing episode about the last act of *Carousel,* which was not in *Liliom.* With trepidation he and Oscar awaited Molnár's reaction when he first saw the rehearsal. "It's the best scene in the play!" he exclaimed.

† Kálmán is now in America; Lehár remained in Vienna; Schnitzler is dead,

To George Middleton
affectionately Ferenc Molnár
N.Y. 1946

FERENC MOLNAR

ARTHUR SCHNITZLER

A merry Xmas
to our author,
"Polly" Claire

INA CLAIRE IN "POLLY WITH A PAST"
Produced by Belasco

To my good friend George Middleton.
Arthur Pinero
17th Oct. 1933.

SIR ARTHUR PINERO

YVETTE GUILBERT

EUGENE BRIEUX

words and phrases—his French, as I recall, being better than his English.

There was thus little evidence of the suave literary style which gave such a glow to those Vienna scenes which had made me yearn for them as a young man. Nor did his conversation convey any of the gayety his earlier comedies had suggested, before he had turned to the deeper tragedies. Extremely high-strung and animated, like Barrie, he had little repose, except that he made me feel comfortable. He was constantly moving amid physical trivialities, pulling down the shades or arranging his books. He steered me to the window to show his garden below.

"I thought I could work out of doors. But I couldn't. The noises distracted me so."

I remember this because Capek had said almost the same in Prague. An airplane droned overhead. Schnitzler loved planes. Just that morning, he said, he had flown from Venice. He was silent for the first time, and my thoughts danced irrelevantly through a phrase he once wrote: "We all play parts, happy he who knows it" —and my recollection of his *Reigen,* considered so naughty that it was twenty years reaching production. I told him how I admired his one-act plays; the thrilling production Mrs. Fiske had made of his *Green Cockatoo,* with its twenty-two speaking parts—that most skillfully constructed of short plays. But he waved aside the *Anatol* before the *Lebendige Stunden* (*Living Hours*) which I, too, cared most for. Perhaps because the three plays dealt with the questionable right of the artist to use the material of his life for copy, I quoted some of his lines I had often used in my one-act play lecture:

You are all alike, you artists, great and small, all alike, so proud of yourselves. Even if you were the greatest genius the world has ever seen, what is all your writing compared to one such living hour, one of those hours when your mother sat here in this armchair and talked to us, or just sat silent? But she was here and she was alive.

And the poet's answer:

Living hours? They live longer than the life of him who remembers them. It is no mean vocation to give such hours an enduring existence beyond the grave.

When I asked him about his method of work, he said (according to the notes I wrote on the back of an envelope in which he had placed the photo he signed for me):

"I generally see the play in its form first. Sometimes I put it aside. When I write it, however, it may fit into another form entirely." He sighed. "But I don't find it easy to write."

I asked him why he wrote novels.

"I began as a playwright. I'm not sure I didn't turn to the other form because of so many difficulties I had in the theatre."

As the talk turned to business I could see he felt very bitterly at what had happened to him during the war: for in America, he said, many of his plays were stolen—and little of the desperately needed royalties subsequently came through.* Further, he told me frankly that his latest plays were not being done in Berlin. He shrugged as though to say, How can a dramatist stop writing?

"I have three plays under way now," he added.

He was tremendously interested in the Guild and asked me to send any articles I had written. Months after I had reluctantly said goodbye, I had a letter about one of the articles:

DEAR MR. MIDDLETON:

I thank you very much to have sent me your article about the Dramatists' Guild in Europe. You are too modest writing that the article contains only information of value for America. The deductions of your essay are interesting also for German and Austrian authors—they are clear and precise.

Auf Wiedersehen hoffentlich

Your sincerely

ARTHUR SCHNITZLER

But I was on my way home.

May 4

I am leaving tonight for Munich, for two days, to try to clear out my brain; and then Paris. . . . I have had no cable of any sort about the play [*The Big Pond*, being tried out in Baltimore], so judge it flopped or the option wasn't taken up. I'm quite prepared. The work here has been so intense that I can't get back into the personal realities concerning the work I once did.

It has been an unforgettable experience here for which I shall probably pay dear in money and work; but no one can take away some of the happy experiences and contacts . . . I'm bone-tired.

No. 20 rue Jacob again, and for the last time! May in Paris. The balcony. Two weeks of it before sailing. Hours with old friends and

* The part this led me to play in the Second World War is explained at the beginning of this book in "Aside to the Reader."

the documents. More authors: Bernstein, big and canny. Missed Marcel Bouteron, the greatest of Balzacians. The play remained in my mind. Lunched with Yvette Guilbert. Wandered about the old places. Would I ever see them again? Now I feel I shan't. "There is always a last time," Barrie once wrote. Always now I recall it, when I say good-bye to the people and places I love. But, as I've said earlier, "Paris is mine as long as I can remember it."

May 11, PARIS

. . . Spent afternoon with Sacha [Guitry] and Yvonne—all alone. Delightful. Please phone Sillcox that I appear before French Authors' Society today (Brieux, president): we are going to work out something and expect important developments. Shall see all the authors here and prepare groundwork for a cooperation. They all want arrangement with us. Tell her, confidentially, that Guitry has promised to join when we want.

I went before the *Commission* of the Society. The building in rue Henner was holding its last meetings before it moved from its old home. It was quite an impressive place. Our Guild rooms seemed so small in contrast. Here the two official agents of the Society, Block and Ballot, had their suites nestling right in the Society's home. Authors always chose which one they were to be *chez*. These agents handled all the plays of the French authors in Paris and generally on tour. I gathered for days all the information as to how the entire agency situation worked.

The Board sat in a formal room with a long table and elegant chairs. In the center was the president, Eugène Brieux. If ever there was a Roman Emperor stepping off one of the old coins it was he. As he greeted me, I felt as though I were being received at court. Charles Méré, and some of the others, were less formal. All seemed to be interested and cooperative. But I made it clear that French authors should deal in America through us. I said my little piece. I even went back for questioning a second time.

But, as one president to another, calls had to be exchanged. I didn't want to have a seventy-year-old try my five flights plus; so, of course, I went to his home. Brieux received me with great courtesy and took me into his study—packed with the books upon which he had based so many of his famous social dramas. Brieux, of course, had especially interested me. He had found so much drama in social inequalities, the injustices brought by law and all the shame of our civilization. He had read and observed, to dedicate himself with passion to the correction of abuses. His play *Damaged Goods* (*Les Avariés*) made history. All the sincerity of his recognized integrity soared above the caviling of those who felt he had made the theatre a platform from which to harangue, and the Academy had received him years back. In the theatre he had performed the important function of tearing it away from tidy themes. I told him how I felt. He received my words with a studied reserve, and I felt chilled; but as I rose to go I mentioned his play *L'Avocat*. He looked puzzled at my knowledge of it, as it had had only twenty-two performances in Paris. When I told him I had adapted it for Belasco a startling change came over him. All the reserve left. He thrust out his hand: no Roman Emperor he!

"Confrère!"

He made me sit again and eagerly asked me all about the American production. Then, with the mask down, he poured out his feelings about the French theatre, the soaring costs of production, the difficulties of casting, motion pictures—the story I had heard everywhere on my trip, which only echoed conditions at home. The theatre all over the world, in fact, was crumpled in the same contortions.

I had long overstayed, at his urging, the time of a formal call; but it had become something more than that. As I was leaving he went to a bookcase and took out a copy of a play which he had had privately printed. He wrote my name in it and gave it to me. He smiled as he said almost wistfully:

"I can't get it produced."

He, too; like Jones, Schnitzler, and Sudermann!

When the *De Grasse* sailed I looked towards the shores of France as I had done four times before. I thought of what stood out in those fast-moving weeks. Denys Amiel had said that my going to Berlin was important, and that all felt so. There were personal satisfactions in what little I had tried to do for the Guild. My quest had been the business of authorship, not the art of it. But I kept asking myself: In this changing world of the theatre, what was ahead for us dramatists? And there came back to me the words of astute André Rivoire:

"The authors must now be prepared to fight big mechanical industries."

At Berlin, dramatists from every part of Europe were aware of the profound changes already taking place in their professional lives. With the perfecting of new inventions—which were using and transforming, by mechanical means, the product of an author's brain—unforeseen dangers were already at hand; and greater dangers were ahead. No one could prophesy what might soon be utilized without payment, and even without consent. Already, everywhere, efforts were being made to shorten copyright restrictions, or to reduce the penalties for deliberate violation of copyright so as practically to negate its legal protection.

Mechanical industries which photograph on films, record on films and disks, and use these for transmission over the air, can sustain themselves on copyright material alone.

What if some of them should take such material without payment, as a deliberate policy, and thus compete unscrupulously with those having higher concepts of fair play? What defense against them could prevail? How could mere individuals talk back to any aggregation of capital and power? Could any legislation whatever serve the needs of individual writers, so threatened?

All the dramatists at Berlin had had the same wish: to guard for the creator the rights which authors had so laboriously won through the years; to permit no encroachments under new and persuasive disguises of expediency. The aloofness of individual authors in every country, who hate to mix the business and the art sides of their profession but willingly accept the advantages others have gained for them, must give way before such a menace.

Yet it would not be enough merely to organize only the authors of one's *own* country. Light and sound waves do not recognize national boundaries. The inherent moral rights of the author remain the same, whatever the flag that flies over him.

The consciousness of a need of *protective unity* was then the big idea back of this convention. The thought was my own dream of an ideal authors' community. I felt so deeply that I would gladly have given further service to that end, had my own circumstances and the coming occasions permitted. The way was clear, and the direction indicated. The future rested in the hands of the writers themselves.

And I thought long of it while my boat moved homeward through tranquil seas.

CHAPTER XXX

HOLLYWOOD: THE STAGE AND
SCREEN FACE IT OUT

HOLLYWOOD!

The question I had asked myself when I took Douglas Fairbanks and Mary Pickford to Sarah Bernhardt's grave, as to what the films would do to the theatre, had already been partly answered. But when sound now began to dominate the film industry I wondered what further result talking pictures would have. What would they do to the dramatist and vice versa? I was now to go West and find out.

PICTURES AND OUR POCKETBOOKS

I had known few film people. William C. De Mille, though, who married Anna George,* daughter of the single taxer, was early my friend. He and I had been at Columbia together, and later there he "put on" *Embers,* one of my little plays. He became a popular playwright with *Strongheart* and *The Warrens of Virginia,* in which both Mary Pickford and Cecil De Mille acted. The two brothers, so closely linked as film pioneers with Jesse Lasky, were, like their parents, theatre folks. But the nearest I ever got to Cecil was sitting beside him when he was in Paris at the Ritz, in bed with arthritis. I knew Jesse first "routing" and staging vaudeville acts. I saw him not long ago with *Sergeant York* in his pocket, one of the great successes in film history—history which he and the De Milles had helped to make, after they and Sam Goldwyn (then Goldfish) had traveled west to a barn in California. In between, Jesse had tasted the bitter and the sweet, smiling as gently with one as with the other. I always felt better when I saw him, especially after a $15,000 picture contract he gave me at Paramount, in 1918, for a half-dozen "originals" in which Pauline Frederick, Mae Murray, Jack Pickford, House Peters, Fanny

* Their daughter, Agnes De Mille, herself an outstanding dancer, has now, with *Oklahoma!* and *Carousel,* established herself as the leading American choreographer.

Ward, Vivian Martin, and other early stars had briefly shone. I might add that picture shares from my Broadway plays had netted me something around $50,000. Aside from this, however, I had never been summoned to Hollywood in state. I went now, in 1928, when the "talkies" themselves were just old enough to give a coming-out party.

Leaving aside a possible Hollywood salary how had silent pictures affected a dramatist's pocketbook? When I began scribbling, stage plays brought no financial return outside the theatre. Then we had road tours, repertoire, foreign rights and, best of all, "stock" weeks. Senility alone killed the earning power of a successful script. Some had yearly netted me a thousand dollars or more, even after the first flight—metropolitan failures, like my *House of a Thousand Candles,* included. These combined to make good concurrent cushions against new production uncertainties. Incomes were less spectacular then, but steadier. On the road then bloomed many a hardy annual that Broadway seldom heard of. Even a half-success might be nursed into a money-maker—impossible today, with a higher infant death rate. For years Owen Davis's earnings averaged $50,000. The rest of us lacked such fertility and industry. When silent pictures first flickered we dramatists, as I have said, considered film rights as so much velvet. Owen, for example, from several hundred scripts thrown into his trunk, bundled together twenty-five, for which he picked up $50,000. Another bundle did even better.

"I was beginning to think I'd sold them too cheaply, George," he said, with his best business twinkle. "But I've a better idea of what became of the money than the scripts. I never saw them again. Maybe they're still doing them."

When D. W. Griffith decided to film *Way Down East,* with Lillian Gish and Richard Barthelmess, he paid Brady $175,000, then the highest price for a stage play. But when it was circused (in thirteen reels) with the two film favorites, to earn $2,000,000 the first year, what did it and all similar films made from our plays, in fact, do to the legitimate theatre, where—as the child described living actors—"round people" traveled with plays and scenery?

In the decade after the Shubert-Syndicate fight, when the newly built theatres had to be filled, numerous companies of a hit sallied forth with a New York endorsement but poor casts. Audiences "on the road" soon tired of paying for such well advertised but badly wrapped products. So stars had to put their trademark on the articles.

Yet there, too, artificially puffed-up personalities were quickly deflated. Empty theatres everywhere soon left a vacuum into which silent films rushed. In addition, the picture firms, vying with one another, built beautiful houses of their own, sporting spacious seats for the work-weary and the neckers. Thus, many small cities, where touring companies had once held forth, were now visited by magnificent star casts expressed in waterproof cans. But the picture was not cheapened in transit; unlike a play, it arrived exactly the same as it left its point of origin. A good silent was soon seen to be less boring and expensive than the average "road show." Our stage audience was thereupon being weaned away; and a new audience, not even theatre-bred, began to be created. While we dramatists thus got "velvet" from a dead or moribund play, its film version was tending to diminish the normal outlets for the play itself. No longer were we without competition as entertainment purveyors. We were, in fact, supplying it through selling our plays to be filmed.

But even this competition did not hamstring the theatre. Many film stars meant nothing to real theatre lovers, while the few stage stars who entered silent pictures seldom had the box-office appeal of stars who had grown up with the film industry. Established playwrights rarely went to Hollywood, since only directors' handy men were needed at first.* So many pictures were "shot on the cuff" that the "title writers" merely inked in some fancy laundry marks on the film or sewed up the story holes. No playwright could pretend to himself he was important, so long as the movie directors could say "Off with its head" about anything in the script. Yet, as the novelty of silent pictures wore off, scarlet ecstatics and purple passions grew boring. Many films were so bad that the customers themselves became selective. Meantime, the stage had largely held its breath and its personalities. Its outstanding stars and authors were loyal. Stock, too, inevitably enough, had even begun to recapture its former outposts. Picture houses were closing and into them new stock companies and road companies were being rushed to pay the landlord.

But in 1927 sound suddenly squelched this healthy revival. I saw at once that stock and road tours, without outstanding personalities, could not compete with fine talking pictures, with star casts now drawn from the stage, offering versions of the very same plays

* See *Hollywood Saga* (New York, 1939), by William C. De Mille. This is the best inside story of practical aspects of an extraordinary industry, by one of its most cultivated participants.

which the corner theatre might be showing at twice the price, with a company of "round actors" who actually had to eat.*

Once again a new invention brought the dramatist unexpected velvet. Film companies, after having bought silent film rights, now had to pay for the "dialogue rights," before remaking the picture. On *Way Down East,* for example, with Janet Gaynor as star, $50,000 more was paid. Yet while the stage authors got windfalls the stock and road income from the plays sold now stopped for good. On new plays, the film companies bought both silent and talking rights, as one was worth nothing without the other. Hence new plays could no longer develop stock value. Another factor now lifted its head, to strike at the dramatist: stars and leading actors rushed to the swimming pools and patios of Hollywood, and were no longer available for his new plays. Many plays either could not be produced or were inadequately cast.

So the loss in cumulative royalties from the shortened life of plays makes it debatable whether the large outright sums paid for the film rights exceed the plays' potential returns under the old conditions. The delirium caused by large checks may easily have blinded playwrights to the sustaining virtues of constant chicken feed. One exceptionally successful colleague, who admits he made $2,000,000 out of stage and screen, told me half had come from theatre royalties alone. The other million, from films, included large weekly salary stretches the companies thrust upon him.

When the camera cleared its throat and films first began to talk every one in Hollywood jumped out of bed. There was an intruder in the family circle! But he was not bringing glad tidings: it was Change! Revolution!! The silent kings and queens rushed about, in contract confusion, trying to hold on to their crowns while testing their tonsils. If pictures must talk, dialogue would have to be written! What was worse; it would have to be spoken! Executives looked at their long-term commitments: what to do with the sky-voiced, kiss-lingering male lover, at ten thousand per, and the vocal twangs of

* Some idea of the shrinkage in stock alone brought about by new conditions can be gleaned from Dramatists' Guild records. When it was first organized, it was partly financed by taxing stock productions one dollar a week. The first year or so, before the full effect of talking pictures was registered, the intake approached $4,000. It is a question, at this writing, whether even $400 a year comes in. However, fees paid for amateur performances have greatly increased, and plays especially adapted for special groups earn many thousands. I have been told that *Adam and Eva,* which we sold outright for a song, has been worth $100,000 to the agent who had the insight to speculate on it.

that starry-eyed bitch, the nation's model of gentility? Would she ever learn how to speak, if the Svengali-Trilby relationship were broken and the megaphone-shouting director were actually reduced to coaxing in pantomime? How were those same dictators, if without previous stage experience, to grapple with the readings, timing, and what not of the theatre?

So the executives sent an SOS for theatre people: *People speak on the stage, don't they? We must get stage actors! Of course: but only the good-looking ones. And keep 'em young. Yet their names won't draw a plugged nickel into our box offices! What to do? Well, we'll mix them with the others: One silent star—not so hot on inflections—with one actor who can spout but may not get on so well with the camera. That's it. Can't our picture dolls be made to talk? Dialogue directors? That's it. They'll coach the dumbbells that contracts and their public compel us to carry along. Stage directors can direct the dialogue for the old picture directors, who will direct the camera angles! That will all tie up fine. And dramatists! Of course. They'll write the dialogue. We'll team them up with our silent continuity stand-bys. Good! So away with the organ tremolos and violin obbligatos of the good old silent days, and up with more soundproof stages.*

Theatre folk, hearing the clink of the ducats, stopped, looked, straightened their halos, and rushed forth: *There is a maiden in distress—with gold in her undies. We must save her!* The stage shook almost to the point of collapse under the rushing feet. The movement swept westward, to where the sun actually set in the ocean! What a sense of mission we pioneers had! *Of course, we'll show 'em. Silent pictures weren't really our forte. But the talkies—all they mean is moving the characters about a bit more, breaking up the scenes: really, in fact, a play in smaller pieces.*

How little we knew what was in store for us! For the silent old-guard directors did not intend to give up silent picture ways to these know-it-alls. Some openly resented us; but the cautious, canny majority put on acquiescent smiles, with the resolve to get what they could out of us—and kept their tomahawks handy.

It was as this seething conflict reached its height that I, in my new Buick, arrived in Hollywood.

An executive job had been offered to me, and I had accepted. If I survived the option my two years would net me $117,000. Since Guild work had kept me from much writing, my bank account was tottering. As to the option I can answer, like the nobleman who was asked what he had done during the French Revolution, "I survived." In fact, I did one hundred four straight weeks without a break except a vacation or two they gave me—I suspect because they needed the rest.

My status in that period of adjustment was confused. In the "screen credits" of the dozen films in my charge I was an "associate producer." Those who didn't like having me over them called me "a supervisor," and on the lot I was generally called a "supervisor." I had reams of responsibility without final authority, and never knew whether I was fish, flesh, or fowl—though the last leaves me wide open. While I did not have to do all stories submitted, my selections had to have "front office" approval. After I had overseen the preparation of casts and scripts, they were subject to a red or green light from my two bosses: Sol Wurtzel and Winfield Sheehan, who later married the famous singer, Madame Jeritza. Winnie had formerly been a reporter on the New York *World*. Having many intimates in the theatre he was almost the first film executive to believe stage folks would have to be used. Sol, being a silent film product, had no love for us dramatists as a class; but he pocketed his prejudices before the new order. I liked him much more than he ever did me.

When Winnie gave me my contract he said: "I can't ask you to give up the presidency of the Guild. Any time you need to give to it will be all right. I know that all authors haven't been happy in Hollywood. If you see anything you don't like, or if we have any disputes with writers on our lot, I'll cooperate with you to clear them up."

I left my resignation, however, with Arthur Richman, asking him to wire when he felt it should be submitted; and I stepped out when certain negotiations arose between the Guild and the film industry.

At that time, I may interject, only the cameramen were organized. Feelers were soon made to me through Sidney Howard, on behalf of Actors' Equity, which was then trying to organize the film actors. But the Dramatists' Guild, owning its own copyrights, had different obligations from those working exclusively on a salary. Managers then, by performing a play for a specified time, acquired a half-interest in its picture sale. I pointed out that the Guild could not jeopardize any manager's right by refusing to deal exclusively with a film company, as was proposed, because it in turn refused to deal exclusively with Equity members. The screen writers I advised, out of our experience, to tie up all the writers before making any demands to improve their work conditions, since they could gain nothing fundamental from the benevolent droppings of a studio-dominated Academy. Vigorous leadership was ahead, and both Hollywood actors and writers are now effectively organized.*

I never worked so hard in my life as at the studio. I did not miss a day in two years. Never before had I been tied in an office, had a salary or a boss. I have my own measure of what I contributed: I will merely record that I "brought in," under budget allowances, all but one of the assignments I had been told to do, whatever their later box-office history may have been. I also know where I fell down. But for the total estimate, I'm more concerned with sketching the contortions of the dramatist in general than with rubbing my own tummy where it ached and cockadoodling where I might. I had keen disappointments, as they had with me: but no rancor remains. It is curious how funny one's own writhings shape in the look back when emotion has left them.

But I must admit a personal weakness. In my previous executive experiences with direction over other people, neither their money nor their jobs were involved. My studio relationships, however, soon troubled me. I grew to like most of those with whom I worked. I felt more a collaborator than an overseer; and I am sure this lessened my executive effectiveness. As Sol once frankly put it:

"George, you haven't been enough of a S.O.B. with that director. He doesn't respect you. Look how I treat him. He eats out of my hand."

But for a year and a half I was the white-haired boy. Even when Sol and I were about to part company, my "doghouse" remained a rubbed-down oak-paneled office, with a shower to supply any cold water the front office might overlook. In my last week I read *Kim* and dictated letters to all the directors thanking them for their cooperation. As they probably suspected sarcasm, none replied. In Hollywood, as in Washington, people are always rushing towards you or away from you. It amused me to recall that Alexander Korda had also been kenneled near me; but he escaped to London, where he

---

* The Screen Writers' Guild of the Authors' League has an enforcible Basic Agreement to expire in 1949, with a 90 per cent Guild shop. In May, 1946, it had 1,027 active and 383 associate members, defined by the number of weeks employed. The studios take on about 350 writers each month. Individual yearly earnings range from $2,500 to $100,000. The present minimum weekly salary is $125. Licensing the authors' original scripts rather than the customary outright sale is now the latest objective of the Guild under its president, Emmet Lavery.

subsequently became famous and a "sir." He and I were talking of my coming over with him when the war broke.

Nine months after my contract expired I wrote farewell notes, like Washington, to Sol and Winnie, saying that Fola and I were on our way to Wisconsin. Immediately both called me to their offices in anguish. They both wanted me to stay or return a coming September morn. They even let me in to see them before they admitted the waiting Louella Parsons! How like Hollywood! But, as I anticipated, Winnie later wrote me:

> Nobody knows your talents, your manifold capabilities, your enthusiastic and able services better than I do; hence I'm going to be very frank in saying that we haven't a place in sight which would please you just now—and I'm not going to offer you something, even tentatively, which I know would not satisfy your energy or your ambitions.

I forgot to add that Sheehan, when he signed me to go out, was general manager of the Fox Film Corporation, whose deal with the managers had precipitated our Dramatists' Guild fight! Either he had admired what I had helped the other dramatists do to Fox, or he had never even heard of it. Neither of us ever brought it up; but it was the most profitable smile I ever had over a turn in events.

My Picture Education

I had realized, of course, that Hollywood was more than an overgrown suburb of the theatre. However much the same were their masonry and plumbing, Hollywood had its own traffic rules. It was a fabulous never-never land which any dramatist simply had to explore —with my salary if possible. But I had one advantage over the later settlers, being in on the talkies' puerperal moment, when they were first looking from perfected silence to the bewilderments of perfecting sound. It was a fascinating period, as we were all trying to reconcile what the stage and the screen could take from and bring to each other. With the artistic and economic friction generated by the contact, neither was ever to breathe the same again.

But what had I thought the dramatist might offer to talking pictures? Both obviously required words, actions motivated with suspense devised as in the theatre. Dialogue, too, must be "sayable" with similar directness for the jab or the laugh. Theatre folks knew how to write or speak lines and "protect" them. Stage writers, and stage actors in films, could better anticipate such dialogue reactions on a film audience. This, I soon saw, was to be our most helpful contribution—even more helpful than situation structure. But while we could bring about better built scenes the tenacious habits of the silent films blocked our special technics of exposition and plotting. My own theories got rough treatment, as I shall show.

I early learned a lesson in the contrasting values of silent and talking picture. When sound hit the industry it had thousands of feet of silent film ready for release or in the making. In theatres not yet wired for sound these found a normal outlet. Here, too, silent versions of even the "all-talking" pictures might still be shown, with old-style imposed printed titles. Where houses were wired, however, the demand for talking pictures was greater than the supply. So, to salvage the millions of dollars unexpectedly tied up in silent films, musical "sound tracks" were added—"synchronized" with the action, like the old "sob" and "snake" music of Granddaddy's melodramas. In addition there was frequently let loose that most horrible contraption called a "talking sequence." On these I cut my eyeteeth—for I had charge of four. One of my few claims to film fame is that I believe I wrote the first lines Janet Gaynor ever spoke. The silent films and the talkies were now to show each other up. The poverty of silence became as obvious as the enrichment that sound could add; but the talkies demonstrated that they could not merely consist of stage scenes, with hunks of dialogue, unrelated to the flow of visual movement which the silent films had perfected.

From Charlie Chan, the famous Chinese detective, however, I further learned what every dramatist in Hollywood had to know. I was in at Charlie's birth: when Earl Biggers' best-seller *Behind That Curtain* was dolled up for the screen. As much as $80,000 had already been spent on "story treatment"; but, reading it, I could not follow the "story line." Yet Irving Cummings, the director, to beat the spring heat of Death Valley, was already there with a hundred supers and a caravan of camels, actually shooting the desert sequences! I told Sol Wurtzel what I thought, and he sent me forth in command, with Sonya Levien, to "fix it up."

I had known Sonya back in her New York editorial days. Since then she had become first aid to every new Fox writer, being an expert on continuity and the mysteries of dissolves, fade-outs, and other film punctuations. So we landed in Death Valley. The rock formation of the distant Panamint Mountains, our English expert said, was just like that of Khyber Pass, through which, for some reason or other, our plot had to squeeze. It was my first experience on location.

Death Valley was an exciting vision. I had, in fact, fallen in love with the West, and during my three years there Fola and I slipped off in its wonders for week ends and vacations. I never could get over orange groves and snowy mountains being within eyeshot; nor the amazing geological formations—the canyons with their book of rocks written in colored erosions; the arroyos, the crater lakes, the meteor holes and black lava beds edging the lush loveliness of unexpected vistas. (To anticipate, when we finally left Hollywood we retraced American migration. For we drove eastward through mining towns, Yellowstone, and the Bad Lands to Wisconsin. And then over the Canadian route to Gaspé, stopping a half-hour to note something the voyageurs never saw in Callander: seventy-five diapers blowing in the morning breeze to indicate the morning wash of the Dionnes! Then to drive down through New England, home of my forebears, to the city where we were once again to find 158 Waverly awaiting. Never before these years had I so fallen in love with America.) Of all my Hollywood experiences, I hold most precious such scenes as I now beheld. For it was this cruel Death Valley, born of tragic convulsions that made it the lowest land in America, which most fascinated me. The stage had never offered me anything like the back curtain drop I gazed at, that first dawn.

After Irving Cummings reluctantly agreed to take only background shots and put the story aside until we found it, I went off with him to learn how wide was the camera's reach. The sand drifts, it could focus to suggest infinities; and small things, too—a desert flower picked up for its flash of beauty, and, by the shift of an inch, a rattler coiled to strike the oncomer. The camera *was* a new personage in drama. When a master turned or directed it, it took on a special life, with a selective visual emphasis unknown to the theatre, impossible on the stage. Here I sensed that something grand had emerged which, in time, could be an art apart. If it could ever be free to record honestly all it could see and hear, it would be the medium some screen Shakespeare might enduringly make his!

When I gazed at the bulging white clouds, rushing in breathtaking formations above the sheer mountains, I knew how dead was "scenic investiture" in our theatre, as well as all the cardboard trappings I had thrilled to as a boy. A camera shot had killed one theatre of yesterday. Might it not kill the others? That day, in Death Valley,

I graphically saw how and why our theatre had been contracting; but when I later came to know all the state laws, and the self-appointed moral, social, and international censorship, constricting the industry I realized that no camera could ever really kill the theatre's soul.

Though we had to write *Behind That Curtain* backward—since Warner Baxter had to be chased into the desert for those beautiful "shots"—we still didn't know the crime or the solution. I will mention only two illustrative factors in that writing-as-we-shot affair. In the popular series of Charlie Chan mysteries which followed ours, the Chinese detective was the star part. But in our script two Hollywood personalities had already been cast for the romantic roles: the love story of Warner Baxter and Lois Moran was made important as poor Charlie became less. Both my bosses also insisted Charlie the First should be acted by a *real* Chinaman. I begged for a real actor, as I had recently been through a similar experience trying to cast a China-man in my *Blood Money*. But I was outshouted.

Natives, who had never acted, have been successfully used in atmospheric films, like Bob Flaherty's *Nanook*, which William Archer had sent Fola and me to see in London: but here the real Chinaman who first played Charlie could not "read" English, which he spoke well enough offstage. So we progressively cut him out of nearly all his scenes. When it was Charlie's cue to speak he had to be kicked under his table to remind him.

I never told Earl Biggers why Charlie Chan was nearly kicked out of the picture: but I assisted, at least, on his first and only appear-ance with a Chinese actor in the role. After that Warner Oland and others took over. This merely illustrates how we all were then groping. The idea of silent films, that so long as a character looked the part he could be made to *act* it, died hard; but it could not survive the coming of words. No longer could Vilma Banky be an American girl of high-bred Boston parentage; her Hungarian consonants unfortu-nately took her rare beauties out of pictures. When Greta Garbo's lovely husky accent proved both intelligible and delightful, hosannas went up. My wire-haired pal, Skippy, gave her a special bark each time we said hello as she strode by our house, all alone, disguised in white sailor trousers, a long peaked polo hat and smoked spectacles that anybody could recognize.

Since my doings with Irving Cummings and others open up the relation of author to director and explain in part the reaction which I found the playwright was soon to acquire toward Hollywood—and still has—I may turn over another reminiscent clod or two from my own plowing.

I had been told by Sol Wurtzel to rehearse my own dialogue so that Cummings could devote himself "solely to camera angles" and the like. As he had worked up through silent films, with some slight stage experience, he resented my intrusions, for which I was nowise to blame. But when I saw what happened to the readings I had given the actors in *Behind That Curtain,* as well as to the scenes themselves, when he shot them, I also got a bit upset—to put my nausea delicately.

Here stage and screen, in fact, met head on. My training had been to build a scene towards a climax: advancing and gaining in effect, by close knitting of phrase and action. The slightest break in the mounting tempo, unless studied, ruined the "punch." In *Behind That Curtain* one scene was a good old cross-examination. Instead of playing it tensely in one room, as it was written, Cummings had them sprinting about the tropical bungalow: in the living room, on each side of a door between and in the bamboo bedroom (so that its beaded curtains could tinkle). As I saw it, the drama had gone out the window.

And yet I came to see, in general, the director was right. The ideal scene would have been constructed with due regard to dramatic dialogue but with breaks properly spaced for his roving camera. It was a motion picture, not a play. Here, I was to confirm my growing suspicion as to a basic difference: sustained stage scenes, even with constant "camera angle" switches, could not hold a picture audience, who go to a movie with eyes as well as ears. The screen cried for what it could best do: move. On the stage, actors must stay in the same room. With the camera's help, screen actors can fade in and out of the house, be wafted on the wings of time or occasion, so that neither age nor geography requires a pause in the story's flow. While the dramatist could still make his contribution, I saw that his art and the camera must marry. The progeny might favor one parent or the other too much: the child of genius will be something beyond either.

Irving Cummings' hostile attitude towards us stage folks was not unique. I also met it in the suave William Howard, director of Paul Muni's first talking picture, *The Valiant,* when I was told to rehearse it. Paul had that same concern for detail which I was to see again when I had charge of his *Seven Faces,* which Berthold Viertel directed. I have never, in fact, seen a more conscientious actor, in all the minutiae of characterization and make-up. We spoke the same language of the theatre and established an unmarred work relationship.

In fact, none of these ordered intrusions made me happy. In my otherwise agreeable contacts with genial Frank Borgaze, the aggressively outspoken Raoul Walsh, the adventurous Victor Fleming, or the cynical John Ford, I soon sensed the quiet determination of these top-notchers not to suffer any interference with their camera domain. I was brought in, for example, when Will Rogers was to do the version Owen Davis made of Homer Croy's *So This Is Paris*—about which I knew something myself. But it soon became plain that Frank Borgaze intended to do all his own cooking, and Sol gently told me so. I used to drop around, to save my dignity, when it (the film, that is) was being shot, chiefly to have Will read me the daily newspaper column which he did between times. He liked to try it on anybody who would listen, and was glad for any excuse not to rehearse. With him I had happy hours at the table or on his ranch—one, in particular, when I took Bob La Follette out and sat back as the two swapped political stories.

The joke was, of course, that these splendid directors, went their own way after the first throw-back or two, used words sparingly except in short bridge scenes, stressed the old silent technics, and soon sailed their cargoes into ports of their own choosing. They always got the big stars, too: so the pictures automatically made money. Sol carefully kept me away from them—for my own protection, I assume. I was forced to recognize that the director was the most important man on the lot. As directors spawned less rapidly than actors and writers the mortality had to be kept to a minimum. I was generally placed with directors who were earning their spurs.

But I soon saw that the silent film directors, also experienced in front-office politics, would outlast even such fine stage directors as Guthrie McClintic, with whom I did two pictures. Of that early crew from the theatre only an occasional George Cukor or John Cromwell has come through. Like the leaves of the black oak, the surviving directors of the silent films will be the last to fall.

And what of the stage actors and dramatists in all this? In those early days, were any of them to feel the theatre was entering into a true marriage with pictures or merely carrying on an affair?

STAGE AND SCREEN ACTING

Actors were to prove the stage's greatest gift to the talkies. They took to it as the duck to his swim. And while some old-line film magnates grouched, as I have said, stage training was obviously more of an asset to the new medium than the plasticities of the silent screen. The industry thus grabbed what it needed most—our actors. Actors, in leaving the theatre, also gave it a body blow. For few who go to Hollywood ever come back to stay; they are becoming, in fact, the casuals of the stage.

No one is to blame, of course. Apparent security always will outweigh financial uncertainties. The stage could no longer hold and support productions, or guarantee more than a few actors even a respectable run. Many a near stage star could with dignity accept small roles in Hollywood, be assured of adequate employment, and feel, on his "personal appearances," he really was still somebody. This has brought to the film ensemble casts no stage play could ever afford or approximate.

Being a picture executive, paid to guard its best interests, I encouraged getting stage actors. On our lot, Paul Muni, Spencer Tracy, Humphrey Bogart, and a score of others then started their upward swing. The other valuable actors who shortly came from the theatre to the various studios, like James Cagney, Fredric March, Edward Robinson, Marie Dressler, Charles Laughton, and Ruth Chatterton, would fill such a fleet of ships as Homer listed. Today we tend to forget how many of them the stage once knew.

At first these actors, used to concentrated characterizations in their nightly performance, missed the creative element a living audience itself supplies. Stage acting is a constant re-creation; each performance is the actor's first interpretation and his last; it is modeled anew by his "in'ards" and the temper or response of his listeners, which the insensitive celluloid strip can never supply. Compared with stage demands, screen acting to them was easy, in spite of physical work in muscular episodes. The actor would each day learn his little sprint, not the long role of the theatre. He had nothing within himself he needed to organize. He rehearsed a bit and the other bits of the whole, often without regard to sequence. Then, as soon as it was screened, he could afford to forget it. He thus became a jigsaw piece in a remarkable and persuasive synthesis.

Yet, in the last analysis, screen acting can only remain this mechanical patching together of the mosaics of emotion, shot at different times and angles: the best of "the day's take," trimmed in the cutting room of any unkind inflection, gesture, or grimace, to be jelled and shown in sorted perfection. Its very nature keeps it immune to the full contagions of histrionic art. The interplay which makes great acting, and in turn moves an audience, cannot exist. But one should be content with the pleasure the skilled actor can and does bring to films. I mean in no way to pooh-pooh the many screen performances I have enjoyed. I could not, however, mistake make-up masterpieces for psychological interpretations, nor be as deeply moved by shadows as by the living substance of great stage personalities.

It was good to hail old theatre friends: Mr. and Mrs. George Arliss, who lived near by; Jack and Lionel Barrymore, an omnivorous reader, with whom I talked of the Balzac and Meredith he knew from cover to cover; and Otis and Maud Skinner, who asked us to celebrate his seventieth birthday. The genial Joseph Urban, scene designer *par excellence,* was a continual joy, with a rare humor which never deserted him amid the chaos in which he was trying to work at a salary of several thousand a week. I had no idea how many members of the Players were weaving in and out of the studios until I was asked to organize a dinner for our president, Walter Hampden, when he played *Cyrano* in Los Angeles. Over forty turned up. In fact, so many have still remained that a sort of branch club was established there under Charles Coburn's initiation. Several actors with whom Fola had played, including Frank Reicher and Henry Kolker, were about, as well as those who had been in my own plays, Fay Bainter, Robert Edeson and . . . But I shan't try to call the roll. Some, frankly, I had forgotten. As I would bump into them, I understood how Mrs. Pat Campbell had blurted out, on meeting the aging Mrs. Leslie Carter: "Why, I thought you were dead." Odd how many ghosts one met in new environments: some doing "extra" work with salaries depending on the extent of their wardrobes.

Fola joined me after my first option had been taken up. I hated to have her quit teaching at the City and Country School, where she had made a place for herself and found deep inner satisfactions. But all life is making choices. Even after twenty years a husband may still have persuasions. Lord knows, I was often to need her accurate measure of Hollywood standards where status was slyly determined by which side you were of a thousand-a-week salary. And she was to find, as usual, interest and amusement in the new world. Mainly, I'm sure, in spite of what some said of Hollywood, because life there was what one chose to make it, outside the glamours and boredoms of the studios.

There were, for example, visits from Bob and Phil, Mary and

Charles Beard, Lincoln Steffens, and others "passing through." It was refreshing, after the klieg lights and hectic story conferences, to hear Ratan Devi (Mrs. Francis Bitter), the distinguished authority on East Indian music, sing to Arbós, the Spanish conductor then engaged at the Hollywood Bowl, who analyzed, over our cordials, the influence the Arabic invasion had had upon his native folk music. Often, too, we would go off to the Walter Arensbergs, to talk of the Baconian theory, to which Walter had devoted years, or to look at their outstanding collection of "moderns." I recall a Brancusi sculpture (which made headlines when the Customs inspector refused to classify it "as a work of art") and the celebrated Marcel Duchamp canvas, *Nude Descending a Staircase,* which has bothered me ever since I first saw it when it startled the American public, at the Sixty-ninth Regiment Armory cubist show, in 1913. Here, too, we became devoted to George Kelly, whose wit and wisdom were so often engaged with Don Marquis at our "conversational bridge" sessions. So, had time and energy permitted, every free hour could have been filled with delightful people who came to Hollywood for one reason or another.

Among studio folks, we went out to our Austrian friends the Viertels, who helped us recapture the continental flavor we at times hungered for. Salka Viertel, who had been a star in the theatre, spoke both French and English. She had keen literary judgment, a tolerant sympathy for human weaknesses, and an appraising humor about her friends. Her husband, Berthold Viertel, with whom I was associated in several pictures, had been a distinguished director and literary figure in Europe. They took us into their home, where their many foreign film connections were always "dropping in." I heard in their own varied accents what each felt sound would mean to the Industry: Lubitsch, the sophisticate; the German Murnau (on one of whose uncompleted pictures I worked), so tragically killed; the French Jacques Feder and his wife, Françoise Rosay, who together, after Hollywood was through with him, were to create the naughty, delectable *Carnival in Flanders.* Also, in and out, was the most distinguished Russian in his world: Sergei Eisenstein, producer of *Potemkin,* wandering confused amid our restrictive immigration laws. Fola was of some assistance, through Washington, so that he could remain in the States to make *Thunder over Mexico,* never finished. Yet later it was assembled in some fashion by Salka and Upton Sinclair, whom I had seen intermittently since college days, between his strenuous political campaigns and novel writing.

Once, when we persuaded Salka to do one scene in a Paul Muni picture, I saw her authority and technical facility. Her theatre training also made her a splendid judge of our stage contemporaries. When Fola and I took her to see Mrs. Fiske, in almost her last performance, we felt Salka's quick excitement, as the most famous of Becky Sharps saltily spoke. She clasped Fola's arm and whispered: "There is the finest actress I've yet seen in America."

At the Viertels' we met Greta Garbo, who lived in walled seclusion near us. We found her simple, without pose, yet guarding a sly humor which peeked out of all she said. When I had a chance to talk with her or watch her—as she would sometimes sit hunched up on the floor of Salka's salon—I tried to analyze her peculiar appeal. For it was ever present in private, as in her films that Salka had a hand in writing and, I suspect, in coaching. Aside from a feminine lure which is never crudely exposed but has its unmistakable outline almost chastely veiled, I believe Garbo's appeal lies in its implications, in her capacity to suggest emotional repercussions. The great lady of the screen has, of course, the perfect mask, so subtly controlled that her face itself is a thousand faces. Like all males I found her disturbingly attractive. Even my dog, Skippy, would run after her when she snapped her finger. I never had the heart to warn the ambitious little fellow.

I speak especially of Garbo because she reached her pinnacle without stage training. She had a native superiority to her vehicles and outshone them, as well as more popular actors who merely "had a way with them." For I would shake my head in amazement over the skimpy gifts of some in Hollywood who had shot to fame. With these, associated stage youngsters of ability who had been hastily crated and sent westwards after a success or two on Broadway, still green with inexperience. What might they not have come to mean in time to the theatre had they stayed in it!

None of these had ever known the searing drudgery, the long grinding apprenticeship which had gone into the making of Julia Marlowe, E. H. Sothern, Margaret Anglin, Alla Nazimova, Eva Le Gallienne, Fay Bainter, and Effie Shannon, among other stars with whom I had worked. How many exacting parts, by comparison, these had learned, struggled over, modeled with nightly care, and often lived with for years. I heard E. H. himself say:

"I have perhaps played sixty or sixty-five parts in my life, and was not able to undertake Hamlet until I was forty. My father played six hundred eighty-one parts before he was twenty-eight; and Irving played over six hundred roles before he had even made his first visit to London."

Was it unkind of me then to be a bit contemptuous of film fame, often so easily bought with a shiny-faced alloy? How could a camera possibly shape an artist's soul, as does a living audience?

DRAMATISTS AT SEA AND DON MARQUIS

And the playwrights in Hollywood?

I believe I was the only one, at the time, in an executive position. Most "supervisors" had been silent picture hang-overs: the dramatists already there stuck to their phrase knitting. I felt my anomalous situation: but I knew I was being helpful to my fellows where their scripts were concerned. Often also they would talk over their personal problems as they tried to function in so strange a land. There were certain broad accords I found when I probed their reactions, though individual estimates were colored if their options were taken up. Nothing, however, could be further apart than Clare Kummer, trying to fit her inconsequential universe into the structural rigidities of the screen, and S. N. Behrman, whose dialogue gifts permitted him to fly in and out, light awhile, drop some deft scene, and flit off again with fabulous fodder.

Among those doing a chore with me at Fox was Don Marquis. His comedy *The Old Soak* showed how he could depict in scenic form humorous aspects of American character. Backed with a long list of books—to say nothing of his zoological masterpieces, archy, the cockroach, and mehitabel, the amorous cat—he more nearly approached Mark Twain than any other writer. With patience and sympathetic handling Don might have been an ideal man to compose enduring films. But he was unhappy in Hollywood. His one venture for Will Rogers didn't jell. Subsequent outside efforts made him cynical. I remember his laughter in recounting how he, for many years the leading columnist on the *New York Sun,* had been "hired," at $1,000 a week, to write a story of Embassy life in Lisbon—to discover, in the next cubbyhole, a former American consul at Lisbon struggling over a scenario about a New York columnist!

Learning that Metro was to do *Kim,* and knowing that Don reread it and Shakespeare each year, I wired suggesting that he make the "story treatment." Only an inadequate pen keeps me from repeating his adjectives when they turned him down. No: he was not happy. But, as Don's experience in the film capital adds perspective to any estimate of it, I linger with one who was a most talented writer and a most lovable man. Though we both had long been members of the Players, I came to know him best in the admitted isolations of spirit he and I were often to experience in this state of mind called Hollywood.

Don's life was a coat of many colors. It warmed with robust, Rabelaisian mirth; for no Anglo-Saxon I ever knew had the Frenchman's gusto, except possibly Waldo Peirce, the painter. Many of Don's letters, like those of Eugene Field, are unprintable. Each of our valued sheaf is a *tour de force*. He would send Fola a most profound and profane letter, telling her to read it first to see whether she thought "it proper for George to hear." But, for some flavor of his quieter humor, I can only give one letter here:

MY DEAR GEORGE:

I am sending you check No. —. One of an account which I hope to see as high, one day, as Mt. Lowe—with my thanks and blessings.

While we are on the subject of checks, I cannot resist telling you a charming little anecdote I heard about Rudyard Kipling. It seems that so many people want his autograph that when he draws a check he never knows whether it will be cashed—people save them for the autograph.

It would be nice if something of this sort were to get started with one of us, wouldn't it? It's merely a thought—scarcely a suggestion—just a vague feeling, you might say, that it would be nice.

Seriously, when I touched you the other day, it was just in time to save a graduate poet from being as dead as his poems. When I arrived at home I found that My Loved Ones—the Little Woman and the Wee Tots—needed bread.

Yours, till Jesus comes to Hollywood,

DON M——

Don would often read us his daily grind, which flowed from his machine in magnificent disarray. His years as a columnist had made him careless: he hated to rewrite. I had often seen him at the Players start his afternoon stint an hour before the messenger was expected. While much of his best work lies in his sensitive verse, the stage always lured him. *The Old Soak* was the only play, however, which brought him large returns. Once, while acting his titular hero, in a stock production, he went up in his lines. Not knowing what to answer on his cue he confidentially put his arm about the actor and, in a husky, alcoholic voice truthfully said: "I don't know *what* to say to you." The play he most cared for, however, was *The Dark Hours,* a deeply felt study of the Christ story. This had been dedicated to Reina, his first wife, when published shortly after her death. Later he himself backed its stage production. As he said to me, "I've always wanted to see it, George." The irony was that while it was in rehearsal he was temporarily stricken blind. It was a dire failure.

Don had one self-preserving quality: he had no repressions: he could suffer straight through his own many dark hours to release. No one otherwise could have dredged such depths as when Reina died, or when their little daughter, Barbara Marquis, likewise left him. Fola and I were with him in Hollywood through that time. I had known her first as a wonderfully healthy child: but soon it was clear she was marked. She faded to a waif and then one night was gently carried off. Don had me ask Fola if she would say a few words at Barbara's funeral. Fola had just come back after her own mother's death, but, of course, did what Don wished. She also read several of the girl's poems, for the child had rare gifts. One was a poem on death itself, written with strange prescience, only a few days before it was so suddenly to touch her. Don came to us after Barbara had been taken away.

Yet it was fortunate that so sensitive a spirit as Barbara did not live to see Don's own tragic end a few years later. Stricken, he may never have known of the death of Marjorie Vonnegut, his devoted second wife, an actress of talent and beauty, who had become a courageous, tragic figure in a domestic situation the Greek dramatists would have relished, inconceivable in its irony. Yet one fact I hope Don did know: the way his many friends, quietly and sufficiently, were later to express, to a helpless comrade, the affection and esteem in which all of his fellow writers and club mates held him. None more than those who were about him during these Hollywood days of which I write.

I am telling this here as testimony of something else I was to learn of Hollywood. For that great sprawling, formless city, which made and ruthlessly crushed so many, was after all only a small town. Its heart, too, was as cruel. But it could also be as kind.

It was another dramatist, however, who best summarized two years' observation of the Film City. Since he so nearly voiced my own conclusions I thought him quite penetrating. From my notes it went somewhat thus:

"Well, George, in the theatre you and I write what we want to. Here we do what we're told. There we may never make a dime out of a play for months of work. Here we get a fat check for everything we do each week. But what we write in the theatre is our own. If we place it we don't have to change a line unless we wish. Our Guild sees to that. If the play's a flop it's strictly our mashed potato. Sometimes a flop may even make money for us—look at your *House of a Thousand Candles.* But if our play *does* get over, we can sit back, as the ads put it, and let it work for us. Best of all, our name does a solo on the program: we are somebody. We get it printed, too.

"But pictures? What's ours? We find a guy down the lane is also writhing over a version of the same story. We've not only got to please the supervisor and the front office but the director who still believes the script is his private preserves. We have no say about the cast, nor who is to direct it; we're not even asked to a rehearsal. In the theater, actors and authors work together: it's a married relation which produces a performance. The stage director merely completes the ceremony. In pictures, the director and the camera move into the ménage and take over the family intimacies.

"Does anybody even know who writes a film, or care? I tell you, George, the reason the stage writer will never feel he belongs out here is because he's a stray soul. He's not lost his tugging vanities, and he knows being a top picture writer won't ever lodge him in *Who's Who.* That is why he soon ceases to care what happens to his scripts, why he takes the cash, and grabs what credits he can. They may need us now and then, like the queen bee does her drone on their nuptial flight. But you know what happens to him, after he hands over.

"I'm making another discovery, George. Soon they won't even need us dramatists out here. No. After they get the hang of what we're supposed to know about, watch and see. Watch the good newspapermen, like Dudley Nichols, and the magazine fellows with a story sense or a gift for lines. Mark my words. The time will come when pictures will be so routine that a clever boss will make any scribbler he can 'handle' turn out a good job. The dramatists will only be called here to do their own plays or for some emergency dental work on the dialogue.

"No. Let's stop kidding ourselves that we dramatists are necessary. It's mighty comfortable out here. I'm enjoying it even though my wife's bored stiff—as most intelligent gals are at the gabble that goes on. I like the palm trees and the patios. They treat me well at the studio, too. But my script? It's anybody's baby. Once in a while I get mad. I'd like just once to be able to wipe my own child's nose in my own way. But until I have that precious parental privilege, they can change its didies themselves as many times as they want to.

"A dramatist in Hollywood! Huh! Count us in ten years."

Mrs. Patrick Campbell Rounds the Circle

In Hollywood, the question of stage and screen was now dramatically to confront me again as it had done when Douglas and Mary stood with me by Sarah Bernhardt's grave in Paris. Around their celluloid orbits these Hollywood stars were actual entities to polyglot millions, known, awaited, and adored. On their more earthly circuits of "personal appearances" they carried their own press-agented plaster thrones wherever they went. The world bowed because their shadows had preceded them, bringing, for a few pennies only—glory be!— unmeasured joy, romance, excitement, and release to many a drab and harried life. Indeed, in the thirty years since Julia Marlowe had done my first play, I had seen profound changes in our world of make-believe. But now, better than any moralizing, I was sharply to realize how wide and varied had also been the span of my professional experiences.

I was called to Winnie Sheehan's office. I then had charge of a dated English drama, *The Dancers,* which we were remaking as a talking picture.

"George, I want you to make a place in the picture for Mrs. Pat Campbell."

I gasped. I knew the celebrated English actress was gliding about Hollywood, with her Pekingese and a quiverful of poisoned darts she would casually let fly with a charming smile. Ignoring my sputtering protest, Winnie went on:

"Make her somebody's aunt or something. Two or three scenes will be enough. It will be her first talking picture. Her name will help the sales in England. Besides, she's broke. We are giving her $8,000. Do the best you can."

I had orders, but my heart was heavy. The script was pried open, and a mature lady edged in. A limousine was sent for her every day, and there were flowers, too, in a star's dressing room reserved especially for the famous actress; however, in the publicity her name was merely to be in support of two youngsters.

She came to my office a day or so before she was to face the camera. She might have been a middle-aged Paula Tanqueray dropping in for tea and muffins. Her face was pale but strangely unlined, though she was then sixty-seven. Her hair, of course, was still its raven-black; she had not let it go as Duse and Ada Rehan had. Her caressing eyes made no effort to conceal their worldly wisdom, and her voice— Well, I could have picked it from a million. I should know it now. I had never met her, and she didn't know me from Adam. She was on the defensive. After all, for twenty-five years one of the most famous of stage ladies, favorite actress of Pinero, Shaw, and others, with the pick of their roles, co-star with Sarah Bernhardt in Maeterlinck's *Pelleas and Melisande,* for years almost an English institution—sitting in an office of a movie man! Not until I mentioned that I was a dramatist, that I had even sent her a play, that we had many friends in common, did she unbend. Only then did I venture a story.

"Mrs. Pat, I want to tell you about a young college lad I once knew who loved the theatre. He hadn't much money. In fact, when he heard you were coming over on your first American tour—"

"Goodness!" she interrupted. "That was nearly thirty years ago."

"Yes. George Arliss made his first American appearance with you then and—"

"I paid him $65 a week. I gave him his first real start in London. Now look where he is. They tell me he is quite important." Of course, she knew he was.

"Well, the lad I speak of wrote to the theatre to reserve a single seat in the gallery for each of the five plays in your announced repertoire. When the doors opened he was first in line at the box office. He eagerly asked for the seats which were to be reserved in his name. For weeks he had saved out of his allowance and lunch money. His heart had been set on seeing you. But his letter had never been received. He insisted he had written it. The line behind grew impatient. He stood there stubbornly demanding the seats. Tears filled his eyes and probably got into his voice; for the manager, in the back of the office, heard his plea. The lad got those seats. I'm that lad, Mrs. Campbell."

I admit, as I told it, my eyes welled up, for all the theatre had been and for my adorations of those far-away heroines of school and college days. She smiled; but I don't think she took in what it had meant to me. Yet I am sure, when greatness kissed her hand in her heyday, she had never been offered a more genuine tribute.

As I sat looking at her my mind flashed freakishly back to an odd intermission during her performance of Björnson's *Beyond Human Power*. The orchestra was playing Grieg's *Peer Gynt Suite*. In front of me sat another young stage enthusiast who gave me a nod but went on reading what I saw was Ibsen's *Ghosts*. Behind me another thin-faced author touched my shoulder and thrust a circular into my hand.

"Middleton, a lot of people are interested to see what the critics have said about my new novel. So I've had the comments printed all together."

The former was Philip Moeller, not only to be one of the Theatre Guild, but actually to write *George Sand,* which Mrs. Campbell herself did years later in London. The latter was Upton Sinclair, with his first novel, *Springtime and Harvest.*

I had brought to my Hollywood office some wooden Virgins and Christs of my French wanderings, though they often seemed to look quizzically at me—that we should both be there. About, lolled a souvenir or two of the stage. Behind Mrs. Pat, in fact, hung a frame, intended for the Players, which held four letters in the manuscript of Shaw, Barrie, Pinero, and Jones: the big figures of her era. She recognized the handwriting of Pinero and Shaw. "Dear Pin," she purred. And I'm sure across her mind rushed the quick panorama of their successful collaboration: the oft revived Paula, Agnes in *The Notorious Mrs. Ebbsmith,* and Phyllis in *The Thunderbolt.* But when I mentioned Shaw she laughed. I'm sure they must have enjoyed rehearsing *Pygmalion* together!

"Here I am broke, and I have in my safe deposit all those letters he wrote me—a hundred and twenty-five of them," she said. "Of course I can't be a cad and sell them, can I?"

But she had already published some in her autobiography—one of the best of stage reminiscences, by the by. In it is that most moving of letters Shaw wrote her when her son was killed in the Boer War. She told me she had tried to get his permission to publish others in her book, but he replied: "No, Stella. I will not play horse for your Lady Godiva." When her will was read, after her death in Pau, France, at seventy-six, it stipulated that the letters were to be "published in proper sequence, not cut or altered in any way, in an independent volume to be entitled *The Love Letters of George Bernard Shaw and Mrs. Patrick Campbell.*" Shaw, when the question of publishing the letters was put up to him, replied: "Forty-five years ago everybody wrote letters to Mrs. Campbell. I know she thought mine the best of the bunch, though personally I thought those of Burne-Jones more interesting." I hope I am around to read them.

And this lady, about whom for twenty-five years much of the best of English drama revolved, was now to appear in several patched-up scenes gashed into a routine picture, directed by a man who had never before directed either a picture or a play! This lady, who had played nearly all the great parts in Shakespeare, was now supporting a star who had acted a scant handful of "sides" and had never even heard of Mrs. Pat Campbell! Except for Winnie, I was the only one on the lot who had ever seen her!

Personally, I never could go out to her with any warmth. Her tongue was too unkind; and there was never a suggestion of more than polite gratitude for what one tried to do. However, in one letter she wrote me: "That was very kind of you to read my play and I will take advantage of your criticisms and improve it, I am sure." I have forgotten whether, towards the end, she was trying to write it herself or not; but I can never forget how cruel it was to watch this great lady, through necessity, do this triviality so many routine screen actors could have done better. She didn't make any one happy at rehearsals—she was not openly contemptuous, and she tried hard to adapt; but she was used to an audience, to moving majestically about, and she could not handle herself in the narrow confines of a camera's angles. She knew nothing of the medium, whose A B C's our star had at her fingertips.

"But what is there about her that is so wonderful?" the wide-eyed little star asked, when I tried to tell her something of what was Mrs. Pat's outstanding quality.

I thought a moment. What one word would convey to a person who had never seen Mrs. Pat the sheer force of her arresting personality, her power to hold and fill the stage?

"She has the one thing nearly all screen actresses lack: *breadth.*"

I am sure the little star didn't understand. Why should she? She would not have recognized it. Further, it wasn't needed in her medium.

When I saw the film put together, most of what Mrs. Pat had done was bad. Yet there was one moment—a second or two—when she read a totally unimportant speech. But from it radiated a thousand meanings. It was a moment as unforgettable as the last time Isadora danced. I used to have that scene run just to recapture a flash of the old Mrs. Pat: an arresting, fascinating woman, a queen I had once bowed to.

For three decades I had done almost everything in the theatre: hackwork, rewrites, biographical as well as unproduced published plays, dramatizations, collaborations, adaptations, one-acters, vaudeville, Paris and London productions, with a few smash hits and numerous big flops. I had been censored here and abroad and even been plagiarized by a friend! Throughout, I had also been concerned with every business aspect of our profession, and was part of the effort we dramatists made to protect our rights and better the trade conditions under which we worked. So at Hollywood I had finally rounded out a journeyman playwright's odyssey. The circle was complete.

As I remembered Mrs. Pat Campbell, near the end of my picture adventure, the theatre I had loved called clearly to me once again across the years.

That, too, will always be mine, the way it was—as long as I can remember.

[*The curtain falls*]

[*But* THE AUTHOR *has been waiting in the wings; his wife has been standing beside him. There is some polite applause which he hastily takes advantage of. He goes and stands before the footlights.*

Outside, a storm has been raging. Rumbles of thunder, like guns, have shaken the theatre. Now there comes another crashing sound. Perhaps those still in the audience had better wait a bit. It may let up.

So they settle back in their seats, while THE AUTHOR *clears his throat and speaks:*]

CURTAIN SPEECH: WITH BALZAC'S ASSISTANCE

The Author

Ladies and Gentlemen:

Thanks for having stayed. Maybe you wonder, as I so often have at a play, about the things not told, or left over. What ever happened to Nora when she left her Doll's House? What of almost any character, in fact, except the dead ones, *after* the dramatist quits them at the final curtain fall?

A truly completed autobiography has only one finish, and its narrator can't be around to supply it. He can but select a rounded experience on which to end. So there is a lot of living and work here left unrecorded, even though my chosen story is all in. But an item or two may still add a final high light to this scribbler's tale in the Hollywood afterglow. What did those two intense and profitable years in executive externals and surface stories do to the writer in me and after?

[*He notices a bit of interest here and there.*]

They left me dry as a summer in Kansas! There had been no time for the slow welling up of inner reserves, out of which alone may any real creation flow. Whatever the purity or potency of such a stream, it must accumulate before it can even trickle over into literary expression. Mere reportorial genius is something else; that gets its quick flash off shiny salient facts. Though fictive creation has its own individual laws, most writers must be cud chewers.

[*He sees he should hasten along; this is getting a bit too analytical.*]

I was hungry for my own work again. Yet I found only parched places. Like the proverbial hen, I kept scratching; but I found nothing to feed upon. Every writer knows this experience. I would never write again! Never would a play take fire within me. I was finished at fifty. I thought it time to take stock of what I felt and thought about this thing called Life, and about my place in it. So I took up verse!

OFFICIALS OF THE INTERNATIONAL CONFEDERATION OF DRAMATISTS AND COMPOSERS
Making a formal call on President von Hindenburg, Berlin, 1928

Arnold Genthe

FOLA LA FOLLETTE

[He notes an incredulous look or two and sees he must explain.]

Each day my Skippy—pal for ten years, and the only dog I ever had—would spring into the seat beside me, his little tail erect, his paws on the open windshield, as the breeze spread his whiskers and his eyes were keen on his own world of interest. We would always drive off to the sea. There I returned to the wonderings of my youth, when I had gazed into its restless waves in search of the far-away future; now, however, I sought meanings in the past. And as I tried to phrase what came out of the depths of me I would scribble its words upon my lap pad. I relaxed. Much to my dog's amazement and disgust, I gave myself for motionless hours to whatever might float slowly up from within. What ugly fish there are in our own deep waters!

[He can see they all have some that they won't speak of either.]

How much of beauty, too! The many-hued friendships, for example, also weaving in and out the recurrent repertoire of riches which my wife had brought me beyond the power of words.

While the weeks and months slipped by, page after page was kept; many just as they rose to verbal form. When I got bored looking within, I gazed out at the pelicans flapping heavily over the water, the browns and greens of the near-by mountain sides or the cloudlike Valkyries rushing godward overhead. All of these visual impressions I also tried to catch in phrase. And then one day, so easily had they now begun to come, I wondered whether here might not be an answer. Maybe I was a poet at heart. Maybe, like my brother, I could find a place in that high body. So I bound some pages together, and sent them off to Horace Kallen, the philosopher, and Hal Witter Bynner—a real poet—for detached opinions. Horace wrote, "It's a soliloquy but not a communication." Here is what came back from Hal.

[He takes from an inner pocket a letter and reads:]

August 8, 1932

DEAR GEORGE:

Your messages have come and the manuscript, which I finally found time to read. About it, I am considerably perplexed. I find plenty of substance in it but, at the risk of cracking a friendship, I must say at the outset that, in my judgment, verse is not your medium. I have heard, in drama, words of yours put together which belong together and made their proper effect through proper prose; but in these pages I feel that you are at sea trying to express yourself in a medium which does not belong to you. You say things heavily which, in your natural prose, you would say with ease. You say things without good verse rhythm which, in your natural medium, you would be saying in good prose rhythm.

All in all, I should not be your friend if I did not plead that you consider this manuscript valuable only for the good it has done you in writing it, and not for the good you might convey to others in this form. I may be wrong in my judgment. Ask some one else.

If you think me harsh, remember I warned you. I am too old to palaver. If I am asked, I answer. And this answer is given with regret, to be sure, but with honesty and affection.

Yours always,

HAL

[*He pauses as there is some applause over the generous spirit of the letter.*]

After that, of course, nobody was ever to see that script again.

[*Some more applause.*]

But Hal was right. There had been good in it for me. It had stirred again the creative processes, such as they were. I sensed it when drama subjects soon began to tap on my attention. Then it was I felt I had to ask myself what I was going to do with them. Now that I had lived a goodly measure, did I really have anything of value to say? Was it worth the seeking? If so, what about it?

I did have an aim. But would the ammunition hold or carry? At least, as Professor Woodberry had put it, I could try to be faithful to my "instincts and impulses" in the hope they would carry me "in the direction of the excellence" I most desired and valued.

So I made a resolve. I held to it at times, I fear, with ruthless irresponsibility.

[*He glances at his wife in the wings, whose face remains inscrutable. He knows there were so many things he may never have known.*]

But there *was* a glittering gamble in it. Something worth while, in satisfactions, *might* come through—possibly also with rewards. So with what temporary financial freedom was left to me, after the crash, I determined to take five years and write exactly what I wanted. That would be the first yardstick; not what I thought might be commercial. The law of averages had always held before. Fola had embarked, after her mother's death, upon the long job ahead, writing her father's biography out of the huge abundance of material in the "La Follette papers" of his forty years in public life. Her course was mapped out, and, before Washington, Wisconsin claimed it. So there we went for two years. In the deep snows and hours of solitude, at the La Follette farm outside Madison, we both began our chosen work.

The next five years were to be the richest in my writing experience. I soon found they were also to be the poorest in money returns. To make this professional playwright's saga complete, I will say that, of the five plays I wrote, one hasn't had a nibble; two, dealing with industrial and political backgrounds—into which I put my long observation of the national scene—have so far failed of production in spite of three rewritings each, though, in fairness to them, I should add there have been offers held up by the old casting difficulties. The two others got published. Time has killed one of these: the other still waits on Time and fortunately can.

Of certain personal aspects of *Hiss! Boom!! Blah!!!* in relation to Senator La Follette, I've already told. But I speak further of this play to illustrate the problem of what to do, in the theatre today, with the experimental script. For this *was* frankly an experiment: an application on the stage, as I've said, of a modified movie technic in fifty scenes: to pack "the outstanding crises through which the various groups in an unnamed community pass—from the intolerances of the World War and the attendant absurdities of the Bankers' Banquet during Prosperity, to the irrationalities of the present Great Dilemma," created by the Depression. In handling the community concerned I went on the theory that an individual may be a spectator of a dramatic episode one moment, and the next himself the active participant. Thus, in the play as in life itself, the heroes are the extras, the extras the heroes. And all are caught in the flashlight of events that, willy-nilly, sweep over them.

Yet, save for one hardy adventurer—Dr. Lester Raines, of the New Mexico Normal University, who directed the amateur groups known as "The Koshare" in it—no one even ventured to produce it in its entirety. He wrote me: "I think you would have enjoyed the audience. They were too stunned to applaud much but have certainly talked and applauded since."

In spite of the more than generous reviews and personal letters from numerous fellow playwrights, no manager in the professional theatre displayed the slightest interest. The reasons are obvious and were anticipated. We have no endowed, state, or municipal theatre in America for such an experiment. Today, indeed, only by putting their own money or that of "friendly angels" into their plays, can the dramatists get some of them on. Few managers finance their own productions as in the old days. This is one of the newest manifestations of changed conditions. Slowly, successful authors who can are becoming more and more, singly or collectively, "inside speculators." I had no more resentment at the conditions which barred this play from a hearing than I had regret over the months of work I gave to it. There are many places in the theatre for regrets: but none for self-pity over an open-eyed course, like my own. I knew what to expect and got it. Though, of course, there was always the outside chance . . .

[*He sees his wife give him a penetrating look, which reminds him he was not so acquiescent at the time. And he suddenly realizes how much she must have put up with, through the years; though life with him was never exactly tame. So he quickly changes the subject.*]

But now came my greatest literary satisfaction. It is perhaps the only play in which I had complete critical accord through press and personal letters. It was *That Was Balzac*. I've talked a lot about that man; for nearly a quarter of a century of this record I know he has kept bobbing up. In the theatre, unless something later comes through, we call that a "false lead." But not until that Wisconsin winter did I feel *ready* to write it. I was eager to dig into the mass of material I had gathered since college days. I sent for my special cases of books and pamphlets. The fine Wisconsin University Library fortunately had a superb supplementary collection. For weeks I reread all Balzac's letters and the autobiographical sections in his novels. Never was I so lost in a job. I came across an early outline of a scene scheme which still held surprisingly well. But I could not begin till I had the answer I later mention in the preface I wrote:

"If one be merely content to exhibit such a character by threading it with glittering incidents here is matter enough at hand. But I believe in a biographical play the scattered particles of a personality should be fused by some unifying principle: and underneath Balzac's incredible surface disturbances there surged emotions that gave a deep consistency to his whole life. His hunger for fame, his passion for his art, his search for permanence in love: and above all the driving power of illusion will hint at what I have felt some of these universals were."

But this play also, for one reason only, has not yet been produced. When my friend and agent Harold Freedman read it, his first words were: "It's grand, George. But whom can we get to play it?" Until the various managers, who have been disposed to do it, and myself are satisfied with the actor for the part of Balzac it will not be done. In the old days, before motion pictures absorbed the one or two who would be acceptable, a Richard Mansfield, as Walter Eaton's lengthy review in the *New York Tribune* suggested, would have been available; or a Belasco could have put an actor under contract a year ahead, as was his custom. Now no manager can so plan, as few outstanding actors will "tie up."

My play may also serve to accentuate the present production difficulties that are encountered by a dramatist who deliberately writes a script so totally dependent upon a star. For my Balzac is a *virtuoso* part that is a challenge to both an actor's natural endowment and a wide range of technical skill. It must have an actor who can excite and sustain an interest in his own personality through the media my scenes offer. For here is no mere interest to be aroused in a plot but in a man.

Several film stars, with stage experience, have been friendly to the play; but they either have hesitated to accept the role or did not wish to leave their green pastures. Sydney Greenstreet, however, would gladly have quit Hollywood, where he has now shot to stardom, to create this part, which he could have interpreted superbly. But, unfortunately, he could not realize visually the early scenes of the very young Balzac. A letter he recently wrote me is one of the rare compensations which come to an author of a published but still unproduced play.

[*He takes out some letters from his pocket—which he has accidentally put there for just such an occasion—and reads one:*]

"I have read your play to so many people, and 95 per cent of them have made me finish it in one reading, which went to two or three o'clock in the morning many times. But when somebody really appreciates it, I enjoy giving them the treat of the wonderful life of Balzac which you have drawn. I defy anybody not to know Balzac thoroughly for the rest of his life after hearing that play. It is an experience which you never forget.

"It is such a difficult part to cast because to have a man young enough for the first episodes it would be rare indeed to get an artist experienced and great enough to play the latter episodes. I would love to see it played by the right man. I would hate to see it played by the wrong man. It is too great. It is by far my favorite modern play. I only hope I can achieve something as great, as an actor, as you have as an author. Then I would indeed be content."

[*Glancing over the other letters as he speaks of them and reads:*]

John Corbin, long the eminent dramatic critic on the *New York Times,* also understood this casting difficulty when he wrote me:

"It is a tremendously vivid character, alive and brimming with gusto, and I can quite believe that you will find it hard to discover an actor for the part. Yet it is *made* for the stage. Perhaps it will discover its own actor."

There is a collateral comment in this letter from Robert Sherwood. For Bob (fortunate in his having Raymond Massey, the inevitable man for his Lincoln) generously tried to find an actor for me in London:

"It's unquestionably a noble piece of work: a labor of love, which everything worth while must be. . . . Don't worry about Balzac. You'll find your man, and it's a rare kind of play (rare at least these days) which can wait for production."

So I wait. But my experience with it, besides revealing sidelights on the difficulty the movies have created in taking most of our stars away from the theatre, suggests the dramatist's problem of obtaining production for a play written out of a deep desire. In the meantime, I was fortunate enough to get it published. Though it has brought no financial returns, my play, I know, has already taken its modest place in the mass of Balzaciana. I'm as content—as an author can be in having written a play which doesn't get acted.

[*He does not look into the wings at this to note his wife's reaction. He knows what she would say to that.*]

But what fun I had had with Balzac in my constant background! When the statue Rodin had made of Balzac has been rejected, what I had him say in my prologue was out of my feeling:

"But to live with a great man like Balzac these seven years, as I have; to read four thousand articles and books about him, all his own novels and thousands of letters, seeking the real man; to know the women he had; to live his dreams for fame and love—that's reward enough for me."

There were also other compensations. They lay in the reactions, not only of literary critics and Balzac specialists—such as William Hobart Royce and Professors W. Scott Hastings and Paul Hazard—but of professional authors who had admired the French novelist, as I had. I was happy when John Masefield wrote:

"For a long while, many years ago, I was a Balzac lover, and your play is bringing back the old enthusiasm."

[*As though suddenly remembering:*]

And I must not overlook these words Dr. Thomas Mann sent me after he had told me he was to lecture on Balzac at Princeton:

"The deep interest which the subject of your play awakens in me, was much increased by the vitality of your handling of it. Everyone who admires this great epic artist will be profoundly grateful to you for the dramatic monument you have erected to him. Your fashioning of the socle figures of that monument, which represent the contemporary characters and spirit of that time, is as fine a plastic work as that of the main figure itself . . ."

I was particularly pleased along this line that Van Wyck Brooks could also write:

"It seems to me a wonderful evocation, and I marvel at your skill in compressing into these few short scenes such a wealth of experience and feeling. All your people are flesh and blood, even those who appear for a moment only, and you've packed a whole epoch of history into a single writer's life, and always with such delicacy and lightness of touch. I hope it is going to be produced. It is so essentially dramatic. Meantime it's a capital play to read and has given me a world of pleasure."

If you won't mind I may venture these three other personal letters —only three, I promise—which naturally did not find their way to the publisher's blurb. There is a certain poignancy in this one from the Austrian, Stefan Zweig (author of *Marie Antoinette* and a host of other biographies, who killed himself in despair over what he had suffered in the war), since it relates to the recent announcement of the posthumous publication of his biography of Balzac, to be edited and completed by a friend.

49, HALLAM STREET, LONDON W. 1
16 July 1938

DEAR MR. MIDDLETON:

You will perhaps be surprised by the rapidity of my answer. But I am a fanatic Balzacian and your book arrived at 7 P.M. I started reading it at nine P.M. and was through with it at 12:30. I had only the intention to read the first scenes, but I was so fascinated that I could not stop.

My dear Middleton, you have done marvelously. You have avoided all sentimentality and exaggerations, and beyond all you have shown Balzac as the genius he was. Of course, we Balzacians know how rich his life was and how many scenes could still be introduced. I have myself had the idea and the offer for a picture three years ago, but never the time of finishing it.

It is one of the dreams of my life to retire once for three or four years and to write the missing great biography of Balzac in two or three volumes. I have much material since years and years and it will interest you that I possess not only the complete proofs (a real marvel) of Balzac's *Ténébreuse Affaire* but also the manuscript of *La Messe de l'Athée*. Perhaps this suggests to you a visit to Europe, and in any case we will meet in January when I come to America for my lecture tour.

In the meantime *all my congratulations* and kindest regards.

Yours sincerely

STEFAN ZWEIG

This from John Buchan, also gone before his time, of my meeting with whom at the White House I have already written.

GOVERNMENT HOUSE, OTTAWA
April 15, 1937

MY DEAR MR. MIDDLETON:

I am greatly in your debt for the gift of your play on Balzac. Both my wife and myself read it with enormous enterest. It is the only thing I know, either in fiction or drama, which attempts to trace the growth of the temperament and the mind of a great novelist, and I am full of admiration for the skill with which you have handled a most intricate subject. Both the philosophical and dramatic interest are sustained throughout.

I have always admired Balzac profoundly. In many ways he seems to me the greatest of all novelists. The only thing I find lacking in him is that element of the "translunary," of high poetry, which seems to me to be indispensable in the greatest art.

It was a great pleasure to see you in Washington, and I hope we shall meet again.

Yours very sincerely

TWEEDSMUIR

Eva Le Gallienne's father was another Balzacian. Though I had not seen Dick for many years I had followed his Balzac articles in the *New York Sun*. Something of his enthusiasm for the great Frenchman shines through his lovely prose:

LA TOURETTE, BOULEVARD DE CARAVAN, MENTON
March 14, 1937

MY DEAR MIDDLETON:

We have been away from home for some little time, and it was a delightful surprise to find *That Was Balzac* awaiting us on our return.

Needless to say that I have read it eagerly and with a deep thrill at your masterly reincarnation. I can sincerely say that you have made Balzac live for me more completely than he had ever done before. The sympathetic imagination which you have brought to your long absorbed study of him has really acted in the manner of an incarnation, and enabled you, so to say, to summon him from the vast deep of his creation and reveal himself before me in the very manner in which he worked and dreamed. Honestly, he seems to be in the room with me as I read!

And I immensely admire the combined concentration and breadth in your romantic treatment, and it seems to me that you have invented something like a new form of dramatic interpretative presentation.

I particularly admire the scene in his printing house. It is amazing how much you have got into that short "episode."

It is like a veritable microcosm of his whole life, all his varied interests and complications, his vast dream, his titanic energy, his earthly frustrations—the tragic humour of the scene with his creditors! And how beautifully you have done Madame du Berny—"Dilecta"—as again in "the final episode" it was an inspired stroke to bring her in, as a phantom of his brain as he is dying. . . .

Always yours sincerely,
RICHARD LE GALLIENNE

Yet, in spite of all the deep satisfactions such letters have brought me, the play—so essentially made for the theatre—is unproduced, after ten years! Even realistically appraising all the reasons that it remains in its red covers, I can never forget that the stage alone could touch it into life. But the robe, at least, is ready when and if the actor comes along who can and cares to put it on.

[*Hoping that he may possibly conclude with one or two more letters, he reaches into his pocket and brings them out.*

But the stage manager is closely watching from the wings. He pulls the switch, and blinks the footlights several times in warning that the hour is late. Under union rules the electricians will soon charge "double time." No theatre will tolerate that— even for a playwright.

His hesitation is embarrassing; for the audience, and his wife, too, wonder why he is so unexpectedly silent. Truth is, he feels the need of an ending. Suddenly he smiles, and holds out his hands: the old playwriting instinct comes to his aid.]

Just one moment more. I—I want to tell you something Balzac once said about the writing profession with which so much of my story is concerned. It's sort of apropos—at the end. As you know, he was one of the first, after Beaumarchais, to try to organize authors. To his home there once came, at his suggestion, Victor Hugo, Théophile Gautier, George Sand, Alexandre Dumas, and the other giants of his day. And over the coffee he spoke of this, as I have him in my play.

The words that follow are my paraphrase of scattered expressions of his indignation at what authors once suffered, but now happily are spared. I think I can remember them by heart.

[He pauses a moment and speaks with the emotion the words waken.]

"We are being plagiarized without redress! Our novels, songs, and music pilfered in France, reprinted by thousands in Belgium. Our stories are stolen for the stage without consent or payment. Publishers hate me because I have stood out for the rights of authors. . . . I asked you here to help me stop it.

"You have all suffered and done nothing to prevent it but complain. You think it undignified to act! I tell you, to submit is the indignity! Crows are feeding on the seeds we plant and bring to flower with our tears and toil.

"It is we writers who dig beauty from the heart of life: we who create the songs, poems, books that feed the hungry spirit of the world.

"We must protect our property against thieves who quench their own thirst in our blood, suck our brains and rob us to feed themselves.

"We must be either scavengers or kings. We must assert the dignity of our profession; for there is none greater than this pen.

"It is a toy to a child, but in the hands of a master, it is a scepter; a lever to overturn a world!"

[*As* THE AUTHOR *again stands silent, with silence now in the world outside, the lights blink again.*

In the wings his wife is waiting. He walks slowly to her. He slips his hand through her arm. They walk across the stage of the theatre they have both loved.

They pass out, through the stage door.]

INDEX

413

Burbage, 69; in film-rights crisis, 315 n.;
friendship with, in Hollywood, 389,
391–393; compared to Mark Twain,
391; unhappy at his chore in Hollywood, 391–392; tragedy in his life and
death, 393
Marquis, Marjorie Vonnegut (Mrs. Don),
393
Marquis, Reina (Mrs. Don), his play
dedicated to, 392–393
Martin, his Lafayette dining room, 10;
his Café, 11–12, 51
Martin, Vivian, 375
Masefield, John, president of Society of
Authors, 333 n.; exhibits his theatre
at Boar's Hill, joins Dramatists' Guild,
praises Scudder Middleton, 341–342
Masks (Middleton), book of one-act plays
including Masks, Jim's Beast, Tides,
Among the Lions, The Reason, The
House, 137, 148; writing of, 177
Masks (Middleton), one-act play, 137, 146
Masses, under Max Eastman, 113, 114
Massey, Raymond, 406
Mather, Margaret, 24
Matthews, Brander, 38, 74, 152, 216; per-
sonality and achievement of, 35–36;
nominates a candidate for the Players,
56; his comment on "closet drama,"
138; his advice on the preface to a first
book of one-act plays, 145; on Their
Wife, 146–147; how he and George
Arliss collaborated, 154; on Brian
Hooker's translation of Cyrano, 244
"Matty," Belasco's property man, 276,
281, 289
Maude, Cyril, 246, 302
Mauget, Irénée, produces Cercle in Paris,
230
Maugham, Somerset, 317, 338, 341
Maxwell, W. B., first impression of, 214
Megrue, Roi Cooper, 39, 76, 315 n.; on
Dramatists' Guild contract committee,
323; on Guild committee conferring
with managers' committee for a settle-
ment, 326 n.; death of, 328 and n.
Meiklejohn, Alexander, 332
Meiklejohn, Helen (Mrs. Alexander), 332
Meilhac, Henry, collaboration with Halévy,
152
Melchers, Gari, 58
Mencken, H. L., accepts one-act plays for
Smart Set, 143; on Criminals, 150

Merchant of Venice, The, 233
Méré, Charles, 231, 371
Meredith, Anne, forgets a scene in Polly
with a Past, 285–286
Meredith, Burgess, 246 n.
Meredith, George, his poetry, 94; the
women in his novels, 122; a me-
mento of, 122–123; creeping neglect
of, 219; his ode to France, 255; presi-
dent of Society of Authors, 333; on
"test of the civilized," 367; Lionel
Barrymore's love of, 388
Merely Mary Ann, 302
Merry Wives of Windsor, The, Ada Rehan in, 78
Messager, André, 355
Metamora (Stone), income from, of its
author, 311
Metropolitan Opera House, 34, 79, 253
Metropolitan Temple, suffrage meeting at,
125–126
Michael and His Lost Angel (Jones), 343
Mid-Channel (Pinero), Ethel Barrymore
in, 219
Middleton, David, 90
Middleton, George: family background,
1–5; childhood adventures in Manhattan around 1890, 5–9; discovery of theatre and thrills of "eating out," 9–12;
atmospheric disturbances in home life,
12–15; permanent influence of childhood insecurity, 15–16; religious influences, 17–19; at boys' boarding school,
19–22; deepening love for theatre, 23–
26; two years at Dwight School, 26–27;
professors and awakening interests at
Columbia University, 27–41; Columbia
affords further background and training for theatre, 33, 35–41; breaking
into play writing, 42–44, 46–47; collaborating with Paul Kester (The Cavalier, Julia Marlowe), 44, 48–52; Abe
Hummel protects interest of, in play,
51–52; learning about Erlanger, Frohman, and theatrical "Syndicate," 53–56,
74; joining the Players, 56–59; following literary and business trails, 59–60;
adventures in reading plays to stars and
managers, 60–62; some privileged theatre associations of early writing days, 62–
65; Margaret Anglin produces A Wife's
Strategy, 65–72, 73; profits by Shubert's fight against "Syndicate," 74–75;